MISBEHAVIOR IN ORGANIZATIONS

Theory, Research, and Management

SERIES IN APPLIED PSYCHOLOGY

Edwin A. Fleishman, *George Mason University*
Jeanette N. Cleveland, *Pennsylvania State University*
Series Editors

Gregory Bedny and David Meister
The Russian Theory of Activity: Current Applications to Design and Learning

Michael T. Brannick, Eduardo Salas, and Carolyn Prince
Team Performance Assessment and Measurement: Theory, Research, and Applications

Jeanette N. Cleveland, Margaret Stockdale, and Kevin R. Murphy
Women and Men in Organizations: Sex and Gender Issues at Work

Aaron Cohen
Multiple Commitments in the Workplace: An Integrative Approach

Russell Cropanzano
Justice in the Workplace: Approaching Fairness in Human Resource Management, Volume 1

Russell Cropanzano
Justice in the Workplace: From Theory to Practice, Volume 2

David V. Day, Stephen Zaccaro, and Stanley M. Halpin
Leader Development for Transforming Organizations: Growing Leaders for Tomorrow's Teams and Organizations

James E. Driskell and Eduardo Salas
Stress and Human Performance

Sidney A. Fine and Steven F. Cronshaw
Functional Job Analysis: A Foundation for Human Resources Management

Sidney A. Fine and Maury Getkate
Benchmark Tasks for Job Analysis: A Guide for Functional Job Analysis (FJA) Scales

J. Kevin Ford, Steve W. J. Kozlowski, Kurt Kraiger, Eduardo Salas, and Mark S. Teachout
Improving Training Effectiveness in Work Organizations

Jerald Greenberg
Organizational Behavior: The State of the Science, Second Edition

Uwe E. Kleinbeck, Hans-Henning Quast, Henk Thierry, and Hartmut Häcker
Work Motivation

Martin I. Kurke and Ellen M. Scrivner
Police Psychology Into the 21st Century

Joel Lefkowitz
Ethics and Values in Industrial–Organizational Psychology

Manuel London
Job Feedback: Giving, Seeking, and Using Feedback for Performance Improvement, Second Edition

Manuel London
How People Evaluate Others in Organizations

Manuel London
Leadership Development: Paths to Self-Insight and Professional Growth

Robert F. Morrison and Jerome Adams
Contemporary Career Development Issues

Michael D. Mumford, Garnett Stokes, and William A. Owens
Patterns of Life History: The Ecology of Human Individuality

Kevin R. Murphy
Validity Generalization: A Critical Review

Kevin R. Murphy and Frank E. Saal
Psychology in Organizations: Integrating Science and Practice

Susan E. Murphy and Ronald E. Riggio
The Future of Leadership Development

Erich P. Prien, Jeffrey S. Schippmann, and Kristin O. Prien
Individual Assessment: As Practiced in Industry and Consulting

Ned Rosen
Teamwork and the Bottom Line: Groups Make a Difference

Heinz Schuler, James L. Farr, and Mike Smith
Personnel Selection and Assessment: Individual and Organizational Perspectives

John W. Senders and Neville P. Moray
Human Error: Cause, Prediction, and Reduction

Frank J. Smith
Organizational Surveys: The Diagnosis and Betterment of Organizations Through Their Members

George C. Thornton III and Rose Mueller-Hanson
Developing Organizational Simulations: A Guide for Practitioners and Students

Yoav Vardi and Ely Weitz
Misbehavior in Organizations: Theory, Research, and Management

MISBEHAVIOR IN ORGANIZATIONS

Theory, Research, and Management

Yoav Vardi
Tel Aviv University

Ely Weitz
*Tel Aviv University
and visiting at
Baruch College, City University of New York*

 LAWRENCE ERLBAUM ASSOCIATES, PUBLISHERS

2004 Mahwah, New Jersey London

Lawrence Erlbaum Associates, Inc., Publishers
10 Industrial Avenue
Mahwah, New Jersey 07430

Cover design by Sean Sciarrone

Library of Congress Cataloging-in-Publication Data
Vardi, Yoav, 1944–
    Misbehavior in organizations / by Yoav Vardi & Ely Weitz.
      p. cm.
    Includes bibliographical references and index.
    ISBN 0-8058-4332-9 (c) – ISBN 0-8058-4333-7 (pbk.)
    1. Organizational behavior.   2. Corporate culture.   3. Business ethics.   4. Work ethic.
  I. Weitz, Ely.   II. Title.

   HD58.7.V367 2003
   302.3′5–dc21   2003044093

Printed in the United States of America
10 9 8 7 6 5 4 3 2 1

We dedicate this work to our loved ones.

Ely also dedicates this book to the memory of his late father Ben Zion Weitz.

Yoav also dedicates this book to his late father Avraham Vardi
and nephew Ori Armon.

Contents

Series Foreword

Series Editors
Edwin A. Fleishman
George Mason University

Jeanette N. Cleveland
The Pennsylvania State University

There is a compelling need for innovative approaches to the solution of many pressing problems involving human relationships in today's society. Such approaches are more likely to be successful when they are based on sound research and applications. This Series in Applied psychology offers publications which emphasize state-of-the-art research and its application to important issues of human behavior in a variety of societal settings. The objective is to bridge both academic and applied interests.

This book fills an important void in the study and understanding of organizational behavior. Work in this field historically emphasized the study of positive, desirable behaviors facilitating the performance of individuals, teams, and systems in furthering organizational objectives. Relatively little attention has been given to research on what the authors call organizational misbehaviors (OMB) that can be dysfunctional in furthering the objectives of the organization.

In this book, Professors Vardi and Weitz present a systematic, careful, and thorough analysis of organizational misbehavior. For the most part, OMB has been indirectly addressed in the organizational behavior literature. There has been some discussion of dysfunctional political misbehavior, negative affect or emotions, or specific negative behaviors. This book is one of the first to organize and synthesize the diverse kinds of misbehavior in organizations.

The authors identify a range of organizational misbehaviors including "soldiering", as described in Taylor's early work, to vandalism and sabotage to modern issues of data theft, substance abuse on the job, sexual harassment, political behaviors such as' whistle blowing, deception and Interpersonal manifestations such as incivility, bullying, and jealousy. Next, antecedents and important correlates of organizational misbehavior are presented, including findings from different job types and organizations, organizational climates, and various control systems. Values and ethics are presented within the OMB context using up to date cases illustrating ethical violations including the Enron affair.

The authors have an impressive history of contributions to the literature of organizational psychology, management, leadership, human resource management., and career development. They have collaborated on research in OMB and related areas. We are very pleased to have this book in our *Series in Applied Psychology.*

The book provides an important framework and typology for OMB, and provides an agenda for future research in this area. The book also highlights the relevance of these issues to effective management of human resources in organizations. The book will appeal to academic researchers in industrial and organizational psychology and to those in related disciplines concerned with the behavior of individuals in organizations. It can serve as a text or supplementary text in upper level I/O psychology and OB courses. The book will also be of interest to thoughtful managers concerned with these issues in a variety of organizations in the public and private sectors.

Preface

Ideas for new constructs come from different sources. The idea for Organizational Misbehavior (OMB) came from a surprise at being caught off guard. The incident was recorded in Vardi's personal file and is quoted from there. It happened during the fall term of 1990 when he taught a course in an Executive MBA program at Cleveland State University. The course title was: Behavioral Sciences for Organizations. All of the 24 students attending the class on those Saturday mornings were either managers or had previous experience as managers in a wide variety of industries. Their real-life experiences, as well as their natural preference for the practical over the academic, were often shared in class vocally and enthusiastically.

Dr. Vardi wrote the following in his notes for an essay on teaching Organizational Behavior to managers:

During the class on work motivation, I posed a general question to the group: How can we design the work to be done so that people will want to expend more effort? Eventually we got to discuss different theories of work motivation. They particularly liked Adams' inequity theory. We also explored the classical job design model by Hackman and Oldham. The students seemed to appreciate it, as many OB students do. It is one of these Organizational Behavior models that makes good theoretical sense and also seems to have practical value because it clearly demonstrates how employees react to their own jobs; as a consequence, it has implications for supervisors and managers. As we explored the model with its different facets and emphasized the role of the intervening "critical psychological states" in eliciting good performance, satisfaction, and motivation, John M. (who at the time ran a large manufacturing department) said, quite cynically: "You know, professor, I like this model, but there is one problem with it." Expecting the usual comments about subjectivity versus objectivity or about the role of individual differences, I was taken by surprise when he said: "The way I see it, the problem is that this model has nothing to do with reality. Excuse me, but only academics who don't really manage people can view the world like this. My job as a manager is not to make work more interesting or more satisfying. My job is to make sure people don't waste time, don't steal, don't cheat their supervisors, don't take drugs, and don't fight with one another. Believe me, I am more of a cop than a cheerleader. I don't want to give them more autonomy, I just want them to be honest and do their jobs."

This quite uncharacteristic outburst started a heated class debate about misconduct at work—issues that had never come up in class before. They all recalled incidents at their organizations. They felt that there is a lot of improper behavior going around. Not only employees do this, they observed; executives engage in it. They even admitted that they, too, stray from time to time (small stuff you know, like making long-distance phone calls, doing their term papers on company time, etc.). I was completely caught off guard and taken aback. The model indeed says nothing about predicting misbehavior on the job. I promised to do a quick search of the OB literature for next class to see whether anybody writes about misconduct at work and why it happens. I was intrigued and spent the week skimming management and OB textbooks and found very little. I read several scholarly reviews of the field in the prominent *Annual Review of Psychology* — not a word.

It was then when I began to suspect that Organizational Behavior as a discipline has for some reason neglected to explore what I decided to call Organizational Misbehavior. Quite apologetically, I told my students that indeed there are no OB models that systematically explain why members of organizations are motivated to engage in misconduct and concluded that they were right to feel quite cynical toward them. If these models indeed fail to account for the negative aspects of work behavior, they offer only partial explanations for the wide range of organizational behaviors in the "real world." I added that because we have a formal concept to describe exceptionally good behavior (OCB—Organizational Citizenship Behavior), we might as well have a new concept to tap "bad" behavior: OMB—Organizational Mis-Behavior).

It caught on.

The next few years were spent conducting graduate-level seminars and work-shops, first in Cleveland with Yoash Wiener and later in Tel Aviv with Ely Weitz, focusing on such questions as: How prevalent is organizational misbehavior? What are the different forms of such misconduct? Who engages in them and why? Over 10 years, we collected hundreds of stories and questionnaires from participants willing to share their experiences and opinions (mostly anonymously, of course). We started to identify a lot of data about the economic costs of such phenomena as theft by employees, corporate fraud, substance abuse, computer and information sabotage, sexual harassment in organizations, monitoring and control, and much more. The evidence is staggering and quite overwhelming. Although many work organizations have had to deal with forms of improper conduct for years, either by choosing to ignore them or battling them, academia seems to be falling behind in realizing the extent of such phenomena. This initial effort culminated in a theoretical article entitled "Misbehavior in Organizations: A Motivational Framework" written with Dr. Wiener (1996) and a number of research papers with Dr. Weitz (2000–2002). At Tel Aviv University, over 30 studies for master's theses were conducted during that period, all devoted to the study of OMB.

The rationale for our book is this. It is safe to assume that most, if not all, members of work organizations, throughout their employment, engage in some form of misbehavior related to their jobs, albeit in varying degrees of frequency and intensity and for different reasons. Certainly unconventional work-related manifestations by employees are not new. Some date employee theft (a major form of OMB), for instance, to ancient times. Scientific Management brought such practices as *soldiering* and *goldbricking* out into the open and the early proponents of the Human Relations production restriction and rate busting (and their consequences) as early as the 1920s. Nonetheless, it appears that most management literature has presented normative, if not plain positive, aspects of behavior at work. We found that only in recent years have organization scholars become more willing to acknowledge that various forms of work-related misbehavior by employees and managers are prevalent, and that their consequences for employers are indeed quite significant and costly.

We wish to emphasize that misbehavior in business is not at all a new phenomenon. We simply wish to reintroduce the topic into mainstream organization studies. As early as 1776, Adam Smith argued that salaried managers would not administer honestly:

> The directors of such companies, however, being the managers rather of other people's money than of their own, it cannot well be expected, that they should watch over it with the same anxious vigilance with which the partners in a private copartnery frequently watch over their own. Like the stewards of a rich man, they are apt to consider attention to small matters as not for their master's honour, and very easily give themselves a dispensation from having it. Negligence and profusion, therefore, must always prevail, more or less, in the management of the affairs of such a company. (Smith, 1937, p. 700)

Thus, the purpose of this book is to delineate a new agenda for OB theory and research. It is intended for students of organizations as well as practitioners who manage organizational behavior. The message is a simple one: For many years we, the scholars aligned with mainstream research paradigms that make up OB have been leaning toward the more positive depiction of organizational reality. For most of us, behavior patterns that are unconventional, so to speak, constitute deviance in the sociological sense or unethical behavior in the managerial sense. We have not come to grips with the fact that certain forms of organizational misbehavior are indeed commonplace, are prevalent, are part of any organizational life, and are not necessarily bad or dysfunctional for either perpetrators or organizations. We must explore misbehavior simply to better understand people's behavior in the workplace. In short, we can no longer dismiss organizational misbehavior as some esoteric form of deviant behavior. To claim that such deviance is indeed pervasive is to use an oxymoron. We know OMB is part and parcel of OB.

We devote this book to the study and management of misbehavior in work organizations. We do not take a pessimistic view of organizational life, just a realistic one. Part I discusses the prevalence of these phenomena. It then searches for typologies and definitions for misbehavior in the management literature using a historical perspective and proposes a general framework of OMB. Part II explores some important manifestations and antecedents of OMB at different levels of analysis—person, job, organization. Finally, Part III presents practical and methodological implications for managers and researchers. Thus, we offer a comprehensive and systematically developed framework for the identification and management of misbehavior in organizations.

Acknowledgments

During the past 13 years, in which this book gradually emerged from unorthodox questions about the field of Organizational Behavior, through numerous graduate seminars and research projects, to this final format, many wise and caring individuals have contributed willingly and enthusiastically to the Organizational Misbehavior (OMB) approach. They all deserve our gratitude and most heartfelt appreciation.

First, we thank Professor Emeritus Yoash Wiener of Cleveland State University with whom scores of most challenging and rewarding hours were spent in conceiving the foundations of the motivational model of OMB. As we began to evaluate various possible answers for the inevitable question of why would employees misbehave on the job, we were struck by the similarities between our explanations of normative and non-normative behaviors. We realized that people misbehave at work because they want to; because they have their reasons just as they do for behaving properly. This intellectual exercise culminated in a 1992 paper presented at the annual meeting of the Academy of Management, in which the motivational framework of OMB was first introduced.

Professor Peter Frost of the University of British Columbia deserves special thanks for his editorial role in reviewing, improving and accepting an early (1996) paper on behalf of *Organization Science*. In his introductory statement he recognized the importance of studying organizational misbehavior. At Cleveland State University professors Stu Klein and Ken Dunnegan carefully read and commented on early manuscripts. Dr. Vlado Dimovski of the University of Ljubljana and other members of the 1990–1991 doctoral seminar, were the first students to systematically search the literature and articulate ideas about OMB. Cornell University ILR professors Tove Hammer and Larry Williams encouraged the project in its earlier stages. Our colleagues at Tel Aviv University commented on various research projects and papers that eventually became the raw material for this book: Yinon Cohen, David DeVries, Yitchak Haberfeld, Dan Jacobson, Gideon Kunda, Guy Mundlak, Amos Spector and Haya Stier. Moshe Semyonov, Ephraim Yaar and Yinon Cohen strongly supported the initial idea to write this book and actually suggested this co-authorship. Professors Hugh Gunz from the University of Toronto, Aharon Tziner from Netanya College, and the late Rami Sagie from Bar Ilan University, contributed helpful commentaries on papers and earlier chapter drafts. Professor Steve Barley of Stanford University deserves special thanks for providing his support and guidance during the early stages of the publication phase. Finally, Ely Weitz's colleagues at the Zicklin School of Business, Baruch College, CUNY, where he has been visiting during this past year, provided valuable insights and support. Special among these are Abe Korman, Allen Kraut, Hannah Rothstein, T. K. Das, Moshe Banai, Richard Kopelman, Don Vredenburgh, Shyam Kumar, Al Booke and the Management Department Chair, Harry Rosen.

Many graduate students in Tel Aviv University's Department of Labor Studies participated in the Unconventional Behavior in Organizations research seminar, which generated over thirty research projects between 1992 and 2003. We wish to warmly acknowledge the conceptual and empirical contributions of the following former students, presented in chronological order of graduation: Orly Goldman, Eran Galmor, Tzipi Gushpanz, Tamar Naor, Tamar Bejerano, Dina Bar-Ulpan, Sara Zangi, Revital Balasi, Tali Cohen-Orenstein, Idit Siton-Avisror, Iris Reshef-Tamari, Halit Kantor, Anat Biran, Sharon Ganot, Tamar Ravid-Robbins, Galit Cohen, Yael Peled, Yael Rubin-Kedar, Yael Lichtenstein, Ateret Malaachi, Hila Yosifon, Dikla Elisha-Michael, Nurit Meltser, Efrat Bareket, Eyal Egozi, Keren Youldus, Keren Tsuk, Limor Davison-Carmel, Anat Schwartz, Einat Bar-Liberman and Rinat Ofer.

A number of research assistants and graduate students were particularly helpful in material search and in managing the project. They deserve our most sincere compliments and gratitude: Tzippi Gushpantz and Danny Tzabbar (the banks shares case), Karni Krigel (the personality variables), Eyal Egozi (the historical review and the OMB management model), Keren Youldus (the OMB measurement dilemmas) and Keren Tsuk (management ethics). Avital Sella and Merav Apirion were very instrumental in the editorial phase. Our thanks go also to Hana Raz and Hazel Arieli for translating some of the material from Hebrew to English, and especially to Yasmin Alkalai for her continuous help with the computer and in data analysis. We wish to thank Anne Duffy and Art Lizza at LEA, and the editors of this book's series Ed Fleishman and Jan Cleveland for patiently, professionally and graciously supporting this project. A grant from the Tel Aviv University research authority and generous support from the Faculty of Social Sciences and the Department of Labor Studies were very helpful.

We also wish to acknowledge the contribution of the hundreds of anonymous managers and employees who volunteered to participate in the many field studies we conducted and to honestly report opinions and behaviors that are, indeed, quite sensitive. They helped us take a good hard look at organizational reality as they know it. When we put the final touches on the management ethics chapter, American corporate giants such as Enron and Worldcom succumbed to their own managers' OMB, creating havoc in the business world. We could not have expected a more clear-cut and painful reminder of the importance of what we were trying to say throughout this volume.

Ely Weitz feels a deep sense of gratitude to his family for their support in this project. Ruth and Daniel Gilan, Ruth Wheat, Marilyn and Lenny Bielory, Cheryl Gilan, Rita Wheat, and Iris and Elliot Schreier who were so supportive and helpful on the USA parts of the project. Ely would like to express special thanks to his brother, Moshe Weitz and Marta Morales, and his sister and brother-in-law, Erela and Doron Goldfeld who supported him in more ways than they can imagine.

We humbly ask forgiveness from our families for being so physically and emotionally involved in the writing of this book over the past three and a half years. We deeply appreciate their indulgence and unrelenting support. With them in heart and mind we embarked on this arduous endeavor. Hugs of love go to Yoav's mother Yehudit, wife Dina, grown children Itai and Yael and Golan Rice, and grandsons Tom and Yonatan; to Ely's mother Chava, wife Einat and daughters Eden and Alissa. Now it seems that it was all worth it. Doesn't it?

Tel Aviv and New York City, June 2003

I

ORGANIZATIONAL
MISBEHAVIOR

1

Organizational Behavior and Misbehavior

Problematic behavioral manifestations in the organized workplace are not new. F. W. Taylor (1895, 1903) brought the practice of *soldiering* or *goldbricking*— deliberately slowing down production—to light. The early proponents of the Human Relations School reported extensively on production restriction and rate busting (and their consequences) as early as the 1920s (Roethlisberger & Dickson, 1964). Greenberg and Scott (1996) dated employee theft (a major form of organizational misbehavior) to ancient times. These phenomena are unquestionably universal. Therefore, it is safe to assume that most, if not all, members of work organizations, throughout their employment, engage in some form of misbehavior related to their jobs, albeit in varying degrees of frequency and intensity. Hence, to achieve a better understanding of organizational behavior (OB), we must study organizational misbehavior as well. *Organizational misbehavior* (OMB) is defined as acts in the workplace that are done intentionally and constitute a violation of rules pertaining to such behaviors. We strongly believe that, to truly comprehend the behavior of people at work and the functioning of organizations, social scientists need to explore and research both the positive and negative aspects of work life. After all, how can we understand the functional if we fail to recognize the dysfunctional and unconventional?

In recent years organization scholars have become more willing to acknowledge that various forms of work-related misbehavior by employees and managers are prevalent, and that their consequences for employers are indeed quite significant and costly (e.g., Ackroyd & Thompson, 1999; Giacalone & Greenberg, 1997; Greenberg, 2002; Griffin, O'Leary-Kelly, & Collins, 1998a, 1998b; Robinson & Bennett, 1997; Sackett & DeVore, 2001). Such behaviors range a full spectrum from minor to serious—a mere perception of violation of the psychological contract (Robinson & Rousseau, 1994), minor workplace incivility (Andersson & Pearson, 1999), insulting behaviors (Gabriel, 1998), workplace social undermining (Duffy, Ganster, & Pagon, 2002), theft of company assets (Greenberg, 1998; Greenberg & Scott, 1996), acts of destructiveness, vandalism and sabotage (Jermier, 1988; Sprouse, 1992), substance abuse while at work (Sonnenstuhl, 1996), and aggression perpetrated against fellow employees or toward the organizations (Fitzgerald, 1993; Neuman & Baron, 1997; O'Leary-Kelly, Griffin, & Glew, 1996).

Although such forms of misconduct appear to be rampant and universal, systematic OB research of these phenomena is lacking (Vardi & Wiener, 1992, 1996). Also there is conceptual confusion in describing them (O'Leary-Kelly, Duffy, & Griffin, 2000). Until recently, OB, as a distinct academic discipline devoted to exploring and expanding our understanding of work behavior, has lagged behind other social science disciplines in exploring this vast domain. This is quite surprising given that OMB, referred to by other scholars as antisocial (Giacalone & Greenberg, 1997), dysfunctional (Griffin, O'Leary-Kelly & Collins, 1998a), deviant (Hollinger & Clark, 1982; Robinson & Bennett, 1995), or counterproductive behavior (Sackett & Devove, 2001; Mangione & Quinn, 1975), is not restricted to certain marginal members. It has been recorded for workers of all types of organizations—for employees at all levels of the organizational hierarchy, salaried professionals and nonprofessionals, and both nonsupervisory and managerial employees (cf. Giacalone & Greenberg, 1997; Griffin et al., 1998a; Robinson & Greenberg, 1998; Vardi & Weitz, 2002a).

This chapter is devoted to the ubiquity of OMB. First, we discuss the prevalence of misbehavior and then employ a historical perspective to search the literature for previously proposed typologies and definitions for employee misbehavior. Second, we address the question why the field of OB has overlooked OMB and has, in fact, evolved into a (positively) "skewed" discipline focusing on more normative aspects of work behavior. Last, we describe the emergence of the current interest in OMB from the early sociological research of white-collar crime, focusing on employee deviance, workplace aggression, and political organizational behavior as selected examples.

PREVALENCE OF MISBEHAVIOR AT WORK

Undoubtedly, OMB comes with a hefty price tag. With the cost comes a growing awareness of it. Estimates of the costs of the most prevalent misbehavior— employee theft—run as high as $200 billion annually in the United States alone

(Greenberg, 1997). Estimates of total costs resulting from problem drinking in the workplace are close to $170 billion (Mangione, Howland, & Lee, 1998). The economics of OMB are indeed staggering once the costs of fraud, sabotage, vandalism, substance abuse, litigation, and so on are factored in, although some costs may be offset by benefits that often follow organizational improvements launched due to misbehavior (e.g., new quality and monitoring practices in the wake of exposure of misconduct by whistle blowers). For example, information concerning employee theft has become publicly available on the Internet by governmental agencies and private security firms (e.g., www.workplacecrime.com). One site (www.etheft.com) offers employees an opportunity to anonymously blow the whistle on fraud, pilfering, and embezzlement in their companies. Case-based and practitioner-oriented literature flourished in the 1990s under such telling titles as *Dirty Business* (Punch, 1996) and *Are Your Employees Stealing You Blind?* (Bliss & Aoki, 1993). Some semi-academic books offer solid practical advice on how to prevent violent behavior in the workplace (e.g., Denenberg & Braverman, 1999) or handle employee problem drinking (Sonnenstuhl, 1996).

During the past three decades, work organizations, research has provided ample evidence for the large variety of such misbehaviors (cf. Ackroyd & Thompson, 1999; Bamberger & Sonnenstuhl, 1998a; Giacalone & Greenberg, 1997; Griffin et al., 1998a; Sackett & DeVore, 2001). Mars (1974) studied deviant work practices among dockworkers, Hollinger and Clark (1982) found it in all sectors of the economy, and Analoui and Kakabadse (1992) conducted a longitudinal study of an entertainment and hospitality organization and found unconventional practices among both managers and employees. Greenberg (1990a, 1997) extensively examined the causes of employee theft in organizations, Trevino (1986) investigated unethical managerial decisions, Raelin (1984) studied deviant behavior among professionals, and Giacalone and Rosenfeld (1987) researched sabotage behavior. In fact, there is a growing research interest in specific OMB phenomena such as incivility (Andersson & Pearson, 1999), lying and cheating (Grover, 1993), insulting (Gabriel, 1998), betrayal of trust (Elangovan & Shapiro, 1998; Moberg, 1997), whistle blowing (Miceli & Near, 1992), concealment of pertinent information (Reimann & Wiener, 1988), substance workplace abuse (Trice & Sonnenstuhl, 1988), sexual harassment (Gutek, 1985), vandalism (DeMore, Fisher, & Baron, 1988), and revenge (Bies & Tripp, 1995). Remember, this is just a sample. As Moberg (1997) observed, both employee virtue and employee vice seem endless.

MISBEHAVIOR IN OB DISCOURSE

OB is an interdisciplinary field of research that explores the behavior of individuals and groups within organizational contexts, as well as the structure and behavior of the organizations (see Greenberg, 1994, on the state of the science). At the macrolevel, OB is rooted in sociology, political science, and economics; it deals with questions of organizational form, design, and action in the socioeconomic context. At the more microlevel, OB stems from psychology, especially industrial and organizational (I-O) psychology, focusing on the individual and dealing with his or her attitudes and behavior and how these affect and are affected by the organizational system (Staw, 1984). During its years of development, OB was primarily influenced by its psychological origins, as may be witnessed by the objects of its research and subjects of its practice (Cappelli & Sherer, 1991; Mowday & Sutton, 1993). The social psychology roots of OB have contributed to the extensive interest in work groups and teams in organizations (the mesolevel).

Most OB research focuses on the individual (micro) level, rather then on the effects of culture and environment on behavior (Cappelli & Sherer, 1991; Erez & Early, 1993; House, Rousseau, & Themas-Hurt, 1995). Some scholars argue that this tendency to emphasize interpersonal differences over situational variables is somewhat of a universal approach in OB (Erez & Early, 1993), which may indeed be its main drawback (Cappelli & Sherer, 1991). This line of thought led researchers such as Mowday and Sutton (1993) to conclude that the field is exhausted—that scholars should redirect their attention to the macrolevel and search for new relationships between the organizational context and its individual members, behaviors. We found, however, that although the research concerning the positive-normative behavior of the individual in the organization seems somewhat saturated, the systematic study of the darker side of human behavior at work (Vaughn, 1999) has only just begun.

An examination and tabulation of nine major reviews of the organizational behavioral literature (Cummings, 1982; House & Singh, 1987; Ilgen & Klein, 1989; Mitchell, 1979; Mowday & Sutton, 1993; O'Reilly, 1991; Rousseau, 1997; Schneider, 1985; Staw, 1984) highlights the tendency of OB theory and research to focus on a positive depiction of organizational life. As Table 1.1 shows, attitudes toward work, motivation, performance, and leadership appear to be main areas of interest in OB research. For example, Mitchell (1979) emphasized that work motivation is a highly popular subject in the field (up to 25% of the articles he reviewed deal with the topic). Although by definition attitudes toward work can be negative as well as positive, the articles reviewed tend to focus on positive attitudes such as job satisfaction and organizational commitment. Later literature reviews (Cummings, 1982; House & Singh, 1987; Rousseau, 1997; Staw, 1984) demonstrate this same tendency.

Even more remarkable is that each writer took a different perspective: Cummings (1982) focused on the macrolevel, whereas Staw (1984) and Mitchell (1979) paid more attention to job satisfaction and motivation, the former also addressing absenteeism and turnover. Even absenteeism and tardiness, which may be considered expressions of negative or dysfunctional forms of behavior, are not addressed within a wider perspective of unconventional or deviant organizational behavior, but from the traditional human resource management viewpoint of organizational productivity. Schneider (1985), who reviewed the literature through the prism of

TABLE 1.1
Main Topics in the OB Literature Reviews (1979–1997)

ARP OB Review	Topics Covered in the Review
Mitchell (1979)	Personality and individual differences, satisfaction, commitment, involvement, motivation, leadership.
Cummings (1982)	Task design, feedback, organizational structure, control, technology, research methodology, emerging trends.
Staw (1984)	Field of OB, job satisfaction, job design, comparison theories, absenteeism, turnover, motivation and performance, other behaviors.
Schneider (1985)	Motivation, satisfaction, leadership, groups, organizational climate and culture, productivity.
House & Singh (1987)	Power motive, leadership, executive succession, decision making, OB in evolutionary context.
Ilgen & Klein (1989)	Social cognition, social information processing, expectancy theories, attribution, control theory.
O'Reilly (1991)	Motivation, work attitudes, job design, turnover and absenteeism, leadership, future directions.
Mowday & Sutton (1993)	Organizational context as an influence on groups and individuals, individuals and groups as an influence on organizational context, interaction of individuals and groups with their organizational context.
Wilpert (1995)	Organizations as constructed realities, action theory, theoretical controversies, methodological approaches, new technology, participation, hazardous work system, organizational learning, organization–environment relationship.
Rousseau (1997)	New employment relations, performance, goal setting, information processing, organizational learning, managing organizational change and individual transition, leisure, nonwork, community, organizational citizenship behavior, **deviant behavior at work.**

Note. ARP = *Annual Review of Psychology.*

organizational climate, addressed the same topics reviewed by Mitchell—motivation, job satisfaction, leadership, and productivity.

Two years later, House and Singh (1987), despite their avowed intent to review new issues, also emphasized the positive aspects of leadership, successful management, decision making, and power and influence in organizations. However, they did not deal with the darker aspects of organizational power and control. O'Reilly (1991) concluded that the four main research topics in OB that were identified by Mitchell (1979) are still the most popular more than a full decade later. Finally, Rousseau's (1997) content analysis of 23 chapters of the *Annual Review of*

Psychology, from 1979 to 1995, clearly demonstrates that the main issues investigated in OB research are performance (mainly performance appraisal), motivation (goals and rewards), and employee reactions to the workplace (mainly satisfaction, commitment, and stress). Nonetheless, Rousseau's is the first comprehensive OB review in which employee misconduct, as a research topic, is referred to, albeit in one short paragraph.

Clearly demonstrating this positive bias, none of the reviews addresses *misbehavior* as an integral facet of organizational behavior. Traditional OB models emphasize normatively desirable behaviors under constructs such as satisfaction, attachment, motivation, commitment, leadership, development, redesign, and enrichment (e.g., Porter, Lawler, & Hackman, 1975) and neglect issues such as indifference, undermining, jealousy, abuse, exploitation, insults, manipulation, lying, betrayal of trust, malice, misinformation, pilferage, harassment, conspiracy, sabotage, and so forth. Even less blatant manifestations of misbehavior, such as white lies, arm twisting, incivility, and buckpassing, are almost ignored. There is no compelling evidence, however, that the former type of constructs better describe the complex realities in work organizations.

The situation is not much better in OB textbooks. A cursory study of some of the better known OB textbooks (e.g., Daft, 2000; Daft & Noe, 2001; Greenberg & Baron, 1997; Hellriegel, Slocum, & Woodman, 2001; Ivancevich & Matteson, 1990; Steers, 1991) reveals that by far most of the terms defined in their glossaries are positively skewed. None of these textbooks seriously relates to negative types of organizational behaviors. Terms such as those used in this book to describe various forms of employee misconduct (*misbehavior, dysfunctional, counterproductive,* or *antisocial behaviors*) are hardly mentioned and certainly not discussed as prevalent work-related phenomena that need to be understood, explained, and controlled. Therefore, the depiction of organizations in most textbooks is incomplete.

Finally, we examined titles of articles pertaining to OB in the leading journals (presented in alphabetical order): *Academy of Management Journal* (1958–1999), *Academy of Management Review* (1976–1999), *Administrative Science Quarterly* (ASQ; 1956–1999), *American Journal of Sociology* (1895–1999), *American Sociological Review* (1936–1999), *Journal of Applied Psychology* (1967–1999), *Organizational Behavior and Human Performance* (1966–1984), and *Organizational Behavior and Human Decision Process* (1985–1999). Not surprisingly, these titles clearly reflect the discipline's inherent positive orientation. The number of titles referring to OMB phenomena (misconduct, deviance, unethical behavior, political behavior, theft, violence, harassment, etc.), compared with the enormous amount of research concerning issues such as productivity, attachment, attendance, motivation, leadership, job satisfaction, and career development, is negligible (less than 5%). Thus, the inevitable question is: How did this happen and where has misbehavior gone?

We suggest that the paucity of empirical research into the darker side of organizational life, and the lack of well-developed mainstream models of organizational misbehavior, may be explained by four interrelated reasons: (a) the field's inherent tendency toward specialization and the predominance of functionalism, (b) the predominance of a congruence paradigm, (c) the tendency to address managerial needs, and (d) the lack of methodologies to adequately capture misbehavior in organizations.

Specialization and Functionalism

OB emerged as an interdisciplinary academic field and has prospered primarily in schools of management and business administration (Kreitner & Kinicki, 1995). It is grounded, however, in traditional I-O psychology, which has had a profound impact on its formation and may have inadvertently limited its areas of research interest (Cappelli & Sherer, 1991; Mowday & Sutton, 1993). Because of its importance in this analysis, we now turn to a brief review of the history of I-O psychology.

During the first part of the 20th century, I-O psychologists concentrated their efforts on recruitment and selection, work methods, and job design (Katzell & Austin, 1992). These new practices became part of the academic discourse during World War I, at which time the U.S. government turned to psychologists for help in developing recruitment and selection procedures for the military (see Cappelli & Sherer, 1991). Their apparent success in this endeavor accorded the emerging field legitimization and gave the new area official and widespread recognition, which in turn helped practitioners market professional tools to the prospering postwar private sector seeking and hiring new employees. During the 1930s, the core practices of the field were employee selection, appraisal, and training. On the whole, academic research in those years was characterized by retesting and reexamining what was already achieved, rather than by breaking new ground and defining new directions (Katzell & Austin, 1992).

The number of universities offering programs in I-O psychology was growing. By 1930, Pennsylvania State College, Ohio State University, the University of Minnesota, and Stanford University were offering PhD degrees in I-O psychology. As the decade progressed, several more academic institutions began offering programs to train students for careers in I-O psychology. Of course this offered additional respectability to the new discipline and was a force in its institutionalization as a professional and academic pursuit. Yet even with this growing recognition, there was no marked change in I-O psychology's objects of inquiry. Researchers continued to further their knowledge in the familiar areas, reassess previous studies, and reexamine well-established theories and models. The core objects of I-O psychology remained employee selection, performance appraisal, and training techniques.

World War II had a significant influence on the evolution and development of I-O and OB. As in World War I, hundreds of I-O psychologists representing a variety of specialties were employed by the U.S. military, developing even more sophisticated selection tests. The war gave rise to additional subspecializations within the areas of appraisal, group processes, and attitude change (Katzell & Austin, 1992). The exposure I-O psychologists received in the military during WWII had once again helped them legitimize and expand their professional endeavors in the rapidly growing postwar economy. The 1950s, 1960s, and early 1970s were characterized by rapid economic growth. I-O psychology scholars and practitioners were again in demand by growing companies, giving them opportunities to expand and test their knowledge of employee selection, appraisal, and training. Human resource management was elevated to an academic discipline in its own right.

Work motivation (Locke, 1968; Vroom, 1964), job satisfaction (Herzberg, 1968), job redesign (Hackman & Oldham, 1980), and career development (Hall, 1976) were also widely addressed both scientifically and in practice. This tendency toward the noneconomic and personal rewards was explained in light of Maslow's (1954) general theory of human motivation. The I-O psychology literature of the postwar era was characterized by writings highly critical of the stultifying nature of most jobs and called for expanding opportunities for self-expression and personal growth (Argyris, 1957; McGregor, 1960). Although the starting point for the need deficiency approach may have been the sense of worthlessness and alienation experienced by employees (e.g., Blauner, 1964), the workplace was fast reframed as the arena in which the employee should fulfill his or her various needs—from security and a decent wage to self-esteem and self-actualization. Less pleasant aspects of the human experience at work were neglected.

Years later, in the first *Annual Review of Psychology* state-of-the-art analysis of OB, Mitchell (1979) rightly noted the saturation of research in some areas as opposed to the nonexistence of study in others. Others (e.g., O'Reilly, 1991) argued that most studies in OB contribute to the progress of already existing areas or methodologies, but tend not to seek new concepts or objects of inquiry. Following this, House et al. (1995) suggested that the field needs new theories and a wider range of objects, and Daft and Lewin (1993) openly called for a new research agenda, including the development of issues such as leadership in flexible and nonhierarchical organizations, employee empowerment, organizational learning, computer communication, and interorganizational cooperation. Still this agenda did not include a call for systematic research, which may shed some light on the less observable corners of organizational life, misbehavior among them.

The exclusion of misbehavior from OB discourse is apparently the result of a long process of institutionalization of several practices leading to a positive-normative bias in the field. This process was further reinforced by the dominant approach in the social sciences, especially at the formative stage of OB development as a distinct discipline—functionalism. As a paradigm, functionalism was neither reflexive nor critical. Therefore, it was not sensitive to the problems and conflicts of the society at large (Smelser, 1999) and the work organization in particular (Bensman & Gerver, 1963).

Although this trend was typical of I-O psychology, sociology was no different. Early on the academic field of sociology also ventured into the workplace.

The famous Hawthorne studies, which seem to mark the shift from scientific management to human relations, have become the cornerstone of every course dealing with industrial sociology. In 1914, when Henry Ford faced grave organizational problems, he founded a sociological department that employed 250 people. Aiming to reduce a daily absentee rate exceeding 10%, compounded by a huge yearly turnover rate, which required nearly $2 million a year just to train new workers, and facing fierce negotiations with one of the most militant unions in the country, Ford designed a new program for commitment, loyalty, and conformity. Every qualified employee was paid $5 per day (Marcus & Segal, 1989). The sociological department was charged with determining who was qualified to receive this remuneration. These agents of social control visited homes and interviewed friends, neighbors, and priests to determine who conformed with the code of conduct stressing family values, community values, thrift, and personal character. They used strict criteria for unsuitability and norms of exclusion: single young men, men who were engaged in divorce, those who did not spend evenings wisely, those who drank alcohol, or those who did not speak English. They also gave lessons in home management to workers and their families and taught them how to shop and preserve moral values (Marcus & Segal, 1989).

Sociology, as a form of social praxis, sought to establish rational control over human nature and society (Shenhav, 2002). Although these social agents focused on improving good and proper behavior and expunging what they considered to be evil or deviant, they, like I-O psychologists, failed to further investigate these darker sides of work life and the reasons for their prevalence. Even when crime and deviance were discussed, they were considered as pathologies or problems to be solved through the mechanisms of equilibrium (hence need not be worried about) or as functional to the system in the long run and thus no longer categorized as a problem (Bensman & Gerver, 1963). In his classic study of the French bureaucracy, Crozier (1964) described an organization in which a lack of integration between the staff and the firm's goals caused negative employee attitudes toward the workplace. However, he concluded that "this lack of integration does not seem to have much influence over other aspects of the staff's behavior and attitudes.... The staff's dissatisfaction and pessimism do not prevent a satisfactory basic pattern of adjustment. Indeed, they can be viewed as a specific way, a grumbling way, of achieving it" (p. 50). Moreover, "they adjust to it [to the bureaucratic hierarchy] in a grumbling way, but, one way or another, they adjust" (p. 55). Although aware of the possibility of irregularities, back-door deals, and subtle blackmail, Crozier argued that no organization could survive if it were run solely by such individual and back-door deals. This was due to "the rational side of the organization and the series of social controls that prevent people from taking too much advantage over their own strategic situation" (p. 166). Management control in the workplace has indeed been a dominant notion for the better part of the 20th century (cf. Edwards, 1979).

A Congruence Paradigm

Functionalism, however, does not stand alone. Later mainstream approaches to the study of organization behavior, emerging from Katz and Kahn's (1966) adaptation of the open system model, also focus on the positive-normative aspects of work and organizational life (e.g., Nadler & Tushman, 1980; Porter et al., 1975). These approaches contend that, for the enterprise to be efficient, there needs to be a fit (a congruence, a match) among its components. The implication that its absence leads to problems, dysfunctional behavior, and underperformance has somehow remained unaddressed, which is our second concern regarding OMB research. The influence of the congruence argument has permeated several key areas of interest in OB. The following are some well- known examples from both macro- and micro-OB.

At the *strategic* level, the best known theory promoting the tenet of congruency is Miles and Snow's (1978) seminal work on the fit between organization types and their environments. In another realm, one of the most influential models of *occupational careers* is based on the assumption that personal career fulfillment is a function of the fit between a person's occupational orientation and a commensurate occupational environment (Holland, 1985). In the study of *organizational careers,* Hall (1976) and Schein (1978) promoted the view that successful careers are a result of a good match between the needs of the employee and opportunities provided by the organization through its career management system. This was in line with the predominant person–environment fit approach to personal adjustment promoted by work psychologists (see Pazy & Zin, 1987). Finally, at the *person–organization interaction* level, the popular notion of the psychological contract promoted the proposition that congruency of expectations and obligations between employer and employee should lead to desirable outcomes (e.g., Kotter, 1973).

Perhaps a good example of the congruence paradigm's influence on OB is Nadler and Tushman's (1980) framework for organizational diagnosis. They (following Katz & Kahn, 1966; Leavitt, 1972) proposed a general model in which organizational effectiveness is a function of fit among key organization components: mission or task, formal structure, informal structure, and the individual. Despite their logical appeal, the weakness of such theories is that they strongly imply that congruence is desirable and incongruence is not. Thus, they portray a normative bias and shy away from dealing with potential or actual misfit. Certainly misbehavior at work may result from such mismatches (e.g., when individual values are incongruent with the organization's policy). Yet they may also emerge when fit between person and work exists (e.g., when loyalty leads to acting illegally or unethically on behalf of the organization).

In summary, traditional research on attitudes toward work, job satisfaction in particular, tended to focus on improving the fit between the individual and his or her occupation. The consequences of lack of fit or mismatch between the individual and his or her work were not adequately explored or researched (Pazy & Zin,

1987). Similarly, the positive consequences of lack of fit, such as certain friction and tension that may enhance creativity and change, were ignored. Such conditions could indeed be important precursors of misbehavior on the job.

OB and Management

The third reason for the lack of OMB research again goes back to the early days of management—namely, the rise of scientific management and, later, the emergence of the Human Relations School. Both focused their attention on issues of productivity and motivation (Farrell & Petersen, 1982; Katzell & Austin, 1992) mostly because, in the wake of the two world wars and the Depression, times of vast opportunities and economic growth unfolded. The main interest was enhancing organizational productivity and developing work organizations and their managers. Perhaps in the search for yet higher levels of effectiveness, especially in the footsteps of the Human Relations School, many of the founding fathers of OB (e.g., Argyris, 1957; Herzberg, 1968; McGregor, 1960; Porter & Lawler, 1968; Schein, 1969) emphasized behavior and deemphasized misbehavior. The models depicting employee behavior at work, which were attractive to practitioners and management, were and perhaps had to be positively skewed. Management fads (Abrahamson, 1996, 1997) such as efficiency improvement, job enrichment and sociotechnical programs, career development, quality circles, total quality management, sensitivity training, and the like caught the public's fancy because they also sounded and sold well. Understandably, programs with more realistic names, such as insensitivity treatment, defect correction, or inefficiency prevention, would not have had the same appeal, although these might have better reflected their learning contents. Most telling of this trend in OB is the way Adams' (1963) theory of inequity came to be commonly known as equity theory. Perceived equity is not a motivator. Rather, the theory subsumes that individuals are driven to cope with cognitive dissonance that results from perceived incomparable worth—not equal worth—and are thus motivated to act to restore an internal sense of balance. Later, in fact, Greenberg (1990a) demonstrated how perceived inequity at work may lead to theft.

Practitioners, consultants, and academics, offering solutions to managers' ever more demanding perceived or real problems, tend to wrap their goods in attractive package and promote positive aspects of behavior while mostly ignoring the negative ones. The venerable Harvard Business Review (HBR), which, during its 75 years of existence, offered managers up-to-date practical programs and prescriptions, designed to increase the firm's efficiency and profitability, and the employees' well-being clearly demonstrates this bias. A thorough review of HBR publications (Sibbet, 1997) reveals that models, research, or practical advice for the daily and cumbersome confrontation with misbehavior in the workplace occupy negligible space if at all.

Many questions come to mind. Does mainstream OB literature portray behavior in organizations accurately? Is it reasonable to assume that management and organizational scholars do not encounter misbehavior in the workplace? Does management seek to not deal with dysfunctional behaviors? Has it not experienced manifestations of theft of company property by employees, aggression, sexual harassment, and the like? Are researchers not aware of these phenomena? Why do managers and practitioners prefer to deal only with techniques such as cooperative management, interpersonal communication total quaity management, and the like while ignoring the more murky aspects of the workplace? Have researchers attempting to study negative aspects of organizational life encountered a total lack of cooperation from management?

It appears that top management generally has had no interest in studying unconventional practices in their firms and even less interest in publishing—going public with—such findings. It may be that they are wary of tarnishing their or the company's reputation (Analoui & Kakabadse, 1992), preferring to sweep the bad news under the proverbial corporate rug. Unquestionably, this lack of cooperation and consent creates difficulties for would-be OMB researchers in the quest for valid data, which leads us to our fourth concern regarding the paveity of OMB research: the methodological problems in the study of OMB (see chap. 10).

Methodological Limitations

The methodology in use by the majority of organizational researchers has no doubt influenced the development of OB. It may also explain OB's tendency to focus on a relatively small number of phenomena. Historically, OB researchers have specialized in cross-sectional correlational designs, whereas experiments were left to psychologists and ethnographic research was left to anthropologists. For example, most of the studies published in the *ASQ* between 1959 and 1979 tended to be empirical—that is, mostly low variety and statistical (Daft, 1980). These methods, using quantitative, precise, and rigorous language to describe organizational phenomena, narrow the scope of organizational issues that can be investigated. That is, they limit research projects to relatively accessible, tangible, a priori-defined characteristics of individuals and organizations, and therefore do not tap the amorphous and often hidden dimensions of everyday organizational life. Thus, generally speaking, OB research sheds light on only a narrow range of the organizational reality. It misses, as Daft (1980) argued, "the complex, intangible, emotional dimensions of organizations [that] probably cannot be processed through the fine filter of linear statistics" (p. 632).

In addition to the lack of agreement among scholars as to the nature of OMB, the tools they use to encompass the dimensions of OB are limited. Most instruments used in OB research tap a fairly limited amount of behavioral variance because of the manner in which behavior is operationalized. In many ways, it is a myopic view of both the fidelity and bandwidth of human behavior in organizations. For example, take one of OB's most studied variables: job satisfaction. Traditionally, research captures this affect or attitude on a preset numerical (i.e., arbitrary) scale. Yet those individuals who are either euphoric or utterly miserable at work, by definition, cannot convey their true feelings toward their job on such a scale. Similarly, organization climate scales (e.g., Litwin & Stringer, 1968) are not designed to assess the extent to which manipulative managerial behavior is predominant in an organization, leadership questionnaires (e.g., Fleishman & Harris, 1962) typically ignore the possible abuse of supervisory power, and most commitment measures tap neither betrayal intentions nor addiction to work or workaholism. We believe our tools, with their limited measures, provide some explanation for the institutionalization of the positively leaning descriptions of organizational life OB has generated.

Qualitative, long-term ethnographic research has definite advantages over quantitative methodology in revealing new fields of knowledge, but it tends to be highly time-consuming and evokes many ethical dilemmas. To conduct such research, generous funding, a commitment by management, and academic support are required. For example, it took Dr. Analoui 6 years of undercover work to record and analyze some 450 incidents of OMB in one particular British organization (see Analoui & Kakabadse, 1992). This may not be suitable for academicians struggling with the pressure to publish within given time constraints and incommensurate with the lack of funding, as well as management's unwillingness to participate in research examining company-sensitive issues and secrets (Analoui & Kakabadse, 1992). In addition to increasing difficulty to publish in leading academic periodicals, these constraints may explain the paucity of rigorous OMB research.

Finally, the lack of agreement among scholars about common descriptions, explanations, and definitions of observed phenomena of misbehavior also makes it difficult for this new theoretical and empirical body of knowledge to be developed. Furthermore, the fact that OB scholars come from varied academic disciplines makes it more difficult to agree on what is instrumental and what is evil (Near & Miceli, 1984), what is prosocial and what is antisocial (Giacalone & Greenberg, 1997), and what is functional and what is dysfunctional (Bamberger & Sonnenstuhl, 1998). We believe the need to resolve such conceptual and methodological dilemmas becomes quite apparent.

A HISTORICAL PERSPECTIVE

After almost five decades of OB research, three distinct phases in the evolution of the newly emergent area of OMB can be identified: mid-1950s to the late 1970s—*the early phase,* a period of sporadic and nonsystematic research; early 1980s to the mid-1990s—*the formative phase,* a period of wide scholarly call for systematic research and the evolvement of the major areas of interest in the new field; and the mid-1990s to date—*the current phase*, toward the full integration of the emerging subfield of OMB into mainstream OB.

The Early Phase

Although OB scholars and practitioners tend to ignore the dark side of organizational life, other disciplines such as industrial sociology, occupational psychology, criminology, and organizational anthropology did in fact deal with it (Hollinger & Clark, 1982). For instance, Quinney (1963) investigated the impact of an occupational structure on its employees' criminal behavior at work. Larceny, in the forms of embezzlement (Altheide et al., 1978; Cressey, 1953), fiddling (Mars, 1973), pilferage (Altheide et al., 1978; Ditton, 1977; Mars, 1973), and employee theft (Horning, 1970; Kemper, 1966; Mars, 1974; Merriam, 1977), was explored extensively. Sabotage, whether referred to as industrial sabotage (Taylor & Walton, 1971), vandalism (Cohen, 1973; Fisher & Baron, 1982), or destruction (Allen & Greenberger, 1980), also received widespread attention mainly because it was harmful, costly, and easy to track. Restriction of output (Collins, Dalton, & Roy, 1946; Harper & Emmert, 1963), goldbricking (Roy, 1952), informal coworker interaction (Roy, 1959), and unauthorized use of time-saving tools (Bensman & Gerver, 1963) were other types of deviant behaviors addressed by scholars, perhaps following management's growing attention to production efficiency and productivity in the 1950s and 1960s.

The only extensive attempt to explore improper work behavior was made by sociologists and criminologists using the concept of white-collar crime proposed by Sutherland (1940) in his presidential address to the American Sociological Society in 1939. Later Sutherland (1949) defined it as "crime committed by a person of respectability and high social status in the course of his occupation" (p. 9). Although the notion was never developed into a full and coherent theory, and despite its inherent deficiencies (for review of the critiques, see Coleman, 1987; Shapiro, 1990), it offered a significant contribution to criminology, sociology, and, later, OB research as well (Braithwaite, 1985).

From an analytical viewpoint, the term *white-collar crime* has three foci: illegality of the act, social status of the actor, and identity of the beneficiary. Most definitions comply with the first—that is, writers (e.g., Coleman, 1985; Horning, 1970) emphasize the formal definition of acts of misbehavior as criminal. However, they often relate it to only one of the other two foci, thus contributing to the concept's proliferation.

Originally, a class distinction was made between white- and blue-collar crime—or more accurately between white-collar crime and blue-collar theft (Horning, 1970). Later, more widely accepted conceptualizations were suggested by Clinard and Quinney (1973) and Coleman (1985, 1987) based on the identity of the beneficiary of the illegal act. Clinard and Quinney decomposed the concept of white-collar crime into *occupational crime,* defined as "offenses committed by individuals for themselves in the course of their occupation and the offenses of employees against their employers," and *corporate crime,* which, in contrast, is defined as "the offenses committed by corporate officials for the corporation and the offenses of the corporation itself" (cited in Braithwaite, 1985, p. 18). The definition of *occupational crime* encompasses many blue-collar, occupational crimes. Coleman (1987) in a somewhat different classification, called for the distinction between *occupational crime,* which he defined as "[crimes] committed for the benefit of individual criminals without organizational support," and *organizational crime,* which refers to "[crimes] committed with support from an organization, that is, at least in part, furthering its own ends" (p. 406). A more clear-cut distinction, supplementing Clinard and Quinney's (1973) work, emphasizes the difference between crimes committed against coworkers and those com mitted against the organization (Greenberg & Scott, 1996). In fact, Greenberg and Scott (1996) took the definition a step further by adopting the distinction made by Hollinger and Clark (1982) between production deviance and property deviance, thus adding a third dimension to the conceptualization of organizational crime.

The evolving definitions of *white-collar crime* demonstrate the long way Sutherland's term traveled during its 60 years of existence. However, the history of the white-collar crime concept has its share of controversy. Sutherland's overarching definition "has been criticized, refined and debated" more than supported (Shapiro, 1990, p. 347). Although Sutherland's conceptualization was incorporated into popular culture, it has proved to be somewhat confusing and obfuscating. Today the term has come to be used generically, dealing with a wide variety of work-related illegal acts by persons at all organizational levels (Greenberg & Scott, 1996; Jensen & Hodson, 1999). "Taken as a whole," Coleman (1987) observed, "the literature on the etiology and development of white-collar crime is a hodgepodge of studies looking at different crimes from different levels of analysis" (p. 408). These studies "confuse acts with actors, norms with norm breakers, the modus operandi with the operator" (Shapiro, 1990, p. 347), resulting in "an unfortunate mixing of definition and explanation" (Braithwaite, 1985, p. 3). Although the white-collar crime construct offers important insights into the darker side of organizations, it fails to develop a systematic theory of OMB. We expanded on it to exemplify some of the dilemmas involved in conceptualizing the phenomenon.

The Formative Phase

Besides Blauner's (1964) seminal work on alienation in the American workplace, systematic thinking about employee reactions to work dissatisfaction has its most profound roots in Hirschman's (1970) *Exit, Voice, and Loyalty: Responses to Decline in Firms, Organizations and States.* Identifying *voice* as employees' political response to job dissatisfaction, and defining it as "any attempt at all to change rather than to escape from an objectionable state of affairs" (p. 30), was a major contribution to the OB field (Farrell, 1983). Not only did Hirschman bring the darker aspects of organizations into the forefront, but he also set the basis for one of the most important conceptual frameworks in OB. The Exit, Voice, Loyalty, and Neglect (EVLN) model, for example, derived from Hirschman's work by Rusbult, Zembrodt, and Gunn (1982), is a useful conceptual framework for analyzing the relationships among responses to job dissatisfaction (Farrell, 1983).

Although Hirschman's conceptualization was developed to explain the responses of organizations to decline, it could also prove useful in understanding how individuals act when things are not going well (Withey & Cooper, 1989). Thus, the EVLN model may serve as a general framework for understanding a variety of workplace behaviors.

We posit that loyalty, may be viewed as organizational citizenship behavior (Organ, 1988), prosocial organizational behavior (Brief & Motowidlo, 1986), extra-role behavior, and the like (for review, see Van Dyne et al., 1994). That is, *loyalty* may be defined as individual acts that are first and foremost supportive of the organization (for a discussion in the variety of meanings attached to loyalty, see Withey & Cooper, 1989). Similarly, antisocial behaviors (Giacalone & Greenberg, 1997) may be viewed as related to *voice* and *exit* and, to a lesser degree, *neglect.* However, unlike Rusbult et al. (1982) and Farrell (1983), we do not view voice as merely a contributive behavior, but more as a variety of behaviors ranging from acts aimed at restoring past situations (e.g., filing a grievance) to destructive behaviors aimed at causing damage to the organization (e.g., sabotage) or its members (e.g., aggression and violence). Moreover, although the EVLN responses were found to be both conceptually and empirically distinguishable, (Farrell, 1983; Withey & Cooper, 1989), their boundaries are somewhat blurred. For instance, exit and voice could be independent, sequential, or co-occurring (Withey & Cooper, 1989). In any case, during the 1980s in particular, with the exception of the EVLN model and some work on workplace deviance (Hollinger & Clark, 1982, 1983; Raelin 1984), interest in organizational misbehavior is still marginal in OB, but the seeds for the rapid development in the 1990s are sewn.

The Current Phase

Interdisciplinary and eclectic by nature, the emerging approach to OMB is in a unique position because it can appropriate and enjoy the fruits of the research conducted in other disciplines. For the sake of parsimony and focus, in this section, we only discuss the evolution of selected OMB subinterests: *employee deviance*, *workplace aggression*, and *political behavior.* Each domain has a somewhat different focus: The employee deviance literature is concerned with the social conditions under which certain behaviors are considered to be counternormative or deviant. Workplace aggression research is limited to exploring mainly harmful and damaging behaviors. Political behavior research attempts to shed light on the use and misuse of power and influence as means to achieve particular individual and group interests. Evidently, these three scientific branches are not totally distinct. In fact, to a large extent, they are interrelated and overlap at times (we explore these topics further throughout the book).

Employee Deviance.   Several early attempts have been made to classify employee deviance, also referred to as *workplace deviance* or *organizational deviance.* For instance, Wheeler (1976) classified forms of organizational rule breaking into serious and nonserious offenses. Mangione and Quinn (1975) proposed two categories of deviance: *counterproductive behavior,* defined as "purposely damaging employer's property," and *doing little on the job,* defined as "producing output of poor quality or low quantity" (p. 114)—somewhat similar to Taylor's (1895, 1903) definition of *soldiering* over 100 years ago.

A significant breakthrough in understanding workplace deviance was made by Hollinger and Clark (1982). They noted, "for the student of occupational behavior a relatively unexplored area of inquiry is the deviance [which] occurs in the workplace, particularly those unauthorized acts by employees which are intended to be detrimental to the formal organization" (p. 97). Following Mangione and Quinn (1974), they classified the findings of Cressey, (1953), Mars, (1973), Ditton (1977), Horning (1970), and others into two distinct categories of employee deviance: *property deviance* and *production deviance.* Property deviance focuses on those instances when employees acquire or damage the tangible property or assets of the organization without authorization, whereas production deviance concerns behaviors that violate the formally proscribed norms delineating the quality and quantity of work to be accomplished. Unlike white-collar crime, their definitions of production deviance and property deviance classify the act as anormative, not as a crime. That is, occupational white-collar crime against the company is now replaced by employee deviance (mostly toward property); however, the former focuses on the illegality of the act (yet possibly normative), whereas the latter underlines it as being counternormative (yet possibly legal).

More than a decade later, Robinson and Bennett (1995) called for expanding this framework, arguing that an accurate typology of employee deviance should consider not only behavior directed at organizations, but also behavior that targets other individuals. Their typology—derived from a statistical analysis of survey-based data—offers two solid dimensions: type of target chosen by the perpetrator (other persons or the organization) and extent of damage inflicted (minor or serious). Bennett and Robinson (2000) further refined their understanding of employee deviance and developed and validated a measure called the Workplace Deviance Scale. Their measure distinguishes between organization and interpersonal deviant behavior. We return to their influential contributions to OMB theory and research throughout the book.

Workplace Aggression. The phenomenon of workplace aggression was rarely studied within OB until the beginning of the 1990s. Perhaps this reflects a more benign work atmosphere in organizations in the post-WWII era characterized by rapid growth and full employment. Since the early 1980s, the workplace in the United States and Europe has become markedly more vulnerable and unsettled, accompanied by new-age forms of employee alienation and the breakdown of the old psychological contract. The term *aggression* is employed to describe many different behaviors, not all of which are necessarily antisocial in either their intents or effects. As Neuman and Baron (1997) noted, for example, there is a distinction between aggressive (with mostly negative connotation) and assertive (with mostly positive connotation) forms of behavior, and the difference is not always clear-cut. Yet most of the more recent literature seems to tilt toward the hostile dimension of the behavior (e.g., O'Leary-Kelly et al., 1996). Again this may not be surprising in view of the rapid growth of reported cases of aggression, homicide included, within the workplace (for a comprehensive review, see Neuman & Baron, 1997).

The proposition that aggression is a plausible outcome of frustration in the workplace is not new (Spector, 1978). Blauner (1964) observed that "machine-breaking was a common response in the early stages of industrialization when new factory conditions appeared oppressive" (p. 106), suggesting that aggression is a result of employees' frustration brought on by their lack of control, perhaps "ways of getting even with a dominating technology" (p. 107). However, despite Blauner's depiction of powerlessness and alienation in industry, and although early work motivation theories (Adams, 1965; Herzberg, 1968; Vroom, 1964) alluded to the possibility of hostile behavior at work, aggression as an intentionally harmful behavior was not fully conceptualized until the mid-1970s (Spector, 1975, 1978). This is quite surprising considering that a significant amount of research outside the organizational context was devoted to factors that cause, facilitate, or exacerbate human aggression or that tend to prevent or reduce it. Unfortunately, Neuman and Baron (1997) observed that there is little evidence to suggest that this large body of knowledge has been systematically applied to the social context in which most adults spend most of their waking time—their work environment.

Workplace violence and aggression are often discussed in the popular literature (for a review, see Martinko & Zellars, 1998), suggesting that a number of workplace factors are associated with these forms of misbehavior (e.g., pressures of widespread job losses and fewer job opportunities, lower levels of organizational loyalty, souring peer relationships, authoritarian styles of management, substance abuse, etc.). Although this literature offers anecdotal evidence regarding elements that have been or are postulated to be associated with workplace aggression and violence, there has been little systematic research explaining their effects. In social psychology, for example, human aggression is considered an adaptive reaction to frustration—an instinct resulting from internal excitation or a learned social behavior that is part drive-based and part learned behavior. The social learning perspective posits that organizational aggression is prompted by external factors (social-situational cues and reinforcers), rather than internal factors (instincts and drives; O'Leary-Kelly et al., 1996).

An early adaptation of the social psychology models to the organizational setting was made by Korman (1971, 1976), who presented a framework relating environmental antecedents to motivational processes and suggested that a high level of aggression toward self and others stems from the workplace's environmental characteristics. This model, although novel, is undeveloped and lacks a definition of aggression. In a similar vein, Spector (1975, 1978) explored the relationship between frustration caused by factors in the work setting and aggression. He defined *aggression* as "behaviors designed to hurt the employer or the organization" (Spector, 1975, p. 635) and noted that aggression was traditionally conceptualized as a reaction to an organization's control and punishment systems. He concluded that frustrating events, which interfere with employees' goal attainment and/or maintenance in organizational settings, may indeed cause aggressive behavior.

Two further distinctions regarding aggression can be made. The first distinguishes organizational aggression and interpersonal aggression. Although the former is intended to harm the organization, the latter is intended to hurt another person and "is primarily verbal" (Spector, 1978, p. 637). The second distinction accounts for the visibility of the act. Thus, it differentiates between *overt* (work slowdowns, grievances) and *covert* (sabotage, withholding of output) forms of aggression. Neuman and Baron (1997) noted that research concerning aggression tends to focus almost exclusively on the covert forms of aggression. In any case, as suggested earlier, except for Spector and a few others (for reviews, see O'Leary-Kelly et al., 1996; Neuman & Baron, 1997; Robinson & Bennett, 1997), workplace aggression and violence per se remained almost unexplored until the 1990s.

Political Organizational Behavior.   Crozier (1964) studied power relations and the problem of control in organizations, concepts that gained respect in the Marxist sociological tradition (e.g., Baritz, 1960; Bendix, 1956; Braverman, 1974; Edwards, 1979). During the 1970s and early 1980s, there was a surge of theoretical and empirical work on the acquisition and exercise of power within complex organizations (e.g., Bacharach & Lawler, 1980; Pfeffer, 1981). This body of research focused primarily on structural and environmental factors affecting the distribution and dynamics of power in organizations. It made clear that power reflects the degree to which organizational members cope with critical demands facing the organization and the degree to which members control critical resources or critical information on which others must depend. However, little research attention was given to the more psychological determinants of individual acquisition of power, let alone its manipulative use in organizations.

Although widely recognized by organizational members, instrumental political behavior of individuals within organizations was not integrated into organizational theory until the mid-1980s. Empirical studies of the processes by which individuals select the target of political behavior in which they engage have rarely been conducted (Farrell & Petersen, 1982; Kacmar & Carlson, 1998). The main reason for this apparent paradox is, as already noted, that the Scientific Management and Human Relations schools, with their managerial perspective and prescriptive biases, focused on issues of motivation and productivity at the expense of understanding resource allocation and the related intraorganizational conflict, which is an integral part of it.

Scholarly interest in the political behavior of individuals stems from waves of growing interest in the way power is used in organizations in the 1970s (Farrell & Petersen, 1982; Kacmar & Carlson, 1998). Other social science disciplines

already demonstrated interest in the roots of such behaviors at various levels. Political scientists addressed unrest as antecedent to political protests, psychologists
considered personality variables such as Machiavellianism as potential antecedents
of political behaviors, and anthropologists studied leveling behaviors—behaviors
that reduce others to one's own level or status within a social context (Robinson
& Bennett, 1997). In addition, sociologists began to explore mechanisms of neutralization, which allow individuals in social situations to justify and rationalize
improper conduct (Sykes & Matza, 1957).

Political behavior in organizations is defined as "those activities that are not
required as part of one's organizational role but that influence, or attempt to influence, the distribution of advantages and disadvantages within the organization"
(Farrell & Petersen, 1982, p. 405). This definition emphasizes the instrumental
nature of political behavior by conceptualizing it as residing in informal structures
and relating to the promotion of self and group interests, especially the expansion
of the available resources for mobilization. Farrell and Petersen (1982) presented
a preliminary multidimensional typology of political behavior in organizations
consisting of three dimensions: internal–external, vertical–lateral, and legitimate–
illegitimate.

The first dimension relates to the focus of resources sought by those engaging
in political behavior. The second recognizes the difference between influence processes relating superiors to subordinates and those relating to equals. The third, and
perhaps the most relevant to our discussion, acknowledges that in organizations
there is a distinction between normal everyday and even positive and beneficial
politics and extreme political behavior that violates the rules. As to the question of
who engages in this kind of behavior, Farrell and Petersen argued that illegitimate
political behavior is likely to be action taken by alienated members and those who
feel they have little to lose.

Over two decades after Farrell and Petersen's (1982) work was published, it
is now clear that the real contribution of their work was not in its adaptation of
political behavior to organizational context, or their definition of the new concept,
or the typology they presented. Their main contribution to OB, with which we
definitely concur, was in identifying an inherent positive-normative bias in its
perspective, thus in effect calling for the expansion of its boundaries to encompass
the more sinister sides of human behavior in organizations.

TOWARD A FRAMEWORK
FOR MISBEHAVIOR

In this chapter, we showed that, since its formation as a distinct discipline in the
mid-1950s, OB research tended to (a) focus on the microlevel, and (b) emphasize the positive-normative side of human behavioral patterns in work organizations. Undoubtedly, the field failed to pay proper attention to the microlevel of the

unconventional side of organizational behavior despite its aspirations to become a scholarly field of inquiry. It is now attempting to rectify this omission.

Today more than ever, we witness a surge in OMB research and literature. Certainly we do not yet have the time perspective necessary to judge its impact on and contribution to management and the OB field. The emergence of this relatively new and distinct body of knowledge is the reason the field has moved from the early, formative stage to its current, developed phase—even if this stage is yet to reach full bloom. Beginning in the late 1970s, and especially during the 1990s, we can clearly identify a *corrective tendency* of the OB field—an increasing awareness of as well as research into OMB. Thus, together with OMB and OCB, the OB discipline forms a new, distinguishable, and expanding body of knowledge rooted in academic discourse as well as practice.

We suggest that the classical models of behavior in work organizations, relating principally to enhancing positive outcomes of work life, be reconsidered and expanded to cover the whole range of human behavior in organizational settings. This is necessary because misbehavior is both a **pervasive** and **universal** phenomenon. It cuts across individuals, jobs, hierarchical levels, occupations, organizations, and geographic borders. Only by further broadening our focus, intensively combining new knowledge to what we already understand, and tirelessly reconsidering our existing theories and our models can OB become the scholarly, multileveled, overarching, and encompassing field it aspires to be. However, to date little is known about the effects of meso-(group) level variables on individual misbehavior at work (Robinson & O'Leary-Kelly, 1998). Thus, we attach relatively more importance to the organizational, positional, and individual determinants of OMB.

The next chapter adopts Vardi and Wiener's (1996) original motivational model and extends it to an overall *Antecedents–Intentions–Manifestations* framework for OMB analysis. The new framework serves as our guide and road map for this book, distinguishing various levels of antecedents of intentional OMB and its large variety of manifestations in the workplace. As is seen, both expositions deal with the challenges and demands presented earlier: They are anchored in classical models of OB, and they allow us to extend the discussion of OMB to the effects of both microlevel (person and job) and macrolevel (unit, organization) factors and variables.

2

A General Framework
for OMB Analysis

The growing awareness of the prevalence of workplace misbehavior, briefly demonstrated in chapter 1, can be coupled with a wide array of scholarly definitions and conceptualizations. Based on a review of the literature, Robinson and Greenberg (1998) identified eight terms and definitions that relate to the phenomenon of *employees behaving badly* at work (presented here in a chronological order):

- Noncompliant behavior (Puffer, 1987).
- Organizational misbehavior (Vardi & Wiener, 1992, 1996).
- Workplace deviance (Robinson & Bennett, 1995).
- Workplace aggression (Baron & Neuman, 1996).
- Organization-motivated aggression (O'Leary-Kelly et al., 1996).
- Antisocial behavior (Giacalone & Greenberg, 1997).
- Employee vice (Moberg, 1997).
- Organizational retaliation behaviors (Skarlicki & Folger, 1997).

Of these constructs, three appear to be especially relevant to our framework: *antisocial behavior*— any behavior that brings or is intended to bring harm to the organization, its employees, or its stakeholders (Giacalone & Greenberg, 1997); *workplace deviance*—voluntary behavior of organization members, which violates significant organizational norms and, in so doing, threatens the well-being of the organization or its members (Robinson & Bennett, 1995); and *OMB*—any intentional act by organization members that violates core organizational or societal norms (Vardi & Wiener, 1992). The other definitions pertain to specific behaviors, such as acts of aggression and retaliation, which are considered special cases of organizational misbehavior.

In addition, two other concepts are relevant: (a) Griffin et al. (1998b) defined *dysfunctional behavior* as "motivated behavior by an employee or group of employees that has negative consequences for an individual within the organization, a group of individuals within the organization, and/or the organization itself" (p. 67); and (b) Sackett and DeVore (2001), taking the employer's perspective, considered *counterproductive workplace behavior* as any intentional behavior by a member that is viewed by the organization as contrary to its legitimate interests.

Evidently, behavioral science scholars view this complex and multifaceted phenomenon of misbehavior at work from different vantage points, which is neither new nor discouraging. Most behaviors in organizations (e.g., employee attachment and leadership) have attracted varied perspectives and interpretations resulting in a wide array of definitions and concepts. Eventually some definitions achieve more acceptance than others, especially as they gain sound empirical support. Thus, at this early stage of conceptual development, we should not expect consensus among scholars. We should be able to recognize the differences in emphases and implications and continue to build on them.

The flux of constructs, typologies, and models emerging in the 1990s, typical of the interdisciplinary and somewhat amorphous nature of OB, makes the mapping of research trends in the emerging OMB field extremely difficult (O'Leary-kelly, Duffy, & Griffin, 2000). However, we define the main issues around which this field is evolving and furnish the necessary historical–epistemological dimension to the plethora of definitions and dimensions of workplace misbehavior (cf. Robinson & Greenberg, 1998; Sackett & DeVore, 2001). We wish to develop a body of knowledge from which various OMB frameworks can be structured, researched, and applied.

Therefore, this chapter is devoted to the development of one analytic OMB framework that integrates our current understanding and exploration of the antecedents and manifestations of intentional misconduct so prevalently exhibited by organization members. First, we discuss the current need for such a framework. Then we describe the initial Vardi and Wiener (1992, 1996) motivational OMB model, and finally we conclude by offering a general framework for OMB. As the book progresses, we break down the model to its component parts and then, in the last chapter, reassemble the parts into a comprehensive model of OMB analysis and OMB management.

NEED FOR CONCEPTUAL CLARIFICATION

The most prominent characteristic of research on unconventional practices within organizational settings is the attempt to define the essence of these phenomena and capture their vitality and the many human behaviors that fall within them (O'Leary-Kelly et al., 2000; Robinson & Greenberg, 1998). Indeed the field is still searching for its unique identity. In the early 1980s and especially in the mid- 1990s, we began to see attempts at defining the field. We saw a flood of related constructs (e.g., organizational aggression, unconventional practices at the workplace, and employee deviance) that describe the phenomenon, typologies (e.g., Farrell & Petersen, 1982; Gardner & Martinko, 1998; Neuman & Baron, 1997; Robinson & Bennett, 1995) designed to encompass its scope and variance, and models (e.g., Martinko & Zellars, 1998; O'Leary-Kelly et al., 1996) that attempt to explain why these behaviors occur (either as a generic phenomenon or specific type of behavior) and how to avoid or contain them. The contribution of this emerging and growing body of knowledge to our understanding of the OMB phenomena is yet to be truly understood and evaluated.

Of course in their attempt to explore the other, darker side of organizational life, OB researchers are not alone. Others have studied related fields including management ethics (e.g., Trevino, 1986) and industrial relations (e.g., Ackroyd & Thompson, 1999). In the field of business ethics, for example, scholars have offered a number of models of ethical and unethical decision making over the last decade (for reviews, see Brass, Butterfield, & Skaggs, 1998; Lewis, 1985; Trevino, 1986). On the whole, these models suggest a number of individual (e.g., locus of control, cognitive moral development, and Machiavellianism) and organizational (e.g., culture, climate, reward systems, codes of conduct, and norms) antecedents that may interact to influence unethical behaviors in organizations.

Some Related Concepts

Several attempts to systematize the treatment of phenomena related to OMB have been reported in the academic literature, especially in the areas of sociology and management. We selected a few to exemplify how different academic perspectives produce different classifications and definitions.

Hollinger (1986) observed that sociological research on employee misbehavior (defined as *workplace deviance*) centers around two foci: production deviance and property deviance. Although both constitute rule-breaking behavior, the first includes various types of behavior that are counterproductive (e.g., substandard work, slowdowns, and insubordination), and the second pertains to acts against property and assets of the organization (e.g., theft, pilferage, fiddling, embezzlement, and vandalism). Based on empirical analyses, he concluded that such individual acts are more likely to occur when personal attachment to the organization (e.g., commitment) is low. Other antecedents found to effect productivity deviance are mostly related to group, peer, and competitive pressures (e.g., Hegarty & Sims, 1978; Zey-Ferrell & Ferrell, 1982), conflict and maladjustment (Raelin, 1986), employee recalcitrance (Ackroyd & Thompson, 1999), or implicit disagreements with organizational goals and expectations.

Similarly, antecedents contributing to property deviance, such as theft, may be feelings of injustice or exploitation (Hollinger & Clark, 1983; Mars, 1974), attempts to ease personal financial pressure (Merton, 1938), moral laxity (Merriam, 1977), available opportunities (Astor, 1972), dissatisfaction with work (Mangione & Quinn, 1975), perceptions of pay inequity (Greenberg, 1990a), and feelings of frustration (Analoui & Kakabadse, 1992; Spector, 1997) or revenge (Bies, Tripp, & Kramer, 1997). Vandalism, as property deviance, was also found to be associated with perceptions of inequity and mistreatment (DeMore et al., 1988).

Trevino (1986) took a useful approach to conceptualizing OMB among managers. She aimed to develop a model that explains the role that personality, job, and situational factors play in determining ethical and unethical decisions taken by managers in organizations. She identified individual-level variables such as the stage of moral development, ego strength, field dependence, locus of control, and situational contingencies, such as the immediate job context and organization culture, as antecedents. Trevino then developed an extensive set of interactional propositionsarticulating specific predictions. Although the dependent variable—ethical–unethical behavior—was not formally defined, one may assume that intentionally making an unethical decision constitutes an important precursor of OMB. Because we attach special importance to managers' actions, we dedicate a separate chapter (chap. 9) to unethical managerial behavior in organizations, its antecedents, and implications. Using a case study approach, we show that personal motivations and lack of social values may interact with organizational circumstances and opportunities to produce behaviors that can cause unprecedented harm (e.g., the Enron case).

An intriguing and comprehensive empirically based typology of deviant workplace behavior was developed by Robinson and Bennett (1995), who conceived of employee deviance as voluntary behavior that violates significant organizational norms and, in so doing, threatens the well-being of an organization, its members, or both. This definition is problematic on three counts: (a) By emphasizing organizational norms, Robinson and Bennett distinguished workplace deviance from unethical behavior as the latter form of behavior relates to societal and moral, rather than local, conventions; (b) they included in their definition the harmful consequences of employee misconduct, thus precluding potential benefits of engaging in acts that defy local norms; and (c) they emphasized the role of significant norms espoused by the dominant coalitions in the organization. This could preclude less crystallized, yet important norms of conduct defined by other stakeholders such as customers or legislators.

Robinson and Bennett's (1995) typology of employee deviance consists of two dimensions: one ranging from personal to organizational targets, and the other from minor to serious infractions. Four types of voluntary and harmful misconduct emerged from a multidimensional scaling analysis: production deviance (e.g., wasting resources), property deviance (e.g., stealing from company), political deviance (e.g., showing undue favoritism), and personal deviance (e.g., sexual harassment). Robinson and Bennett's collaboration recently culminated in the development of a workplace deviance scale specifically devised to measure organizational and interpersonal targeted misbehavior (Bennett & Robinson, 2000). This fairly concise and useful measure taps into forms of both personal and organizational misbehavior (chap. 10 further discusses OMB measurement issues).

Robinson and Greenberg (1998) proposed an integrative model of workplace deviance consisting of five sequential components: (a) perpetrator (insider–outsider), (b) intention (intentional–unintentional), (c) target (internal–external and individual–organizational), (d) action (direct–indirect, active–passive, and verbal–physical), and (e) consequences (harmful–beneficial). This scheme allows for the identification of a variety of workplace activities that violate agreed on organizational norms of proper conduct. However, the model fails to provide a major component in the process—the motivation to violate accepted organizational norms (i.e., what forms the inclination or intention to misbehave?). The motivational question is dealt with at length in this book.

These models reflect an ongoing debate as to whether the decision to misbehave (e.g., to make an unethical decision) is more a function of bad apples or bad barrels (Trevino & Youngblood, 1990). That is, are misbehaviors a function of the personal characteristics of individuals (the bad apples perspective) or organizational and societal variables (the bad barrels perspective)? However, Granovetter (1992) argued that neither the undersocialized perspective of individuals acting in isolation nor the oversocialized perspective of individuals obedient to norms and culture is adequate to explain behavior. Following this argument, many researchers argue that neither the individual nor the organizational and societal perspectives alone fully explain OMB. Indeed most propose integrative explanations (e.g., O'Leary et al., 2000; Vardi & Wiener, 1996).

OMB

Our review of the literature suggests that misbehavior in organizations should not only be viewed as **pervasive,** but, for the most part, as **intentional** work-related behavior mostly (yet not necessarily) bearing **negative consequences** for both individuals (perpetrators and targets) and the organization. Thus, we view OMB as an integral and common aspect of organizational reality and an important facet of individual, group, and organization conduct, not as a marginal, deviant organizational occurrence. It is as real and important as proper and conventional workplace behavior.

Definitions of behaviors considered as workplace misbehavior may take a variety of approaches and properties depending on theoretical positions concerning

(a) the criterion against which OMB is determined, (b) the agent(s) who decide what constitutes OMB, and (c) the personal and organizational consequences of OMB. The position we take in this book concerning these requirements is guided by one overriding principle: The resulting definition should be broad enough to integrate various types of misbehavior, yet capable of providing a foundation for a constructive and explanatory model of OMB. Thus, we selected the concepts of values and norms as the criterion determining OMB and viewed both society at large and the organization as the defining agents. Because consequences of OMB can vary in different situations (e.g., functional or dysfunctional, negative or positive, and short term or long term), we do not include them in the definition, but rather as a dependent variable in the overall model.

The term OMB has its roots in the industrial relations field. Our conceptualization and definition of *misbehavior,* however, is quite different from the Marxist conceptualization (Edwards, 1979). Ackroyd and Thompson (1999) referred to it as "anything you do at work you are not supposed to do" (p. 2). They claimed misbehavior occurs when there is a mismatch between what is expected from the employees by their employers and what they are actually willing to do. This conceptualization of OMB deals with noncompliance, counterproductivity, and sabotage as part of employees' attempts to increase their own control over their work lives in today's capitalistic labor market. The authors presented four dimensions of appropriation in the organization on which owners and workers may agree or disagree: appropriation of work, appropriation of resources, appropriation of time, and appropriation of identity. Inherent conflicts between employees and employers about these dimensions is what may lead employees to misbehave; the various forms of misbehavior reflect different levels and intensity of disagreement.

This Marxist explanation of OMB posits that it is an expression of employees' resistance to managerial control. Hence, misbehavior is an endemic condition produced by the organization resulting from the inevitable class conflict and is by no means new. Although it is reasonable to believe that OMB is widespread, there is no reason to treat it as an inevitable product of class conflict. For example, in some cases, employee theft may reflect an employee's attempt to take revenge for maltreatment and a means of protest against employers. Undeniably, it may also be motivated by personal needs and intended to benefit the perpetrators (Greenberg, 1993).

Our view is that OMB is voluntary and committed by choice. Thus, we adopt Vardi and Wiener's (1996) definition for OMB as "any intentional action by member/s of organization/s which defies and violates (a) shared organizational norms and expectations, and/or (b) core societal values, mores and standards of proper conduct" (p. 151). Clearly this definition requires some qualification. Before we do that, it is crucial to emphasize that we explicitly rule out unintentional acts of misbehavior such as accidental damage to a machine or injury to a coworker. Such mishaps are a result of human error. However, accidents resulting from intentional violation of rules and procedures are indeed considered as OMB. That is, we include in the OMB construct only those acts that are intentional and purposeful regardless of their eventual consequences.

First, the violation of organizational norms and values is a fundamental component in the OMB construct. Work organizations are complex social entities often comprising multiple subunits and constituencies, thus the term *organization* does not necessarily convey a determinate entity. Rather, it represents the relevant unit of analysis of an investigator, manager, or consultant interested in the OMB phenomenon. Depending on their perspectives and special interests, researchers and practitioners may refer to a work organization as a whole or any significant sector within it, such as a work group or one of the divisions or strategic business units. Choice regarding the identity of the unit of interest must be made explicit to identify the relevant core values against which a violation (and therefore OMB) may occur. Thus, whenever the term *organization* is used herein, it is meant to convey exactly this meaning.

Second, both the overt action and its underlying intention(s) are necessary to identify misbehavior; to define OMB without its antecedent intention(s) may result in erroneously including behaviors that may be unintentional or accidental. Hence, work-related actions that involve errors, mistakes, or even unconscious and unintended negligence (e.g., a harmful mistake in a surgical procedure that is committed unintentionally) do not constitute OMB despite their similar consequences to the organization as well as to the actors involved.

Third, in studying OMB, we focus on the individual level of analysis rather than the group or organization level. Although it may be possible to apply the concept of OMB to misbehavior by groups (cf. Trice & Beyer, 1993, on deviant organizational subcultures) or organizations (cf. see Baucus & Near, 1991, on illegal corporate behavior), we direct our attention to individual members who are intentionally, actually, and directly involved in some form of OMB because the role of individual motivation and choice is the source and driver of OMB.

Fourth, for OMB to occur, it needs to run counter to existing core values and norms. These pertain to both formal (laws, rules, regulations, standard operating procedures, etc.) and informal organizational or social expectations. Our definition acknowledges the importance of both internal (intraorganizational) and external (societal) value systems in determining OMB.

The Role of Values

Personal and organizational values play a central role in the understanding of OMB. Therefore, a quick review of the concept is necessary. In the social-psychology literature, there are some inconsistencies in the definition of the concept and the distinctions between values and related constructs such as attitudes, beliefs, and norms. Nevertheless, certain formulations, which allow for operational definitions and empirical measurement, have gained a fair degree of acceptance (cf. Brown,

1976; Fallding, 1965; Meglino, Ravlin & Adkins, 1989; Wiener, 1988). One such definition, first proposed by Rokeach (1973), states that "a value is an enduring belief that a specific mode of conduct or end-state of existence is personally or socially preferable to an opposite or converse mode of conduct or end-state of existence" (p. 5). To Rokeach, values are forms of beliefs that may stem from social expectations particularly when shared. Thus, social values may indeed be viewed as normative beliefs complementing instrumental beliefs as antecedents of behavior (Fishbein & Ajzen, 1975). Further, values may be construed as internalized normative beliefs. Once established, they may act as a built-in normative compass— a guide for behavior independent from the effect of rewards and punishments that result from actions (Wiener, 1982).

The concepts of values and norms apply to various types of social units, including the three most congruous with the definition of OMB: work groups, work organizations, and society at large. Rokeach's (1973) definition suggests that values shared by group members, particularly values concerning modes of conduct, become similar to norms guiding members toward uniformity in behavior. Others (e.g., Kilman, 1985), however, distinguish between norms and values, arguing that the former offer more specific and explicit behavioral expectations, whereas the latter are broader in scope than norms (for a more extensive review of organizational value systems, see Wiener, 1988; for a discussion on societal level values, see Rokeach, 1973).

DEFINITIONAL IMPLICATIONS

The definition of OMB implies four important and distinct features that are useful for constructing an integrative model of misbehavior, measuring the variables, and deriving relevant predictions as well as implications for management in dealing with OMB. Indeed, these are the main goals for this book. Thus, we raise some key definitional issues pertaining to OMB as a theoretical construct and variable in terms of meaning, scope, and effects.

The Construct

Our definition of OMB does not necessitate that the act violate both societal and organizational values to be categorized as such. Although such behaviors are not uncommon (e.g., unauthorized use of company property), it would be theoretically too narrow and not constructive to limit OMB to just those acts. According to the proposed definition, a behavior that may be consistent with organizational expectations, but that violates societal values (e.g., misleading customers), would be considered OMB. Such organizationally condoned misbehaviors may be detrimental to the employee involved and the organization in the long run. Similarly, member behavior that is consistent with societal values but violates organizational

expectations would also be classified as OMB (e.g., whistle blowing in an organization that does not sanction such a behavior). Unacceptable as these behaviors
may be at the time and particular location, they may indeed be beneficial to organizations in the long run. We deem this definitional broadness as essential in any
attempt to construct an integrative and inclusive OMB model. Our definition also
provides a solid basis for a meaningful typology of misbehaviors that would be
useful in the overall understanding and prediction of organizational outcomes.

OMB—Pernicious or Beneficial?

Another feature of the OMB construct is that it does not necessarily equate the
violation of norms or values with negative and undesirable behavior. First, our
definition does not make reference to the consequences of misbehavior. Second,
the desirability of any value-breaking behavior is inherently a matter of judgment.
In general, value-violating behavior would be deemed undesirable by a collective
of individuals sharing that value, but it may be perceived as desirable by another
collective that views this behavior as desirable and beneficial. If we examine the
all too prevalent phenomenon of cheating customers, it may be valued as undesirable by members of society at large, while it may be deemed acceptable and
even necessary in an organization strapped for cash. By the same token, whistle
blowing may be viewed as commendable action by members of society at large,
but unacceptable to the top management of a particular organization.

Consequences of OMB

Unlike some definitions (e.g., Robinson & Bennett, 1995), our definition does not
deal with eventual or real consequences of misbehavior. We argue that the consequences of OMB may be only evaluated by their degree of constructiveness or
destructiveness for any given organization. The basic premise is that an organization may not be successful, in the long run, if it expects or even permits members to
violate values and norms of the larger society within which it operates. Thus, using
the same example, in the long run cheating customers would tend to be detrimental
to organizations that allow it, but whistle blowing may prove constructive (Miceli &
Near, 1992). OMB which violates both societal and organizational values, such
as undermining and harassing members, engaging in corporate fraud, sabotaging
work, or vandalizing equipment, is clearly destructive.

OMB as a Complex Variable

Because OMB is defined in relation to a set of core values of a particular social
unit, and because such core values can be measured, OMB can be considered
a variable. Moreover, because of the complex phenomenon it may tap, OMB
should be treated as a multidimensional construct. Such an approach is useful to

improve the model's precision and it is necessary to generate significant predictions about the phenomenon. In general, OMB may range from a low (benign) degree of misbehavior, such as minor workplace incivility, to a high (severe) degree of misbehavior, such as the murder of coworkers, and the measurement may take two forms: behavioral and attitudinal.

The behavioral aspect of OMB can be measured using frequency counts of acts of misbehavior with respect to a given organizational unit or to individual members. This frequency measure can also be weighted by an index of severity of the observed misbehavior. Such an index may be comprised of two facets: (a) the centrality of the violated norm or value (for proposals related to the measurement of the centrality of a core value, see Wiener, 1988), and (b) the degree of premeditation, preoccupation, or planning involved in the misbehavior.

The attudinal aspect of OMB may tap the individual's strength or intensity of the intention, predisposition, or propensity to engage in work- and organization-related misconduct. Although people tend to be quite reluctant to openly express intentions to misbehave, instruments that tap into these intentions could be designed and developed (e.g., in a questionnaire form. For a discussion on OMB measurement issues, see chap. 10). Multifaceted indexes (behavioral and attitudinal) are routinely used by OB researchers to measure specific work behaviors that individuals hesitate to report—withdrawal behavior (e.g., actual incidents of turnover and intentions to leave the organization) or organizational citizenship behavior (e.g., actual altruistic deeds and prosocial attitudes). Indeed using both behavioral and attitudinal observations may facilitate a more meaningful classification of the misbehavior phenomenon.

Basic Types of OMB

An examination of a broad range of norm-violating behaviors suggests that all such actions may be classified into three basic categories based on the underlying intention of the misbehaving individual:

1. Misbehaviors intended to benefit the self (*OMB Type S*). These are mostly internal to the organization and usually victimize the employing firm or its members. Such behaviors may have three categories of internal targets: (a) the work (e.g., distorting data); (b) the organization's property, resources, symbols, or regulations (e.g., stealing and selling manufacturing secrets); and (c) other members (e.g., harassing peers). An exception is a member's behavior that appears to benefit the organization (e.g., overcharging customers), but is in fact intended to eventually benefit the individual (e.g., gaining a promotion).
2. Misbehaviors that primarily intend to benefit the member's employing organization as a whole (*OMB Type O*). These (e.g., falsifying records to improve

chances of obtaining a contract for the organization) are usually directed toward external victims such as other organizations, social institutions, public agencies, or customers. If the intention underlying this form of behavior is not primarily to benefit the organization, but is self-serving (e.g., for career considerations), it should not be classified as OMB Type O; more likely, this would be OMB Type S.

3. Misbehaviors that primarily intend to inflict damage and be destructive (*OMB Type D*). Targets of these behaviors could be both internal and external. Whereas the intentions underlying Type S and Type O misbehaviors are to benefit either the individual or organization, the intention underlying OMB Type D is to hurt others or the organization. Such intentional misbehaviors (e.g., sabotaging company-owned equipment) may be perpetrated by members either on their own initiative (e.g., as revenge or a response to perceived or actual mistreatment) or on behalf of significant others (e.g., interfering with organizational operations to comply with a union's expectations). However, the underlying intention must be to cause some type of damage whether it is minor or considerable, subtle or visible.

Although OMB classification is based on an internal psychological state (intentions), the classifying task should not be overly subjective. In most cases, the proper classification can be accurately derived from the act. As a rule, when more than one intention seems to underlie an act of OMB, and when observations yield equivocal data, the predominant intention would determine the classification. For example, when a part-time fireman sets a national forest on fire to generate work for himself, this would be OMB Type S because benefiting the self, rather than causing damage, was the primary intention (*New York Times,* July 2002). Again to emphasize the intention principle, which is at the core of the OMB classification, it is necessary to analyze OMB within a behavioral-motivational framework. Therefore, we elaborate on this in the following section.

Conceptual Anchors

Any willful (motivated) violation of shared expectations (norms and values) constitutes misbehavior regardless of its consequences. Therefore, mainstream OB paradigms that make distinctions between normative, value-based processes, and instrumental-calculative ones in determining individual behavior in organizations might be useful as a basis for an individual misbehavior model. One such paradigm, which has been used effectively to explain determinants of individual behavior in organizations, is Fishbein and Ajzen's (1975) reasoned action theory.

Fishbein and Ajzen's conceptualization focuses primarily on predicting and understanding behavioral intentions. It hypothesizes that an individual's behavior is a function of the intention to perform that behavior. A person's behavioral intention, in turn, is determined by two basic components: (a) the person's attitude toward performing the act and (b) the subjective norm or, specifically, perception of the totality of the normative pressures concerning the behavior.

The first component—the person's attitude toward performing the act—is a function of beliefs concerning the consequences of the act and the value of the outcomes as the specific individual perceives them. These can be referred to as instrumental-cognitive beliefs. The second component—the subjective norm—is a function of a person's beliefs about what referent others think he or she should do weighted by the motivation to comply with them. Such significant others may include specific individuals, a particular reference group, the work organization, or society at large.

The manner by which members of a social unit acquire norms and values is not a simple one. How do members know when they act in defiance of existing norms? How do they identify situations in which they engage in certain forms of OMB? Salancik and Pfeffer's (1978) social information theory may be particularly helpful. To them the social context affects a person's behavior by shaping his or her perceptions and beliefs about organizational situations. Yet one can argue that sense-making cues, transmitted through both formal and informal social interactions, pertain not only to desirable behavior but also and perhaps more dramatically to misbehavior. Such cues may carry important symbolic and affective meanings, as well as instrumental ones. Thus, individual attitudes and beliefs, which are formed through such socially constructed realities (Berger & Luckmann, 1966), may determine the intentions that lead to the various types of OMB.

In addition, several researchers (e.g., Jaccard & Davidson, 1975; Pomazal & Jaccard, 1976; Schwartz & Tessler, 1972) have suggested that the subjective norm is determined not only by social normative beliefs (i.e., a person's beliefs of how others expect him or her to act), but also by personal normative beliefs—personal moral standards (Jones, 1991) concerning a particular mode of conduct are established when a person internalizes expectations of others concerning a particular behavior. These determinants of the subjective norm may be termed *internalized subjective beliefs*. When behavioral acts are guided by internalized pressures, they are no longer dependent on their linkage with the reinforcements and sanctions on which they were initially based (e.g., Jones & Gerard, 1967). To Fishbein and Ajzen, attitudes and subjective norms may be viewed as predictors and the behavioral intention as the criterion. The model incorporates both cognitive and affective components because attitudes, by definition, include affective or evaluative considerations concerning ensuing acts (in our case, intentional acts of misbehavior).

Because in our proposed framework one major determinant of OMB is the rational calculations of utility of the behavior to the employee, it is important to determine the considerations that go into this decision-making process. March and Simon's (1958) seminal book on organizations offers important insights (e.g., inducement-contribution trade-offs) about causes of work-related behavior.

According to their paradigm, individuals in organizations decide not only to join or leave but also how to perform and how much effort to exert in any given circumstance. Granted these decisions are constrained by imperfect (bounded) rationality, yet individuals are by and large aware of both constraints and opportunities in their organizational environment. For instance, they use such information in their decisions to come to work or call in sick. This rationale can be readily adapted to explain forms of misbehavior because individuals are aware (albeit imperfectly) of the opportunities as well as the consequences of engaging in misconduct. Such knowledge, in turn, provides the sources of most instrumental or calculative considerations that, like any sort of work behavior, may be limited. Thus, March and Simon's paradigm provides us with an essential attribute of the major cognitions contributing to the formation of individual interests that determine certain types of OMB.

OMB AS INTENTIONAL BEHAVIOR

A motivational OMB framework is shown in Fig. 2.1. The core relationships are based on the Fishbein and Ajzen model as adapted by Wiener (1982) to form a normative–instrumental framework of individual commitment and by Wiener and Vardi (1990) to conceptually integrate organizational culture and individual

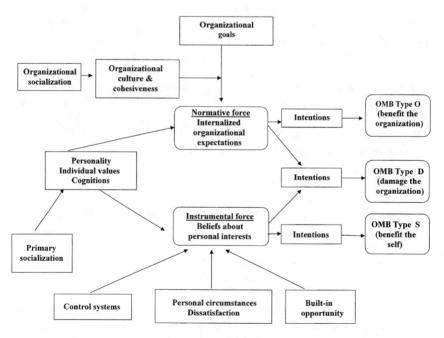

FIG. 2.1. A motivational OMB model.

motivation. In the basic OMB system, misbehavior is not always a function of the two predictor categories: instrumental and normative. Instead, depending on its type, OMB may be determined by either one of the two predictors or simultaneously by both.

OMB Type S

OMB Type S reflects intention to benefit the individual rather than the employing organization. It is determined primarily by attitude, which in turn is a function of the sum of the beliefs concerning the consequences of the individual's misbehavior. Because such misbehavior is self-serving, it stands to reason that it would be influenced by a person's beliefs concerning the extent to which the misbehavior is likely to result in favorable or unfavorable outcomes. For instance, the probability of misusing company resources is reduced if the person believes that punishment may readily result from such act than when no sanctions are anticipated. Thus, the motivational process underlying OMB Type S is primarily calculative-instrumental. Nevertheless, although this type of misconduct is a function of instrumental processes, these behaviors may be constrained by factors, such as the degree of the cohesiveness among members, the organization culture, and organization control mechanisms.

OMB Type O

Although less common, OMB Type O reflects the intentions to benefit the employing organization rather than the individual directly. It is primarily determined by subjective norms that are a function of the totality of internalized normative beliefs concerning expectations from organizational members. As a rule, Type O misbehaviors are anchored in ideology and values and are carried out by individuals who strongly identify with their organization, its mission, and its leadership, and who are often willing to sacrifice self-interests for greater causes. Intentionally breaking the law to protect company interests while knowingly risking personal well-being is a case in point. Although normative pressures determine this type of OMB, one could also argue that certain instrumental factors serve as constraints (e.g., situations in which the potential actors refrain from misbehavior because they estimate the likelihood of being punished by external agencies as being too high for them). Of course it is possible that an individual may break the law on behalf of the company for personal interests. This form of misbehavior should be classified as OMB Type S because the predominant motive self-serving.

OMB Type D

Unlike OMB Types S and O, Vardi and Wiener (1996) classified acts as OMB Type D as reflected by the intentions to damage and hurt a particular individual, organization asset, or social unit. Underlying such intentions may be normative forces as in the case of speaking publicly against the employing organization or damaging company property as a show of solidarity with striking union members. Concurrently, this kind of behavior might be largely determined by instrumental forces: deriving personal satisfaction from an act of revenge or vandalism. This is why we contend that, in principle, both normative and instrumental forces may converge simultaneously to determine Type D misbehavior.

ANTECEDENTS OF MISBEHAVIOR

Our definition of OMB and proposed conceptual framework, which emphasizes the distinction between normative and instrumental determinants of misbehavior, suggests the existence of identifiable antecedents that may affect the formation of the motivational components in the model. We believe that antecedents contributing to the instrumental component would primarily influence Type S misbehavior, and antecedents contributing to the normative component would affect Type O misbehavior. Both forces may influence OMB Type D. We now offer general categories and a selected sample of determinants that may contribute most to the variance of the normative and instrumental components of the model and, consequently, to OMB. The antecedents are categorized according to levels of analysis: organization, group, task, and individual.

Organization-Level Antecedents

Clearly organizations differ in terms of the contextual conditions, at different levels, that may affect the propensity of an individual member to engage in work-related misbehavior. Groups of such factors are listed as follows.

Organizational Goals. Organizational goals—those implicit and declared targets that serve to translate organization strategy to actual plans, closely reflecting top management values and expectations—are likely to strongly influence members' job performance and productivity levels. However, the pursuit of organizational goals may also encourage employee misbehavior particularly when they are conflicting, highly demanding, vague, or unrealistic (Reimann & Wiener, 1988; Stein & Kanter, 1993) and supported by a strong culture or neurotic (Kets de Vries & Miller, 1984) executives. For example, Ackroyd and Thompson (1999) posited that employee misconduct is mostly a form of protest against arbitrary managerial control.

Control Systems. Control systems are not uniform across organizations and may not be similar across departments within the same workplace. Control systems are physical or procedural entities within the workplace designed specifically to reduce the occurrence of events judged to be detrimental to the organization. Typically they serve to increase the risk of detection and thus the likelihood of the perpetrators of such acts to be sanctioned (Sackett & DeVore, 2001). Although methods of control permeate the workplace (Sewell, 1998), there is still little sound empirical evidence of their effectiveness. Nonetheless, it stands to reason that oppressive as well as lax controls, performance appraisal, reward, disciplinary systems, and special monitoring arrangements may contribute to the emergence of OMB (cf. Ackroyd & Thompson, 1999; Hegarty & Sims, 1978). Certain jobs and work organizations involve operations for which external control of employee behavior is inherently difficult. Home delivery, operating cash registers, professional or food services, operations in which cash transactions cannot be directly monitored by receipts, and inventory counts are only a few examples of work processes that may be difficult to monitor at times. Thus, control systems may have a direct impact on members' instrumental considerations of whether to engage in or refrain from acts of misconduct (Vardi & Wiener, 1996). On the one hand, when confronted with extreme control (e.g., surveillance), employees might attempt to resist and protest through damaging behavior (OMB Type D). On the other hand, lax controls might be perceived as a sign of trust and lead to exemplary behavior— or the same signals may be viewed as a form of organizational weakness and present a built-in opportunity to misbehave.

Organizational Culture and Climate. Organizational culture is widely regarded as a construct denoting the extent to which members share core organizational values (Trice & Beyer 1993; Wiener, 1988). Several writers (e.g., Kunda, 1992) demonstrated the power of culture as a tool used by certain dominant groups (e.g., top management) to shape members' values and reduce counterproductive behavior (Boye & Jones, 1997; Vardi, 2001). An organization's *climate of honesty,* defined by Cherington and Cherington (1985) as employees' perception of the presence of an enforced code of ethics, the perceived level of top management honesty, the internal controls, the punitive system, and the perception that that those caught engaging in counterproductive behavior will in fact be punished, acts to reduce misbehavior. Unequivocally, organizations that develop ethical climates enhance ethical rather than unethical behavior (Victor & Cullen, 1988).

Furthermore, the ways employees perceive the fairness of their treatment and the perceived equity of the distribution of resources are important antecedents of misbehavior. Skarlicki and Folger (1997) posited that procedural justice may be further broken down into the fairness of the decisions, the manner in which they are presented, and the treatment accorded the effected employees once the decision has been made. This is termed *interactional justice.* Organizational policies and practices clearly influence the ways in which employees work and misbehave. For example, an employee may choose to sabotage the assembly line in reaction to a perceived injustice. Inequity theory (Adams, 1963) posits that workers compare the sum of the intrinsic and extrinsic rewards they receive for the effort they put into the remuneration others get for their work. If the effort–reward ratio is not proportional, some will feel that they are overpaid, whereas others will feel they are underpaid. The former may experience feelings of guilt, whereas the latter group's sense of inequity may lead to feelings of resentment and anger. This felt inequity—the sense of organizational injustice—may serve as an antecedent to misbehavior. Greenberg (1990a), following Skarlicki and Folger, showed that inequity alone may not be enough to trigger misbehavior. He argued that when there is an interaction between the perceived inequity and the manner in which the manager chooses to explain and deal with it, the likelihood of the worker to misbehave increases.

Organizational Cohesiveness. Cohesiveness refers to the degree of social bonding and normative closeness. In cohesive work environments, the pressure to adhere to norms of work conduct is especially high. Therefore, cohesiveness may affect misbehavior in a manner similar to the way organizational culture affects OMB. Indeed it may be more powerful. We regard this organization characteristic as a significant antecedent that may strongly contribute to wrongdoing in the name of ideology and organizational causes. Also drawing on the concept of *groupthink* (Janis, 1982), it is logical to propose that extreme organizational cohesiveness could also produce some kind of *organizationthink*, potentially leading to misguided strategic behavior.

Group-Level Antecedents

As Goffman (1959) vividly demonstrated, the self only exists in relation to others. In the workplace, the work group is indeed a significant other. The importance of groups and work teams and their relationship to individual behavior and organizational performance has been widely documented, beginning with the early human relationists (Mayo, 1933; Roethlisberger & Dickson, 1964). Griffin et al. (1998b) emphasized the importance of groups in terms of both the causes and consequences of what they called *dysfunctional behavior* in organizations. They argued that group misbehavior is both intentional and damaging and has internal as well as external antecedents.

Internal Pressures. Since group affiliation was demonstrated to be a major determinant of work behavior, it has received significant research attention (Homans, 1950). Studies on groups and their effects within the organizational setting have exposed both positive (productivity) and negative (restriction) effects. Most theorists (for a thorough review, see Feldman, 1981) and researchers (e.g., Gladstein, 1984; Tziner & Vardi, 1982), however, have posited that work groups bear a positive influence on individual work behavior by reinforcing normative performance and attitudes. Such influential social-psychological approaches as Bandura's (1973) social learning theory and Salancik and Pfeffer's (1978) social information-processing theory, attempt to explain why and how groups exercise (positive) power over their members. Social information-processing theory argues that if one is a member of a work group in which misbehavior such as pilfering or false reporting go unsanctioned, he or she is more likely to engage in such misbehavior as well. That is, this theory posits that individuals adapt their behavior based on consequences that are observed and not experienced directly. If a worker is aware of misbehavior by a fellow employee and knows that he or she was punished for it, that worker may change his intention toward that misbehavior.

Furthermore, employees who are inclined to misbehave may be attracted to and selected by work groups that support and reinforce this behavior. Indeed, Robinson and O'Leary-Kelly (1998) found that the group aggregate measure of counterproductive behavior has a significant effect on individual misbehavior. Concomitantly, another body of work demonstrated that groups may create internal dynamics that may be considered negative. Janis (1982) showed the effects of groupthink on decision making, and others have demonstrated such consequences as performance restriction and social loafing (see Karau & Williams', 1993, meta-analysis). Hollinger (1986) showed that the more attached an employee is to non-deviant workers, the less likely he or she will engage in misbehavior. Following Hirschi's (1969) social bonding theory, Lasley (1988) argued that the existence of a common and shared value system in the work group may act to frame misbehavior in a permissible and legal manner. Similarly, the more cohesive the work group, the more likely it is to condone or prohibit misbehavior by its members.

External Pressures.   Interest in group behavior has received a significant boost from situational (Fiedler, 1967), contingency (Hersey & Blanchard, 1982; Reddin, 1967), leader-member exchange (Liden & Green, 1980), charismatic leaders (Shamir, House, & Arthur, 1993), and team leadership theories (Avolio, 1999). These approaches, however, tend to emphasize the role of the manager leader in influencing subordinate (individual and group) normative behavior. Overlooked is the fact that leaders may also encourage negative attitudes and behaviors. Bandura (1969) applied social learning theory to explain how aggressive behavior may be learned from significant others. In much the same vein, Greenberg (1997) explicated the role of groups in enhancing not only prosocial but also antisocial (e.g., stealing) work behavior. Robinson and O'Leary-Kelly (1998) found that the group's antisocial behavior may actually serve as a model for individual members' work-related OMB (e.g., damaging employer property, purposely hurting a colleague, and deliberately breaking rules).

Task-Level Antecedents

Job Design.   Some built-in opportunities to take advantage of or misuse various organizational resources (e.g., time, office equipment, telephone and mail, work tools, Internet, etc.) exist in most jobs. In many cases, the degree to which such built-in opportunities exist may enter into the instrumental calculations concerning the benefits, consequences, and risks of capitalizing on such opportunities (Bliss & Aoki, 1993). Some work organizations apply stringent mechanisms to determine what their employees are doing at any given moment, whereas others employ lax systems or none at all. Clearly these may affect employee behavior and misbehavior in the workplace. For example, Vardi and Weitz (2001) demonstrated that job autonomy may be a potential source of misbehavior—they found a positive correlation for measures of OMB and job antonomy.

Individual-Level Antecedents

Personality.   Although there is no doubt that personality affects behavior, Robinson and Greenberg (1998) argued that there is little if any empirical evidence for the relationship between personality variables and misbehavior. We disagree. Our reading of the voluminous body of literature regarding personality and organization behavior suggests otherwise.

Two personality variables in particular affect motivational components and, in turn, the intention to engage in OMB. The two variables are the normative process of value internalization and the calculations involved in forming instrumental beliefs about personal interests. First is the level of moral development of an organization member (Kohlberg, 1969). Trevino (1986) already demonstrated the usefulness of this factor in the context of unethical behavior among managers. Second is the degree of sociopathic predisposition—the state characterized by disregard for social norms and obligations without the inhibiting experience of guilt. Of course extreme degrees of sociopathic tendencies characterize only a marginal portion of any organization's workforce.

Significant relationships between certain personality traits and workplace delinquency were reported by Ashton (1998). Trevino (1986) proposed the usefulness of such traits as *locus of control* and *field dependence* in predicting unethical decision-making behavior among managers. Griffin et al. (1998) also included individual ethics, values, and morality as antecedents of dysfunctional work behavior. Certainly sociopathic predispositions (Vardi & Wiener, 1996) or pathological tendencies of organizational members (Griffin et al., 1998) are important antecedents. Fox and Spector (1999) found that personality variables affect misbehavior. They reported significant relationships among irascibility, anxiety, impulsiveness, and OMB.

Similarly, Raelin (1986, 1994) reported on the relationship between personality variables and OMB. He found that professionals with low self-esteem tend to express their frustration by counterproductive behaviors. Moreover, he found that achievement motivation is negatively related to employee deviance. That is, the higher the employees' achievement motivation, the lower their tendency to misbehave. Also professionals who feel depressed at work are more likely to misbehave (Raelin, 1994). Galperin and Aquino (1999) found a significant relationship between personality variables and misbehavior. A tendency to behave aggressively moderates the relationship between the perception of injustice and organizational deviance. Thus, people with a strong tendency to behave aggressively are more likely to respond negatively (e.g., to fake sickness, be late for work, etc.) as a result of their perception of injustice than those with a low tendency toward aggression.

Personality researchers (cf. Barrick & Mount, 1991; Digman, 1990) agree that it is possible to organize the noncognitive dimensions of personality. The five major components are *extroversion, agreeableness, conscientiousness, neuroticism,* and *openness to experience.* This categorization is useful for OMB research: It lends itself well to the generation of research questions. A person high on neuroticism is expected to exhibit misbehavior toward the organization and fellow workers, and an employee low on agreeableness is expected to engage in interpersonal misbehavior (Krigel, 2001). In this vein, Barrick and Mount (1991) provided meta-analytical evidence that personality traits (e.g., conscientiousness) are consistently predictive of several job behavior measures—the conscientiousness dimension is consistently related to counterproductive behavior in the workplace. Clearly personality plays a role in determining whether a worker will misbehave. This is further explored in chapter 6.

Value Congruence. This antecedent refers to the degree to which personal values held by the individual are consistent with core organizational and group norms and values (Vardi & Wiener, 1996). The higher such congruence is, the more likely a member is to identify with a referent social unit and be guided by its values and norms (Chatman, 1989; Hall & Schneider, 1972). However, individual values, when incongruent with those of top management, may lead to adaptive behavior characterized by frustration and aggression and may have harmful consequences to the organization (Acroyd & Thompson, 1999; Argyris, 1964). Moreover, extreme commitment and identification may also lead to blind loyalty, which might bear negative behavioral consequences as well (Wiener, 1982). Hence, this variable represents a strong contribution to the normative component of the model and, in turn, to OMB.

The generalized value of loyalty and duty is a personal value acquired in the process of primary socialization. It represents a generalized sense of duty and obligation—namely, the belief by individuals that they have a moral obligation to exhibit loyalty in all significant social situations in which they are involved (Wiener, 1982). Regardless of their other values, individuals who rank high on *generalized loyalty and duty* would tend to identify with their organization and behave accordingly.

Attitudes. When individuals perceive being mistreated by their employing organizations, the valence of self-benefiting misbehavior may increase (e.g., Analoui & Kakabadse, 1992; Greenberg, 1990b; Hollinger, 1986; Mangioni & Quinn, 1975). This may indirectly influence the way organizational expectations

are learned and internalized; it is less likely for a member to be successfully socialized by and identify with an organization when mistreatment of self and others
is perceived. Thus, dissatisfaction of members' needs by an organization primarily affects the instrumental component of motivation to misbehave, but it can
indirectly contribute to the normative forces as well. Job satisfaction, especially
dissatisfaction, has long been associated with counterproductive behaviors. In his
synthesis and review of the literature, Hackett (1989) found, not unsurprisingly,
a stable relationship between job dissatisfaction and absenteeism. Klein, Leong,
and Silva (1996) posited a relationship between dissatisfaction and sabotage in the
workplace.

   Personal Circumstances.   When an individual faces a compelling need
or deprivation—material or otherwise—he or she might be more inclined to engage
in misbehavior that may help resolve such a need (e.g., Merton, 1938). Conversely,
when anticipating being at risk of losing membership and employment, both workers and managers may be less inclined to misbehave. Thus, specific personal circumstances partially determine one's tendencies to engage in OMB—primarily by
shaping instrumental beliefs about the value of the ensuing consequences of any
given misbehavior. When individuals perceive being mistreated by their employing organizations, the valence of self-benefiting misbehavior may increase (e.g.,
Ackroyd & Thompson, 1999; Analoui & Kakabadse, 1992; Greenberg, 1990b;
Hollinger, 1986; Mangione & Quinn, 1975).

A GENERAL FRAMEWORK

Our discussion of OMB thus far focused on the wide range of antecedents that
may lead individuals to choose some form of misconduct. Following Vardi and
Wiener's (1992, 1996) typology, we classified such behaviors into three types
based on their predominant motive for choosing this mode of behavior. We now
expand this initial conceptualization to a more general framework articulating both
antecedents of the intention to misbehave and the actual forms of misbehavior as
manifested in organizations. Thus, our extended model (Fig. 2.2) formally depicts
the multilevel effects on the intentions to misbehave at work. It also provides a
new categorization of manifested behaviors regarded as acts of OMB. It subsumes
that each manifestation can indeed result from any one or more of the antecedents,
and it is mediated by the intention to misbehave. Certainly any determination as
to the actual cause, of course, is a matter for empirical investigation.

OMB Manifestations

Trying to list all possible expressions of OMB seems is an endless and perhaps futile task because, as discussed earlier, the perception of a certain act as
counternormative is highly contingent on situational factors. Moreover, researchers

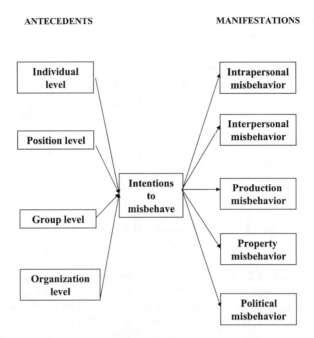

FIG. 2.2. A general framework for OMB.

often use different designations for the same or similar classes of actions. For instance, embezzlement (e.g., Altheide et al., 1978; Cressey, 1953), fiddling (e.g., Mars, 1973), pilferage (e.g., Altheide et al., 1978; Ditton, 1977; Mars, 1973), and theft (e.g., Greenberg, 1990b, 1997, 1998; Horning, 1970; Kemper, 1996; Mars, 1974; Merriam, 1977) all refer to the same behavior, albeit in varied degrees of severity. Much the same, industrial sabotage (Taylor & Walton, 1971), vandalism (Cohen, 1973; DeMore et al., 1988; Fisher & Baron, 1982), and destruction (Allen & Greenberger, 1980) all refer to intentional sabotage.

We organized the expressions of OMB in five categories that are consistent with current writing: intrapersonal misbehavior (e.g., workplace problem drinking, drug abuse, and workaholic behavior), interpersonal misbehavior (e.g., incivility, aggressive behavior, bullying, and sexual harassment), production misbehavior (rule breaking, loafing, absenteeism, and tardiness), property misbehavior (e.g., vandalism, theft, espionage, and computer hacking), and political misbehavior (e.g., misuse of power, impression management, politicking, and favoritism).

OMB Antecedents

Our model (Fig. 2.2) categorized OMB antecedents into classes representing four levels of analysis: individual, position, group, and organizational. The choice of variables is based on studies and models that have previously established some evidence for the role these factors have in explaining misbehavior.

Individual Level.   This category includes personality variables such as the *Big Five* (Barrick & Mount, 1991) and locus of control (Trevino, 1986); attitudes such as job satisfaction (Farrell, 1983; Mangione & Quinn, 1975), frustration (Fox & Spector, 1999; Spector, 1978), and organizational commitments (Blau, 1987); affect and emotion (e.g., Beugre, 1998); and stress (e.g., Spector, 1975, 1978).

Position Level.   This category consists of variables considered to be relevant properties of the job, such as job type and design and built-in opportunity to misbehave (e.g., Vardi & Weitz, 2001) .

Group Level.   This category, includes such variables as norms (e.g., Robinson & O'Leary-Kelly, 1998) and leadership styles (e.g., Ashforth, 1994).

Organizational Level.   This group of determinants consists of variables such as climate and culture (e.g., Ackroyd & Thompson, 1999; Vardi, 2001), socialization, and control systems (e.g., Griffin et al., 1998b; Vaughan, 1998).

Mediators

All current models dealing with OMB subsume intentionality (O'Leary-Kelly et al., 2000). That is, they automatically exclude acts—even those that may be harmful—that are accidental. Robinson and Greenberg (1998) identified five defining characteristics of any behavior that would be considered antisocial in the workplace: perpetrator, intention, target, action, and consequence. The intention to engage in the act would be the mediating variable. Thus, in O'Leary-Kelly et al.'s (2000) terms, *antisocial work behavior* is defined as any attempted behavior that is intentional and potentially harmful.

Following Vardi and Wiener (1996), the intention to misbehave is assumed to mediate the relationships between the antecedents and expressions or manifestations of OMB. This intention, in turn, is assumed to be the result of two major independent—yet possibly correlated—forces: the instrumental force, reflecting the actor's beliefs about his or her own personal interests; and the normative force, reflecting the actor's internalized organizational expectations. These two forces may influence the intention to misbehave as well as the specific type of misbehavior decided on independently or in conjunction. That is, the intention to misbehave may be translated into action in more than one form of misbehavior reflecting two different sets of considerations. For example, an aggravated employee may seek to harm his supervisor to satisfy his own need for revenge (instrumental force), restrict his output in protest, like his fellow employees do (normative force), or do both.

General Propositions

Following the prior review and the models depicted in Fig. 2.1 and 2.2, the process of OMB engagement by organizational stakeholders can be summarized as follows:

- OMB is a motivational process in which the intention to misbehave is assumed to mediate the relationship between the antecedents of the intention and the expressions of the ensuing act.
- The intention to misbehave reflects two different yet possibly interrelated sets of considerations—normative and instrumental—which in turn are a function of one or more antecedents at one or more levels.
- The intention to misbehave may translate into action in one or more manifestations of misbehavior.

A ROAD MAP

The framework described in this chapter serves as our conceptual road map for the entire book. We embark on our journey with a description of the expressions of OMB and work our way back to the various antecedents that may account for them. We begin with three chapters devoted to the numerous OMB manifestations found in work organizations. Chapter 3 deals with intra- and interpersonal manifestations, chapter 4 with production and political manifestations, and chapter 5 with property manifestations—both tangible and intellectual. Three chapters dealing with OMB antecedents follow. Chapter 6 deals with individual-level antecedents, chapter 7 deals with job and group-level antecedents, and chapter 8 is devoted to organization-level antecedents. We then devote chapter 9 to unethical managerial behavior that illustrates our approach to explaining the manifestations and causes of OMB. This leads us to the research dilemmas facing anyone who studies these phenomena, whether as a scientist or practitioner (chap. 10). In the closing chapter (chap. 11), we come full circle and anchor the strategic implications we draw for OMB management in this extended framework.

II

OMB MANIFESTATIONS AND ANTECEDENTS

3

Individual-Level Manifestations of OMB

Men who are drunk are likely to prove a danger in dock work.

—Mars (1987)

Violence has been a recurring nightmare in organizations through the United States.
—Baron (1993)

How does OMB manifest itself in work organizations? What are the overt signs of OMB? What are the actual OMB phenomena? Members of organizations misbehave in every imaginable, sometimes unimaginable, way. To cite one leading study, Analoui and Kakabadse (1992) identified 451 incidents of unconventional practices committed in a service organization over a period of about 6 years and distinguished six major patterns: pilferage and theft, rule breaking, destructive practices, noncooperation, disruptive practices, and misuse of facilities. These were recorded for supervisory as well as nonsupervisory employees, both overt and covert behaviors, and manifested not only by individuals, but also by groups of employees.

Gruys (1999) went a different route. Based on the relevant literature published between 1982 and 1997, the researcher identified 87 different behaviors of categorized counterproductive behaviors—acts that were recently defined by Sackett and DeVore (2001) as intentional workplace behaviors viewed by the organization as contrary to its legitimate interests. By use of statistical techniques (factor analysis), Gruys grouped the items describing misbehavior into the following 11 clusters:

1. Theft and related behavior (theft of cash or property, giving away of goods or services, and misuse of employee discount).
2. Destruction of property (damaging, defacing, or destroying property and sabotaging production).
3. Misuse of information (revealing confidential information and falsifying records).
4. Misuse of time and resources (wasting time, altering time cards, and conducting private business during work time).
5. Unsafe behavior (failing to follow safety procedures and failure to learn safety procedures).

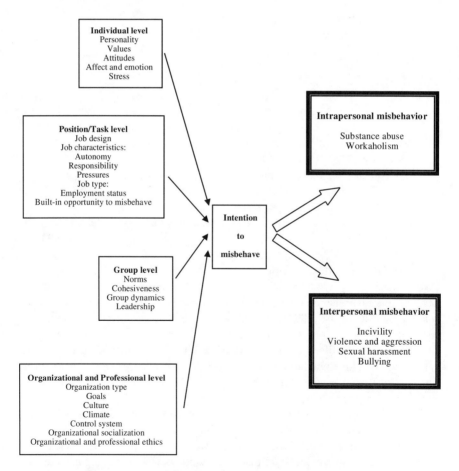

FIG. 3.1.   Intrapersonal and interpersonal manifestations.

6. Poor attendance (unexcused absence and tardiness and misuse of sick leave).
7. Poor quality work (intentionally slow or sloppy work).
8. Alcohol use (alcohol consumption on the job and working under the influence of alcohol).
9. Drug use (possession, use, or sale of illegal drugs at work).
10. Inappropriate verbal actions (arguing with customers and verbally harassing coworkers).
11. Inappropriate physical actions (physically attacking coworkers and physical or sexual advances toward coworkers).

To better understand the abundance and variety of dark-side activity following the OMB model presented in chapter 2, we organized our review of OMB manifestations around three logical parts: intrapersonal and interpersonal (chap. 3), production and political (chap. 4), and property (chap. 5) manifestations. Although we discuss possible causes, these three chapters focus on the behavior, not its antecedents or consequences. Following chapters 6, 7, and 8, we examine the next key issue: What makes organizational members decide to engage in such behaviors? Thus, these chapters are devoted to antecedents of OMB. Figure 3.1 serves as a framework for this chapter. Assuming that both intra- and interpersonal misbehaviors are intentional and a consequence of multilevel antecedent factors, we begin our review at the individual level of analysis.

INTRAPERSONAL MANIFESTATIONS

Substance Abuse

One of the critical problems of intrapersonal misbehavior in the workplace is substance abuse—excessive use of substances such as alcohol, tobacco, and illegal drugs (Bacharach, Bamberger, & Sonnenstuhl, 2002; Gruys, 1999). Evidently substances are addictive and harmful to the user; they usually have negative effects on the work environment and may be hazardous to nonusers as well. Workers' drug abuse is perceived to be a growing problem for the American labor force. Assembly line workers, long-haul truck drivers, and young professionals—disparate groups in terms of socioeconomic factors, education, income, and job conditions— are among those singled out most frequently for abusing illicit drugs on the job. The scant research available on the subject focuses on the role of the work organization in detecting and treating substance abuse through employee assistance programs, rather than focusing on the work context's role in alleviating the problem.

Mensch and Kandel (1988) investigated the relationship between job characteristics and use of illicit drugs in early adulthood. They wanted to determine whether certain ostensibly stressful features of the work environment contribute to substance abuse on and off the job. The relationships between job conditions and use of four classes of drugs (e.g., alcohol, cigarettes, marijuana, and cocaine) were investigated in 1984 among a nationally representative sample of young adults ages 19 to 27. Because the data failed to uncover any relationship between substance abuse and work conditions or occupations, the researchers concluded that workers' substance use is directly attributable to the workforce and less so to the conditions of the workplace.

In an investigation of alcohol abuse in the workplace through the Cornell University Smithers Institute for Alcohol-Related Workplace Studies, Bacharach et al. (2002) found that the costs of problem drinking (as a form of counterproductive behavior) in the United States are prohibitive to both employers and employees. Dollar amount estimates run in excess of $150 billions annually. These costs result from poor quality work, absenteeism, accidents, medical expenses, and so on. Drinking per se is not necessarily perceived as evil or dysfunctional. In fact, some forms of drinking in the workplace are considered socially acceptable, such as in workplace parties, business dinners, and ceremonies. It is the excessive and irresponsible consumption that is bothersome to management and often damaging to drinkers, their families, and their peers. When such conduct is willful and drinkers are aware of the potential harm, problem drinking in the workplace is classified as OMB Type D.

For their empirical research, Bacharach et al. (2002) used survey data collected from thousands of union employees to identify the causes of problem drinking. They posited both organizational and personal antecedents: workplace culture, policy enforcement, alienation, and stress. Problem drinking, the dependent variable, was measured by asking respondents a direct question adopted from Ewing's (1984) medical instrument for detecting alcoholism. The four-item question relies on honest self-report. The respondent is asked whether, in the last month, he or she felt he or she should cut down on drinking, were annoyed by people criticizing their drinking, or felt guilty about drinking, or had a drink first think in morning to steady nerves or get rid of a hangover. The researchers found that, among the aforementioned antecedents, workplace culture (in terms of perceived permissive drinking norms) is the single most important risk factor that drives employees to drink. By implication, when employees think the organization is permissive in terms of tolerating social drinking during and after work hours, there are good chances for drinking to become problematic and abusive.

The reasons for substance abuse on the job may be summarized by three categories as follows:

1. *Social control*—a weakened work structure with limited supervision and low visibility may contribute to substance abuse on the job.
2. *Alienation*—lack of interest on the job, absence of challenging work, and inadequate control over work may cause stress, which in turn may lead to substance abuse.

3. *Social availability*—simply put, certain occupations or work environments encourage leisure-time drinking and drug use among employees.

Perhaps the best known study of workplace drug abuse and its correlates was reported by Mangione and Quinn (1975). They examined whether counterproductive behavior and drug use at work are symptoms of job dissatisfaction. Data were collected from a U.S. national sample of 1,327 wage and salaried workers. The findings show a significant negative association between job satisfaction and self-reported counterproductive behavior among men ages 30 years or older. For the same age group, similar results were found for drug use at work.

Harris and Greising (1998) presented a review of drug and alcohol use as dysfunctional workplace behavior. The authors first summarized the results of a recent survey of organizational practices regarding drug and alcohol, followed by an overview of prior research on the topic. They then described two recent studies that examined the effect of drug and alcohol use on employee wages, reporting that individuals who are more likely to use these substances also tend to earn higher wages. Surprisingly, they found that the two variables, wages and drug and alcohol use, are indeed positively correlated. Harris and Greising, noted several explanations for such relationships: (a) this is just a statistical artifact (spurious relationships); (b) for certain individuals, substance use offers a form of relaxation and diversion from job-related stress, which in turn contributes to better performance and income; and (c) certain users are also good performers who follow opportunities for better jobs and thus may actually earn higher income.

An interesting question arising from the substance abuse literature relates to its nature: Is the use of alcohol and drugs in the workplace dysfunctional or merely behavior meant to be diversionary? Perhaps due to the negative connotations associated with alcohol and drug abuse, there is a tendency to lump together different substances and thereby assume that the effects of use will be the same regardless of the substance. That is, there is often an implicit assumption that different drugs have similar effects for different users in the workplace. Most of the literature has focused on organizational outcomes such as accidents, absenteeism, performance, and turnover. However, it appears that the use of substances at work is a complex phenomenon not only because of the variety of substances involved, but because their use is associated with a wide variety of causes and outcomes. Use also varies for different work environments and occupational groups (e.g., Shain, 1982; Sonnenstuhl, 1996).

A unique study of drug use within a specific occupational group was reported by Dabney and Hollinger (1999). They focused on pharmacists who, on average, spend 6 years in college studying the intricacies of prescription medicines and their effects on the human mind and body. After graduation, they embark on a career in which their expertise and familiarity with the proper use and dangers of prescription drugs continuously grow. Despite this wealth of experience and knowledge, pharmacists may become prescription-drug abusers. Based on in-depth interview data obtained from 50 recovering drug-dependent pharmacists to understand the process by which these professionals come to abuse the tools of their trade, Dabney and Hollinger concluded that, ironically, the knowledge and expertise may actually contribute to progressive prescription drug abuse. They argued that being and becoming a pharmacist presents a paradox of familiarity, wherein technical knowledge and the built-in opportunity, in the absence of proper appreciation of the risks of substance abuse, may actually delude pharmacists into believing that they are immune to the harmful effects of prescription drug abuse to their person and careers.

Substance use and job behaviors were assessed in a sample of municipal employees in the southwestern United States (Lehman & Simpson, 1992). Job behaviors included psychological and physical withdrawal, positive work behaviors, and antagonistic work behaviors (a form of counterproductive and perhaps retaliatory behavior). The employees who reported substance use at or away from work were found to more frequently engage in withdrawal activities and antagonistic work behaviors than did nonusers, although users and nonusers did not differ on positive work behaviors. Hierarchical regression models were used to determine whether substance abuse contributed unique variance to the prediction of job behaviors after controlling for the variance associated with personal and job background. Not surprisingly, the primary finding was that substance use added unique variance to the prediction of psychological and physical withdrawal behaviors.

The seemingly trivial question of whether workplace absenteeism and alcohol use are indeed positively related was addressed by McFarlin and Fals-Stewart (2001). They argued that nearly all investigations examining the link between alcohol use and absenteeism have been generally marked by three characteristics: (a) they have been correlational, cross-sectional studies examining the relationship between one or more global measures of alcohol use and absenteeism; (b) they have been cross-sectional in nature, with little to no information collected about the temporal relationship between alcohol use and absenteeism; and (c) they typically use samples consisting of problem drinkers.

The actual day-to-day relationship between alcohol use and workplace absenteeism was examined by McFarlin and Fals-Stewart (2001). They selected a random sample of 280 employees of one of the three large companies located in the northeastern United States. Using psychometrically sound, semistructured interviews, they gleaned information from employees about specific days of drinking during a 1-month period and actually marked the day(s) on a calendar. Data about employees (absences during the same target time period) were collected from the firm's human resource department and were also marked on an actual calendar. A significant day-to-day relationship emerged between alcohol use and workplace absences; workers were roughly two times more likely to be absent from work the day after they consumed alcohol. The researchers concluded that, given its staggering costs to business each year, identifying a powerful predictor of workplace absence is a necessary first step in developing proactive strategies to reduce alcohol-related absenteeism.

Drug testing may be one such strategy. Although management's use of drug testing programs is becoming a critical organizational issue, no systematic conceptual framework has been applied to the study of employee reactions to drug testing. Konovsky and Cropanzano (1991) dealt with this issue from the employee perspective. They focused on the way employees perceive the drug testing program and its fairness and on how this perception may influence both their job performance and how they feel toward their employer. They used an organizational justice framework to explain and predict the relationships among two types of justice (procedural justice and outcome fairness): employee attitudes (satisfaction, commitment, and management trust) and behavior (turnover intentions and performance). Survey data from 195 employees in a pathology laboratory indicated that perceptions of justice predict employee attitudes and performance. Specifically, procedural justice, but not outcome fairness, predicted all five criterion variables. These results demonstrate the importance of procedural justice perceptions for predicting employee reactions to drug testing.

Certainly when members of organizations behave in ways that are personally abusive in both intra- and interpersonal terms, employers must look for ways to monitor and curb such trends. This calls for three types of strategies: (a) formal management control—applying strict policy and discipline measures, (b) organizational redesign—restructuring work processes to reduce stress and isolation, and (c) cultural engineering—promulgating a normative value system that condemns abuse and condones proper behavior (Bacharach et al., 2002). In principle, these broad strategies are relevant to most other forms of misbehavior and should be considered relevant as we continue to explore other manifestations. How to apply them (as single strategy, in combination, at what level, etc.) is up to the organization because there is no single panacea. Local solutions should be a function of the specific diagnosed problems and the circumstances that naturally differ among organizations (see chap. 11).

Workaholism

Individuals may also choose to abuse themselves at work in other ways. For example, they may exaggerate the role work plays in their lives. For different reasons, some become increasingly devoted to their jobs, work, and careers. Such overcommitment and overinvolvement has been dubbed workaholism to denote some type of addictive behavior. The term *workaholism* is derived from another concept related to addictive behavior—alcoholism. The difference between the two concepts is that addiction to work, as far as the organization is concerned, is generally considered a virtue or positive attribute of the employee, whereas addiction to alcohol is considered a fault or negative characteristic, which could cause suffering not only to the worker, but also to his or her work environment. Thus, although organizations recognize the need to combat substance abuse, they tend to encourage employees, managers in particular, to engage in excessive patterns of work (e.g., long and intensive hours) and often reward such devotion.

We tried to trace the phenomenon's genealogy. The very first usage of the term *workaholism* we found is in Oates' (1971) book, *Confessions of a Workaholic: The Facts About Work Addiction.* Oates treated workaholism as negative behavior, an addiction to work, and the compulsion of an uncontrollable need to work incessantly. Although workaholism has been considered to be a positive organizational phenomenon (e.g., Machlowitz, 1980), it has also been treated as a negative and rather problematic issue (e.g., Killinger, 1991; Porter, 1996). It is considered positive because, regardless of costs, such immersion in work may enhance productivity and organizational performance. However, workaholism may be equated with other addictions; thus, employees afflicted with this addiction may be viewed as frustrated, unhappy, tense, uncooperative, troubled, and pressured individuals (e.g., Naughton, 1987). Assuming that in most cases workaholism is a habit of choice, it is regarded here as an intrapersonal expression of OMB.

A close examination of workaholism's negative aspects was undertaken by Porter (1996) who, like Oates (1971) and Naughton (1987), viewed excessive work as addictive behavior and suggested that, as such, it will have a negative impact not only on the setting in which it occurs, but on the individual employee as well. To properly address dysfunctional behavior patterns that interfere with organizational operations, she called for a total change in perspective. For her, the similarities with other addictions include identity issues, rigid thinking, withdrawal behaviors, progressive involvement in the behavior, and denial. These factors influence the workaholic's decision making and goals. They also interfere with effectiveness by distorting interpersonal relations.

To better understand the phenomenon of workaholism, many researchers have spent considerable resources mapping its dimensions. Scott, Moore, and Miceli (1997) suggested that, although much has been written about the phenomenon, rigorous research and theoretical development on the topic is in its infancy. In their ground breaking article, they integrated literature from multiple disciplines and offered a definition of *workaholic behavior*. They identified three types of workaholic behavior patterns: compulsive-dependent, perfectionist, and achievement-oriented. They also proposed a preliminary model that identifies potential linkages between each type of workaholism pattern and important outcomes such as performance, job and life satisfaction, and turnover. Scott et al.'s argument is that, depending on the type of workaholic behavior pattern, workaholism can be good or bad, and its consequences may be experienced or evaluated differently by individuals, organizations, and society at large. They concluded that researchers and managers should avoid making judgments about positive or negative effects of workaholism until more rigorous research has been conducted and published. We concur. OMB in general is a relative phenomenon; therefore one should refrain from making value judgments before assessing the long-term consequences for all parties involved.

Attempts have been made to operationalize workaholism (Cherrington, 1980; Machlowitz, 1980; Mosier, 1983). Some of the early definitions relate to the number of hours of work invested by the worker as a major characteristic of the addict (Mosier, 1983). Yet other studies found that the amount of time devoted to work does not necessarily distinguish between the workaholic and others—not everyone who puts in many hours is addicted to work. Some work more hours than usual due to a temporary need (Helldorfer, 1987; Machlowitz, 1980), whereas others work more just to survive. A different definition refers to workaholics as people who always devote more time and thought to work than the situation requires. What distinguishes them from their colleagues is their attitude—the way they relate to their work rather than the actual time they spend working (Machlowitz, 1980).

Another thorough attempt at defining the term *workaholism* and its measurement was made by Spence and Robbins (1992). They noted that the addicted worker feels a strong inner urge to work, as well as guilt if he or she does not work. Thus, the workaholic is a person who exhibits three properties: He or she is highly work involved, feels compelled or driven to work because of inner pressure, and is low in the enjoyment of work. The authors chose to contrast the workaholic with what they labeled the *work enthusiast*. Work enthusiast, as they defined it, is a person who, like the workaholic, is highly involved at work but, unlike the latter, is high in enjoyment and is not driven as hard. The researchers identified three patterns based on their workaholic triad notion consisting of three motives: work involvement, driveness, and work enjoyment. Hypothetically then, a workaholic is a person who "is highly work involved, feels compelled or driven to work because of inner pressures, and is low in enjoyment at work" (p. 62). Yet there is also the work enthusiast (high on work involvement, low driveness, and high on enjoyment) and the enthusiastic workaholic (high on all three motives). For their validation study, Spence and Robbins developed questionnaire scales for all three patterns. These were sent via mail to a sample of male ($n = 134$) and female ($n = 157$) social workers. As predicted, those that fit the workaholic profile were higher than work enthusiasts (among other groups) on measures of perfectionism, nondelegation of responsibility, and job stress. Not surprisingly they were also higher on a measure of health complaints.

The question of whether workaholism is related to the construct *meaning of work* (i.e., how central is work in a person's life) was examined by Snir and Harpaz (2000) in two samples of the Israeli labor force. Compared with nonworkaholics, workaholics were higher on measures of work centrality and intrinsic work orientation. They perceive work as the most important facet in their lives and are constantly motivated to get more and more personally and directly involved in it. They also attribute less importance to interpersonal contacts at work. When Snir and Harpaz examined their data for gender differences, they found that workaholism is primarily a male phenomenon—women had significantly lower workaholism scores. Working women apparently balance their different life obligations better than do men.

An interesting attempt to relate workaholism to personality, attitudinal, and affective measures was made by Burke (1999) who collected data from 530 women and men in managerial and professional roles using anonymous questionnaires. Workaholism types were determined using Spence and Robbins' (1992) measures. Three personal beliefs and fears identified by Price (1982) in her cognitive social learning model of Type A behavior (we elaborate on this trait in chap. 6) were assessed as well, suggesting a possible overlap between Type A personality and workaholism. Burke reported that most beliefs and fears measured in his study were positively and significantly related to workaholism.

In a similar vein, Goldschmid-Aron (1997) conducted a field study among Israeli female directors of adult-education centers ($N = 93$). With self-reported workaholic behavior as the dependent variable (measured with a translated version of Spence & Robbins', 1992, scales), she investigated the influence of three personal variables (Type A behavior pattern, work centrality, and career commitment) and perceived climate as an organizational effect. Most significant, she found a positive relationship between Type A behavior pattern and workaholism. She also found that the relationship between workaholism and the potential for hostility and irritability was positive and significant, perceived job pressures were significantly related to workaholism, and career commitment and workaholism were correlated as well. In other words, the more the managers perceived the work as pressured and overloaded, the more they reported work-addicted behaviors; and the higher the managers commitment to their careers, the more they will be overly devoted to work. At this point we speculate that work environments saturated with overload and pressure may also be conducive to extreme modes of behavior, some of which may be defying organizational expectations of proper conduct. Furthermore, certain individual traits may actually exacerbate such behaviors.

Different types of workaholic behavior patterns, each having potentially different antecedents and associations with job performance, work, and life outcomes, were also proposed. For example, Naughton's (1987) classification is based on the two dimensions of career commitment and obsession–compulsion behavior pattern. Such a classification may shed some light on the variety of work and nonwork behaviors expected from both workaholics and nonworkaholics:

1. Job-involved workaholics (high on work commitment and low on obsession–compulsion) are expected to perform well in demanding jobs, be highly satisfied, and have little interest in nonwork activities. These individuals could easily engage themselves out of sheer commitment in committing acts of misconduct that benefit their employer (OMB Type O).
2. Compulsive workaholics (high work commitment and high obsession–compulsion) are potentially poor performers (probably due to staff problems resulting from impatience and ritualized work habits). These individuals' behavior may be characterized by harassment of others, rule breaking, and ignoring safety regulations (OMB Type D) when they become impatient with obstacles at work.

3. Nonworkaholics (low work commitment and low obsession–compulsion) spend more time on nonwork interests. These employees may neglect important work-related duties, which could result in negative consequences for themselves or others.

4. Compulsive nonworkaholics (low commitment and high obsession–compulsion) are individuals who compulsively spend time in nonwork activities. These individuals may intentionally sacrifice work performance and effort for the benefit of their outside interests and activities—a conflict of resources that could bear grave results for peers and the work process.

Finally, Peiperl and Jones (2001) elaborated on the distinction between *workaholics* and *overworkers* by proposing two underlying independent dimensions: perceived effort and perceived return. Workaholics are those who work too much but feel the rewards arising from their work are at least equitably distributed between themselves and the organizations that employ them. Overworkers, by contrast, are people who work too much (in their own terms) just as workaholics do but feel that the returns are inequitably distributed in favor of the organization. Workaholics have a clear reason to continue their extreme work behavior. Overworkers, by contrast, may be trapped in a pattern of work that is neither sensible nor equitable. In addition, two interesting categories of employees emerge: *withholders*, those who work too little as their organizations reap most of the benefits, and *collectors*, those who reap relatively more rewards for less effort than their peers. The pathology, if there is one, is less about addiction among people who work too much but are satisfied with the outcomes and more about overengagement, and possibly denial, among people who are not addicted to work but rather dissatisfied with its utility. Peiperl and Jones viewed workaholics as hard workers who enjoy their work and get a lot out of it, not as work addicts. They argued that, although there may be few people who are genuinely and pathologically addicted to work, they are the exception.

In summary, organizations should pay closer attention to the overworkers who continue to exhibit excessive work behavior while perceiving the balance of rewards they accrue as negative. We argue that such individuals are prime candidates for engagement in OMB Type S, attempting perhaps to purposely restore such perceived negative imbalances (e.g., by embezzlement or theft from their employers).

INTERPERSONAL MANIFESTATIONS

Incivility

Interpersonal on-the-job misbehavior runs the gamut from minute and insignificant acts of incivility that could, by some measures, go unnoticed to blatant acts of violence and terror. Examples of incivility in the workplace abound: answering the phone with a "yeah," neglecting to say "thank you" or "please," using voicemail to screen calls, leaving a half cup of coffee behind to avoid having to brew the next pot, standing impatiently over the desk of someone engaged in a phone conversation, leaving food trays behind for others to clean up, and talking loudly on the phone about nonwork matters (Martin, 1996). Such conduct in the workplace is annoying.

According to Baron and Neuman (1996), the business world was thought by many to be one of the last bastions of civility. For decades the relationships among coworkers was characterized by formality, marked by collegiality and friendliness, and distant yet correct and polite interactions. However, the business world has started to reflect the casualness of society at large. Scholars (see Neuman & Baron, 1997) have cited employee diversity, reengineering, downsizing, budget cuts, continually increasing pressures for productivity, autocratic work environments, the use of part-time employees, and contingent labor for the increase of uncivil and aggressive workplace behaviors.

We begin with the lighter side of the interpersonal aggression scale, with what Andersson and Pearson (1999) so aptly called *workplace incivility,* but we stress that even miniscule expressions of impoliteness or rudeness may lead to more blatant aggression. Indeed Anderson and Pearson explained at length how marginal manifestations of incivility can potentially spiral into increasingly aggressive behaviors. To gain a full understanding of the mechanisms that underlie the incivility spiral, they examined what happens at key points of this process, the starting and tipping points, factors that can facilitate the occurrence, and the dynamics of escalation from incivility to violence.

For Andersson and Pearson (1999), workplace incivility involves acting rudely, discourteously, or with disregard for others in the workplace in violation of workplace norms of mutual respect. Surprisingly, relatively little field research has been done on lesser forms of mistreatment such as rude comments, thoughtless acts, or offensive gestures. A survey of about 180 employees conducted by Baron and Neuman (1996) revealed that a majority of the aggression in the workplace is actually relatively mild. These acts are mostly verbal rather than physical, passive rather than active, indirect rather than direct, and subtle rather than overt. Similarly, Ehrlich and Larcom (1994) reported that half of a sample of over 300 workers admitted having experienced some interpersonal mistreatment within a 3-year period.

Certainly what is considered uncivil in a particular organization, let alone society, may not be perceived as uncivil in other firms. American tourists visiting a Mediterranean country like Greece or Israel often find the lack of a welcoming smile on a salesperson's face as rude. Yet in some cultures smiling at customers is neither common workplace conduct nor is it expected.

Hence, there is great importance in recognizing relevant (group, unit, or organization) cultural normative systems (Wiener, 1988). Workplace norms are those core local or community codes or standards of conduct that reflect tradition and wide acceptance. These norms are transmitted to new and veteran members through both formal and informal communication and via organizational rules, regulations, and policies. Some describe the process as organizational socialization (e.g., Van Maanen & Schein, 1979). However, not only norms of proper conduct are transmitted in this process. Apparently newcomers also learn both formally and informally how to violate them (Ofer, 2003). When members of an organization learn from others and knowingly engage in what can be regarded as low-intensity behavior with an intent to harm, and this form of behavior violates local workplace norms, incivility occurs. According to Andersson and Pearson (1999), such acts, although not necessarily aggressive, may begin a tit-for-tat cycle that, beyond a certain tipping point, eventually become violent.

Such incivility spirals in organizations were already conceptualized by Masuch (1985). Spirals are caused by organization actors because they are unwilling or unable to change their behavior. The escalation takes place when an action by an employee stimulates the negative action of another employee. The ensuing actions in a work setting constitute acts of misbehavior that increasingly violate norms of acceptable behavior. When they get out of hand, such interpersonal conflicts may indeed result in extreme forms of violence—breaching not only local norms but societal codes of behavior as defined by the legal system. This would be the case when a simple exchange of insults turns to an aggravated assault.

Following this conceptual framework, Pearson, Andersson, and Porath (2000) conducted interviews and workshops across the United States with more than 700 workers, managers, and professionals representing different types of organizational and occupational environments. They accumulated a wealth of incidents of what they regarded as mild incivility, such as receiving nasty or demeaning notes, being treated as a child by others at work, being cut off while speaking, being berated for an action committed by another employee, being excluded from a meeting, and having one's credibility undermined in public. These are all minor offenses, but they are also perceived as ambiguous. This ambiguity, unlike cases of overt aggression or sheer vandalism, is open to interpretation by the target and may lead to the spiraling effect (even when the actor did not originally intend to be derogatory). Thus, we need to be on the alert when such exchanges flare up. When unchecked, they can turn nasty, ugly, and dangerous.

Insults

One of the most common forms of workplace incivility is, without a doubt, insults. A unique insight into the social psychology of insults in organizations is offered by Gabriel (1998), who explored insults as a phenomenon that stands at the crossroads of emotion and narrative. Gabriel charted different forms of insulting behavior such as exclusion, stereotyping, ingratitude, scapegoating, rudeness, and being ignored or kept waiting. More potent insults may involve the defamation or despoiling of idealized objects, persons, and ideas. Obviously people react differently to such acts of insult. Thus, among the outcomes these experiences are resigned tolerance, request of an apology, and retaliation. Gabriel, like Andersson and Pearson (1999), distinguished among insulting, bullying, and harassing, which are considered the accumulation, over time, of consistent and unrelenting insulting behavior.

What then are insults in organizations? In Gabriel's (1998) terms, they include behavior or discourse, oral or written, which is perceived, experienced, construed, and at times intended as slighting, humiliating, or offensive. Readers can easily attest that insults are a fairly commonplace phenomenon in organizational life. They are featured in organizational narratives whenever expressions like "rubbing salt into the wounds" or "adding insult to injury" are invoked. Insults may be verbal and gestural, consisting of rude or mocking diatribes, cutting remarks, negative stereotypes, or outright swearing. They can also be performed in deed, such as refusing an invitation or ignoring another person's presence. They may be subtle, residing in verbal innuendo or the facial expression of the actor, or they can be brutal, unambiguous, and direct and abusive as in cases of sexual, ethnic, or racial harassment. To supplement these propositions with empirical evidence, Gariel cited insightful and quite emotional narratives generated by students who were asked to recall their own work internship experiences.

Workplace insulting behaviors are an important organizational phenomenon because they evoke powerful emotions and often affect people's personal lives. Particularly convincing is the argument that insults frequently lead the targeted party to engage in retaliatory and vengeful acts. Such acts are consistent with our definition of OMB Type D—the intentional infliction of damage on others or the organization in general.

Revenge

Retribution and revenge are well documented in human history ("eye for an eye") and are, not surprisingly, prevalent in OB. McLean Parks (1997) wrote extensively about the *art and science* of revenge in organizations. She explored retribution from the perspective of internal justice, and the reciprocity norms on which as-sessments of organizational justice and injustice are based. She focused on a type of reciprocal behavior that is relatively neglected: retributive justice. This form of justice is available to those in organizations who are relatively less powerful but feel mistreated. She explained:

> As a justice mechanism available to the relatively powerless, retribution (as the broader construct, encompassing revenge, which generally has a pejorative conno-tation) can restore justice stemming from a variety of source of injustice: getting less than expected or deserved (distributive justice), being the victim of unfair rules (procedural justice), or being ill treated as a human being (interactional justice). (p. 114)

Following McLean Parks (1997) there are three primary mechanisms of organizational retribution:

1. *Retributory recompense*—Based on inequity theory (Adams, 1965), this includes behaviors intended to balance the scales once a perceived wrong has been done or is anticipated. It returns a positive valence to individuals (who perceive themselves as victims) in exchange for what was lost. For example, Greenberg (1990) showed that employee theft is related to feelings of underpayment, and Boyd (1990) showed that it increases following mergers and acquisitions.
2. *Retributory impression management*—As shown earlier, impression management is a powerful tool individuals use to influence public view of them and their behaviors. This form of retribution is quite subtle and can include both positive and negative impressions. On the one hand, tactics of flattery and ingratiation can be used to retaliate against figures of power in the organization, setting them up for future reprisal. On the other hand, individuals may apply revengeful acts while posing as victims and having no other ways available to restore injustice. In any case, such tactics are often used by organizational avengers for deterrence.
3. *Retributive retaliation*—This tactic adds the component of punishment. Here the victim receives no other recompense other than the simple satisfaction of knowing that accounts have been settled ("don't get mad—get even"). Several years ago, a technician at a Tel Aviv municipal hospital shut down the central oxygen flow to some units to avenge a perceived mistreatment from his superior. Sprouce (1992) recorded cases of retaliatory vandalism such as the one inflicted by a fired computer programmer who registered employees' names as historical figures in the *Encyclopedia Britannica's* computerized system.

Such perpetrators of violence often see themselves as victims of injustice in the workplace. For example, Folger and Skarlicki (1998) suggested that interactional injustice (especially when perceived as a lack of interpersonal sensitivity) is particularly important in predicting retaliation and aggression in the workplace. Before we discuss these manifestations, we bring up the following note concerning the ideological underpinnings of revenge in organizations. The current view of organizational revenge is biased: It is only viewed as a bad, destructive act committed by deviants and malcontents. Bies and Tripp (1998) discussed the ideological sources of this bias and the consequences of it for the theory development and research on workplace revenge. Nonetheless, when multiple actors often involved in such incidents are considered—avenger, perpetrator, and bystander—revenge may be actually constructive. They claimed that their research provides ample evidence that avengers are often prosocially motivated, frequently effect positive outcomes, and consider multiple beneficiaries of their actions. We concur with that insight given our premise that not all OMB manifestations are to be automatically regarded as inherently dysfunctional to the organization.

Hostility, Aggression, and Violence

One of the main sources for assessing the extent to which organizational members are exposed to different forms of violence are surveys conducted yearly by the Society for Human Resource Management (SHRM) and the American Management Association (AMA). The cumulative data demonstrate how prevalent violence was during the 1990s. For example, in 1993, the SHRM surveyed about 480 managers about violence in their companies. Seventy-five percent reported fistfights, 17% reported shooting, 7.5% stabbing, and 6.5% sexual assault. One year later, the AMA found that of 500 general managers surveyed, about 10% reported fistfights and assault with weapons and 1% reported workplace rape. The 1996 SHRM survey shows that 48% of respondents reported violent incidents in their companies compared with 57% in the 1999 survey (Denenberg & Braverman, 1999).

As today's organizations become complex work environments, they become an arena of not only productive behavior and individual excellence but also of enmity, hostility, and aggression. Although precise data concerning these attitudes and behaviors are hard to get, and because some of it highlights the more extreme forms such as homicide, which may be misleading (Neuman & Baron, 1997), it appears that work life has become more tense and hazardous than before (Denenberg & Braverman, 1999). Human resource managers are increasingly expected to be familiar with the phenomenon and supply diagnostic and intervention solutions to cope with it. Thus, how-to literature on the violent workplace has become more available (e.g., Baron, 1993; Denenberg & Braverman, 1999), as well as informational publications by government agencies such as the U.S. Department of Justice (e.g., Bachman, 1994) and the U.S. Department of Labor (e.g., Bureau of Labor Statistics, 1999).

Workplace violence became an important issue in the last decade of the 20th century and the first years of the new millennium. Incidents of work-related homicides frequent the media, citing emotional upheaval, stress, drugs, and layoffs as just a few of the factors that trigger such crises (Mantell, 1994). In the 1990s, incidences of workplace violence increased both in number and intensity involving current and former employees as well as current and former customers. Some argued that one of the characteristics of the modern society is that violence is moving from the streets to the workplace (Johnson & Indvik, 1994). It is not surprising that OB researchers' interest in these phenomena has been rising in recent years. A review some of this conceptual and empirical work is presented next.

Many organizational observers (cf. Greenberg & Barling, 1999; Johnson & Indvik, 1994; Martinko & Zallers, 1998) agree that aggression is more pervasive in new age organizations than those in the second half of the 20th century. Contemporary society is replete with examples of human aggression (individuals intentionally harming or injuring others). In less severe forms, it may involve verbal insults, sarcasm, spreading rumors, and withholding information—workplace incivility. The more extreme forms involve inflicting physical damage and causing workplace homicide (Neuman & Baron, 1997)—or as it came to be known following such incidents at the U.S. postal service, *going postal.* This change may reflect cultural shifts within and outside organizations, which have coincided with economic and work environment upheavals of the latter part of the 20th century. We believe external social pessimism has been matched by internal antagonism among individuals, groups, and subcultures, some of which is translated into hostile attitudes and aggressive behaviors.

Aggression in organizations can take many forms. It can be directed against the source of frustration either verbally or physically. It can also be directed covertly against a person; that is, an individual can secretly perform behaviors that can hurt another person. Aggression can also be directed against the organization. This organizational aggression would be manifested as any behavior intended to hurt the organization, which again could be overt or covert. Much of the recent treatment of workplace aggression emanates from Buss' (1961) classic typology based on three general dimensions: physical–verbal, active–passive, and direct–indirect. Neuman and Baron (1997) provide a comprehensive list of organizational acts of misbehavior organized according to Buss' typology. The examples included demonstrate the wide range of behaviors that can be construed as aggressive, some mild and passive (e.g., withholding pertinent feedback) and some extreme and active (e.g., inflicting bodily harm).

An extensive review of the organizational aggression literature led Beugré (1998) to conclude that, although many studies have underscored the multifaceted nature of workplace aggression, the vast body of research does not point to an integrative model of aggressive behaviors at work. Earlier he proposed that workplace aggression may be directed toward four targets: superiors (upward aggression), peers (lateral aggression), subordinates (downward aggression), and the organization (systemic aggression). Drawing from this literature, Beugré suggested an integrative model of workplace aggression that is much in line with our approach to OMB—that both misbehavior and behavior are products of the same forces. Beugré's (1998) model posits that workplace aggression stems from three sets of variables: (a) individual characteristics, including demographic variables (age, ethnicity, and gender), personality traits (negative affectivity, Type A behavior pattern, and the Big Five personality dimensions), and cognitive factors (hostile attribution bias and locus of control); (b) organizational factors, including socioorganizational dynamics (perceived fairness, organizational punishment, organizational frustration, and organizational stressors) and physical organizational environmental factors (lighting, temperature, and crowding); and (c) socio/cultural factors such as collectivism–individualism, power distance, and cross-cultural perceptions.

In a similar vein but with a cognitive appraisal perspective, Martinko and Zellars (1998) developed another conceptual framework for workplace violence and aggression. They suggested that numerous practitioner-oriented articles have documented concern about this issue, and some practical suggestions have been offered reflecting an increase in the number of violent and aggressive incidents perpetrated in the workplace. Their work places the extant empirical and conceptual literature relating to workplace violence and aggression within a social learning framework, emphasizing the individual cognitive appraisal as the key explanatory variable driving both affective reactions and aggressive behaviors. It offers valuable research propositions regarding the relationships among environmental variables, individual differences, attributions, emotions, and incidents of workplace aggression and violence.

Greenberg and Alge (1998) used an organizational justice perspective to explain workplace aggression. Aggressive acts are influenced by the receipt of unfavorable outcomes as qualified by personal beliefs about the fairness of the procedures used to attain them. Aggressive reactions to unfair outcomes are believed to take more extreme forms of behavior, such as expressions of hostility, when unfair procedures (e.g., discrimination and favoritism) are used by the organization. The enactment of aggressive behavior, however, is thought to be moderated by the presence of various aggression-inducing and aggression-inhibiting psychological cognitions. These cognitions are considered primary when people focus on interpreting the fairness of what has already occurred (e.g., "Was it really unfair?") and secondary when people focus on deciding how to respond to unfairness that they already perceive (e.g., "Can I just forget about it?"). As a result, Greenberg and Alge advocated increased efforts at promoting justice in the workplace, which should serve as mechanisms for reducing workplace aggression. In other words, the more the organization is adamant about actually maintaining such systems, the more likely it is to be perceived by employees as a justice-prone workplace, and the better the chances that any intentions to act aggressively will be minimized.

A somewhat different approach was taken by Diamond (1997), who offered a psychoanalytic perspective of violence and aggression in the workplace, with particular focus on public sector organizations such as the postal service. Diamond posited that shame and injustice are at the core of the problem. Following a statistical summary of workplace violence and an overview of the social and behavioral science research, Diamond provided a psychodynamic schema for analyzing the potential of violence at work. The model combines what he called a *toxic mix* of oppressive cultures and persecutory identities at work.

One particularly influential consequence of low organizational justice is frustration. Spector's (1978) seminal work on frustration in organizations promoted the plausible connection between the experience of frustration and the ensuing reactions of aggressive behavior. Behavioral reactions to organizational frustration (frustration occurs when an instigated goal response or expected behavioral sequence is interrupted or interdicted) include negative effects on job performance, absenteeism, turnover, organizational aggression, and interpersonal aggression. To the extent that these behaviors interfere with the organization's task, climate, or effectiveness, they may tangibly damage the organization. As such they may be thought of as counterproductive, antirole, antisocial, maladaptive, or dysfunctional behaviors. These behaviors may consist of attempts to find alternative paths to goal achievement, withdrawal from efforts to achieve organizational goals (turnover or absenteeism), interpersonal hostility or aggression, or organizational aggression.

Of particular concern is *organizational aggression,* which is defined as any behavior intended to hurt the organization. It can be overt, such as wildcat strikes, demonstrative work slowdowns, and lawsuits, or covert, such as sabotage, withholding of output, or theft (Spector, 1978). Thus, on the whole, Spector's research is geared at developing a general model of the behavioral effects that result from frustration at work, including such OMB manifestations as decreased job performance; organizational aggression such as sabotage, strikes, work slowdowns, and stealing; and absenteeism and turnover.

A good example of this approach to the frustration–aggression connection is Fox and Spector's (1999) study, which sought to investigate the situational, dispositional, and affective antecedents of counterproductive (i.e., aggressive) work behaviors. Fox and Spector regarded any counterproductive behavior on the job as a form of aggression either against other persons or the organization, and they lumped together aggression, deviance, and counterproductive behavior. As mentioned, frustration occurs when a goal-oriented behavior is interrupted, foiled, or interdicted. When this takes place, the individual seeks ways to overcome this block. Organizational aggression is one of them.

Using self-report questionnaires, Fox and Spector (1999) collected data from 185 people from a variety of organizations. The dependent variable (aggressive behavior) consisted of four scales: (a) *minor organizational,* such as purposely wasted company materials or supplies, daydreamed rather than did your work, and purposely did your work incorrectly; (b) *serious organizational,* such as purposely littered or dirtied your work station or your employer's property and stole something from work; (c) *minor personal,* such as failed to help a coworker and played a practical joke on someone; and (d) *serious personal,* such as started an argument with someone at work and was nasty to a fellow worker. In support of the frustration–aggression proposition, a positive relationship was found between employees' experience of situational constraints (those events frustrating the achievement of organizational and personal goals, e.g., a dependence on untrained coworkers) and the behavioral responses (those personal and organizational aggressive acts). Most important, Fox and Spector clarified the role of felt frustration and dissatisfaction as affective reactions that mediate the relationship between the event and act. Thus, they concluded that the initial tenet should be revised into a constraints–frustration–aggression model.

Finally, when it comes to analyzing and predicting organization-motivated aggressive behavior, O'Leary-Kelly et al.'s (1996) framework is considered the leading one. Their review of the literature focused on those aggressive actions and violent outcomes that are instigated by factors in the organization, labeled *organization-motivated aggression* (OMA) and *organization-motivated violence* (OMV). That is, O'Leary-Kelly et al. conceptually differentiated between the actions of an individual who attempts to physically injure a coworker (aggression) and the resulting injury to the coworker (violence). In formal terms, OMA is the attempted injurious or destructive behavior initiated by either an organizational insider or outsider that is instigated by some factors within the organizational context. OMV includes those significant negative effects on people or property that occur as a result of OMA. As intended activity on the job that seeks to inflict damage on others and to elements in the work setting, OMV is similar to OMB Type D. It may be instigated by individual, positional, or organizational factors and be motivated by either instrumental considerations (e.g., revenge) or normative beliefs (e.g., blind loyalty).

Bullying

Workplace bullying (a term used especially in Great Britain) can be defined as repeated, unreasonable behavior directed toward an employee or group of employees that creates a risk to the health and safety of the targets. Within this definition, *unreasonable* means behavior that a reasonable person, having an awareness of the situation, would willingly engage in to victimize, humiliate, undermine, or threaten another individual or group of individuals such as colleagues or clients.

Bullying usually stems from a source inside the workplace. The perpetrator, however, may vary: An employee (including a manager or supervisor) may bully another employee, or an employer may bully an employee. Bullying behavior may also originate from a source outside the workplace (e.g., from a customer making incessant, repeated, and unfounded complaints about a sales agent's attitude). However, bullying is not always intentional. Sometimes people do not realize that the way they treat others may actually have a detrimental effect and be perceived negatively. For instance, when employees of different cultural backgrounds engage in a dispute, they might not realize the effects of seemingly innocent gestures or words on others. Therefore, we do not regard this form of conduct as OMB because it is unintentional.

The essential elements of intentional bullying are that the behavior must be unreasonable and repeated over time. Thus, the following types of behavior that meet these criteria would be considered bullying: verbal abuse, excluding or isolating employees, psychological harassment, assigning meaningless tasks unrelated to the job description, giving employees impossible assignments, deliberately changing work rosters to inconvenience particular employees, and deliberately withholding information that is vital for effective work performance.

Lately, bullying has captured more research attention because of its increasing prevalence in organizational life and the growing awareness of its effects. For example, the *International Journal of Manpower* devoted a whole issue (1999, vol. 20) to the topic. It includes 10 articles devoted to bullying, which present conceptual frameworks and empirical findings from various types of organizations. In addition, there is a growing interest in a new type of bullying in our work lives originating from the information superhighway, Internet, and intranet systems. It appears that employees increasingly feel they are being abused by messages of all kinds, many of which are intrusive and offensive (Baruch, 2000). According to Crawford (1999), more subtle, less detectable actions and behaviors are employed by the current bully, as demonstrated by the emergence of e-mail hate messages and spamming techniques in the workplace. This type of covert bullying in the workplace is clearly a form of psychological violence. Therefore, it should be identified as immoral—an abuse of loyalty and trust. On the practical side, Crawford compared two cases of bullying interventions. Although the two organizations described in the study had detailed employment policies, personnel departments, and occupational health departments in place, their ability to manage bullying was determined by more lax organizational cultures.

The crucial role of organizational culture in breeding bullying behavior was demonstrated by Archer (1999). He investigated the *bullying culture* in the U.S. Fire Fighting Service—which may be characterized as a paramilitary organization. He discovered bullying in two distinct contexts: inappropriate behavior by managers, such as intimidation, threats, and the intimidating use of discipline; and bullying within groups, which is the most influential and potentially the most damaging to individuals. These types of bullying behavior occur particularly in groups and organizations that are heavily dependent on exclusive socialization processes, strong indoctrination, and strict adherence to hierarchy (e.g., military units). Finally, Archer argued that the bullying of individuals, because of their gender or race (albeit immoral and illegal), remains a feature of the Fire Service culture and is perpetuated by some to ensure the continuation of the White male culture. This proposition leads us to one of the most pervasive forms of interpersonal bullying in organizations: sexual harassment.

Workplace Sexual Harassment

In its recent newsletter, the Academy of Management (August 2002) informed its thousands of members, academics and practitioners from around the world, about its newly formed Credo (or code of ethics). In it the Academy reiterates the commitment of its members to provide work environments free of sexual harassment and all forms of sexual intimidation and exploitation. Sexual harassment consists of unwelcome advances, requests for sexual favors, or physical conduct of a sexual nature. One of the inherent difficulties of course is to determine if a behavior is indeed a harassing one. Therefore, the Credo specifies:

> The determination of what constitutes sexual harassment depends upon the specific facts and the context in which the conduct occurs. Sexual harassment takes many forms: subtle and indirect or blatant and overt; conduct affecting an individual of

the opposite or same sex; between peers or between individuals in a hierarchical relationship. Regardless of the intention of the actor, the key question is always whether the conduct is unwelcome to the individual to whom it is directed. (p. 13)

Thus, the primary test in this case is not the intention of the perpetrator, but rather how the specific behavior is perceived by the target. This clearly exemplifies the difficulty in monitoring this type of OMB.

Flirting, bantering, and other sexual interactions are common in the workplace (Williams, Giuffre, & Dellinger, 1999). Certainly not all social exchanges that have a sexual flavor constitute harassment or assault. Cleveland, Stockdale, and Murphy (2000) clearly differentiated between workplace romance and sexual harassment. *Consensual sexual relationships,* defined as those reflecting positive and autonomous expressions of workers' sexual desires, are also prevalent in the workplace. Nonetheless, our interest here is specifically on those overtures, gestures, contacts, and acts that defy organizational and societal codes of proper conduct and thus constitute harassment and bullying. As such sexual harassment is a pervasive phenomenon in work organizations. According to Schneider, Swan, and Fitzgerald (1997), to cite just one credible source, close to 70% of female employees report that they had been the object of sexually harassing behaviors in their workplaces. Thus, to a large extent, sexual harassment is regarded primarily as a male misconduct. According to Welsh (1999), who took the legal perspective, regardless of gender there are two forms of behavior regarded as sexual harassment, and both are considered sexual discrimination: Quid pro quo harassment, involving sexual threats or bribery that are made conditional for key employment decisions (hiring, promotion, evaluation, and dismissal), and hostile environment harassment, involving acts that interfere with the employees' ability to perform or are offensive to them, such as innuendo, lewd jokes, nasty comments, and physical contact. For an extensive and through discussion of sex and gender issues in organizations, see *Women and Men in Organizations* by Cleveland et al. (2000).

Systematic research on sexual harassment is still in its infancy (Welsh, 1999). Over the past 20 years, research has moved from prevalence studies to more sophisticated empirical and theoretical analyses of the causes and consequences of sexual harassment. For example, Cleveland and Kerst (1993) studied sexual harassment and perceptions of power. Their review of the research suggests that the relationships among facets of power and types of sexual harassment are underarticulated. They viewed power as a multifaceted, multilevel construct. Men and women differ in both their use of power and their perceptions of power and powerlessness. Although power issues in sexual harassment have been discussed largely in the context of supervisory harassment, Cleveland and Kerst described the power concerns involved in both coworker and subordinate harassment. They concluded that, to understand the role of power in sexual harassment, researchers need to consider the level of power, sources of power, context of the harassing situation, and reactions of the harassed victims.

Fitzgerald and her colleagues (1997) proposed and tested empirically an integrative model of sexual harassment in organizations. To them both the organizational climate for sexual harassment and the job gender context are critical antecedents of harassment. The first variable taps the level of tolerance toward sexual harassment in an organization; the second variable assesses the gender ratio in a job class, as well as how recent women's entry is into the job class. The model proposes that sexual harassment consists of three facets: gender harassment (crude expressions and offensive behavior), unwanted sexual attention (advances deemed unwanted and unreciprocated), and sexual coercion (quid pro quo harassment). It also proposes that perceived sexual harassment has negative consequences on job satisfaction and mental health, which in turn lead to withdrawal behavior.

An integrative-interactive approach to sexual harassment as aggressive behavior was also employed by O'Leary-Kelly, Paetzold, and Griffin (2000). They claimed that, quite surprisingly, researchers have given only scant attention to the study of sexual offenders. Therefore, they chose to present an actor-focused model of sexual harassment. In the model, which is based on interpersonal aggression research, the authors framed sexual harassment as one form of behavior an actor might choose for pursuing valued goals. The model is interactive in that it elaborates on the effects of sexually harassing acts on the target's perceptions, motives, and behavioral response choice.

Sexual harassment is also considered a workplace stressor with serious consequences for both individual members and their employing organizations. Empirical evidence from two organizations on job-related and psychological effects of sexual harassment in the workplace was presented by Schneider, Swan, and Fitzgerald (1997). Criticizing previous research, they argued that evidence regarding the outcomes of sexual harassment in the workplace has come mainly from self-selected samples and inadequate measures. They obtained sexual harassment experiences, coping responses, and job-related and psychological outcomes from 447 private-sector employees and 300 university employees (all women). Discriminant function statistical analyses indicate that women who had not been harassed and those who had experienced low, moderate, and high frequencies of harassment could be distinguished on the basis of both job-related and psychological outcomes. Overall, their results suggest that even relatively low-level but frequent types of sexual harassment can have significant negative consequences for working women.

Attitudes toward sexual harassment were examined in research conducted in Israel. By using in-depth, semistructured interviews that permitted glimpses into rather personal and intimate experiences, Yanai (1998) found that most subjects encountered sexual advancements at work, although they had only seldom interpreted them as intentional harassment. Nonetheless, they were bothered by them and experienced concomitant negative emotions. Concurrently, most of the victims tended to ignore the implications of the resultant feelings and tended to minimize the behavior of the harasser, including joking about the advances. In general, respondents tended to blame the harasser and his macho personality, as well as an organizational culture too tolerant of harassment.

Peled (2000) used questionnaires to ascertain the attitudes toward sexual harassment held by physicians and nurses in a large public hospital. Following Fitzgerald et al.'s (1988) five-tier classification of sexual harassment (hints, seduction, bribery, coercion, and assault), Peled asked subjects about their attitudes toward such acts and the frequency in which they take place in their departments. Her most striking finding is that, regardless of rank, position, and medical specialty, participants regarded all such acts as sexual harassment. However, some minor contextual differences did emerge: Women were more strict about any form of coercion than men, nurses reported more harassment than physicians, and smaller units (e.g., intensive care) displayed a more permissive attitude toward such behaviors. Such findings suggest that harassment on the job may be partially explained by work environment factors. This is consistent with Gutek's (1985) notions that work environments can indeed become sexualized (e.g., in male-dominated jobs) and that a sexualized ambience can strongly affect attitudes and behaviors. In addition, it supports a finding reported by York (1989) who used a policy-capturing approach to ascertain the way organizational members conceive sexual harassment compared to its formal and legal definition. In that study, university equal employment officers were asked to judge 80 incidents of possible sexual harassment. Their interjudge agreements as to what constituted harassment were indeed high, and they tended to agree on the type of action to be taken in such cases.

The impact of workplace experiences on employee attitudes toward sexual harassment was examined by Konrad and Gutek (1986). They proposed three theories to account for individuals' perceptions of sexual harassment. First, there is a basic difference between men and women in personal orientation toward sexual harassment and how they define it; second, differential sexual experiences at work account for differences in perceptions; and, third, differences in perceptions are accounted for by gender-role spillover—that is, when a job is seen as primarily a man's or woman's job, the gender role spills over into the position. Their analysis of data from a representative sample of 1,232 American working men and women showed some support for all three propositions.

Undeniably, organizational leadership is clearly an important contextual factor. Yet research had been inconclusive in establishing its role empirically. For example, Murry, Sivasubramaniam and Jacques (1999) studied the leader's role in sexual harassment. The purpose was to examine the role the immediate supervisor plays in mitigating the negative consequences of sexual harassment environments when he or she is not the perpetrator of the harassment. They examined a competing mediating–moderating effects model of episodic leader support and social exchange relationship on the consequences of perceived sexual harassment experiences. Using survey data gathered from military personnel, they found support for direct effects of perceived sexual harassment and leadership on individual outcomes, but they failed to confirm the initial hypothesis of perceived leadership as a moderator. However, post hoc analyses indicate strong support for a moderating effect when the sample was subgrouped by the leader's gender. There was also partial support for leadership as a mediator of the relationships between sexual harassment and individual outcomes. More research is needed in this area.

Finally, Glomb et al. (1997) studied at sexual harassment using a group-level perspective. They defined *ambient* sexual harassment in terms of the frequency of sexually harassing behaviors experienced by others in a women's work group. Glomb et al. showed that ambient harassment is as potent as direct experiences in predicting negative emotional health and behavioral consequences. This is an important notion because it clearly indicates the level of indirect harassment individuals are exposed to at work even when not directly victimized. In other words, sexual harassment, as an interpersonal OMB, is hazardous to employees' health. Organizations must do their utmost to curb it—not only because they might face expensive legal charges, but because it strongly reflects on their standings as socially responsible agents of society.

4

Production and Political Manifestations

Many hands make the work lighter!

—Common knowledge about social loafing.

The previous chapter described how individuals who engage in acts of misbehavior may target themselves (e.g., by drinking or overworking) or other persons (e.g., by manipulating or harassing) in their work setting. They may also choose to target their own job as well as the work of others. Furthermore, individuals may target the organization as a whole or any of its components—material or symbolic. This chapter describes conceptual frameworks and empirical research dealing with work process misbehavior and the use of political means for promoting individual or group agendas. Again we emphasize the manifestations more than their causes. We also assume that such behaviors exist in all work organizations, albeit in different degrees of pervasiveness and intensity. We begin with what has been termed as *counterproductive workplace behavior* or *production deviance*. Then we delve into manifestations of misbehavior that are more political in nature. Figure 4.1 depicts these manifestations.

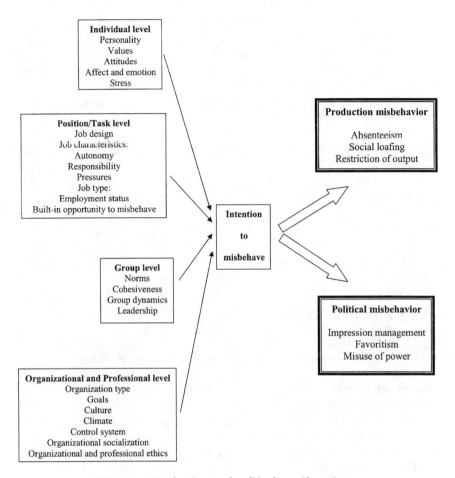

FIG. 4.1. Production and political manifestations.

COUNTERPRODUCTIVE WORKPLACE
BEHAVIOR

A recent review in the *Handbook of Industrial, Work and Organizational Psychology* (Sackett & DeVore, 2001) distinguished between *counterproductive behavior* and *counterproductivity*. Counterproductive behavior is any intentional behavior that is deemed by the organization to run counter to its legitimate interests. This behavior is considered a facet of job performance. Counterproductivity, in contrast, refers to the outcomes of those counterproductive behaviors. Sackett and DeVore illustrated this distinction with the following example: Employees who intentionally ignore or violate safety regulations (regulations they know should be abided for their own protection and the protection of others) behave in a counter-productive way; negative consequences that may arise from these behaviors—in this case, accidents and lost work days—are regarded as counterproductivity. This definitional distinction has some merit but could also pose some problems. Often employees choose to ignore safety rules to enhance their personal productivity or speed up their work or because they perceive management is lax about enforc-ing these rules. In such cases, the organization does not necessarily view this as counterproductive behavior or counterproductivity if there are no clear negative consequences.

Our approach is different. We suggest that a specific misbehavior is catego-rized as OMB if it violates the local core norms of behavior. Thus, regardless of the consequences, intentionally violating safety regulations constitutes OMB—in this case, OMB Type S—because the main motive is self-benefiting (i.e., higher earning). The difference between the two approaches is that we choose to fo-cus on the behavior, whereas Sackett and DeVore took a more organizational perspective.

Withdrawal Behavior

Behavioral violations at work were identified as production deviance by Hollinger and Clark (1983) because they interfere with local norms regarding work proce-dures and processes (sloppiness, low quality, slowdowns, and unjustified absence). Robinson and Bennett (1995) also identified work process misbehavior as produc-tion deviance (intentionally committed acts with the potential to harm the orga-nization). In their statistically generated four-type categorization, such behaviors are classified as minor or not serious and organization- (rather than person-) di-rected forms of misconduct. Undoubtedly, the most prevalent production-related misbehavior is the physical as well as the psychological absence or withdrawal from work. In human resource terms, we refer to these as *dysfunctional late-ness, absence,* and *turnover* (we emphasize the term *dysfunctional* because certain withdrawal behaviors, e.g., turnover by unproductive or deadwood employees, may actually be regarded as desirable by the organization).

A thorough review of the literature on withdrawal from work was undertaken by Johns (2001), who concluded that a general construct of organizational withdrawal behavior does not yet exist, and thus it may still be more useful to distinguish among the different expressions of withdrawal. Moreover, there is no definite evidence indicating that lateness, absenteeism, and turnover are necessarily positively re-lated behaviors. In some cases, employees who intend to quit may have high rates of absenteeism due to time spent on job search or being psychologically less com-mitted to the current workplace, whereas in other cases, the intention to quit may lead employees to maintain regular work schedules and sustain good performance so as not to jeopardize their reputation.

In certain organizations, especially where work arrangements are flexible and work processes are not sequentially dependent, lateness and absence may actually be quite acceptable. A good example of such units would be some research and development settings that may tolerate individual idiosyncratic work habits. Similarly, absenteeism is highly influenced by the social context. For example, group cohesiveness was found to be a major determinant of absenteeism rates (Gale, 1993; Johns, 1997). Organizational politics (discussed later) also play an important role in withdrawal behaviors, especially among employees whose relationship to the organization is not well developed such as new recruits.

Unjustified absence from work and excessive tardiness, if they are acts of defiance of such norms regardless of their consequences, are indeed a form of production and work process-related OMB. The literature on withdrawal behavior in organizations is extensive, both in terms of conceptual models (e.g., Hanisch & Hulin, 1991) and empirical analyses (e.g, Sagie, 1998). One clear conclusion from existing research is that it yields rather equivocal evidence for causes and consequences of withdrawal behavior. Simply put, the models, conceptualizations, and research into absenteeism and lateness offer little to further our understanding of the causal relationships and increase our ability to predict these behaviors.

Thus, on the one hand, withdrawal behavior has been extensively documented and researched; on the other hand, relatively little is known about the intentions underlying the choice to be absent. In other words, we know withdrawal behavior is common; we do not know whether it is an intentional defiance of norms. Certainly it is rarely intended to harm others or the organization. If at all, it is most frequently a self-benefiting form of misconduct. Therefore, we chose to focus our attention on lesser known forms of production-related misbehavior. Next we explore the topics of social loafing and whistle blowing. Both are related to the group cohesiveness effect mentioned previously.

Social Loafing

Modern and humanistic management styles call for establishing various teams of workers in nonhierarchical organizational structures to psychologically empower workers and involve work teams in the processes of decision making (see review by Guzzo & Dickson, 1996). Terms such as *product development teams, marketing teams, multidisciplinary teams, planning teams,* and *virtual teams* are fast becoming familiar to managers and workers alike. The prevalent view governing organizations' activities is that teamwork is typified by mutual learning and coordination and the team members' collective contribution to the final product's completion. Much emphasis is placed on the investigation of the qualities of the team and its contribution to the enrichment of workers' role and life. Teams have invariably been considered an asset.

However, before deciding to redesign the workplace to allow for team empowerment, managers must also consider the quality and quantity of the collective output. For example, one needs to determine whether the team output is in fact greater than the sum of individual members' inputs, is the investment that members of the group are willing to contribute to the collective task smaller, and is identical or greater than that which they would otherwise make on their own. The importance of intrinsic and psychological needs of workers, partly satisfied by teamwork, should not be underestimated, and the actual output, productivity, and organizational efficiency should not be neglected.

Clearly teamwork has many advantages, both from the point of view of the workers and in terms of organizational efficiency. Thus, during the days of Fredrick Winslaw Taylor and scientific management, at the height of the efficiency craze that swept the United States in the first decades of the 20th century, managers were thought to be capable of efficiently supervising 10 to 15 direct reports. Today it is clear that they can manage a much larger number of subordinates if the organization is properly structured, authority is delegated, and effective teamwork is facilitated. Moreover, enabling many groups to become self-managed grants the team members greater autonomy and opportunities to demonstrate their contributions to the organization. Modern communication and technology make it possible to distribute the tasks among individual workers and teams as never before. It is not unheard of to have a team of programmers work on a project in California's Silicone Valley all day and go to sleep at night while another group of programmers, say in India, continues where their American counterparts left off. Therefore, it is not surprising that most research studies dealing with group work emphasize such advantages. Human resources professional and organizational consultants also stress the importance of teamwork in enhancing the workers' role and their satisfaction, promoting solidarity among the workers, and thus increasing organizational productivity.

Despite these important organizational benefits, there is also a need to be aware of the difficulties arising within the teams, which may even constitute factors liable to be detrimental to the work processes. Through collective effort, teamwork may indeed ease the load and creatively enhance productivity. However, a teamwork may also cause individual members to exert less effort than they may otherwise. In the now classic experiments conducted by social psychologists at Ohio State University (Fleishman, 1953), social loafing was clearly evident. When subjects were asked to perform the simple tasks of hand clapping and shouting, those in the group condition tended to decrease their individual efforts compared with when they performed them alone. The decrease in individual effort was interpreted by the researchers as loafing—a choice by an individual team member to reduce his or her individual contribution to the team's effort. These findings are consistent with what is known in the literature as the *Ringelmann effect*, named after an unpublished German researcher who used a rope-pulling game to demonstrate the withholding of individual effort in a team (Kravitz & Martin, 1986; Latané, Williams, & Harkins, 1979).

A work team is characterized by ongoing interaction among its members to facilitate the attainment of a shared goal or execution of a collaborative project. That is, the emphasis shifts from individual to collaborative effort, which calls for mutuality and full cooperation among the members and the ability to contain and resolve personal and professional differences of opinion. The question, again, is whether all team members are willing and able to invest as much effort in the collective task as they would in an individual one. Will they feel committed to its success although they may not always be rewarded based on merit or effort? Are there workers who exploit their participation in a team? The answer to these questions is neither clear nor unambiguous because, unlike in a primary group (e.g., a family) where the relations constitute the aim of the group, the survival and success of a team are greatly dependent on members' belief that their participation is beneficial to them, more so than if they worked on their own. When this belief is lacking, the willingness of team members to contribute their relative share (sometimes more than their share) to the success of the collective task diminishes.

OB researchers have recently begun to question whether, in fact, individuals working as a team experience full cooperation from their peers in the attainment of collective goals. Other possibilities do exist. Are they preoccupied with comparing their own efforts to those made by the other participants and wonder whether they should make the effort while others may be loafing? Do team members really benefit from cross-fertilization and personal development, or are they more concerned about the manner of distribution of collective rewards? Should compensation be individually based or based solely on group membership? Such questions led OB researchers to develop concepts like the *propensity to withhold effort*, denoting the probability that the individual will invest less than maximum effort in a group task (Kidwell & Bennett, 1993). Let us examine how and why this happens.

First, note that, although some of the negative aspects of the group framework and cohesion have already been examined, the focus was mainly on the negative implications of overly high group solidarity (cohesiveness) and groupthink, which describe the tendency toward conformist behavior inherent in such solidarity (Janis, 1982). In the corporate world, there are increasing numbers of well-documented cases of top management teams that have been responsible for illegal and, at times, disastrous policies and activities (Daboub et al.,1995). Such collusion among top executives has recently resulted in corporate collapses (e.g., Enron). One reason for this is that members of cohesive groups tend to prefer to foster and preserve good personal relationships, rather than invest all its resources in the collective mission and task. Moreover, in overly unified groups, pressures are felt toward exaggerated conformity in attitudes and behavior, which may be detrimental to the members' capacity for independent thought and readiness to deal with uncertainty and assess and absorb new data. As a result, the group's potential is not fully realized. For instance, research has revealed that overly cohesive groups affected by groupthink may make faulty decisions despite feeling confident about their choices (Janis, 1982).

We view groupthink as a special case of OMB Type O (misbehavior intended to benefit the organization), but we stress that this phenomenon should be distinguished from workers' propensity to withhold effort. Although groupthink stems from an exaggerated sense of team solidarity, members' propensity to withhold effort usually stems from feeling that they are not recognized or unfairly rewarded for their efforts and from their individual tendencies. Thus, because social loafing is driven by instrumental considerations, it is regarded as a special case of OMB Type S (self-benefiting). In this case, we believe a reasonable level of group solidarity is likely to minimize individual loafing at the expense of peers.

Three main concepts used in the discussion and research of the phenomenon can be identified in the literature: *shirking, social loafing,* and *free riding.* The management literature tends to treat them interchangeably. Researchers of organizational behavior recently suggested that it would be more productive to study the basic behavioral trait underlying all these concepts—namely, the propensity to withhold effort (e.g., Kidwell & Bennett, 1993). The distinction between these concepts is related to the cause or context of the occurrence of lack of cooperation or diminished effort. *Shirking,* usually defined by economists as an increase in an individual's tendency to invest less effort, may have a variety of causes such as lack of supervision, personal interest, and/or opportunism. The concept of *social loafing* is broader because it includes the social context. These processes may occur within the group framework because individual performance is less easily identifiable and the employee is less visible and identifiable in the crowd. *Free riding* is usually defined as a passive reaction of individuals who want to benefit from the group but are unwilling to contribute their share of the costs. In this case, the individual makes a rational decision to withhold effort owing to the belief that even if the work is left to the others, he or she will enjoy the fruits of the final product (see Kidwell & Bennett, 1993).

The similarities among the three concepts—shirking, loafing, and free riding—are evident: All stem from workers intentionally investing less than maximum effort, and they can be studied both experimentally and within the context of a work team. The distinction between them is mainly due to the researcher's specific point of view. For instance, economists tend to focus on shirking as an unproductive action, lowering the output of the group; social psychologists tend to relate to loafing within a social framework, stemming from the decreased likelihood of singling out the loafer; and sociologists emphasize the phenomenon of free riding. Moreover, the models describing the phenomena of free riding and shirking mostly use a rational analysis of cost-effectiveness to explain why workers avoid investing efforts. This emphasis led to neglect of social processes as probable contributive factors. However, many of the activities of teams working in organizations contain elements unexplainable by purely economic criteria: Accepted norms, behaviors and work patterns, feelings, and a sense of solidarity develop among the group members, thus affecting their behavior in both positive and negative ways.

According to the rational choice approach, workers weigh the costs and benefits in material terms to maximize the gains accruing from their contribution. In this case, the workers adopt an effort level consistent with their belief that eventually the rewards will surpass their investment. Rational employees, in deciding whether to invest personal effort or avoid making it, will usually take into account such situational factors as the size of the group and whether the supervisor is able to discern the individuals' efforts or contributions to the task. They will consider to what extent they are dependent on the other group members in fulfilling the task, how dependent they are on this employment, and what the current conditions are of the labor market. The investment of effort is then a function of some or all of these factors (cf. Knoke, 1990).

Unlike the economic approach, the normative approach maintains that individuals act in accordance with the values and social norms of the team. That is, if the norms relating to investment of effort, fairness, and distributive justice are high among the members of the group, they are more willing to invest effort and make individual contributions toward the attainment of collective output. Another approach, which attempts to explain why individuals contribute to collective activity in an organization, emphasizes the emotional ties developing among the team members. According to this approach, individuals' motivation to invest effort stems from the emotional ties to the others in the team, and it increases as the group's identity develops. We return to the antecedents related to social loafing in chapter 7.

POLITICAL MANIFESTATIONS

Whistle Blowing

Typically whistle blowing is an act undertaken by an employee in which he or she decides to inform internal or external authorities, or members of the media, about illegal, unethical, or unacceptable practices in the workplace. This is an extremely important issue because it can result in grave and sometimes tragic results for individuals who opt to blow the whistle and for the organizations (Vinten, 1994). Vardi and Wiener (1996) viewed this phenomenon as a case of intentional OMB because in many settings it may constitute a violation of core norms of duty expected from members. Moberg (1997) actually classified it as a form of treason or betrayal.

Blowing the whistle on the organization or specific members (e.g., superiors) would be considered OMB Type O if it is motivated by a strong sense of identification with organizational values and mission and, thus, by a genuine concern for its well-being and success. However, acts of whistle blowing that are retaliatory and revengeful would be considered OMB Type D because they are intended to cause harm. Nonetheless, many researchers suggest that whistle blowing is an act of good citizenship (cf. Dworkin & Near, 1997) and should be encouraged and even rewarded. Proponents of this approach maintain that whistle blowers should be protected both by organizational sanctions and the law (Near & Miceli, 1995). Protection, they argued, is necessary because often the organization considers the whistle blower as an outcast—an employee who broke the ranks and should be castigated.

Whistle blowing is often viewed as misbehavior: Employers consider this practice as a subversive act and sometimes take vicious retaliatory steps against the perpetrators (Near & Miceli, 1986). Such employers may argue, for example, that even when instances of unethical behavior are discovered, they should be dealt with internally. Near and Miceli's research indicates that whistle blowers reported that they were more likely to suffer retaliation if they did not have the support of their superiors, if the reported incident was a serious matter, and if they used external channels to report the wrongdoing. Of course retaliation by the organization is even harsher if it is not highly dependent on the whistle blower, if the charges are deemed frivolous, or if there are no alternatives to the activity in question. We can clearly see a pattern of escalation of OMB: An improper act is committed in or by the organization, and a member decides to defy organizational norms of loyalty and discloses the wrongdoing to an external stakeholder. As a result, the organization commits further misbehavior by taking retaliatory actions against the whistle blower.

Organizational whistle blowing behavior is on the rise for the following reasons: First, shifts in the economy are closely related to the increase of more educated, more skilled, and more socially aware employees in the workforce. Second, the economy has become information intensive and information driven. Third, access to information and ease of disseminating it leads to whistle blowing as an unanticipated outcome of these shifts (Rothschild & Miethe, 1999). Furthermore, this type of disclosure by members represents a new and fast growing form of employee resistance that can become quite costly for organizations, such as in the widely publicized case of exposing unethical addiction-producing practices in the tobacco industry.

Because of its nature, it is difficult to determine the prevalence of whistle blowing. Rothschild and Miethe (1999) provided some interesting information. Using a national sample of U.S. working adults, they found that 37% of those surveyed observed some type of misconduct at work and that, of those, 62% blew the whistle. However, only 16% of the whistle blowers reported the misconduct to external stakeholders, whereas the vast majority elected to disclose the information only to the internal authorities. Rothschild and Miethe justifiably concluded that, when faced with clear incidents of organizational misconduct, the vast majority of members remain silent observers—only about 25% of the whistle blowers do so to external agents. Thus, in any organization a sizable portion of employees are aware of, or at least have the potential of knowing about, substantial waste, fraud, and crime in the workplace.

Two of the most prominent researchers and writers on whistle blowing, Miceli and Near (1997) viewed it as antisocial OB. An early definition of *whistle blowing* is the disclosure by present or past employees of practices under the control of their employing organizations that they believe to be illegal, immoral, or illegitimate to persons or organizations believed capable of effecting action relevant to the disclosure (Near & Miceli, 1985). *Antisocial organizational behavior* means an act intentionally performed by a member of an organization directed toward an individual, group, or organization with the intent to cause harm. For whistle blowing to qualify as antisocial behavior according to this definition, it must be pursued with the intent to inflict damage or harm others. This behavior then is consistent with OMB Type D (Vardi & Wiener, 1996), and it is also regarded as an act of retaliation or revenge (Miceli & Near, 1997). We may expect that it is this type of whistle blowing that would be mostly met by reprisals or punitive action on the part of the employing organization. Such whistle blowers are considered to be dissidents rather than reformers raising a voice of concern and motivated primarily by pure intentions to help the organization improve itself (Near, Baucus, & Miceli, 1993).

The aptly titled volume, *Whistle Blowing: Subversion or Corporate Citizenship?* (Vinten, 1994) accurately reflects the debate among scholars regarding the nature and moral justification of whistle blowing. Vinten provided a working definition for the act: "The unauthorized disclosure of information that an employee reasonably believes is evidence of the contravention of any law, rule or regulation, code of practice, or professional statement, or that involves mismanagement, corruption, abuse of authority, or danger to public or worker health and safety" (p. 5). Undoubtedly there is a built-in asymmetry between the actor (the whistle blower) and the target (the organization). Thus, there is a greater need to protect the actor who, whether committing an act of citizenship or revenge, exposes wrongdoing, thereby contributing to the welfare of others often at great personal sacrifice. The organization, which is by far more powerful in every way, should accommodate this action, although at first it may be construed as misconduct or an act of disloyalty.

The dilemma facing the whistle blower was clear to De George (1986), who suggested three criteria for what he deemed morally justifiable whistle blowing: (a) The organization, left to its own devices, will inflict some damage on its employees or the public at large; (b) the wrongdoing should first be reported to an immediate superior, emphasizing the moral concern of the would-be whistle blower; and (c) if, after reporting the misconduct to superiors within the organization and exhausting internal procedures, the phenomenon persists and no action is taken, whistle blowing to external agents is regarded as good citizenship behavior.

A starker picture was portrayed by James (1984). He vividly and bleakly described the risks involved when employees choose to blow the whistle on their employers. His description supports the view that whistle blowing is considered an act of OMB by the organization. Whistle blowers almost always experience some form of retribution. In for-profit organizations, they are most likely fired. In addition, they are likely to be blacklisted and often leave their organization with damaging letters of recommendation. In not-for-profit organizations and public utilities, where management may not have the discretion to dismiss them, they are likely to be transferred, demoted, or denied promotions and bound to have their professional reputation shattered in the process. Worse yet, because whistle blowers are perceived by employers as a threat, they are often attacked on a personal basis, including threats to their families. Typically they are branded and treated as traitors, receive negative publicity, and are framed as troublemakers, disgruntled employees, or publicity seekers. In short we believe organizations do not go the distance against their own personnel unless they view their behavior as extremely damaging and a serious breach of acceptable behavior.

When faced with such high risks, two alternative propositions with regard to the motivational forces that affect an employee's decision to engage in this type of misbehavior (as defined from the organizational perspective) should be evaluated. Somers and Casal (1994) suggested examining this issue from the commitment-behavior perspective. This allows for alternative propositions with regard to the expected relationship between organizational commitment and the propensity to blow the whistle. One alternative is that individuals who are highly committed (loyal) to their organization are less inclined to blow the whistle and thereby damage it. The second alternative is that committed employees identify strongly with their organization and are willing to blow the whistle when they believe such an act benefits the organization. The results of the Somers and Casal study, drawn from about 600 management accountants, reveal an inverted-U relationship. Namely, individuals with moderate levels of organizational commitment are the most prone to act as whistle blowers.

Is the intention to blow the whistle predictable? An interesting attempt to answer this question empirically was reported by Ellis and Arieli (1999). Because of the unique military setting, in lieu of the term *whistle blowing,* the authors referred to this behavior as reporting administrative and disciplinary infractions. Conducted among male combat officers of the infantry of the Israel Defense Forces (IDF), the officers' conduct as information transmitters was assessed. Specifically, the researchers examined the extent to which organizational norms of conduct and individual attitudes toward these norms influence (predict) officers' decision to inform their superiors or remain silent and allow observed irregularities to go unchallenged. The military advocates reporting and promotes a culture that promulgates the need to and virtues of complete honesty and accountability; it also provides personnel with a number of official channels through which any individual can transmit such information through appropriate channels. At the same time, the IDF also inculcates values of extreme loyalty to one's unit. Such strong values of loyalty often influence the intention to pass any information that might endanger the unit's reputation. Moreover, there are fairly strong social mechanisms in place that negatively sanction violation of such codes. Thus, any officer engaging in such conduct faces a dilemma between extreme feelings of loyalty to the unit and the moral obligation to divulge any knowledge of irregularity to the military authorities.

Using hypothetical scenarios, Ellis and Arieli (1999) tested assertions derived from Fishbein and Ajzen's (1975) reasoned action theory to predict officers' choice of conduct (see further discussion of the role of reasoned action in chap. 6). It was expected that the intention to report is predicted by the officer's attitude toward the act of reporting (a rational attitude based on instrumental considerations) and a strongly internalized norm of expected behavior (beliefs by significant others). Regression analyses indicate that the norms were stronger than the attitudes in accounting for whistle blowing. In simpler terms, this means that officers who intend to report irregularities do so because of strong identification with prevailing values.

In summary, social influence and organizational culture appear to be extremely important influences on whistle-blowing behavior. For this type of job-related conduct to move from being considered as OMB to a normative form of conduct, it must first be integrated into the organization's cultural value system and then become an essential part of the socialization process—of learning the ropes.

Deception

Two distinct forms of deceptive behavior in organizations may be identified: personal and work related. The former tends to produce deceptive behaviors that create energy in the organization and may be functional. The latter is characteristic of power-acquisition behaviors designed to maintain an impression of rationality but they are really designed to cut corners to get things done or promote the well-being of one's own career or unit at others' expense. Viewing organizations as political environments, Schein (1979) examined the nature and function of deceptive behaviors. In particular, she stressed such concepts as the power-acquisition behaviors of individuals and the differential exhibition of these behaviors within high- and low-slack organizational systems. To Schein, deceptive behaviors are a function of three variables: the form of power-acquisition behaviors inherent in a given system, the potential benefits to the actors involved, and the potential benefits for the organization.

Machiavelli, while advising his prince, stressed the importance of deception in management. To him the illusion of being honest, compassionate, and generous is important to gaining and maintaining power, but so is the necessity of breaking one's word, being cruel, and being parsimonious. Be a lion *and* a fox was his counsel.

Unquestionably, power-acquisition behaviors have many deceptive aspects. Deceptive behaviors are viewed as behaviors designed to present an illusion or false impression: actions or appearances designed to present an illusion that belies the reality of the situation. Deception has more than one medium.

- *Communication*—may include false or partial information presented as full and accurate information.
- *Decision making*—a manager may present an illusion of giving in to a demand when he or she was actually trying to gain something else.

- *Presentation of self*—many managers exude confidence while masking a high level of uncertainty or insecurity.

Managers may create an impression of participation but in reality it is a facade of a highly autocratic management style, which leads us directly to the next related topic: impression management.

Impression Management

Consider the following scenario: Ron submitted his monthly report way behind schedule. It looked quite sloppy. To shift the blame from himself, Ron played down his own role in writing the report and put the responsibility squarely on the shoulders of his new team members. He said, they were extremely unprofessional and uncooperative. He also implied that the computer program that they had installed failed to work properly. Based on this input (tardiness, sloppiness, and blame of peers and equipment), Ron's supervisor is now forming her judgment about the behavior. Moreover, she is going to follow this judgment with her own actions (feedback, evaluation, and sanctions). However, she should be aware that she may have been a target of deceptive impression management (IM) on the part of Ron.

The study of IM in organizations is important in that self-representation may detract from or contribute to organizational effectiveness (Giacalone & Rosenfeld, 1991). IM by individuals in organizations consists of behaviors displayed by an employee with the purpose of controlling or manipulating the attributions and feelings formed of that person by others (Tedeschi & Reiss, 1981). It was defined as "any behavior that alters or maintains a person's image in the eyes of another and that has as its purpose the attainment of some valued goal" (Villanova & Bernardin, 1989, p. 299). Such behaviors, according to Gardner and Martinko (1998), may be regarded from the organization's perspective as dysfunctional IM. For example, Caldwell and O'Reilly (1982) studied the use of IM as a response to failure. They demonstrated that when confronted with failure, subjects may attempt to justify their position by manipulating the information that is presented to others. They also found that respondents who were more sensitive to social cues (known as *high self-monitors*) were more likely to engage in IM.

The prominent scholar, Irwing Goffman, identified the role of IM in OB when he conceptualized this interpersonal phenomenon within his dramaturgical model of social life (Goffman, 1959). Persons in social interaction, he posited, function as actors whose performances depend on the characteristics of both the situations and audiences at hand. The actors on the stage of life strive to control the images and identities that they portray to relevant others to obtain desired end states, be they social, psychological, or material. In this sense, IM is purposive and goal directed. It consists of strategic communications designed to establish, maintain, or protect desired identities.

Three key IM strategies—requests, accounts, and apologies—were observed by Goffman (1971). There are two types of accounts (statements that emphasize the role of certain personal or situational forces responsible for the failure): excuses and justifications. Use of excuses typically entails an actor who recognizes that the act is improper, but assigns responsibility to someone or something else. Justifications are made when a failing person attempts to convince others that, although the act was inappropriate, certain conditions exist that justified it. Apologies, or statements of remorse, are viewed by Goffman as a gesture through which the individual splits him- or herself into two parts: one that is guilty of an offense and one that disassociates itself from the deceit. Apologies by a subordinate are usually expected to lead the manager to have lower expectations of future failures, thereby not necessitating close supervision. In addition, apologies imply remorse, which is a form of self-punishment or self-castigation. Thus, the apology lowers the likelihood of additional punishment.

To test the effects of subordinate IM on the appraisal and responses of a manager following an incident of poor performance, two classic experimental studies were conducted by Wood and Mitcell (1981) on experienced nursing supervisors. Two common impression management tactics, *accounts* and *apologies,* were manipulated in each of the studies. On the basis of the discounting effect reported in attribution literature (Weiner, 1974), it was hypothesized that accounts of external causes for poor performance (excuses) would lead subjects to attribute less responsibility to the subordinate, be less personal in their responses, and be less punitive in their responses. Because of their equity restoration effects, apologies were expected to influence subjects' disciplinary responses to the poor performance without necessarily affecting their attributions of responsibility. Their data tend to support these hypotheses.

Similarly, another laboratory experiment (Wayne & Kacmar, 1991) was designed to tap the influence of subordinate IM on two aspects of the performance appraisal process: supervisor rating of subordinate performance and supervisor verbal communication in a performance appraisal interview. It was hypothesized that subordinate IM would inflate performance ratings, and both IM and objective performance would influence the supervisor's style of verbal communication during the interview. Subjects consisted of 96 undergraduate students who were assigned supervisory roles. Each subject interacted with a confederate subordinate who engaged in high- or low-level IM and performed at a high, average, or low level. Overall the results support the positive influence of subordinate IM on performance ratings done by their superiors. In practical terms, this effect should be carefully considered when implementing any performance appraisal program in an organization.

The consequences of dysfunctional effects of IM tactics were illustrated by Bolino (1999), who posed an intriguing question: Are members of organizations regarded as good citizens actually good at work or are they, in fact, good actors?

Previous research on organizational citizenship behavior suggests that employees who engage in such behavior are *good soldiers,* acting selflessly on behalf of their organizations (Organ, 1988). However, although such behaviors may indeed be innocent and even altruistic, they could also be manipulative and self-serving. This effect notwithstanding, we should consider that IM may actually lead organization members to engage in good citizenship behavior (Bolino, 1999).

A fascinating study of IM was reported by Becker and Martin (1995). The article's title piques one's interest: "Trying to Look Bad at Work: Methods and Motives for Managing Poor Impressions in Organizations." Drawing on the employment experiences of 162 individuals, the authors documented different forms of behavior such as purposely decreasing performance, playing dumb, or self-depreciating. Clearly it is possible that people at times choose to intentionally look bad, inept, or unstable. Becker and Martin viewed intentionally looking bad at work as a form of IM and/or self-handicapping behavior, whereby an employee purposely attempts to convey an unfavorable impression. For a behavior to be identified as such, the person engaging in the behavior must believe that a specific person or group will perceive the behavior as bad and the ultimate target of the behavior is that person or group. To ascertain which behaviors fall within the category of looking bad, the researchers posed the following open question:

> Can you think of any real life examples when someone (yourself or someone else) intentionally made him or herself look bad at work (that is, stupid, greedy, or in some way ineffective)? In the space below, describe, if you can, a very specific situation where someone tried to look bad on *purpose*. Be sure to (1) explain the situation clearly, and (2) describe *why* the person tried to look bad. (p. 180)

Their findings are interesting indeed. The ways organizational members choose to create bad impressions of themselves are almost as varied as human nature. Becker and Martin generated the following classification to ascertain actual methods used at work:

1. *Decrease performance*: Employees restrict productivity, make more mistakes than formerly, do low-quality work, or neglect to carry out their tasks.
2. *Not working to full potential*: Employees feign ignorance of job knowledge or restrict quantity or quality of their work.
3. *Withdrawal:* Employees engage in tardiness, faked illness, or unauthorized or long breaks.
4. *Display of negative attitude*: Employees complain; act angry, upset, strange, or weird; or are hard to get along with or insubordinate.
5. *Broadcast limitations*: Employees let others know of physical or health problems, errors, mistakes, or other personal limitations curtailing effective performance.

A cybernetic model of IM processes in organizations was developed by Bozeman and Kacmar (1997). They argued that recent theory and research suggests that a large portion of human behavior in organizations is motivated by IM concerns—that is, by the desire to be perceived by others in certain ways. However, the complex interpersonal dynamics of IM in organizations remain largely unexplored. Their model allows for the integration of multiple concepts and content areas relative to IM, and it treats self-presentation from a decidedly motivational and behavioral perspective. To them IM is centrally concerned with acquiring positive images and avoiding negative ones. It suggests that the motives, type of information processing used, and behaviors displayed may exist on a continuum rather than being an either–or proposition. In addition to those situations involving relatively large discrepancies between desired social identity goals and target feedback, IM may also be motivated by the desire to reduce positive discrepancies between one's desired image and the way one is perceived by others. Last, IM is also likely to occur in relatively neutral situations to maintain behavioral consistency with the social identity or sense of character already created and established in past interactions with a given target. Given all of this, you will understand why we turn directly from IM to political behavior.

Political Behavior

Organizational scholars have pursued different avenues in their explorations of the intricacies of political action within work organizations. For most the emphasis has been on the ways individuals and groups use power and influence to obtain desired resources. Some of the tactics actors choose are legitimate and part of the local normative system, and most are within the rules of the organization. At times, however, these tactics may be negative, manipulative, and exploitative. In this chapter, we emphasize those behaviors that are self-serving and manipulative and are not sanctioned by the organization. Such behavior has many potentially negative consequences, including conflict and disharmony, which occur when elements in the organization are pitted against each other. The resultant work environments are typically replete with tension and hostility. Specifically, we explore both actual manifestations of organizational political behavior and the way the political environment is perceived by its members.

The nature of the organizational context offers numerous opportunities, rewards, and threats that provide individuals with circumstances and motives to manage the impressions that others form of them (by manipulating information, distorting facts and withholding and filtering certain information; Fandt & Ferris, 1990). This formulation of IM is akin to the way we treat *organizational politics,* which has been defined as "opportunistic behavior engaged for the purpose of self-interest maximization" (Ferris & Kacmar, 1988, p. 4).

Research in the area of organizational politics has centered on the effectiveness of political behaviors, as well as on identifying the conditions under which employees behave opportunistically. Fandt and Ferris (1990) examined the effects of two situational conditions (accountability and ambiguity) and a personal characteristic (self-monitoring) on the management of information and impressions. When accountability was high and ambiguity was low, there was greater use of defensive information and more emphasis on positive aspects of the decision than in any other condition.

From a theoretical standpoint, using internal politics is all about the complex, often subtle, forms of exercising power and influence in organizations (Bacharach & Lawler, 1980). To examine this proposition empirically, Vigoda (1997) conducted a longitudinal investigation into organizational political behavior among public sector employees in Israel. His wished to ascertain the causes and consequences of employing political strategies on the job. Following the much-cited work of Kipnis, Schmidt, and Wilkinson (1980), Vigoda viewed organizational politics as those intraorganizational influence tactics deliberately used by organization members to promote self-interests or organizational goals. He identified 10 workplace behaviors that qualify as political strategies employees use to promote these interests:

- *Assertiveness*—Putting demands, requests, and strict deadlines.
- *Ingratiation*—Satisfying the wants of others and making them feel important.
- *Rationality*—Planning ahead and using rational and logical arguments.
- *Sanctions*—Using protest, punishment, and negative feedback.
- *Exchange*—Tacitly bargaining for exchange of favors and mutual support.
- *Rank*—Pulling rank and position and appealing to higher ranking superiors.
- *Blocking*—Putting obstacles in front of others and obstructing others' performance.
- *Coalition*—Obtaining the support of others against an organizational target.
- *Manipulation*—Controlling the flow of information, depriving others, and scanning.
- *Networking*—Developing informal social connections and recruiting supporters.

Analyzing close to 1,000 questionnaires collected at three different times, Vigoda (1997) found that: (a) Men and highly educated employees tend to use these political tactics more extensively and frequently than women and less educated employees; (b) use of political tactics is negatively related to job satisfaction and positively related to participation in decisions; (c) use of political tactics targeting subordinates and coworkers is much more than their use against superiors; and (d) managers use such tactics more frequently and more extensively than do nonmanagement employees. Certainly using political tactics to influence others is a legitimate and socially acceptable mode of behavior in work organizations.

When they involve the violation of core organizational or societal codes of proper conduct and acceptable human interaction, however, they are regarded as OMB. The study also revealed that perceptions of organizational politics were positively and significantly related to intentions to quit ($r = .29$, $p < .001$) and intentions to misbehave ($r = .27$). Interestingly, this measure of perceived organizational politics explained employees' job performance: The less employees perceived their work environment as political, the better was their performance (as appraised by their immediate supervisors).

We agree with Vigoda (1997) that, although the measure of politics (the Perceptions of Organizational Politics Scale, adapted from Kacmar & Carlson, 1994) is limited to employee perceptions, the findings are valuable because individuals act on the way they perceive their environment. When employees feel strongly that the organization is replete with discriminating favoritism, rewards are not contingent on effort and performance or that certain individuals or units always get things their way because nobody challenges their influence, they will act accordingly.

Generally speaking, organizations are social entities that, by their nature, involve inherent struggles for resources and the use of different influence tactics by individuals and groups for obtaining them (Ackroyd & Thompson, 1999). In much the same vein, Ferris, Russ, and Fandt (1989) viewed organizational politics as behavior designed to maximize self-interest. When such behavior contradicts organizational norms of proper conduct (e.g., peaceful, harmonious conflict resolution and compromise), it is OMB Type S because benefiting the person or group is the underlying motivation to use political maneuvering.

Often when employees are asked how they view organizational politics, they associate it with self-serving behavior, manipulation, subversive acts, defamation, and misuse of power and authority with no regard for others' welfare. Drory (1993) found that the negative effects of organizational politics are stronger for employees of lower status who are more vulnerable and more easily victimized by such manipulative behavior. Therefore, they exhibit more negative attitudes and behaviors toward the organization than higher status employees.

Concluding Remarks

The view that organizations are actually political arenas, in a negative sense, was well articulated by Mintzberg (1983), who referred to organizational politics as individual or group behavior that is informal, ostensibly parochial, typically divisive, and, above all, illegitimate—sanctioned neither by formal authority, accepted ideology, nor certified expertise (although it may exploit any one of these). Other researchers such as Drory and Romm (1990) also viewed political behavior as self-serving activities that are contrary to organizational effectiveness designed to attain power at the expense of other stakeholders. Thus, when individuals resort to political tactics that are in violation of organizational codes of acceptable conduct, they clearly engage in acts of OMB. Moreover, when their work environment becomes too politically oriented or politicized, it may inadvertently become an arena for the kinds of manifestations of misconduct discussed throughout this chapter, such as social undermining and subversion, incivility and insult, and betrayal and revenge. The danger for the organization is not so much the existence of such conduct, some of it undoubtedly typifies any work organization, but in turning it into a way of life and making it normatively acceptable.

5

Property Manifestations

Malfeasance is usually just a matter of opportunity.

—Bliss and Aoki (1993)

Princeton Pries Into Web Site for Yale Applicants.
—Headline in the *New York Times* (July, 2002)

It should come as no surprise to those familiar with human nature and behavior patterns in organizations that organizational members steal (take, pinch, borrow, lift, pilfer, filch, etc.) from their organizations and other organizations almost any of their assets, material, or intellectual. Employee theft is by far the most pervasive and intriguing form of OMB and one of the costliest (Cornwall, 1987; Greenberg, 1998). Employees at all levels take home some office supplies such as paper clips, return late from breaks, misuse computer time, falsify reimbursement requests, embezzle monies, cheat customers, and use a design idea for private business. We believe both employees and managers may not always be aware of the magnitude of theft around them and/or they may not always be willing to deal with it. By the same token, mainstream OB researchers have also shied away from including measures of theft in their field studies.

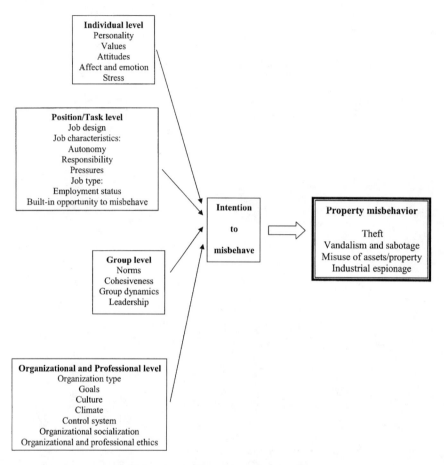

FIG. 5.1. Property manifestations.

In addition to employee theft, we discuss other manifestations of misbehavior including sabotage and vandalism, and we pay special attention to new-age misbehavior such as data theft, cyberwars, pirating, and hacking. Figure 5.1 depicts the types of intentional property misbehavior we discuss in relation to the variety of possible antecedents that might account for them. In this chapter, the phenomenon (the behavior) is emphasized, and in chapters 6, 7, and 8 some of its personal, positional, social, and organizational antecedents are explored. In chapter 9, U.S. and Israeli cases of unethical managerial behavior in which grand theft and fraud of enormous proportions are presented. In chapters 10 and 11, the focus shifts to measurement issues and overall managerial implications.

PHYSICAL MANIFESTATIONS

As we begin to explore forms of damaging OMB such as theft of organizational resources, we approach the fine line between employee misconduct on the job and illegal, criminal activity. Although in managerial terms the distinction is important because it carries implications for dealing formally with specific cases of misconduct, from our theoretical perspective it is less crucial. Conceptually, we regard theft, vandalism, or espionage as OMB when the act violates core organizational or societal rules. Thus, if the company specifies that using the company car for private use is not permitted, then its use may be regarded as OMB Type S if the purpose was to benefit from it.

Criminology as a scientific discipline has been struggling with such definitional issues from its inception (Shapiro, 1990; Shoham, Rahav, & Adad, 1987). Nonetheless, we can benefit from some of its contributions, which are particularly helpful in clarifying some of the confusion in our domain. One such contribution is Clinard and Quinney's (1973) seminal work on criminal behavior. They posited that criminals differ by the type of crimes they commit, their social organization, their social background, their personal value, and their self-image. They also developed a universal typology for criminal activity, which over time has gained prominence and support. It consists of eight categories arranged by degree of seriousness, which are relevant to OMB:

1. Personal violence including some types of homicide. In many cases, perpetrators are not criminals because they have no record, lead normal working lives, and identify with societal norms. Their crime is often a result of circumstances.
2. Incidental property offenses. Included are most individuals engaging in such acts as petty theft or vandalism of public property. These too would be considered crimes of circumstance.
3. Occupational crime. These are acts of theft, fraud, or embezzlement, ranging from a small business owner overcharging customers to a company's chief executive officer (CEO) who authorizes spurious accounting practices to deceive the authorities and investors and other stakeholders, or misuse of public funds.
4. Political crimes. These include actions that are politically or ideologically motivated. Many such activities are performed within formal institutions by individuals who strongly believe in what they do and what their organizations represent.
5. Immoral crimes. These acts are considered illegitimate as well as immoral because they may hurt the public. For example, companies that conceal pertinent data about risk factors inherent in their products leave the public defenseless and exposed to danger.

6. Conventional crimes. This category consists of the typical crime activity (burglary, theft, and robbery) that is mostly carried out by career criminals. Such activity is often organized and planned and, in some cases, involves acts of aggression and violence.
7. Organized crime. This is akin to any organizational activity because it is systematic, planned, coordinated, monitored, rewarded, and often competitive. It is also highly territorial and specialized and involves high levels of hidden networking, secrecy, and isolation from public scrutiny.
8. Professional crime. These include the elite, highly reputable, professional, well-trained criminals who are regarded as real professionals. They are held in high esteem by criminals and authorities alike.

Employee Theft

Sennewald (1986), a former president of the International Association of Professional Security Consultants, offered some insights into the realm of employee theft, referring to them as *theft maxims*. No business, industry, institution, or enterprise is immune to internal theft:

- Employee theft is a social disease and, as such, is contagious.
- Many organizations protect their property against theft by outsiders, but they neglect to protect it against theft by insiders.
- Theft is a combination of attitude and act. Organizations tend to emphasize dealing with acts rather than attitudes.
- Forgiving theft because of severity of damage or because of rank or seniority is tantamount to licensing more theft.
- Organizations lose more from embezzlement and fraud than from armed robberies.

Other maxims pertain to the employees:

- Everyone who is caught stealing says he or she is stealing for the first time.
- Theft in organizations is often a retaliatory act against management.
- Success in stealing often becomes addictive.
- Employees who are known to lie are also prime candidates to steal.

These maxims bear some important theoretical significance for any student of OMB and attest to the phenomenon's pervasiveness.

Buss (1993) is frequently cited for estimating that organizations in the United States lose $120 billion annually to employee theft. Greenberg (1997) estimated the loss to be close to $200 billion annually. Others suggest lower figures (e.g., Zeitlin, 1971). Greengard (1993) estimated that 20% of U.S. businesses fail because of excessive rates of employee theft. The numbers themselves are not really critical because it is impossible to precisely calculate such damages on the national level. What is important is the message. Employee theft is a pervasive and daily workplace behavior (Delaney, 1993).

It is estimated that 75% of organizational members steal something of value from their workplace at least once, and that most damage is not due to isolated grand theft cases, but to the accumulation of petty theft (Lipman & McGraw, 1988; McGurn, 1988). According to Halverson's (1998) survey of the retail industry in the United States, which covered 29 retailers with over 11,000 stores and close to 2 million employees, 1.76% of sales income was lost because of employee theft ($4.4 billion for 1 year). Over 780,000 employees were caught stealing an average of $903.18 worth of merchandise. About 40% of the workforce admitted the temptation to steal, and 20% admitted taking some cash from stores. Using direct and experimental measurement techniques to elicit valid reports of past theft behavior, Wimbush and Dalton (1997) questioned approximately 800 employees and ex-employees of theft-prone workplaces such as stores and restaurants. The direct questions elicited a positive response from 28% of the employees, whereas the more subtle, indirect methods revealed that 58% admitted to stealing from their employers.

No wonder theft by members of organizations is considered to be a widespread and costly phenomenon in work organizations in the United States and perhaps in most other countries as well. However, one problem that researchers and practitioners face in light of such varied statistics is the absence of a theft base rate, which would indicate how much theft is a high rate in different types of industries. In any case, we acknowledge the pervasive existence of employee theft and need to articulate ways to both observe and controll its various manifestations. Indeed organizations have become more aware of this phenomenon; with the advancement of technology, many attempt to use electronic surveillance methods to thwart or catch perpetrators or monitor computer abuse. Others use selection testing (e.g., honesty or integrity tests) to identify theft-prone candidates before they enter the premises.

Establishing the base rate is difficult and related to the problem of defining the theft phenomenon. The term *theft* is not limited to the stealing hard equipment or property. Merriam (1977) defined *employee theft* as unauthorized taking, control, or transfer of money, goods, or services of an employer committed during the work day. Greenberg's (1995) definition is more inclusive: "any unauthorized appropriation of company property by employees either for one's use or for sale to another. It includes, but not limited to, the removal of products, supplies, materials, funds, data, information, or intellectual property" (p. 154).

Unauthorized is a hard concept to define organizationally. In restaurants, for instance, employees who consume unauthorized quantities of food or drink may actually be stealing from the owners. However, they may believe, perhaps coached by peers and others, that these are customary job perks, not theft. Furthermore, a lax atmosphere may exist that creates a sense among employees that such behavior, if not condoned, is at least not frowned upon. Such an atmosphere, of course, may be reflected in employees' ambivalence as to what is considered theft and what is not. When the norm is not clearly defined and communicated, it is hard to distinguish misbehavior from acceptable behavior. We recently overheard hushed debate among some university administrative employees in the cafeteria during lunch. Apparently some employees come in early in the morning, clock in, and then leave the workplace to carry out personal errands without clocking out. The hushed debate was about the legitimacy of this misconduct. When one person said that it is improper, the others agreed, but how can they know? How can those in authority findout? And besides, many people do it.

In their practitioner-oriented book entitled *Are Your Employees Stealing You Blind?* Bliss and Aoki (1993) admitted that most people do not look for ways to cheat, but when an opportunity presents itself they may not be quick to brush it aside. The authors illustrated this with a list of some remarkable white-collar thefts recorded by a fraud investigator: A bookkeeper in a doctor's office had been skimming over $250,000 a year in payment to a fictitious supplier; an apartment building manager found a way to pocket most of the cash received as rent by adjusting the books to conceal the theft; a partner loaned himself nearly $800,000 of partnership funds without the knowledge of the other partners, eventually forcing the firm into bankruptcy; a bookkeeper embezzled over $300,000 in 5 years by using the company president's signature stamp to sign checks made out to nonexistent firms and cashed them with the help of a bank teller.

These cases may sound like rare instances of big-time theft. They indeed are. Yet we regard the daily misuse of organizational resources in the same category—theft—and thus as OMB. This may include the vast majority of organizational members who take time off from work, use equipment for personal use, or consume goods that should be sold. You may regard this as petty. Yet if it violates any rule or norm, by definition it is OMB. Thus, we discuss employee theft as a common and prevalent form of organizational behavior.

Workplace theft by blue-collar employees has been a concern to owners, managers, and labor representatives from the beginning of productive systems (Horning, 1970). Although practitioners such as security officers, insurance agents, and arbitrators have been burdened by the problems arising from theft and its damages, academic interest has lagged. Horning suggested that, despite its costs and prevalence, theft has not been accorded much attention by either students of deviant behavior or organizational analysts, stating that "Even sociologists, with their empirical, analytical, and theoretical interest in normative behavior, have been conspicuously neglectful of the non-legal activities of industrial operatives" (p. 46).

The many references to theft—pilfering, misappropriation, peculation, filching, mulcting, poaching, embezzling, stealing, petty thievery, petty larceny, grand theft, and purloining—illustrate the range of acts in question. However, they do not reveal the nature of the relationship between thief and victim, and they do not tell anything about the motivation behind them or whether they where committed to inflict damage or benefit the self, group, or organization. Horning (1970) thus laid the foundation for the present distinctions among OMB types. For example, an employee admits in an interview: "Occasionally I'll bring something home accidentally. I'll stick it in my pocket and forget it and bring it home. I don't return that 'cause it's only a small part and I didn't take it intentionally" (p. 55). How should one characterize such behavior? What is the motivation? Benefiting self? Inflicting damage? Doing what is customary? Is it a prosocial or an antisocial activity? We turn to the individual-level antecedents of theft in the next chapter. Suffice it to say that employee theft could be regarded as both prosocial behavior when it is motivated by a desire to adhere to some group norms and antisocial when it is motivated by some desire to harm and inflict damage.

Horning (1970) proposed some important conceptual distinctions between white-collar and corporate crimes and between blue-collar crime and blue-collar theft. The categorization of white-collar crime should be reserved to acts by salaried employees that victimize the organization, whereas corporate crime pertains to acts that benefit the organization. Blue-collar crime includes all illegal acts committed by rank-and-file employees (nonsalaried) that involve the organization's assets (e.g., theft and destruction of property) or the misuse of the location for engaging in such acts as gambling on company premises during work hours. Specifically, Horning defined *employee theft* as the "illegal or unauthorized utilization of facilities and removal and conversion to one's own use of company property or personal property located on the plant premises by non-salaried personnel employed in the plant" (p. 48) .

Employee theft is considered a major component of what is known as shrinkage (the totality of goods and materials missing due to shoplifting, vendor theft, misplacement, accounting or bookkeeping manipulation, or error as well as employee pilferage). Rosenbaum (1976) studied employee theft and tried to find ways to predict its occurrence. He suggested that worker theft especially in the private sector is largely undetected, unreported, and underprosecuted. Based on data on employee selection and theft data collected from two samples drawn from privately owned merchandising companies, Rosenbaum concluded that organizations might be able to use data from employment application blanks to distinguish between employees who may pose a risk (and thus would need more surveillance on the job) and those who pose less threat of stealing (and thus do not require special surveillance). Humphreys (1977) harshly criticized this study for failing to account for the base rate for theft in these organizations, which renders such conclusions and implications premature (see further discussion of methodological problems in OMB measurement in chap. 10).

Understanding the pervasiveness and importance of this form of behavior, Hollinger and Clark (1982, 1983) studied employee theft quite extensively, and their research is frequently cited. They analyzed questionnaire data from over

9,000 employees representing retail, hospital, and manufacturing organizations. They operationally defined *theft* as the unauthorized taking of organization property by employees who generally have a nondeviant self-concept. They also assumed that for most employees theft is a function of perceived deterrence. Lax controls, they argued, lead to more prevalence of theft. Using direct questions, Hollinger and Clark (1983) asked their respondents to anonymously report their past year's level of participation in thefts of merchandise, supplies, tools, equipment, and other material assets belonging to their employers. Retail sector employees were asked about the frequency (from daily to 1–3 times a year) of misuse of discount privileges, taking store merchandise, receiving pay for hours not worked, borrowing or taking money without approval, claiming false reimbursements, and damaging merchandise to buy it on discount. In all, 35.1% of 3,500 individuals admitted being involved in theft. Of the 4,111 hospital personnel about 33% were involved in such acts as taking supplies, misusing medication intended for patients, and taking hospital equipment or tools. About 28% of the 1,497 manufacturing sector employees admitted to taking raw materials used in production, taking finished products, taking precious metals, and receiving some undeserved pay. Such questions, although pertaining to stealing from the organization, may not be interpreted that way by employees who may regard their behavior as quite acceptable.

A fascinating discussion of the fine line between taking and stealing is offered by Greenberg (1998), who wrote on the geometry of employee theft that there is a cognitive "gray area" regarding what various members of the organization considered theft. He presented a conceptual analysis to explain this ambiguity following two lead questions: (a) When do members take company property, and (b) when is taking such property regarded as theft? His goal was to develop a framework for theft deterrence.

Although managers tend to frequently complain that "everybody's stealing the company blind," workers tend to conceal or deny knowledge of it. This gap could be attributed to two sources. One is the actual difference in day-to-day experiences among job holders at different levels. Another stems from the ambiguity inherent in the way different individuals interpret theirs' and others' behaviors. Thus, what constitutes theft may be subjective. Greenberg (1998) cited a legal definition of *employee theft* that helps explain this issue. According to the National Council on Crime and Delinquency (1975), employee theft is a "rational crime of opportunity, done as an intentional act that involves a breach of trust, resulting in a direct economic benefit to the actor, against the employing organization, within varying degrees of localized tolerance" (p. 7). That is, certain acts (e.g., unauthorized consumption of food and beverages in a restaurant) may be perceived differently by owners and employees and in other ways at various locations.

Following Lewin's (1951) force-field theory, Greenberg (1998) suggested that taking behavior be conceived as resulting from the net strength of individual, group, and organizational-level forces that both encourage and inhibit acts of taking. To the extent that people desire to present themselves as behaving in a morally appropriate manner, they attempt to negotiate the legitimacy of their acts of taking with others who threaten to impose labels (e.g., thief) that challenge their moral self-images. Efforts to dissuade others from interpreting one's taking behavior as acts of theft involve different mental mechanisms and tactics known as *neutralization*. Greenberg proposed that employee theft may be deterred by efforts to counter these cognitive strategies as well as attempts to strengthen inhibiting forces and weaken encouraging forces.

Can such tendencies be detected? Can we indeed predict engagement in theft activity? It is hard to say, but some attempts have been made. For example, Jones and Terris (1983) designed a predictive validity study to test the claim that employees with dishonest attitudes who heavily employ neutralization and rationalization to justify their behavior engage in counterproductive activity and theft in particular. They used the Personnel Selection Inventory–Form 1 (London House Press, 1980) as a measure of workplace dishonesty; it assesses perceptions and attitudes toward theft. The measure presumes that theft proneness is exhibited by (a) more rumination over theft activities (e.g., "How often in recent years have you simply thought about taking money, without actually doing it?"), (b) more projection of theft in others (e.g., "How many executives steal from their companies?"), (c) greater rationalization of their acts (e.g., "Will everyone steal if the conditions were right?"), (d) less punitive attitudes toward thieves (e.g., "A young person was caught stealing $50,000 in cash from an employer. If you were his employer, what would you do?"), and (e) more interthief loyalty (e.g., If you were caught stealing, would you tell on the people who helped you?"). They found that employees with higher dishonesty scores were also rated higher by their supervisors on counterproductive acts. Additionally, units with the worst theft records were staffed with personnel with higher dishonesty scores. Thus, tolerant personal predispositions toward this misbehavior and its justification may well be predictive of actual conduct and could be utilized in the design of personnel managerial tools, such as selection tests (to read more on the prevention of OMB, see chap. 11).

What are some of the behavioral signs to look for when monitoring employee theft? According to Bliss and Aoki (1993), the signs exist and are too often ignored by both superiors and peers. In fact, "when embezzlement or some other internal rip-off is discovered, management's usual response is an embarrassed confession that certain early warning signs were ignored, that a 'hunch' that something was wrong was shrugged off" (p. 23). Such signs can be an abrupt change in lifestyle, excessive use of alcohol or drugs, close social ties with suppliers or customers, refusal to take a vacation, unusual and obsessive neatness, and frequent borrowing from other employees. Obviously this approach addresses management concerns about subordinates. However, with the growing evidence that managers are not immune from engaging in improper behavior that amounts to large-scale theft and fraud, employees should be aware of the early warning signs for organization members at all levels, such as a sudden sale of company stocks and options.

Sabotage and Vandalism

Undoubtedly the most blatant manifestations of employee misconduct that targets the organization's products and property with an implicit intention to inflict some damage are vandalism and sabotage. These fall within the realm of workplace aggression, but are often not considered violent behavior. Giacalone and Rosenfeld (1987) suggested that employee sabotage occurs when people who are currently employed in an organization engage in intentional behaviors that effectively damage that organization's property, reputation, products, or services. Nonetheless, there is no consensus as to what exactly is considered sabotage (Giacalone, Riordan, & Rosenfeld, 1997). Some mild forms of sabotage and vandalism, such as graffiti or spreading rumors maligning the employer, are quite often dismissed by management and may at times even be tolerated. The question, again, is where one draws the line between acceptable and unacceptable damaging behavior. As we pointed out, any act that purposely inflicts some damage on the organization as a whole, its assets, or its stakeholders is regarded as OMB Type D—damaging, destructive, or disparaging behavior committed intentionally.

Vandalism at work is not a newly discovered phenomenon. It may take on new forms because of technological advances and changes, but employees' physical tampering with their work environment is well documented. Crino and Leap (1988) offered several basic reasons why employees engage in workplace sabotage:

- Make a statement or send a message to others.
- Take revenge.
- Have an impact on a large faceless system.
- Satisfy a need to destroy.
- Seek thrills.
- Avoid work.

A fascinating depiction and analysis of industrial sabotage was presented by the French sociologist Dubois (1976) in his book *Sabotage in industry*. Dubois distinguished two prototypes of sabotage: instrumental and demonstrative. Instrumental sabotage is aimed at a limited or total transformation of the present situation. Demonstrative sabotage is an expression of protest, dismay, or rejection of management values, policies, or actions; it is not aimed at achieving certain demands. That is, it is by and large political in nature. To illustrate an industrial context that enhances such actions, Dubois (1976; akin to Blauner's, 1964, depictions of mass production settings that produce worker alienation) vividly described the plight of a quality control worker in a tire factory: "Tires by the thousands. Fifteen thousand a day. Several hundred pass the quality controller in every eight-hour period, on every forty seconds. His job is to examine and test each one for faults: any tire that is defective must be set aside. Suppose he does not do his job properly—what then? ... It is easy enough not to check: just a matter of doing nothing" (p. 13).

Thus, sabotaging the work process and disrupting the organization could be easier if more individuals engage in such behavior. If, Dubois remarked, in this type of setting many individuals engage in such behavior and the organization is forced to increase its means and resources devoted to control it, this could be "the first indication that sabotage is going on."(p. 13)

Dubois (1976) further (p. 13) demonstrated that destructive sabotage, such as the machine-breaking phenomenon in industrializing societies during the 18th and 19th centuries, is mainly a defensive reaction by employees resisting the mechanization of their work.

For example, F. W. Taylor (1911) identified management's responsibility for the go-slow type of sabotage. His logic was that such employee behavior is a direct result of the piece-rate method of pay. Intuitively, such a method should increase productivity because of the clear effort-to-pay contingency. However, the reality is different: Employees restrict their performance for fear that, as a result of their productivity, management will redesign work or establish new, yet higher standards. Deliberate absenteeism (i.e., absenteeism not justified by illness, family obligations, etc.) is typically an intentional act in which the employee rejects a given work situation. In another classic portrayal of industrial organizations of the mid-20th century, Turner and Lawrence (1965) showed that absenteeism was the highest in settings where jobs had little or no variety, were not intellectually stimulating, and demanded low levels of personal responsibility. Such absenteeism is regarded as sabotage because when it persists over time and spreads through the organization it may cause substantial disruptions, real losses, and a possibility for some kind of chaos.

Giacalone et al. (1997) offered a useful approach to the identification of sabotage. They suggested a series of questions that address practical concerns of deterrence and apprehension and that may represent the inception of a potentially fruitful alliance between scholars and practitioners. The answers that managers provide offer a more reality-based picture of sabotage behavior. This in turn extends the researchers' ability to formulate a scientific understanding of what is mostly described by explanatory metaphors of sabotage. Based on the sabotage literature (e.g., Dubois, 1976; Giacalone & Rosenfeld, 1987; Linstead, 1985; Sprouse, 1994; Taylor & Walton, 1971), Giacalone et al. (1997) stipulated that deterrence or apprehension of employees engaged in sabotage require specifying (a) a proper definition of what it is, (b) the number of perpetrators and the internal organizational support for sabotage, (c) the history of sabotage in the organization, (d) the provocation of the acts, (e) the targeting of the acts, and (f) the extent of damage done.

Definition of the Act of Sabotage.   There is an inherent difficulty in defining an act of misbehavior as sabotage because there is no consensus as to exactly what it is, and because it may apply to a wide variety of actions such as the damage done to equipment, spreading a virus over the Internet, stealing goods or knowledge, harming products or services, vandalizing property, and so on. Scholars have offered different classifications. In addition to Dubois' (1976) typology, Strool (1978) identified the following types of sabotage: informational, chemical, electronic, mechanical, fire related, explosive, and psychological. Giacalone and Rosenfeld (1987) proposed four groups: slowdowns, destructiveness, dishonesty, and causing chaos. Obviously one major problem is distinguishing between intentional (e.g., spilling coffee on your computer on purpose) and accidental sabotage (e.g., spilling coffee on your computer by accident); although the outcome may be the same, qualitatively these should be construed as different behaviors. It is important to correctly identify the act because inaccurate assessments often lead to improper management reactions, which may not only be unfair to the employees, but could actually exacerbate the situation and indeed cause retaliatory sabotage.

Who Is or Are the Perpetrator/(s)?   It is important to ascertain whether sabotage is an individual or group act because this determination may lead to different interpretations and reactions. Individual sabotage (usually committed covertly) is regarded and treated as such, but collective sabotage is different. Giacalone et al. (1997) proposed three types: (a) independent group sabotage is performed by a number of individuals in the organization who may not be aware of each other's activity, (b) conspirational group sabotage is committed as a result of a specific group decision, and (c) blind-eye group sabotage occurs when a number of individuals know of or witness an act of sabotage and choose not to inform management about it. This complicity is sabotage as well.

What Is the History of Sabotage in the Organization?   Occasional sabotage is certainly important. Yet a pattern of sabotage behavior is consequential for both perpetrators and organizations because they indicate that there may exist a persistent and most probably an unresolved problem. Thus, both the extent and history of the observed phenomenon should be examined. This knowledge is bound to make the organization's reaction less haphazard and more effective.

Was the Act Provoked?   It is extremely important to understand that there is a vast difference between acts of sabotage perpetrated by employees identified as suffering from personality or emotional disorders and acts perpetrated by employees motivated to engage in them for reasons such as defiant reaction to managerial control or abuse. Sociopaths or psychopaths should obviously be treated as employees in need of help. However, the personal or organizational causes of such behavior for psychopaths, which make up the lion's share of saboteurs, requires careful investigation.

Who Is Targeted?   It is important to distinguish among personal, group, and organizational targets. Often the results of sabotage or vandalism can be deceiving. Although the consequences could be organization-wide, the intended target could be a specific manager or decision. This distinction is important because again a misreading of the situation might lead to inappropriate action such as removing the cause of the activity from the scene.

What Type of Damage Was Done?   Aggressive acts of sabotage or vandalism, in addition to causing physical damage, may spill over to indirect, long-term psychological effects such as increased stress and uncertainty (cf. Painter, 1991). Therefore, it is useful to identify both types of consequences-personal and organizational because this sometimes leads to the identification of hidden motives for aggressive sabotage acts.

According to a recent *workforce on line* article geared at human resource managers (Laabs, 2000), angry, bitter, bored, frustrated, envious, and resentful employees are sabotaging employers' equipment and operations in increasingly sophisticated and creative ways. Employees and managers often use sabotaging tactics (e.g., agreeing to carry out a task, but then stalling) when they covertly resist imposed changes. The variety of options seems endless. Sabotage can range from simple pranks to the most sophisticated financial fraud. The media has reported numerous cases in which angry employees tampered with products in unimaginable ways—from putting rodents in food product to needles in baby food, set their company on fire, or wiped out entire databases. Sabotage is taking on new forms as computer networking becomes available to most employees. Workers are overtly and covertly setting computer bombs, erasing databases such as customer lists, or tampering with personnel files. Writers on sabotage behavior (cf. Analoui & Kakabadse, 1992, 1993) claimed that sabotage is the tool of the disgruntled employee who feels discriminated against, taken advantage of, and ignored by the organization. They see it mostly as retaliatory behavior whereby members, alone or in groups, take revenge on the system.

In an *Industry Week* article, Caudron (1995) illustrated what he called *get even* employees—a new breed of workers who will do anything to sabotage the company, be it by antagonizing customers, assaulting the computer system, or damaging critical pieces of equipment. These, he assumed, are employees who react strongly to their feeling resentful, alienated, or fearful about job security and being wary of management. He presented the following cases:

Case 1—Tired of constant overwork and lack of management appreciation, employees at an industrial plant punch a hole in a drum of toxic chemicals. Slowly the air seeps into the drum, pressure builds, and the drum explodes, spewing dangerous chemicals into the workplace. Work comes to a standstill until the hazardous substance can be cleaned up. The perpetrators, hiding a smile, head home for a much-needed day of rest.

Case 2—Disgruntled over the lack of recognition of his work and fearful of an impending layoff, a computer programmer for a major defense contractor plants a logic bomb in the information system. His plan is to destroy vital data on a rocket project and then, in the event of a layoff, get hired as a high-priced consultant to reconstruct the lost information.

Case 3—Angry over reconstructing, reengineering, and never-ending management platitudes, a hospital employee infects the computer system with a virus that destroys the last word in each file. The problem is, once the virus works its way through the system, it turns around and starts all over again. Slowly but surely, each file is erased from the end to the beginning. Managers seldom scroll all the way to the bottom of their documents. Volumes of data are damaged before the virus is detected.

However, sabotage can also be OMB Type S—a result of misconduct motivated by greed. Laabs (2000) reported a case filed by City of New York (NYC) in which charges are being levied against 29 individuals, including former employees with the department of finance, which handles tax payments and landlords. The city claims that the employees manipulated a computerized system for recording real estate tax payments from property owners by wiping out millions of dollars in taxes. The landlords paid back substantial bribes. NYC is seeking to recover some $20 million in lost taxes and interest. Overall, in the United States, the losses from employee fraud cost more than $400 billion annually, which amounts to 6% of the organizations' revenue. Moreover, it is estimated that episodes of serious workplace violence (including serious acts of sabotage) can cost employers a quarter of a million dollars in lost time and legal expenses. Morin (1995) portrayed a rather bleak picture of the corporate world, which is inflicted by what he termed *silent sabotage*. He blamed the spread of sabotage on a valueless society and a sense of anomie, and he urged organizations to instill value systems and codes of ethics with which employees can better identify.

INTELLECTUAL MANIFESTATIONS

Data Theft

One of the most frightening documents we read on computer-related misbehavior is Cornwall's (1987) book, *Datatheft*. It chillingly describes the endless opportunities to misbehave, the unlimited possibilities that computer and telecommunication systems provide, and the incredible repertoire of activities they generate. Cornwall richly illustrated types of activities relevant to OMB researchers:

- Crimes made easier by the computers—fraud (false inputting, fake inventorizing, and fake outputs), forgery, impersonation, information theft, and eavesdropping.
- Crimes not possible without a computer—computer manipulation (data files, application software, expert and system programs, attack on hardware,

compromised hardware, compromised measurement devices, and vandalism/sabotage), theft of software, theft of hardware and peripherals, theft of computer resources, and hacking (by employees and by outsiders).

One of the reasons that computer systems have made misbehavior so easy is their nature: (a) there is a general absence of direct human involvement; (b) most, if not all, of the organization's assets are computerized or at least managed through the system; (c) contents of files are invisible; (d) managers and administrators tend to trust experts in handling computers and data not realizing the level of risk to which they are exposed; (e) raw data, such as documents, are mostly handled by nonexperts and are mostly unprotected while being processed; and (f) basically all systems are breakable and, because they are ever changing, never becoming fully protected. Certainly with the Internet's infinite capabilities of handling data, the opportunities to steal and manipulate other people's data have risen significantly.

New-Age OMB

The term OMB was used by Punch (1996) in his captivating book *Dirty Business* to denote corporate misconduct and deviance at the macro-, organizational level. To Punch, corporations *behave* because certain top managers make certain strategic choices, but they also misbehave. For example, when he analyzed the collapse of the once venerable financial institution BBCI, he cited Kochan and Whittington's (1991) study saying that the bank apparently had its own secret security service that operated as a global intelligence operation and enforcement squad. Namely, the bank acted as a global villain. However, most of its rank-and-file employees went about their daily chores and tasks unaware of the bank's activities. In this respect, our use of the terms is somewhat different because we emphasize OMB at the individual level. Admittedly, the distinction is a bit fuzzy because, after all, it is not BBCI that ended up in British jail, but its top executives, who were found guilty of wide-ranging crimes. We face the same conceptual tension later in chapter 9 when we discuss unethical managerial conduct in the Israeli Banking system and the case of the recently collapsed Enron Corporation.

Espionage and cyberwars among organizations also appear to be fast growing due to global computer interconnectedness (Cornwall, 1987; Guinsel, 1997). To gain a better understanding of the realities of today's technology-based organizational misconduct, we scanned the *New York Times* during several months in 2002. As expected, we found evidence about the financial and accounting scandals that swept sweeping through the corporate world (Enron, WorldCom, Xerox and Tyco) and Wall Street.

As we were writing the draft of this chapter, the academic world received a firsthand reminder of the potential threat of Internet espionage right at the heart of one of its most respected Ivy League institutions. Apparently the Yale University admissions office Web site was breached by an outsider who scanned through

11 files of applicants. The spied-on files were placed in a special site that could be accessed by applicants checking on the status of their applications. Entry was possible only by using birthdates and Social Security Numbers. One month later, in a meeting of Ivy League admissions officials, the story broke: Curious about whether certain applicants had been rejected by the rival, the Princeton University admissions director visited the site and examined files he was not supposed to see. This was no complicated hacking job: He simply used the numbers of students who had registered at both universities. The director was removed, and Princeton hired the services of a Newark law firm to investigate. Mr. D. G., dismayed by this scandal, wrote a letter to the editor: "As a member of Yale's class of 2006, I am appalled by Princeton's violation of fundamental privacy of its applicants ... it is plausible that Princeton changed the admissions status of prospective students based on whether or not those students were admitted to Yale" (*New York Times,* July 28, 2002). The director's misconduct would be classified as OMB Type O if his primary motive was to spy on behalf of his organization, OMB Type S if the motive was to gain some personal benefit, and OMB Type D if the intention was to harm the competition.

The Internet, together with the advance of sophisticated cellular, satellite, and tracking technologies, undoubtedly has changed the way business is conducted around the world. For example, an auto part can be located, ordered via Internet, identified, located, packaged, and shipped automatically to anywhere in the world. Global networks of delivery ship it instantly and track it via satellite as it makes its way to its destination. Thus, parts and products travel the world, completely changing the old warehousing and transportation concepts of the later part of the 20th century. Zero-level inventory, for example, has become a reality. At a different level, drug traffickers today, are not outcasts hidden behind an iron curtain. They use cellular phones for communications and the Internet for encoding secret messages, they travel freely, and they have multiple bank accounts in the finest financial institutions around the world (Guinsel, 1997).

However, the Internet has made industrial espionage, misinformation, and subversion big businesses. Well-paid hackers are often the brains and soldiers in these wars among corporations. Hacker newsgroups have emerged as communities of experts who generate, shuffle, and disseminate important information. This is now called *espionomics*. If one knows how, one can find almost any pertinent information needed to make strategic and tactical decisions for any company—who filed the most recent patent on polymers, how project teams are operating in your competitor's research and development units, what they publish and what they hide, where certain executives traveled recently, or how the weather in Columbia affects the quality and quantity of coffee beans next year. Of course with the availability of information, a whole new counterespionage and protection industry has emerged as well. Big brother has become a world giant, albeit taking different shapes in different countries. In France, for instance, financial documents pertaining to the state of business organizations are available for public or private scrutiny, whereas information pertaining to individual citizens is not. In the United States, it is pretty much the other way around (Guinsel, 1997). What worries most countries and institutions is the relative ease with which subversive individuals and organizations can penetrate information networks and use them for illicit purposes.

One of the most harmful and dangerous forms of new-age misbehavior is known as *Internet piracy* (Jennifer Lee, *New York Times*, July 11, 2002). Mr. John Sankus, a 29-year-old computer technician, was sentenced to 46 months in prison. He was charged by the U.S. Customs Services as being a ringleader of an international gang of software pirates that deprived companies of millions of dollars through illegal distribution of copyrighted software, games, and movies on the Internet. His group, known as DrinkorDie, is just one of thousands that engage in such pirating. Many operate from within their work organizations, using company resources to download and distribute protected material. What seems especially interesting about the new-age pirates is their motive. Many of them, Mr. Sankus suggested, are not out to cheat anybody or benefit financially. Some do it for fun, for the challenge, for the competition, or because they cherish the feeling of mastering the technology. Nonetheless, according to the Business Software Alliance, software Internet piracy, costs about $10 billion per year in lost sales worldwide (*New York Times*, July 11, 2002).

Why do the new-age pirates, hackers, and saboteurs do what they do? Using qualitative research techniques of observation and interviewing, Turgeman-Goldschmidt (2001) penetrated the hackers' culture in Israel and studied, from their own stories and accounts, not only how they operate, but also how they justify and rationalize their misbehavior. She contacted 54 hackers who were located through a snowball networking process and interviewed them at length. All fit a particular profile: young men around 24 years old, single, educated, working in the computer industry, above-average income, secular, and urban. They all presented themselves as nonconformist, computer freaks from a young age, who were talented and smart. Contrary to the public image of the lone hacker and his computer, it appears that these hackers and their colleagues use their network for social bonding. What starts as a virtual contact often develops into close, collegial, and professional friendships.

So what do hackers do on the Internet? Their illicit activities can be divided into three categories: (a) misconduct related to breach of copyright regulations (duplicating, disseminating, and trading protected programs), (b) misconduct related to hacking (breaking into browsing and using protected data banks or Internet sites, using Internet services without pay, writing and disseminating viruses, stealing information, retrieving or changing official documents, causing the collapse of computer systems, and misusing credit card information), and (c) misconduct known as *freaking* (mostly using international phone services without pay).

Hackers rationalize their misconduct mostly by using self-benefiting rationalizations. Unlike other offenders who use economic deprivation reasons (e.g., Analoui & Kakabadse, 1992; Greenberg, 1997), hackers claim they use computers for competition, kicks, fun, thrill, satisfying curiosity, and control. They steal because they can and because they enjoy the excitement. They do, however, use neutralizing tactics (Sykes & Matza, 1957) such as denying responsibility, denying damaging the victim, blaming the accusers for creating the opportunity, and resorting to higher values.

In summary, as with the whole cyberworld, what is known as this type of OMB is only beginning to emerge. What we do know is probably just the tip of the iceberg of endless opportunities for untold individual and organizational forms of misconduct. One reason that this and other forms of illegal and immoral forms of misconduct are spreading so rapidly is the perpetrators' ability to live with it. To do so, they engage in the process of neutralization.

Neutralization

In a seminal article on neutralization, Sykes and Matza (1957) described a series of strategies that individuals employ to cognitively justify their misbehavior. Neutralization and rationalization techniques play an extremely important role in helping individuals justify wrongdoings. Accordingly, there are several techniques employed by individuals who misbehave:

- *Minimization*—People think or say things like "it's only a paper clip," "it's just one phone call," and "they'll never miss it." The theft would be justified on the grounds that the value of such items is negligible.
- *Externalization*—Misbehaving individuals blame others for their OMB. This technique is used when employees, when caught stealing, would say things like, "this is not stealing, my boss let me take it," or when blaming others (e.g., peers) for pushing them to act in an inappropriate manner.
- *Normalization*—This may best be summed up by the often heard phrase: "Okay, but everybody around here does that." This reflects the internalization of strong social (e.g., work group) norms that act to legitimize improper behavior. The potency of such norms justifying theft has been documented in field research (Mars, 1982) and theory (Greenberg, 1997). There is evidence that people steal to be socially accepted—to receive their peers' approval as full-fledged members.
- *Superordination*—This is a cognitive mechanism of justifying wrongdoing by attributing it to some particular higher goal. Employees may justify using company resources to help others in need, or they explain their misbehavior by blaming the organization for unfair policies, discrimination, maltreatment, and monopolizing the industry. Blaming the organization is typical when the inequity argument is used to justify improper actions such as stealing ("I took it because they owe me").

An empirical study of the use of neutralization techniques to justify theft was reported by Hollinger (1991), who drew from the same large data bank on employee deviance described earlier. He found a significant relationship between rule breaking (stealing property and time) and the use of neutralization techniques. Following Sykes and Matza's (1957) typology, Hollinger operationalized three techniques as independent variables:

Denial of the victim—This technique is similar to Greenberg's (1997) superordination, in that it reflects an attempt by the perpetrator to justify misbehavior on the grounds that the victim (employer) is no victim and actually deserves the fate because of his or her own wrongdoing (e.g., treating the employee unfairly). The scale included items pertaining to satisfaction with certain employment conditions such as pay and promotion.

Denial of injury—Employees tend to minimize the harm they inflict and rationalize that the victim can afford this inconsequential loss. To study this, researchers used items that measure how each respondent perceived the degree of social control directed toward use of company property. The rationale is that employees can more easily excuse their own-rule breaking acts when they have concluded that the company does not seem to care much about the potential harm caused by workplace theft.

Condemnation of condemners—This neutralization technique is used by wrongdoers when they recognize their wrongful activity and let themselves off the hook by accusing the condemner of being hypocritical. They might blame an employer for being dishonest in the first place. To measure this technique, items of perceived corporate honesty are used, hypothesizing that the more employees perceive their employers as conveying the message that honesty is of paramount importance, the more wrongdoers will condemn them for being hypocritical, thereby justifying theft.

Generally, organization members' ability to engage in deviant behavior despite organizations' often intensive efforts to remove it is facilitated by the use of these verbal, behavioral, or cognitive techniques, which serve to reduce or eliminate the perceived discrepancy between a deviant action and the norms it violates. Drawing on existing literature from psychology, sociology, communications, and organization theory, Sykes and Matza, (1957) propose a simplified typology of neutralization strategies and generate a number of hypotheses regarding the conditions or factors likely to determine their use and effectiveness.

A FINAL OBSERVATION

We offer a rather humorous depiction of the same manifestations so tediously described in the preceding section. To do this, we consulted *The Dilbert Principle* (Adams, 1996). We seriously consider it an important and insightful explication of the modern workplace. The definition of what Adams so vividly described as the *virtual hourly compensation* is the total amount of compensation one receives per hour including:

> Salary, bonuses, health plan, inflated travel reimbursement claims, stolen office supplies, airline frequent flyer awards, coffee, donuts, newspapers and magazines, personal phone calls, office sex, telecommuting, illegitimate sick days, Internet surfing, personal e-mail, use of laser printer for your résumé, free photocopies, training for your next job, cubicle used as a retail outlet. (p. 92)

This reflects the kind of property misconduct we encountered in our own research and careers. Furthermore, in a recent *New York Times* article (July 11, 2002), Adams commented on the public astonishment at the discovery that giant corporations collapse or file for bankruptcy because some CEOs engage in gross misbehavior. People seem surprised that captains of industry are stealing vast amounts of money at every opportunity. He suggested, again using his unique sense of corporate humor, that we put things in perspective: "Every employee I ever worked with in my cubicle-dwelling days was pillaging the company on a regular basis, too. But the quantity of loot was rarely noteworthy. . . . The CEO's aren't less ethical than employees and stockholders; they're just more effective" (p. 92).

We cannot refute Adams' astute observation.

6

Individual-Level
Antecedents of OMB

Aggression is not anger, but it often accompanies anger.

—Allcorn (1994)

Acts of OMB are committed intentionally by members of work organizations. Thus far, our goal was to venture into the darker side of these organizations and enumerate and describe the many forms and manifestations of OMB. The repertoire is indeed impressive. We begin to address the inevitable questions: Why do employees intentionally misbehave? What motivates them to violate accepted norms and standards of proper conduct—to intentionally inflict damage and take advantage of resources that belong to others? How can we account for this conduct? Earlier we suggested that any explanation for unacceptable work behaviors has to be as complex and multidimensional as the explanation of behavior designed to directly contribute to the well-being of the organization and its stakeholders.

To begin, we need to consider that any human behavior can seldom be accounted for by a single direct cause. For example, to predict ethical and unethical decisions by managers, Trevino (1986) enlisted a number of personality, job, and organizational variables that may interactively account for the dependent variable—the type of decision made. Because of this multidimensionality and for the sake of effective presentation, we present our discussion about the causes of OMB by level of analysis. In this chapter, we identify selected individual-level antecedents; in chapter 7, we discuss position- and group-level influences; and in chapter 8, we present organizational-level antecedents.

We believe that the ability to predict intentional misbehavior patterns would be an important contribution to OB research. However, systematic empirical research on misbehavior is still lacking. We realize this is quite problematic because of management's reluctance to provide researchers full access to systematically observe misbehavior and researchers' reluctance to engage in long-term investigations. It is also difficult because most misconduct is a low base-rate phenomenon, and much of it is hard to observe. Such obstacles often require indirect, subtle observation methods. For example, we can measure OMB directly as well as through the intention to misbehave. Dalton (1999) discussed at length both the limitations and usefulness of using intent-to variables in OB research. These variables are useful in misbehavior research because such conduct is mostly the type of low base-rate behavior that presents problems of sampling and limited range on scales. For example, in their research of organizational whistle blowing, Ellis and Arieli (1999) and others (cf. Near, Dworkin, & Miceli, 1993; Somers & Casal, 1994) used

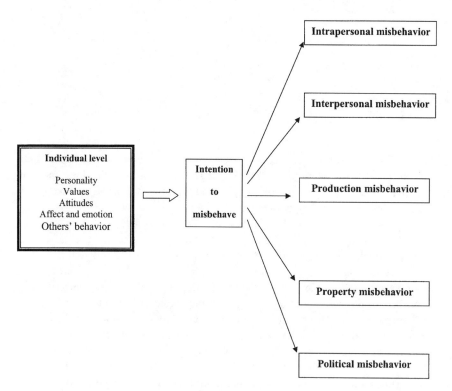

FIG. 6.1. Individual-level antecedents.

the intention to blow the whistle as a proxy for actual reporting of irregularities in the military.

In this chapter we present selected theoretical contributions as well as evidence from empirical studies that suggest ways in which personality traits, predispositions and attitudes, and affect may contribute to the intention to misbehave. Our goal is to gain a better understanding of the phenomenon and generate plausible propositions for future research, anchored in a solid theoretical statement that captures the essence and complexity of OMB, its manifestations, and antecedents. Clearly the number of individual-level antecedents of misbehavior is large, and it is impossible to discuss all of them here. Therefore, we selected antecedents that adequately represent the main individual difference levels: personality, values, attitudes, affect and emotion, and others' behavior. The overall scheme is depicted in Fig. 6.1.

PERSONALITY TRAITS

Personality in OB

Although personality variables played a fundamental role in the research of attitudes, feelings, and behaviors from the mid-1960s through the early 1990s, in theories of OB they only had minor importance (Mount & Barrick, 1995; Murphy, 1996; Weiss & Adler, 1984). For example, Mitchell (1979) emphasized that personality variables in studies of OB mainly serve to play down the connection between a situational variable and some other criterion. Although his survey clearly indicates that personality characteristics predict attitudes, motivation, and leadership, he pointed out that the studies' main foci are attitudes, motivation, and leadership, not personality attributes. Mitchell (1979), much like Weiss and Adler (1984), concluded unequivocally that, although personality measures appear to be clearly related to behavioral outcomes, they do not play a leading role in OB research.

This neglect of personality research during this period, described by Hough and Schneider (1996) as "the dark period" of OB, apparently stemmed from the dominance of the situational approach, which maintains that personality characteristics are illusive and personality can account for only a small part of the variance in OB compared with situational factors (Guion & Gottier, 1965). Studies carried out from the 1960s to the 1990s, explaining the variance of some behavioral outcome criterion by means of these two components, almost always highlighted the weight of situational variables (Mitchell, 1979; Vardi, 1978). Naturally this led many OB researchers to focus on situational factors as having the greatest influence on attitudes and behavior in the workplace. The evidence provided by Landy (1985) is that, in the course of 20 years after Guion and Gottier's conclusions were published, only a small number of studies related personality measures to performance at work.

This can also be attributed to personality research, its slow and inadequate conceptual development, and the poor quality of the methodology employed (Weiss & Adler, 1984). Ozer and Reise (1994) suggested that OB researchers have not invested sufficient effort in conceptualizations and theories defining the psychological elements that comprise the human personality. That trend has led to long-term disagreements among researchers regarding the definition of *personality* and the ways it differs from values, interests, and emotional responses (Murphy, 1996). Nevertheless, researchers and practitioners in the field of industrial and occupational (I/O) psychology made use of personality variables in empirical research, particularly for the purpose of employee classification selection. Hough and Schneider (1996) claimed that I/O practitioners have indeed played an important role in the eventual revival of personality research.

The 1990s saw changes in both OB and personality research. Students of OB started to explore OMB, deal with its domain and dimensions, and carry out empirical studies (e.g., Giacalone & Greenberg, 1997; Robinson & Bennett, 1995; Vardi & Wiener, 1996). Concurrently, a renewed interest in personality variables occurred, attributed by many researchers to the emergence of a wide framework for the examination of personality, called the *Big Five* (see Judge, Matocchio, & Thoresen, 1997; Mount & Barrick, 1995; Seibert & Kraimer, 1999). This led to the publication of numerous studies examining the validity of predicting of workplace behavior by means of personality measures (Hough & Schneider, 1996). To date, however, only scant attention has been paid specifically to the personality–OMB relationship, which we explore in the next section.

The Big Five and OMB

Personality traits are commonly conceived as those inner structures directing an individual's behavior in a relatively stable and typical manner (e.g., Allport, 1961). Such hypothesized structuring requires that we find parsimonious ways to organize such traits conceptually. Otherwise identifing those characteristics and using them to explain behavior becomes tedious. A good example of this potential confusion may be borrowed from Moberg (1997). In trying to describe *employee vice,* Moberg generated a list of 32 terms that purport to be a variety of similar traits such as: cowardice, lawlessness, dishonesty, disloyalty, insincerity, unreliability, callousness, lack of civility, indecency, uncooperativeness, bluntness, intolerance, and selfishness. Therefore, many social scientists believe that logically organizing specific traits into clusters that tap some commonality is more useful.

Support for the Big Five categorization stems from various studies using a variety of questionnaires with both self-reports and descriptions of others using different samples ranging from children to adults in different languages and cultures (Digman, 1990; Mount & Barrick, 1995). Although a universal consensus has yet to be reached as to the exact nature and content of these traits, there is widespread agreement with regard to the significance of the dimensions of *extraversion, agreeableness,* and *neuroticism* and somewhat less agreement as to the significance of the dimensions of *conscientiousness* and *openness* (Hough & Schneider, 1996). Thus, the core Big Five literature (Digman, 1990; Mount & Barrick, 1995; McCrae & John, 1992) provides us with definitions of the five basic dimensions of human personality:

> *Extroversion* includes traits such as sociability, talkativeness, assertiveness, adventurousness, daring, vitality, and drive. At the other end of the spectrum are people described as *introverted*—shy, quiet, inhibited, and reserved.
>
> *Agreeableness* consists of traits such as courtesy, friendliness, and flexibility. Agreeable individuals are described as trusting, cooperative, forgiving, considerate, and tolerant. This dimension thus comprises the more humane aspects of personality, such as altruism and caring for others as opposed to hostility, apathy, and lack of compassion (Digman, 1990).
>
> *Neuroticism* represents differences in people's disposition to feel tense, anxious, depressed, angry, excitable, insecure, nervous, and fearful. People ranked low on this scale are characterized as emotionally stable.
>
> *Conscientiousness* is defined by traits such as responsibility, trustworthiness, and efficiency. People who score high on this dimension are regarded as well organized, good planners, and achievement oriented. Some researchers maintain that this dimension typifies persons who are reliable, prudent, methodical, efficient, and good planners, and others stress ambitiousness and competitiveness. In several surveys, researchers (cf. Mount & Barrick, 1995) concluded that conscientiousness consists of both aspects: self-discipline and competitiveness. McCrae and John (1992) argued that this is the most value-laden dimension, describing good persons (as opposed to bad ones)—those highly desired by work organizations.
>
> *Openness* to experiences represents individuals with a wide range of interests who are receptive to new experiences, imaginative, curious, responsive to the arts, and intellectually stimulated. Researchers (e.g., McCrae & John, 1992; Mount & Barrick, 1995) pointed out that of the Big Five this dimension is the most controversial. Although some define it as culturally based (e.g., Norman, 1963), others view it as more intellectual (e.g., John, 1989). Recently, following Costa and McCrae's (1988) lead, there is a growing consensus that this dimension comprises traits such as: imagination, inquisitiveness, originality, aesthetic sensitivity, and wide horizons (Hellriegel et al., 2001)

The emergence of this approach and the broad consensus regarding its effectiveness prompted many researchers to conduct empirical studies to examine its validity as a predictor of traits. Although the early studies were mainly directed at clinical assessment of flawed personality (Wiggins & Pincus, 1992), with time a great deal of research was conducted with the intention to predict a variety of work behaviors. Although traditionally the main criterion variable was performance, subsequently a variety of other criteria came under scrutiny, such as job satisfaction, career success, and some forms of misconduct.

Extroversion. Most of the studies attempting to predict behaviors by means of the extroversion trait report a positive relationship between extroversion and positive behaviors or attitudes in the workplace. These may range from a high level of performance to career success and satisfaction at work. Barrick and Mount (1991) examined the predictive validity of the Big Five and work performance among five different occupational groups. Extroversion predicts work performance characterized by a great deal of interaction with others, such as managers and salespeople. The researchers concluded that traits such as sociability, zestfulness, and assertiveness, which are included in the dimension of extroversion, contribute to success in these occupations. Vinchur et al. (1998), who focused on salespeople, reported that vitality (also a subtrait of extroversion) has the highest predictive value for success at selling. An additional positive criterion related to extroversion is career success. Seibert and Kraimer (1999) found that personality traits explain additional variance in career success apart from situational variables. They particularly stressed the positive relationship between extroversion and an inner sense of success (satisfaction) and external career success (pay and advancement). Furnham and Zacherl (1986) also reported a positive relationship between satisfaction and extroversion—namely, that extroverted people tend to report greater work satisfaction, especially with regard to pay, and a high level of overall satisfaction from work.

These studies thus demonstrate that extroverts (i.e., active, assertive, energetic, and sociable individuals) tend to report a higher level of satisfaction derived from their work and career, and they also tend to display higher levels of performance especially in occupations demanding interaction with others (managers and salespeople). However, some studies report a positive relationship between extroversion and misbehavior in the workplace. For instance, Collins and Schmidt (1993) found that the personality profile of white-collar offenders (convicted of offenses such as fraud, embezzlement, and forgery) was typically more extroverted, compared with employees in similar hierarchical levels who were not convicted of such acts. Judge et al. (1997) reported that their research indicates a significant positive correlation between extroversion and absenteeism. However, they qualified this finding by saying that this relationship can only be confirmed if situational variables, such as the type of occupation or its characteristics, are controlled because they may affect the willingness of an extrovert to invest in work.

Agreeableness. According to Graziano and Eisenberg (1997), one of the components of agreeableness is a prosocial disposition or voluntary behavior directed toward the well-being of others. Being agreeable is also referred to as being likeable, generous, pleasant, and considerate (Goldberg, 1992). Employees ranked high on this trait are more likely to perform well at work (Tett et al., 1991), and display less hostility and aggression toward others (Graziano & Eisenberg, 1997).

Tett et al. (1991) found that, in general, agreeableness is positively related to work performance. This result differs from that of Barrick and Mount (1993), who found that in occupations characterized by a high level of autonomy, less amiable managers (those ranked lower on agreeableness) display a higher level of performance compared with more amiable managers. One of the possible explanations for this finding is that in such positions overly amiable managers are perceived by their supervisors negatively. Another possibility is that managers, tending to cooperate and assist others, perform better in the less vague and more structured aspects of their roles (Barrick & Mount, 1993). Additional studies show that the traits characterizing an amiable person are related to teamwork (e.g., Hough, 1992). That is, the more employees tend to cooperate, help, and behave pleasantly with others, the better they are suited to teamwork and the more likely they are to succeed in it. Thus, in general terms, these traits explain why friendly, agreeable, and sociable workers are less prone to delinquent behavior such as theft, absenteeism, vandalism, substance abuse (Ashton, 1998) and vindictive behavior even when they feel that organizational justice has been breached (Skarlicki et al., 1999).

Neuroticism.   A neurotic person tends to experience tension, anxiety, depression, anger, and insecurity and is more nervous and high strung than others. Most of the studies researching this trait report that neurotic employees tend to feel dissatisfied with their work and career, perform at somewhat lower levels than expected, and at times behave vindictively toward their organization. More specifically, people ranked high on neuroticism tend to be less satisfied with the amount of work demanded of them, their fellow workers, and their salary. Reinforcing such findings, Seibert and Kraimer (1999) reported a negative correlation between neuroticism and internal (subjective) career success. Overall, according to Tett et al. (1991), neuroticism is significantly related to performance in a negative way: The higher the score on this personality dimension, the lower the performance.

Skarlicki, Folger, and Tesluk (1999) examined the relationships among negative affectivity, perceptions of organizational justice, and vindictiveness. Negative affectivity was measured on a scale composed of six personality traits (calm, apprehensive, tense, nervous, depressed, and irritable) also included in the neuroticism dimension of the Big Five (Goldberg, 1992). Their findings clearly show a relationship between negative affectivity and organizational vindictiveness. They also show that the tendency to act vindictively is high when the level of negative affectivity is higher and the perception of justice is lower. Because of the way negative affectivity is measured, it may be possible to project these findings onto people describing themselves as neurotic. Thus, it is reasonable to suggest that the higher people are ranked on the neuroticism scale, the more likely they will be to act vindictively especially when they also perceive low levels of organizational justice (e.g., discrimination, favoritism, and inconsistency).

Conscientiousness.   Many researchers have pointed out that, among the Big Five, conscientiousness most effectively predicts a variety of criteria in the workplace and its environment (Barrick, Mount, & Strauss, 1993; Hough & Schneider, 1996; Mount & Barrick, 1995). Moreover, some researchers (see e.g., Schmidt & Hunter, 1992) have gone so far as to argue that conscientiousness plays an important and central role in determining performance levels at work. Therefore, this trait must be taken into consideration when attempting to predict and explain factors related to this criterion. OB researchers who focus on personality variables conclude that there is a positive relationship between conscientiousness and work performance (e.g., Barrick & Mount, 1991; Fallan, Kudisch, & Fortunato, 2000; Hough et al., 1990; Tett, et al., 1991; Vinchur et al., 1998).

The most comprehensive research on this topic, conducted by Barrick and Mount (1991), clearly indicated that conscientiousness consistently predicts a higher level of performance in all five occupational groups studied (professionals, policemen, managers, salespersons, and trained or partially trained workers). These findings were confirmed by Barrick and Mount (1993) in a study focusing on managers. This research also revealed that conscientiousness is the most valid factor in predicting a high level of managers' performance. Whereas Barrick and Mount (1991) examined the level of performance according to the workers' professional skills, guidance skills, and the way they were assessed according to labor force data, Vinchur et al. (1998) took a different approach. They studied workers' performance according to supervisory reports (calling this criterion *objective success*) and arrived at similar findings. More specifically, they found that achievement orientation is the main component of conscientiousness in predicting objective success. However, Fallan et al. (2000), who examined the relationship between the Big Five and the performance level of cashiers in a large organization, found that the general conscientiousness scale better predicts work performance than each component of this trait separately (pride at work, perfectionism, accuracy, and diligence). In the wake of these studies, Fallan et al. (2000) concluded that this personality trait—describing a person with achievement orientation, commitment, responsibility, and perseverance—is indeed conducive to task performance in all types of occupations.

The predictive validity of this trait was also examined in relation to additional criteria, such as tests of integrity and teamwork, irresponsible and nonfunctional behavior, replacement, and absenteeism of workers. Ones, Viswesvaran, and Schmidt (1993) reported a particularly strong positive relationship between conscientiousness and integrity tests. For instance, they found that people who are responsible, compliant, and reliable (i.e., conscientiousness) also tend to be graded high on integrity, sincerity, and trustworthiness. Hough (1992) argued that conscientiousness is the personality trait with the strongest relationship to teamwork. She also examined the negative aspect of the workers' behavior dubbed irresponsible behavior. She found that two components of conscientiousness (achievement orientation and dependability) were most highly (negatively) correlated to workers' irresponsible behavior. Additional studies support the claim that the less conscientious workers are (i.e., they score low on traits such as responsibility, compliance, achievement orientation, organizational ability, and orderliness), the more they are prone to exhibit dysfunctional behaviors in the workplace, such as delinquent activities and substance abuse (Sarchione, Cuttler, Munchinsky, & Nelson-Gray, 1998) or theft, vandalism, and absenteeism (Ashton, 1998). Moreover, negative relationships were found between withdrawal behavior as turnover (Barrick, Mount, & Stauss, 1994) and absenteeism (Judge et al., 1997) and workers' scores for conscientiousness.

Therefore, we propose, as did Hogan and Ones (1997), that conscientious workers (responsible, achievement oriented, and dependable) tend to be good corporate citizens and invest exceptional effort at work without expecting rewards because they care. Conversely, workers low on this personality trait do not perform well at work and may be more inclined to get involved in a variety of behaviors that may be dysfunctional or even harmful to the organization.

Openness. People in this category actively seek out new and different experiences. Openness is comprised of inquisitiveness, aesthetic sensitivity, intellectual curiosity, wide-ranging imagination, and originality (McCrae & Costa, 1997). Studies have shown that people open to new experiences tend to support liberal parties and social causes, and this behavior is consistent with their quest for knowledge and their natural inquisitiveness. Moreover, their willingness to question existing values and seek out the unfamiliar (McCrae & Costa, 1997) leads to the development of high moral values. In light of this, we presume that people adhering to such values will be less prone to behave in unethical ways and actively participate in misbehaviors in the workplace (Trevino, 1986). Tett et al. (1991) reported a significant relationship between openness and performance at work. However, studies (e.g., Hough, 1992) show that openness (termed *intelligence*) is positively related to workers' irresponsible behavior apparently due to their inquisitiveness and originality, which at times may lead to irresponsible actions.

In summary, most of the studies attempting to predict behavior at work by means of the Big Five indicate that conscientiousness (i.e., responsibility, accuracy, and achievement orientation) is highly appreciated in the work world. Apparently workers ranked high on this trait perform their work better, are valued by their supervisors, tend to display good citizenship behavior, and are less prone to engage in some forms of OMB. As in the case of conscientiousness, the studies examining the predictive validity of agreeableness report stable relationships with positive behaviors at work (e.g., satisfaction and performance, teamwork, and career satisfaction) and negative relationships to misbehaviors (i.e., delinquent behavior and organizational vindictiveness). Likeable, generous, and amiable workers are less prone to misbehave toward the organization or its workers. In contrast, neurotic workers who appear to experience high levels of tension, anxiety, depression, nervousness, and anger perform less well on their professional tasks, are less satisfied with their work, and are more likely to behave in vindictive ways. To demonstrate the research opportunities inherent in the search for the role of personality in explaining and predicting OMB, we turn to the Ashton Study.

The Ashton Study

To test the predictive power of personality traits, Ashton (1998) conducted a study of 50 male and 77 female undergraduate students with summer job experiences. This study is of special interest because, unlike most research into the predictive validity of employee selection measures, Ashton used a measure of OMB as a job performance criterion. The study comes in the wake of the methodological debate (e.g., Ones & Viswesvaran, 1996) known as the *bandwidth-fidelity dilemma*. The issue involved is the utility of using broad personality traits (e.g., each of the Big Five or a general integrity factor) rather than narrower, more specific traits (i.e., particular scale components) in predicting workplace behavior. Ashton sought to determine whether narrow rather than broad traits better account for what he called *workplace delinquency*.

Ashton (1998) asked participants to recall their recent summer work as waiters, fast-food servers, messengers, and the like, and to relate their actual work behavior. The students were advised that, because the responses are completely anonymous, there was no need to try and make a good (or bad) impression. (Note that a discussion of impression management and the problems researchers face when seeking to obtain data regarding sensitive issues such as stealing from or vandalizing one's workplace appears in chap. 10.) Ashton's Workplace Behavior Questionnaire contains behavioral, direct, self-report, and quantitative questions that tap the following behaviors: unjustified absenteeism, lateness, alcohol use, safety violations, goldbricking, theft, freebies (the total dollar value of goods or services that you have given to your friends or relatives for free), and vandalism.

Most of the students indicated some involvement in misbehavior. Also, as in the Vardi and Weitz's (2002c) study, some gender differences emerged: The mean score for male students was significantly higher than that for female students. This may indicate that either male students committed more OMB and/or they were more willing to admit such conduct.

Further findings are also interesting. First, there was no integrity-related general factor of personality. It was assumed that if there were such a factor, then responsibility, low risk taking, conscientiousness, and agreeableness should demonstrate high loadings on a single factor. However, the factor analysis yielded high loadings for unrelated traits such as breadth of interests, complexity, self-esteem, conformity, extraversion, and emotional stability. Second, there was no correlation between that factor and the overall delinquency composite score. Third, the Big Five model received strong empirical support with all five traits emerging as distinguishable factors. Fourth, only two of these traits—conscientiousness and agreeableness—negatively and significantly correlated with misbehavior. Fifth, two of the narrow traits—risk taking and responsibility—correlated with misbehavior, and these relationships were stronger than the two predictive broad traits. Yet the somewhat equivocal findings, the ambiguity of currently available personality measures, and the limited validity of the criterion measure only under-score the difficulties of obtaining hard empirical data on real workplace misbehav-ior. Nevertheless, these findings reinforce our conviction that further systematic investigation of the impact personality traits have on the intentions to engage in different types of OMB is needed.

Integrating Personality, Organizational Justice, and OMB

To demonstrate a potentially interesting research direction, we suggest that OMB be studied as a function of the interaction between the Big Five and the three types of perceived organizational justice, the former representing the personality and the latter the situation. Assuming that the strength of the relationship be-tween personality and actual behavior is influenced by situational factors, this model regards *organizational justice* as a moderator variable. Basically, organi-zational justice reflects a person's evaluation of the kinds and levels of equity existing in the employing organization (Greenberg, 1990b). Three types of justice are proposed following the justice literature: (a) *distributive justice*—employee perceptions concerning equity of the organizational reward system, (b) *procedural justice*—employee perceptions concerning equitability as reflected in organiza-tional policies, and (c) *interactional justice*—employee perceptions concerning the quality of interpersonal treatment by authority figures within the organization.

During the past decade, researchers investigated these variables in relation to a variety of work behaviors including improper behaviors. For example, Greenberg and Alge (1998) discussed extensively the relationship between organizational justice and aggressive behavior. Skarlicki et al. (1999) tested the role of personality as a moderator of the perceived justice–misbehavior relationship. Our rationale is that, given certain personality traits, a person's inclination to engage in a certain type of OMB (especially Types S and D) might change as a result of perceiving different levels of justice. Thus, in the proposed model, the organizational justice perception construct serves as a moderating effect on the relationship between personality traits and OMB. We argue, for instance, that the relationship between agreeableness and OMB toward others is enhanced when the person perceives a violation of interactional justice. Similarly, a neurotic person's tendency toward organizational OMB will be mitigated when the person perceives that procedural justice is strictly maintained.

The potential of this model and additional propositions derived from Bennett and Robinson's (2000) distinction between workplace misconduct aimed at others and misconduct aimed at the organization are presented in Table 6.1. The terms specify probable interactions among the three types of justice perceptions and each of the five personality traits. For instance, we may expect that individual

TABLE 6.1

Research Propositions for the Moderating Effects of Perceived Organizational
Justice on the Personality–OMB Relationship

	Justice Perception		
Personality Traits	Violation of Distributive Justice	Violation of Procedural Justice	Violation of Interactional Justice
Neuroticism (high level)	OMB toward others	OMB toward organization	OMB toward others and organization
Agreeableness (low level)	OMB toward others	—	OMB toward others
Conscientiousness (low level)	—	—	OMB toward organization
Extroversion (high level)	—	—	OMB toward others
Extroversion (low level)	OMB toward organization	OMB toward organization	—

employees who score high on neuroticism will be inclined to misbehave toward
the organization (e.g., steal, loaf, and be counterproductive) when they perceive
low distributive, procedural, and/or interactional justice. We may also expect such
persons to target other individuals in their work setting (e.g., undermine, insult,
harass, and manipulate) when they perceive low distributive and/or interactional
justice.

INTENTIONS AND ATTITUDES

Predicting the Intention to Misbehave—An Investigation

Unquestionably, the decision to deal with ethical dilemmas in a certain way is a
complex cognitive process (e.g., Trevino, 1986). We conducted a study designed
to specifically test some hypotheses regarding the prediction of the intention to
engage in different types of OMB (Vardi & Weitz, 2002c). Here we briefly report
the rationale, method, and findings of this study to illustrate the need to better
understand the kind of cognitive calculations one makes when an intention to act
in a way that violates organizational codes of proper behavior is formed.

Individual behavior follows a cognitive process that leads to the formation
of behavioral intentions (Fishbein & Ajzen, 1975). By understanding how such

intentions are formed, one can explain and predict behavior. The theory of reasoned action (TRA) is predicated on several basic assumptions: (a) the individual is an organism that utilizes available information to form opinions and values and make judgments and decisions; (b) most behaviors are voluntary, and thus controlled by the individual; and (c) in most cases, individual attitudes and behaviors are in congruence. Hence, a negative form of behavior toward a person or an object follows a negative attitude toward that person or object. Accordingly, the factor that determines whether a person will or will not carry out a particular behavior is the behavioral intention to carry it out. The behavioral intention is determined by the person's attitude toward the behavior and his or her subjective norm—the person's belief about whether significant others think that he or she should engage in such behavior. Significant others are specific individuals whose expectations and preferences in this particular domain are important to the focal person such as family members, colleagues, or superiors at work. Hence, the behavioral intention is considered to be a linear regression function of attitudes toward the behavior and subjective norm. The weights of the two predictors are determined empirically. According to Fishbein and Ajzen, attitude toward behavior is a function of the individual's important behavioral beliefs that represent the perceived consequences of the behavior and the value he or she attaches to those consequences. The subjective norm is a function of the individual's beliefs about the degree to which referent others believe that he or she should carry out the behavior weighted by his or her motivation to comply with the referent's opinions (see Ajzen, 1985; Ajzen & Fishbein, 1980; Fishbein & Ajzen, 1975). This theory is useful in explaining most social behaviors, including both functional and dysfunctional work-related behavior (Ajzen & Fishbein, 1980; Kurland, 1995; Sheppard, Hartwick, & Warshaw, 1988; Vardi & Wiener, 1992; Wiener, 1982).

Vardi and Wiener (1996) postulated that the intention to misbehave, which is the immediate cause of an eventual act of misbehavior, is formed differently when the psychological forces that precede it are primarily instrumental or normative. Specifically, OMB Type S (self-benefiting misbehavior) is assumed to be mostly motivated by an instrumental judgment as to the utility of engaging in such an act for the individual, the positive and negative values accruing from it, and eventual personal consequences (attitude according to the Fishbein and Ajzen's (1975) theory of reasoned action). OMB Type O (organization benefiting misbehavior), in contrast, is primarily motivated by affective as well as normative forces within the person. For instance, strong affective or normative commitment (Meyer & Allen, 1997; Wiener, 1982) to the organization may lead an individual member to engage in forms of misconduct to protect it. Thus, the theory of reasoned action would suggest that, in this type of misbehavior (e.g., an unethical decision), the subjective norm has a higher weight in determining the preceding intention. Finally, OMB Type D (intentional acts that inflict damage) is assumed to be motivated by either attitude or subjective norm. At times it may be motivated on a calculative basis (e.g., getting even), and at times it can be a result of an ideological identification with a cause or group. Three research hypotheses follow these suppositions:

1. The weight of a person's (instrumental) attitude toward OMB Type S is higher than the subjective internalized norm toward such conduct in predicting the intention to engage in such behavior at work.
2. The weight of the subjective norm toward committing OMB Type O is higher than the person's instrumental attitude when predicting the intention to engage in OMB Type S.
3. There are no difference in the weights of attitude and subjective norm when predicting the intention to engage in OMB Type D.

Our sample included individuals who, at the time of the data collection, held either a full-time (70%) or part-time position in different types of work organizations. Two hundred questionnaires were distributed in graduate classes of management and OB at our university. During class time, 129 students filled out the questionnaire on a voluntary basis. About one third of the participants were rank-and-file employees, 19% were professionals, and 48% held managerial positions. The questionnaires included the following measures.

Intentions to Engage in OMB.   To measure the intentions to perform Types S, O, or D acts of OMB, we presented three different hypothetical scenarios accompanied by this question: If you were in that situation, would you have acted similarly or differently? To develop these scenarios, we generated 12 narratives representing workplace circumstances and specific behaviors that supposedly deal with them designed to represent the three OMB types. These were then submitted to eight participants in graduate seminars who were asked to read all the stories and identify the primary motivation behind each behavior. The three stories selected were those receiving the most votes as representing Types S, O, or D intentions. The students were also presented with the methodological dilemma of whether it would be preferable to ask a direct question (how would you handle the situation) or an indirect question (how would the person in the story handle the situation). After discussing the pros and cons of each approach, the group voted for the direct approach, which was adopted for the study. The scenarios were as follows:

(a) *OMB Type S Scenario*—As part of your monthly salary, you receive reimbursement for using your own car for visiting your customers. Like many others in the company, you think the real costs you incur are not covered by this extra pay. Occasionally you join a fellow employee for the ride to visit customers. In such cases, would you report those trips for reimbursement to increase your income?

(b) *OMB Type D Scenario*—You work as an engineer in the research and development department of a high-tech company. Your team is highly cohesive, but you do not really feel part of it. Actually you are quite bitter because you think people are talking about you behind your back. Recently you had a brilliant idea that could improve the product your team is working on, but you have no desire to share it with them. Your good friend from college works for a competing firm. Would you tell your idea to him so his team could beat your company in the competition?

(c) *OMB Type O Scenario*—You are a veteran and loyal salesman in a company that markets technological products. You are proud of your company, although at this time it is not doing too well financially. In addition, it was recently discovered that one of the most popular products that you sell has a defect (albeit not a critical one). Headquarters issued a directive to the salesforce to stop marketing the product until further notice. You know that such a move will hurt the financial conditions of the company. Would you keep selling the product to your customers to minimize the economic damage to your company?

Attitudes Toward OMB.   Following Fishbein and Ajzen (1975), we surmised that individuals evaluate the eventual consequences of certain behaviors, as well as their importance and significance. Thus, each scenario was followed by a list of potential positive and negative outcomes: I will gain financially, I will feel guilty, my actions will lead to my dismissal, I will be appreciated by my family, my colleagues will follow my lead, I will feel that I betrayed my values, and my reputation might be tarnished. For each outcome, the respondent was asked to assess how certain he or she is that these outcomes would follow the described act. Scores were calculated for each of the three types S, O, and D.

Subjective Norm.   Following the list of positive and negative outcomes, we presented a list of seven significant others (spouse, relative, immediate superior, manager, colleague, customer, and friend). The respondent was asked to consider how three of the most important of the figures would suggest he behave in the described situation and to what extent he or she would be ready to follow their suggestion. The computation of scores followed the same procedure as before. Thus, the more positive the score, the more the respondent internalized a tolerant subjective norm toward the misbehavior and vice versa.

So what did we find? Descriptive statistics for the three components of the TRA scale (intention, attitude, and subjective norm) for each of the OMB types are presented in Table 6.2. The strength of the intention to misbehave differs by type in a descending order: self-benefiting > organization benefiting > damaging. This is paralleled by the strength of attitudes toward those behaviors: OMB Type S is the most tolerated and Type D is the least. Table 6.2 also presents Pearson correlations between the intention to misbehave and the two precursors (attitude and subjective norm) for each of the OMB types separately. All six correlations (three OMB types and the two precursors) are of moderate size and are statistically

TABLE 6.2

Means, Standard Deviations, and Correlations Among Behavioral Intentions,
Attitudes, and Subjective Norms Toward OMB Types S, O, and D

| | | | r | |
Variables	M	SD	Intention	Attitude
Type S				
Intention[a]	3.15	2.31	—	
Attitude[b]	−1.41	2.72	0.31**	
Subjective norm[b]	−0.26	4.69	0.33**	0.23*
Type O				
Intention	1.95	1.51	—	
Attitude	−2.01	2.30	0.37**	
Subjective norm	−2.36	4.40	0.37**	0.24*
Type D				
Intention	1.87	1.42	—	
Attitude	−2.52	2.63	0.40**	
Subjective norm	−2.31	5.20	0.26*	0.12

[a]Range = 1 to 7.   [b]Range = −9 to +9.
*$p < .05$.   **$p < .001$.

significant, supporting the proposition that both the attitude toward the behavior and
the subjective norm may be conceived as precursors of the intention to misbehave,
tapping related but different psychological decision processes.

Results presented in Table 6.3 show only partial support for our hypotheses.
All three regression models in which intention is predicted by both attitude and
subjective norm are significant. The variance explained by the two predictors alone
is quite substantial—ranging from 15% to 24%. However, only the intention to
engage in OMB Type S was predicted as hypothesized. That is, the (instrumental)
attitude had a higher weight in forming the intention than the (normative) subjective norm. Type O was predicted evenly by both precursors, whereas the Type
D intention was mostly accounted for by the attitude toward the act of inflicting
damage.

Because the sample included a majority of female (65%) employees, we decided
to test an a-posteriori hypothesis that TRA scale predictions will not differ between
the two groups. Table 6.4 shows significant differences between female and male
students. Men's intentions to perform acts of misbehavior on the job were higher
than women for Types S and O. Most important, women's subjective norms appear
to be much less (all three t values were significant at $p < .001$) tolerant toward
any type of OMB than among the working men in this sample.

TABLE 6.3

Multiple Regressions of Attitudes and Subjective Norms on Intentions to Engage in OMB Types S, O, and D

Intentions	Type S			Type O			Type D		
	Beta	T	R^2	F	Beta	T	R^2	F	Beta	T	R^2	F
Attitude	0.26	3.03**			0.35	4.31***			0.35	4.25***		
Subjective norm	0.23	2.90**			0.36	4.33***			0.17	2.10*		
Model			0.15	11.99**			0.24	21.85***			0.18	15.07***

$*p < .05.$ $**p < .01.$ $***p < .001.$

TABLE 6.4

Means and Standard Deviations for the Research Variables for Women and Men
and t Tests[a] for Differences Between the Groups

	Women		Men			
	M	SD	M	SD	N	T
OMB Type S						
Intention	2.78	2.20	3.73	2.46	119	2.20*
Attitude	−1.40	2.71	−1.30	2.87	117	0.16
Norm	−1.00	4.94	1.54	4.10	120	2.80**
OMB Type O						
Intention	1.80	1.30	2.20	1.80	119	1.30
Attitude	−2.90	2.72	−1.77	2.40	120	2.21*
Norm	−3.60	5.15	−0.40	5.00	119	3.30***
OMB Type D						
Intention	1.80	1.30	2.53	2.01	119	2.60**
Attitude	−2.11	2.51	−2.10	1.97	120	0.02
Norm	−3.30	4.40	−0.40	4.46	118	3.40***

[a] Two-tailed test for independent groups.
* $p < .05$. ** $p < .01$. *** $p < .001$.

Our results confirm the TRA based prediction that each one of these behaviors would be predicted by the instrumental considerations with regard to such an act, as well as the internalized subjective norm reflecting the assumed values of significant others. In addition, the separate regression models for each of the three types provided some support for the supposition that the relative weights of attitude and subjective norm depended on the specific stimulus or situation. This finding sheds light on the cognitive processes involved in making decisions to behave in two distinct manners that knowingly violate organizational and/or societal norms: chosing to act within the work environment in a way that enhances personal or organization-wide outcomes and chosing to purposely inflict some damage on elements of the work environment such as other individuals, the work itself, or organizational resources. It appears that Types S and D intentions to misbehave are more heavily influenced by the person's assessment of both positive and negative eventual consequences than by the internalized subjective norm.

As discussed in the next sections, we need to incorporate into this line of research personality and affect variables to better understand the role of emotion in explaining workplace behavior (George & Brief, 1996; Fisher & Ashkanasy, 2000). Certainly strong emotions such as dissatisfaction (Hollinger & Clark, 1982),

anger, or envy and jealousy (Vecchio, 2000) should play a significant role in energizing job-related misbehavior. For instance, one can extend such models as
Weiss and Cropanzano's (1996) affective events theory to study how different
patterns of misbehavior emerge. This would show that the intentions to misbehave have both cognitive and affective antecedents. For example, although OMB
Type S may be better predicted by intentions that emanate from cognitive instrumental considerations, it stands to reason that OMB Type O is motivated by
affective states such as strong identification with the organization's goals and culture and does not necessarily reflect only the more cognitively based subjective
norms.

Cynicism

Attitudes toward work are reflected in the way individuals act on their jobs. The
OB literature, as shown in chapter 1, has been especially attracted to their role
in predicting behavior (e.g., O'Reilly, 1991). Thus, we have a relatively good
understanding of how job satisfaction (e.g., Spector, 1997a) and commitment (e.g.,
Meyer & Allen, 1997) operate in relation to job performance. Generally speaking,
they have a positive motivational relationship with work-related behavior (Wiener,
1982). We refrain from delving into those well-documented work attitudes, but
note that we also found overall satisfaction (Yosifon, 2001) and organizational
commitment to be important determinants of misbehavior. Cohen (1999), found
that they negatively correlated with self-report measures of workplace misconduct.
Thus, we selected a less researched, yet prevalent attitude—cynicism at work—to
represent a key attitudinal antecedent.

Cynicism, according to Kanter and Mirvis (1989), a form of disparagement of
others, is becoming an inherent characteristic of as much as 43% of the American
workforce. Like most other complex attitudes (e.g., its counterpart, trust), it can
be considered as having affective, cognitive, and behavior intention components.
Cynicism is both a general and specific attitude characterized by frustration and
disillusionment, as well as negative feeling toward and trust of a person, group,
ideology, social convention, or institution (Andersson, 1996). Not surprisingly,
cynicism was described in various studies as a personality trait, emotion, belief,
or attitude. Most researchers, however, have viewed cynicism as an attitude of
contempt, frustration, and distrust toward an object or objects. Some argue that
it reflects a basic philosophy about human nature, an antithesis to idealism, or
a general attitude that one cannot depend on other people to be trustworthy and
sincere. Cynicism toward work is a specific attitude—that work is oppressive,
unrewarding, and unworthy of effort. For instance, if the firm does not truly care
about its employees, it does not really merit their commitment to it.

Whitener (1999) reported two studies that investigate the interaction of employee cynicism and managerial behavior on how employees trust their superiors.

In much the same vein, Reichers, Wanous, and Austin (1997) investigated employee cynicism about formal organizational change. They argued that, although such change is indeed necessary in most organizations and a condition for their survival, many of its targets (i.e., the affected personnel) tend to remain cynical about both its importance and effectiveness. Cynicism about organizational change, they maintained, often combines pessimism about the likelihood of successful change, accompanied by casting the blame for the current and future bad fortunes on the incompetent or lazy managers responsible for the change.

Data from their study and previously published research suggest numerous factors that contribute to the development of such cynicism. These include a history of change programs that were not successful, a lack of adequate information about change, and a predisposition to cynicism. Results also suggest that cynicism about organizational changes carries negative consequences for the commitment, satisfaction, and motivation of employees. Thus, we consider cynicism behavior as an important precursor of all types of OMB.

Cynicism about organizational change is distinct from skepticism and resistance to change (Reichers et al., 1997). Skeptics doubt the likelihood of success, but they are still reasonably hopeful that positive change will occur. Resistance to change may result from self-interest, conservatism, misunderstanding, and inherent limited tolerance for change. Yet cynicism about change involves a real loss of faith in the leaders of change, and it is more often than not a response to a history of change attempts that have not entirely or clearly been successful. More important, cynicism frequently arises despite the best intentions of those initiating and managing the change process. It can actually become a self-fulfilling prophecy if cynics refuse to support change. Thus, cynicism is recognized as an important barrier to change and has the potential to spill over into other aspects of work and personal life.

To determine the causes and consequences of cynicism in the workplace, Andersson and Bateman (1997) conducted a scenario-based experiment. Their results reveal that high levels of executive compensation, poor organizational performance, and harsh immediate layoffs generate cynicism among white-collar workers. These authors believed that cynicism relates negatively to intentions to perform good citizenship behavior which is conceptualized (as noted earlier) as individual behavior that is discretionary, not directly or explicitly recognized by the formal reward system, and that, in the aggregate, promotes the effective functioning of the organization (Organ, 1988). These behaviors (a) do not explicitly lead to rewards or punishment, (b) are not part of an employee's job description, and (c) do not require training to perform. Yet Andersson and Bateman also proposed that cynicism is positively related to employee intentions to comply with requests to engage in unethical behaviors.

We propose that cynicism may indeed affect OMB Types S, D, and O. Chapter 9 analyzes some cases of major unethical executive behaviors that are strongly related to cynicism with regard to the public at large.

AFFECT AND EMOTION

Understanding the causes, characteristics, and implications of various emotions emerging in the workplace constitutes an important, yet relatively neglected aspect of OB (Muchinsky, 2000). As Lazarus (1991) pointed out, despite the assumptions expressed throughout the ages by philosophers, theologians, and writers as to the role of emotions in human experience, the study of emotions as a component of academic research is a relatively new phenomenon (cf. Fitness, 2000; Weiss & Cropanzano, 1996). Over the last two decades, affect and emotions attracted the attention of researchers interested in the social psychology of the workplace—an environment typified by complex power structures and dynamic relationships and saturated by emotions (Ashforth & Humphrey, 1995). At the same time, the rapid advent of emotional intelligence provided an additional impetus for OB researchers. The studies by Salovey and Mayer (1990) and Gardner (1983) popularized this notion, and Goleman (1995, 1998) published bestsellers by that name. Goleman and Cherniss (2001) recently expanded emotional intelligence to include work-related behavior, selection, and employee development.

We strongly believe that emotions are an integral component of daily life in organizations. The work experience is permeated by feelings ranging from moments of frustration or joy, through sadness or fear, to an enduring sense of dissatisfaction or commitment (Ashforth & Humphrey, 1995). Research has shown that affect (emotion) influences motivation, performance, satisfaction, commitment, and other organizational outcomes (George, 1989; Lewis, 2000). There is ample evidence that negative emotions have an important detrimental effect on employees, including absenteeism and dissatisfaction (George, 1989; Staw, Sutton, & Pelled, 1994). Despite the prevalence of emotions in the workplace, researchers have just begun to study and form theories on the subject. This dearth of empirical studies coupled with the important role played by emotions in affecting behavior act as powerful motivating factors promoting research on the phenomenon.

The starting point of modern research on emotions in organizations is Hochschild's (1983) book, *The Managed Heart*, which skillfully deals with what she called *emotional labor*. Hochschild studied the work of flight attendants and maintained that wearing the mask dictated by the organization—smiles, pleasantness, cordiality, and neatness—actually required a real emotional effort. She found that obeying the organization's emotional rules, as set during the socialization and training processes, can have a deep emotional impact. Some flight attendants adopt a pattern of naïve enthusiasm for their work, but they may feel and behave differently after work. Others define their emotional role as "being on their best behavior": They smile, laugh, and express concern in a persuasive manner when this is required—in other words, they expertly manage the impression they wish to make. In any case, with the passing of time and the mounting pressure, emotional labor extracts a price: It may cause burnout, and, at times, authentic emotions penetrate through the mask in the form of irritability, anger, or actual revolt.

Hochschild's (1983) work inspired OB researchers. Rafaeli and Sutton (1987, 1989) focused their attention on the expression of emotions as a component of the role played at work. Staw, Bell, and Clausen (1986) studied *dispositional affect* to predict work satisfaction. Their work soon promoted the adoption of *trait affectivity* as a useful variable in the study of organizations. Isen and Baron (1991), dealing with the influence of moods, turned the attention of researchers to more transitory aspects of emotions in the workplace.

Thus, interest in emotions in the workplace gained momentum during the last decade. Although the body of research is still not fully developed, it is promising and suggests that the study of emotions in the workplace has enriched the understanding of human behavior in organizations (Fisher & Ashkanasy, 2000). George and Brief (1996) maintained that emotions are central to our understanding of motivation in the workplace. Persistent negative emotions such as anger (Allcorn, 1994), frustration (Spector, 1978), and fear (Burke, 1999) no doubt exert a strong influence employees and organizations. Employees experiencing such emotions may act in ways that harm the organization or its workers. Therefore, it is important to better understand the role of affect in determining the intentions to act. We now describe some key emotional factors related to misbehavior and propose ways to incorporate them into the OB research agenda.

Emotions are easy to comprehend intuitively, but they are difficult to define. Van Brakel (1994) provided a list of 22 definitions of the term *emotion*. Ashforth and Humphrey (1995) simply defined emotion in broad and comprehensive terms—a subjective feeling state. This definition includes the basic emotions (e.g., joy, love, and anger) and the social emotions (e.g., guilt, shame, envy, and jealousy), as well as related concepts such as affect, sentiments, and moods. The difficulty in developing a definition apparently stems from the awareness that an emotional response is a combination of related reactions. Thus, several researchers (e.g., Lazarus, 1991) stressed that the best way to relate to emotions is to perceive them as processes, as opposed to states, because emotional responses develop with the passing of time and usually include a sequence or series of emotional reactions. Plutchik (1993) proposed a serial model of human emotions in which specific factors generate the sequence of events we call *emotions*. The stimulus tends to be certain events that upsett a person's equilibrium at a specific point in time. These events create a state of emergency. Even joyful states can be conceptualized as related to an emergency. Joy tends to be related to the receipt of rewards and the attainment of aims, increasing the individual's power and prestige. Moreover, most of the elements in the sequence are not conscious. People are usually not aware why they become emotional and do not identify the factors affecting their emotions. Each person tries to interpret other people's emotions as well as his or her own. Our feelings are indicators of our evident or unconscious judgments as to the importance of events. Our emotions provide information about our responses to situations we would otherwise not be aware of, and they reveal to us our needs, worries, and motives. Our emotions tell us about unfinished business and trigger action.

The conclusion that may be drawn from the literature is that an emotion is a response to an event (Weiss & Cropanzano 1996). It is not a personality trait, although there may be different levels of affect chronically accompanying responses to specific events. As pointed out by Frijda (1993), emotions always have an object; they are related to something. There is a reason that a person is happy, angry, or frightened. For example, if someone threatens me, my emotional response may be fear. Similarly, if someone abuses my trust, my response may be anger, which can engender a desire to retaliate. If a hungry person sees food he may be happy If a peer gets a promotion, I may become envious, perhaps leading to attempts at discrediting the person. Such a definition poses interesting questions about the existence of a relationship between the emotional response and misbehavior.

Assuming such a relationship does exist, which emotions cause an employee to misbehave? What leads a person in a certain emotional state to misbehave in an organization? We studied in some depth two particular affective reactions that, based on our reading and work experience, are powerful antecedents of OMB: jealousy and envy.

Jealousy and Envy at Work

We first distinguish between jealousy and envy. The terms *jealous* and *zealous* are both derived from the same Greek root meaning an enthusiastic devotion and care for a person or an object. Jealousy relates to a concern that what was attained or cared for is in danger of being lost. The term *envy* is derived from the Latin *invidere*, meaning to look at a person maliciously. In this sense, envy represents the desire to possess the assets or qualities of another (Bryson, 1977). We may compare it to *rivalry*, from the Latin *rivalus*: the person competing for access to the same source of water. The *Oxford Dictionary* relates to these Latin roots in defining *jealous* as troubled by the belief, suspicion, or apprehension that the goods one seeks to preserve for oneself will pass to another, and anger toward another person because of existing or suspected rivalry. *Envy* is defined as a feeling of dissatisfaction and resentment aroused by another person's possession of coveted benefits such as greater happiness, success, prestige, or possession of anything desirable. Although the concepts of jealousy and envy are distinguishable, we often find that they are used interchangeably, with *jealousy* often used to describe both situations.

On the basis of the theoretical work carried out by White and Mullen (1989), Vecchio (1995, 2000) viewed jealousy as a pattern of thoughts, feelings, and behaviors stemming from a blow to a worker's self-esteem due to a loss of outcomes related to workplace relationships. The loss or mere threat of such loss is perceived as an intrusion by a rival. The rival has the potential to lower the worker's self-esteem or undermine important social relations. Jealousy is essentially a tripartite relationship because it involves three elements: the worker, the rival, and the person esteemed (the target). An important aspect of worker's jealousy is the real or imagined threat. This threat identifies jealousy at work as a type of reaction to stress (e.g., a strong emotional reaction, including the wish to behave defensively or withdraw). Unquestionably, organizations are replete with such stress-producing, jealousy-provoking situations.

Although jealousy can be defined in general terms, jealousy among workers calls for a separate discussion because of the unique factors characterizing social relationships at work. For instance, the norms prevalent in social relations in such an environment differ from those within a family unit (as between parents and their offspring) and between two people who love each other. In the work setting, the difficulty inherent in breaking off a relationship is not so great, and the degree of acceptability of the use of physical violence is generally lower than elsewhere, whereas social pressure to deliberately ignore rivalry is greater (Gayford, 1979). Such differences in norms limit acceptable responses to the experience of jealousy. Moreover, the types of rewards implemented at work differ from those used in other social situations (Foa & Foa, 1980). For instance, the fact that a supervisor is able to grant status and recognition by publicly expressing appreciation of a subordinate and change concrete extrinsic outcomes creates rewards unlikely to be found in other environments.

Because envy and jealousy are emotions with negative social connotations and constitute sources of stress, there is a tendency to perceive them as dysfunctional. However, in a certain sense, these emotions among workers may indeed be functional in that they promote specific behaviors and act as discriminating cues, resulting in healthy competitive responses. Nevertheless, reports of a rise in violence in work situations (including the murder of workers and their supervisors) and the common ways of harassment of rivals show that work situations are not exempt from pathological responses to envy and jealousy (Sprouse, 1992). Apart from responses considered pathological (e.g., obsessive thoughts), envy and jealousy tend to create cognitive dissonance, producing adaptive coping behaviors (Festinger, 1954). From this viewpoint, envy at work can be socially effective as a goal when attention is directed to a specific situation and steps are taken to reach a specific target. It may be inferred from the prior discussion that envy can arouse a range of reactions, ranging from adaptive responses to destructive or pathological reactions.

On the basis of the model of affective events proposed by Weiss and Cropanzano (1996) and Vecchio's (1995) model of envy and jealousy in work situations, we posit that events in the course of work arouse feelings leading to various behaviors. Such events constitute antecedents to the arousal of envy or jealousy, leading to the activation of both positive and negative coping strategies. Vecchio (1997) actually found that coping with envy and jealousy encompasses a wide range of behaviors. He carried out an analysis based on multidimensional grading of the perceptions of 160 students and found that responses related to coping with envy and jealousy could be classified along two dimensions: a constructive–destructive continuum and an assessment of the extent to which others are involved.

People may respond to envy and jealousy in a destructive way and, within the context of the workplace, engage in OMB. Not surprisingly, there is a growing interest in the way negative emotions trigger violence (Delgado & Bond, 1993). In this context, envy and jealousy are especially relevant to the workplace: There is evidence that violence and aggression at work, which have recently increased considerably (Baron & Neuman, 1996), are frequently triggered by workers' feelings of envy and jealousy (National Victim Center, 1994). People motivated by envy and jealousy may cause harm to their rivals, for instance, by embarrassing them or spreading malicious rumors and gossip about them.

Employees may also be expected to respond to envy and jealousy by using hostility and anger, sabotaging their rivals' work, and bothering or ostracizing them (behavior classified as personal aggression). Such responses are motivated by the desire for revenge against the rival. They stem from people's need to preserve their perception of the organizational world as a familiar, just, and fair world (Lerner, 1980). When something occurs that threatens this perception (e.g., an event arousing envy or jealousy), it motivates people to restructure such occurrences and assists with psychological closure (Janoff-Bulman, 1992), which may arouse the desire for revenge. Moreover, people are motivated by the need to preserve their positive personal and social identity and their sense of control over their world. When events threatening their self-esteem occur (e.g., episodes arousing jealousy), they act to confirm their self-worth and preserve their sense of control. Such actions may be channeled into harmful directions. Revenge as a response to jealousy or envy may be turned directly against the rival, but it may well be directed against the organization, perceived as responsible for unfair treatment (e.g., unfair distribution of rewards), and may take the form of sabotage or theft of the organization's resources.

From our review of the literature, we conclude that in work organizations employees may be expected to respond to jealousy and envy with various intentional misbehaviors. Thus, we formulate the following proposition: Overall, there is a positive relationship between jealousy and OMB and between envy and OMB. More specifically, jealousy is more strongly related to OMB Type O, and envy is related to both OMB Type S and Type D.

OTHERS' INFLUENCE

Thus far, we suggested that OMB may emanate from personality traits, attitudes, and emotional states. Yet we should also consider the active conduct of other persons with which we interact at work as a major individual-level determinant of misbehavior. (Group-level effects are explored in the next chapter.) We already considered such effects when we discussed emotional reactions such as cynicism, envy, and jealousy. Now we explore what others actually do that triggers the intentions to misbehave. We selected two fairly unique constructs that represent powerful behavioral effects: breach of the psychological contract and social undermining. Both have the potential to generate intentions to misbehave at work.

Breach of the Psychological Contract

Making and keeping promises are the heart and soul of any mutual voluntary interrelationship. This is the basis for trust in any relationship in general and at work in particular. These simple and fundamental precepts underlie the psychological contract approach. Although its sources can be traced to early OB literature (Argyris, 1960) and research (Kotter, 1973), it was Rousseau's work (e.g., 1989, 1990; Rousseau & Parks, 1993; Rousseau & Tijoriwala, 1998) that elevated the idea to a solid, universally accepted, theoretical framework. The theory is fully described in Rousseau's (1995) seminal book, *Psychological Contracts in Organizations.*

Psychological contract are implicit, unwritten agreements between two agents who wish to be connected in some kind of social exchange (e.g., employee–employer, supervisor–subordinate, and mentor–trainee). The contract enumerates, negotiates, specifies, and communicates mutual expectations to give to and receive from each other (Kotter, 1973) or specific mutual obligations and promises (Rousseau, 1995). Although such an implicit understanding may not be legally binding, it is believed to be a strong antecedent of any social exchange within the organization.

The problem begins when one or both sides to a contract sense a violation—a reneging on promises or a breach. Unlike the concept of unmet expectations (Porter & Steers, 1973), which denotes, for example, a new employee's frustrations because real promises are not actually delivered by the organization, a psychological contract violation occurs when one party perceives that its counterpart is unable or unwilling (or both) to keep its promises (Robinson, 1996; Rousseau, 1995; Turnley & Feldman, 1999, 2000). The psychological effects of breaking promises in organizations are often exacerbated because the contract comes with a sense of entitlement. This develops because over time the psychological contract becomes more emotionally binding: I have taken your word for a promotion as promise, so now I feel I am entitled to it. Such implicit entitlements, of course, make feelings of contract violations more pronounced (Setter, 2001).

Violations of psychological contracts in organizations are not the exception, but the rule, as demonstrated by Robinson and Rousseau (1994). They are often associated with negative outcomes (Robinson, 1996). Such outcomes range from disappointment and dissatisfaction to reduced trust, withdrawal, turnover, and decreased efforts (Rousseau, 1995). These arguments should come as no surprise in the rapidly changing organizational world in which we live. In fact these changes enhance the likelihood that organization members increasingly realize their implicit agreements about work and careers are being violated (Rousseau, 1998). As these personal (basically cognitive) experiences become acute, we can expect negative emotions to follow: frustration, disappointment, anger, feeling let down, and betrayal. These emotions amount to a fairly strong affective reaction of being mistreated or even violated. Hirschman (1970) predicted that such emotions push individuals to react by both passive resignation and active protest. Robinson and Rousseau (1994) found empirical support for such reactions. In their study of 128 management alumni who were surveyed at graduation and 1 year later while employed, they found that the occurrence a psychological contract violation correlated positively with turnover and negatively with job satisfaction.

We extend these ideas and findings to predict that contract violations will also affect members' intentions to engage in OMB. The more and longer organization members perceive their implicit psychological agreements with a relevant agent of the organization (a colleague, supervisor, or human resources representative) as breached, the stronger will be the negative emotional reaction and the higher the likelihood they might engage in OMB (Type S) and/or Type D.

As shown in previous chapters, both self-benefiting and damaging misbehaviors can materialize in variety of forms, manifestations, and levels: Intra- and interpersonal, property, production, and political. For example, one can suspect that a strong sense of frustration about entitlements will lead to thoughts about getting even (retribution), which might in turn lead to the intention to inflict some real damage on those perceived as breaking a promise. We hope that future research on these prepositions will result in a better understanding of the specific effects that varying degrees of perceived contract violation may have on the intention to engage in OMB.

Social Undermining

Despite the emotions described in previous sections, interpersonal relationships at work, we contend, are mostly quite congenial. When you ask employees about their reasons for coming to work, almost invariably you hear about how friendly and helpful people are around them. Moreover, employees tend to recognize the importance of being cooperative as part of the reciprocal relationships that are so necessary for their own task performance. Yet employees are also aware of the other side of the coin: negative exchanges, interference, hindrance, cover-up, rumor mongering, and back stabbing. Organizational realities are replete with both types of interpersonal exchanges.

Recently, Duffy et al. (2002) reported an investigation of social undermining in the workplace conducted among Slovenian police officers. Participants were asked about the behavior of their supervisor and coworkers. With regard to the immediate supervisor, they were asked: How often has your supervisor intentionally hurt your feelings? Put you down when you questioned work procedures? Undermined your effort to be successful on the job? Belittled your ideas? Did not defend you when people spoke poorly of you? Concerning their peers, the subjects were asked how often the coworker closest to you intentionally insulted you? Spread rumors about you? Delayed work to make you look bad or slow you down? Talked bad about you behind your back? Gave you incorrect or misleading information about the job? After a statistical analysis of the items, the first set of questions indeed clustered as supervisor undermining and coworker undermining.

Duffy et al. (2002) defined the overall construct of *social undermining* as "behavior intended to hinder, over time, the ability to establish and maintain positive interpersonal relationships, work-related success, and favorable reputation" (p. 332). Undermining can evidently take different forms. It can be a direct act, such as saying derogatory things and rejecting or belittling somebody's well-intended offer, or it can be done passively by withholding something desired by the other party, such as concealing information, not revealing a plan, excluding the person from important engagements, and so on. By the same token, the act may be explicit, verbal, or physical, such as a vocal refusal to give assistance, or it may be done by avoiding contact and giving the silent treatment.

As expected, the study demonstrated that high levels of perceived undermining were related to measures of active (e.g., stealing) and passive (e.g., absence from work) counterproductive behavior which they derived from previous work on misbehavior (Raelin, 1994; Robinson & Bennett, 1995; Skarlicki & Folger, 1997). This claim, according to Duffy et al. (2002), would be quite consistent with some similar conceptions of antisocial behavior at work (Giacalone & Greenberg, 1997), workplace deviance (Robinson & Bennett, 1995), and workplace aggression (Neuman & Baron, 1997). Therefore, we see willful and intended undermining as conducive to OMB Types S and D because, like violation of psychological contracts, it too may trigger processes of negative affect, aversive emotions, retaliatory sentiments, and, consequently, a decision to engage in different forms of OMB.

7

Position and Group-Level Antecedents

Lead us not into temptation.

—The New Testament

The need to better understand the reasons for workers' voluntary acts of misbehavior (e.g., theft, fraud, bullying, or vandalism) has led researchers to develop integrative causal models that explain these behaviors (e.g., Goldman, 1992; Griffin et al., 1998a, 1998b; Trevino, 1986; Vardi & Wiener, 1996). As an example for such conceptual effort, Goldman (1992) presented a comprehensive process model combining situational and personal factors that influence the development of what she called *workplace deviant behavior*. The model subsumes three main stages:

1. *Stimulation:* This includes the perception of aversive organizational circumstances at work that may lead to deviant behavior, such as ambivalence in expectations, incompatibility between ends and means, large size, and formal structure of the organization.
2. *Response:* This includes the resultant inclination to misbehave as a response to such perceptions. Different variables at the individual level may affect the cognitive process that leads to this inclination: personality traits, beliefs, values, and attitudes as well as personal characteristics as gender or age.

143

3. *Outcome:* This refers to the actual behavior, its positive or negative consequences, and the reactions by the organization to them. Such outcomes, in turn, feed back on both the stimulus and response stage factors, making this a cyclical and dynamic process.

Conditions that affect members' behavior at work are found at different levels. In this chapter, we explore how the characteristics of the job and how membership in a specific work group may enhance the intention to misbehave (see Fig. 7.1).

It was mentioned earlier that job characteristics play an important role in enhancing good performance, as well as creating crucial forces that stimulate misbehavior. Thus, in the first part of this chapter, we argue that lax controls may be construed by employees as an organization's weakness or indifference, which in turn may be interpreted as a license to misbehave. To support some of our claims, we present data from field research designed to test such suppositions especially as they pertain to job-level attributes as antecedents of OMB. In the second part of the chapter, we shift our focus to the group level of analysis by looking at the way certain group dynamics, such as the strengthening of internal cohesiveness and the group pressure to conform, also influence how individual team members

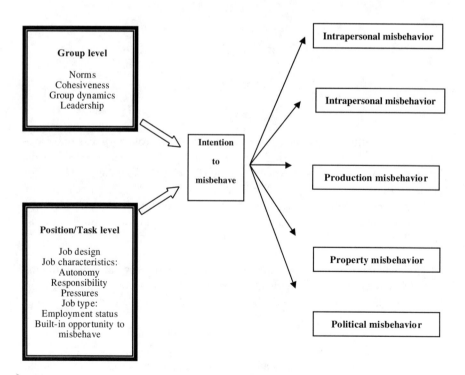

FIG. 7.1. Position-level and work group antecedents.

operate. For example, work groups, by pressure or modeling, may induce and enforce social loafing and withholding effort or damaging manifestations such as theft and aggression. Recall that in the previous chapter we discussed some of these as manifestations. Now we look at them as antecedents. We start with the job as a potential antecedent of OMB.

JOB LEVEL ANTECEDENTS

Our readers probably do not recognize the names Terry Lynn Barton and Leonard Gregg, but both received a lot of media attention during the hot summer of 2002. Ms. Barton has been a seasonal employee of the Colorado State Forest Service for 18 years. Mr. Gregg was a part-time fire fighter from Cibecue at the Fort Apache reservation in Arizona. These two individuals, federal employees paid to control forest fires, were both charged with actually ignited them, generating wildfires that went out of control causing extensive damages. On June 18, 2002, federal investigators concluded that 10 days earlier, while alone on routine patrol, Ms. Barton intentionally started a fire that eventually burned nearly 120,000 acres in central Colorado. Fueled by temperatures in the mid 90s and swirling winds, the fire went out of control, burning in its wake 25 homes and forcing thousands to flee (*New York Times,* June 19, 2002). Judging from the amount and direction of underbrush, investigators concluded that the fire was deliberately set and had been staged to look like an escaped campfire. They did not buy Ms. Barton's story of innocently burning a letter from her estranged husband at the campsite. If convicted, Ms. Barton faces up to 20 years in prison and fines in excess of $500,000 for damaging federal and private property as well as misleading investigators.

Mr. Gregg was arraigned on June 30, 2002, in a federal court in Flagstaff, Arizona. He was charged with setting a blaze that burned vast lands of natural vegetation and over 400 homes. If found guilty, Mr. Gregg faces 10 years in prison and $ 500,000 in fines. His prosecutors argued that he purposely started the fire to make money fighting it (*New York Times,* July 1, 2002).

Both cases of misconduct on the job are certainly extreme and very serious because of the disastrous outcomes. However, it is important to account for job factors that contribute to this kind of behavior. We now focus on the role that job autonomy may play in presenting employees with opportunities to carry out damaging acts such as the ones just described. In these two cases, performing their jobs in isolated areas and having the know how and means to set the fires, are important contributing factors to the employees' decision to engage in such acts.

The Job Autonomy Study

One of the factors conducive to misbehavior is the actual opportunity to engage in it (i.e., the degree of freedom or latitude allowed for individual members to intentionally act in ways that violate core organizational norms that specify what is considered proper work conduct). The level of prescribed job autonomy, although designed to create a structure of opportunity that facilitates desirable and normative behaviors, may also contribute to people's engagement in misbehavior. Paradoxically, this may be an unanticipated consequence of management's good intentions. Most research on the effects of job autonomy on the employee has focused on examining its link to positive work outcomes such as performance and satisfaction (e.g., Breaugh, 1985). We identified few studies that dealt with negative outcomes. Thus, we decided to explore this for ourselves.

By expanding on a study we conducted from 1998 to 1999 on the possible negative effects of job autonomy on work-related behavior among Israeli employees (Vardi & Weitz, 2001). We wished to determine whether employee-perceived autonomy should be regarded not only as a positive aspect of their positions but also, under certain conditions, as an opportunity to defy norms of proper conduct. We asked 250 managers and nonmanagers from different organizations, occupations, and ranks to fill out questionnaires concerning their own as well as their colleagues' actions on the job, which are considered to be OMB. Results show that autonomy and its components were positively related to both self and others' reported incidents of OMB. In addition, we tested hypotheses concerning the role of autonomy in explaining OMB relative to selected individual and organizational variables. We found that certain personality (Type A), attitudinal (job satisfaction and professional identification), and organization (position) variables were directly and indirectly related to OMB. Based on these findings, a model incorporating autonomy as an antecedent of OMB is presented.

The literature on job autonomy as an organizational variable can be divided into two domains: control theories and job design theories. Control theories treat organizational control as a variable that influences worker's attitudes and behavior. Because researchers view autonomy as a type of control, they attempt to understand its effect on employee behavior by examining the effects of types of control (Ganster, 1989; Karasek & Theorell, 1990; Spector, 1986; Thompson, 1981). The job design theories include approaches that regard autonomy as part of work enrichment and assume that job autonomy will positively influence the individual's attitudes and behavior (Abdel Halim, 1978; C. Lee, Ashford, & Bobko, 1990; Pines, 1981). The Job Characteristics Model (Hackman & Oldham, 1976) is by far the best known model dealing with job design.

One of the core job dimensions that contributes to motivation and satisfaction in a specific job is *autonomy*. This dimension is viewed as the way in which the position provides individuals with meaningful discretion, independence, and personal initiative in organizing their work and controlling performance. According to the model, autonomy is assumed to engender a certain critical psychological state (experienced responsibility for results of the work), which, in turn, may contribute to the coveted work outcomes: high internal work motivation, high-quality work performance, high satisfaction with the work, and low absenteeism and turnover.

The model also subsumes a moderator effect of the strength of employees' growth needs. For instance, one could expect that increasing autonomy for low-growth needs employees will actually result in adverse outcomes because of the expectation that autonomous employees would make more work-related decisions and take more initiative. These expectations should actually make the work more stressful for such individuals, resulting in lowered satisfaction and motivation, possibly enhancing misconduct as an unanticipated consequence.

Combining the job design and control theories, Breaugh (1985) defined *job autonomy* as workers' level of freedom to decide on work methods, schedules, and the criteria for evaluating their work. To assess these characteristics, he developed a research instrument that measures the degree of judgment the individual has with regard to various dimensions of his or her work as follows: (a) autonomy in work method—the degree to which individuals are free to conduct and choose processes and methods for performing the work, (b) autonomy in scheduling—the degree to which workers feel that they have control over their schedule, and (c) autonomy in performance criteria—the degree to which workers are able to set or choose the standards for evaluating their own performance. We adopted his definition for our study.

Autonomy. To date few studies have suggested job autonomy as a possible cause of OMB (Vardi & Weitz, 2001). Those researchers who did so (e.g., Allen & Greenberger, 1980; Wortman & Breham, 1975) believed that a low level of job autonomy is likely to increase the tendency for misconduct. For example, Analoui and Kakabadse (1992) noted that one of the motives for the unconventional practices they observed both managers and subordinates commit was actually the aspiration for more autonomy. In another study, Molstad (1988) found that, when faced with routine work and extensive supervision, workers developed various action strategies to give themselves a sense of control and autonomy. For example, they created an impression among the managers that they were working hard and were not free to take on more work, or they developed a private language that the managers could not understand. This autonomous behavior gave the workers a sense of control despite the attempted management supervision.

Yet one might argue that a great deal of job freedom is precisely what might lead to misbehavior. Extensive job autonomy leaves room for action and performance that actually creates opportunities for deviance. For example, Mars (1982) found that differences in the level of supervision over employees' attendance at work were related to the opportunity structure for deviance. According to Vardi and Wiener (1996), organizations with a sensible work control system are more effective in controlling their employees' behavior than organizations with either very restrictive or very flexible systems. The latter, they proposed, are liable to increase the motivation for exhibiting OMB Types S and D. Thus, we suggest that, at least conceptually, both high and low autonomy might, albeit inadvertently, enhance improper conduct on the job.

A recent review of literature on job autonomy (Biran, 1999) indicated that the possibility that the extensive freedom and variety of opportunities for action that stem from job autonomy will lead to negative or deviant behavior in the workplace had yet to be examined empirically. Therefore, we assumed that these job characteristics, along with their known positive effects, are also apt to encourage manifestations of OMB. Autonomy, by definition, gives the worker a great deal of latitude in performing tasks, scheduling, and evaluation of output. When employees perceive their positions as autonomous, such perception may facilitate misbehaviors such as working slowly, stealing time, engaging in private activities during working hours, and abusing other organizational resources. Based on this basic argument, we hypothesized that job autonomy and OMB are positively correlated: The higher the job autonomy, the stronger the tendency for OMB (Hypothesis 1).

Hierarchical Level. There is no doubt that employees at various hierarchical levels differ in terms of work needs, sources of motivation, expectations and aspirations, and the degree to which they desire job autonomy. More specifically, differences were found in the ways employees at different job levels cope with autonomy and job pressures (Greenberg & Strasser, 1986; Savery, 1988; Westman, 1992). Salancik (1977) argued that employees at more senior levels develop a higher sense of responsibility than lower ranking individuals. Steers and Spencer (1977) and Schein (1978) suggested that a higher ranking manager is more involved in decision making and identifies more with the organization and its core values. Thus, although managers are more exposed to temptations by virtue of their formal position, greater independence, contacts with external agents, broader knowledge of the organization, and easier access to resources, the inherent responsibility, moral development, authority, and observance of rules and procedures should mitigate tendencies for misbehavior. Additionally, managers are expected to adhere to the normative system to which they subscribe and serve as role models for others, especially their own subordinates. Therefore, we hypothesize that the tendency for OMB is lower for those in a managerial role than in a nonmanagerial role (Hypothesis 2).

Type of Job. Following Schein's (1978) model of organizational careers, Gaertner (1980) characterized the types of jobs in an organization by the extent to which they permit examination of the employees' skills and attitudes. She defined an *assessment position* as one that requires great administrative and managerial responsibility and exposes the individual to various career management bodies in the system. Thus, the performance of these role holders is put under greater scrutiny. For example, Holtsman-Chen (1984) examined career progression in a governmental security agency. She found that service in field positions increased workers' chances of advancing in the system because agents' behavior was closely monitored. In contrast, Vardi and Wiener (1996) noted that in many peripheral jobs, it is difficult to supervise and control the worker's behavior. For instance, messenger services or services at the client's home are jobs with built-in opportunities for misbehaviors such as cheating, loafing, and stealing (e.g., Rubin-Kedar, 2000). In other words, such types of jobs are liable to increase the tendency for misbehavior (particularly OMB Type S). Therefore, we hypothesized that in field positions there is a greater tendency for OMB than in staff or for employees located in company headquarters (Hypothesis 3).

To test these hypotheses, data were collected in a private personnel placement center in the greater Tel Aviv area. The sample comprised 250 employees from various organizations and diverse jobs. It included 134 men and 116 women ranging in age from 23 to 35. Their last jobs were in sales (13%), computers (10.8%), engineering (16%), economics (8.4%), or occupations such as clerks, manpower, and advertising (about 52%). Thirty-six percent worked in field positions, 64% in staff positions, and 50% had administrative roles. Most of them had spent up to 5 years at their last job.

The research instrument was a self-report paper-and-pencil questionnaire especially designed and compiled for this study.

OMB. We used items characterizing production deviance for this scale that were adopted from Robinson and Bennett (1995). In addition, we included two types of lead questions—one pertaining to behavior by others and one to behavior of the subject. In this part of the study, the items were presented as indirect questions relating to other people in the organization. For example, "To what extent do workers at your workplace lie about their work hours or make deliberate mistakes?" In a separate section, we presented the same items as direct questions relating to the employee and his or her behavior at work.

Job Autonomy. Job autonomy level was examined by the subject's self-report about his or her last job. Items were adopted from a questionnaire by Breaugh (1985). The first three items relate to the work methods (e.g., "I could decide how to do my work"), the next three items examine the degree of autonomy in setting work schedules (e.g., "My work allows me to decide when to do each action"), and the last three items refer to autonomy in evaluating the outcomes (e.g., "I could choose what goals and tasks to accomplish and complete").

Job Type. Job type was examined by this question: "Did you perform your job in the office (staff position) or outside the office (field position)?"

Job Level. Each subject was asked two questions pertaining to whether they had been in charge of other people. Those who answered positively were coded as *managers,* whereas others were coded as *nonmanagers.*

To test the main hypothesis, we correlated OMB with job autonomy and found a positive correlation both in reporting on others ($r = .26$, $p < .001$) and on the self ($r = .14$, $p < .05$). Thus, we surmise that job autonomy is the antecedent of OMB

TABLE 7.1
Relationships Between OMB and Job Autonomy

Variable	OMB Self	OMB Others
General autonomy	***0.26	*0.14
Autonomy in work methods	** 0.16	*0.14
Autonomy in scheduling	***0.27	0.09
Autonomy in setting performance standards	***0.24	*0.15

$*p < .05.$ $**p < .01.$ $***p < .001.$

because it is a structural feature of the job. In addition, a positive correlation was found between each individual dimension of autonomy (in the "general autonomy" variable) and OMB reported of the self and others, with the exception of the relation between autonomy in scheduling and OMB reported of others, which was not found to be significant (see Table 7.1). We also found a positive correlation between hierarchical level and reporting OMB of others. This may mean that managers, who are responsible for other employees, report on others' misconduct more than nonsupervisory employees. However, no correlation between job type and OMB was found.

Finally, to test the assumption that job autonomy is a predictor of OMB, we regressed the misbehavior measures on job autonomy while controlling for some attitudinal measures we collected. As expected, job autonomy, employee satisfaction, and employee professional identity explained about 16% of the variance of the self-report OMB variable. Does all this make sense? Some possible explanations for the positive correlations found between job autonomy and OMB are discussed next.

Opportunity to Misbehave.   This concept relates to the characteristics of the job or the organization that pave the way for deviance. The positive correlation between job autonomy and OMB described earlier supports the hypothesis that the structure of opportunity, availability of varied avenues for action, and extensive freedom on the job may increase the tendency for OMB (Goldman, 1992; Vardi & Wiener, 1996). Moreover, if autonomy is perceived by subordinates as the absence of close supervision or, alternatively, as managerial weakness, it may actually increase the tendency to commit OMB.

Sense of Inequity.   A job characterized by a great deal of autonomy inevitably entails more tasks and personal responsibility. Individuals who think they are not adequately rewarded for their great investment in the job may feel a sense of inequity that may lead to an increased tendency for OMB. They may attempt to compensate themselves in less conventional ways, such as decreased output, slow work, resting, and doing private work on the job. The freedom of action they possess may enable them to adopt these behaviors. Research on inequity and distributive injustice support this claim (e.g., Greenberg, 1990a, 1993). In addition, Ackroyd and Thompson (1999) suggested that most OMB is driven by employees' sense of organizational and managerial maltreatment. When despair and opportunity coexist, misbehavior may be enhanced.

Need for Autonomy.   Most researchers who have dealt with the negative effects of job autonomy have attributed their results to differences in the need for autonomy (Harrell & Alpert, 1979; Langer, 1983). For people with a low need for autonomy, a job characterized by a great deal of autonomy will create a sense of tension, overload, and at times decline in their work satisfaction. Moreover, autonomy may decrease their sense of control and arouse a feeling of confusion. In other words, autonomy is a positive job characteristic if and when the individual is interested in and capable of handling it. Hackman and Oldham (1976) considered personal growth needs as having a moderating influence on the worker whose job is enriched. Yet they did not raise the possibility that an individual with low growth needs may react to autonomy—not only by a decline in motivation or satisfaction, but also by venting their frustration and misbehaving. For example, Spector (1997b) showed how such job context frustrations can lead to antisocial work behavior.

Managerial Responsibility.   A significant positive correlation was found between managerial role and OMB (reported of others). In other words, managers report more OMB (of subordinates, colleagues, and other managers) than do workers in nonmanagerial roles. The hypothesis regarding the negative correlation between managerial role and OMB was not supported. By virtue of their role, managers are responsible for enforcing the rules, regulations, and procedures; are more involved in decision making; are required to prevent employee OMB; and identify more with the organization and its values (see e.g., Salancik, 1977; Savery, 1988; Steers & Spencer, 1977). Thus, they are less likely to misbehave.

The Fast-Food Study

The management of the Burger Farm (fictional name) fast-food chain in Israel announced that, according to the standards established in the code of behavior of the worldwide corporation, no workers with long hair would be hired. As one of their executives commented: "The chain forbids workers with pony-tails to serve as messengers... for reasons of hygiene, cleanliness and aesthetic appearance.... We accept employees with long hair if their hair is gathered under a cap, but this rule is not valid for messengers, for when they go on deliveries, we have no control over them, and they may take off their caps and let their hair down" (Rubin-Kedar, 2000 p.16).

Home deliveries are attractive to customers. Due to the competition among businesses, many organizations adopt the policy of including home deliveries among their services. Among these are food chains, home appliance businesses, cellular phone companies, personal computer stores, and so on. Although the number of jobs involved is growing, there are few studies of the behavior of employees working outside the organizations' physical space. Therefore, we wished to examine the relationship between various types of jobs, including those of messengers, and OMB. This study is unique because we used an ethnographic approach following Kunda (1992) and Analoui and Kakabadse (1992), in which qualitative data were collected through participant observation and onsite interviews (interview citations that follow are adapted from Rubin-Kedar, 2000).

The study was designed to examine on-the-job misbehavior characterizing fast-food employees. It distinguishes between levels of OMB of various groups of employees within this organization and investigates how the organizational values of these groups affect their relationship to OMB. The Burger Farm in Israel has over 70 branches, 40 of which provide home deliveries. Branches providing home deliveries employ, in addition to the messengers, a person responsible for this service and telephone operators receiving the orders. Although the performance of branch employees is closely monitored by the manager and deputy, the behavior of the messengers working outside the branch is of great concern for the chain's management, who are apparently aware of the difficulty in directly supervising these employees' behavior.

The sample included seven branches that provide home deliveries. Branches employ 15 to 70 workers (the number of employees depends on the size and location of the branch) fulfilling the following functions: cashiers, kitchen staff, telephone operators, messengers, employee in charge of the kitchen, employees responsible for the shifts and home deliveries, a deputy manager, and a manager of the branch. The various jobs are classified in three categories: (a) branch workers, (b) messengers, and (c) management functions. The average age of the branch workers is 15 to 18; the messengers are mostly older, between the ages of 18 and 24; the age of the management staff varies from branch to branch, but most of them are over 25.

The participating branches had approximately 40 branch workers (i.e., employees working within the branch precincts, among them cashiers, telephone operators, and kitchen staff). In addition, they employed some 20 uniformed messengers on scooters. The cashiers' job included dealing with the customers, receiving orders and payment by the customers, and handing them food. The kitchen staff was responsible for preparing the food and bringing it to the cashiers. The telephone operators received orders from customers wishing to have food brought to their homes or workplaces and passed the orders to the kitchen staff. Although sometimes there was rotation among the workers in the various jobs, most of the cashiers and telephone operators were women, whereas the kitchen staff mainly consisted of men. When we inquired about this division, one of the (male) managers asserted that "the female employees' behavior to the customers is more pleasant and courteous; they are also more mature and serious than the men's."

Messengers, all young men mostly employed right after their military service with a motor scooter driving license, hold a coveted position at Burger Farm. They are responsible for checking the order before leaving for the designated address to ensure that the food prepared in the kitchen matched the order received by telephone. Then they rush through the city traffic, deliver the order, and receive the cash payment. Therefore, it is surprising that messengers' conduct outside the branch is of great concern to management while they appear to be aware of the supervisory difficulties. For example, the manager responsible for home delivery throughout the country explained: "We operate covert customer services in order to check the behavior of the messengers when they are outside the branch. Sometimes we also receive information from customers who complain about unsatisfactory service by a messenger, or people report reckless driving. But apart from these measures, it is difficult to find out how they really behave; the fact that they work outside the branch reduces the possibility of supervision."

Employees of higher rank than the branch workers and messengers fulfill various management functions (responsibility for the kitchen, shifts, delivery, deputy managers, and branch managers). Shift supervisors (about three in each branch) are concerned with the ongoing work of the shift and are responsible for discipline, training new staff, and dealing with customers' complaints. They also serve as linking pins between rank and file and management. For every shift, there is also someone responsible for the kitchen; he or she is mainly concerned with ordering and maintaining the stock and food preparation. In some of the larger and busier branches, home delivery became a separate administrative unit with a person in charge who also holds the rank of branch manager. These are the top positions which are usually filled by trained and more senior employees. Their main areas of responsibility are keeping contacts with the headquarters, recruiting new workers, dealing with wages and bonuses, running the training programs, presiding over staff meetings, promoting sales through special events, and providing for the welfare of the employees. One of their biggest worries, we found, was discipline and proper service behavior.

We hypothesized the existence of a relationship between the job type and OMB. For example, we suspected that the tendency toward engaging in OMB would be higher among messengers than branch employees. Our findings generally support this hypothesis particularly when it comes to self-reported OMB. This is consistent with theoretical propositions made by a number of researchers regarding the relationship between the job type and OMB (Hollinger, 1986; Van Maanen & Barley, 1984, 1985). These researchers related the built-in opportunities provided by the job as a factor likely to explain OMB. According to Vardi and Wiener (1992, 1996), the concept of *built-in opportunity* refers particularly to activities that are difficult for the organization to control, such as home deliveries, cashier work, and food service, which make misconduct relatively easy.

Delivery messengers working for a food chain apparently have many more built-in opportunities for OMB than branch workers because they spend most of their time outside the branch and are not closely supervised. Therefore, they may think that they "can do whatever they feel like." One participant remarked that sometimes there are no deliveries during his shift ("down time") so, "why not go and see friends, instead of vegetating at the branch. No one can find out, and if they do ask questions, there are plenty of excuses for the boss:' 'There were traffic jams,' 'I couldn't find the house,' 'they didn't give me the correct address,' and a lot of things like that. Sometimes we fix up beforehand to meet with friends, when there is no work—that's what everybody does."

Taking a break between deliveries is just one example of the variety of misbehaviors the messengers mentioned. "It's much better to be a messenger," one of them said. "They don't push you around all the time. For instance, it's different for the cashiers—they [supervisors] stand beside them every minute insisting about cleanliness, 'put your cap on,' and so on. I am away most of the time. Who'll tell me off if I don't put my cap on? We don't bother about such nonsense."

At the same time, branch workers said that there were few opportunities for OMB: "Apart from having more sodas than we are supposed to, what else can we do? There are plenty of finks to run and tell the manager. Sometimes it looks as if they were training us for the military. They are so intent on discipline."

Interviews with branch managers, the training director, and the home delivery manager revealed that they were aware of these differences and that the messengers' behavior preoccupies many of them. That is why the branch managers hold periodic meetings ("home deliveries' forums") to think of ways to cope with this issue. One of the attempts designed to motivate messengers to fit in more home deliveries— prevent long breaks between them and "taking a turn on the motorbike to see friends"—led to a change in the payment method. As an alternative to payment by the hour, it was decided (in some of the branches) to pay by delivery. However, because volume of orders varies by branch, messengers in many cases preferred payment by the hour, and the motivating element of the new method of payment disappeared.

Job Level.   Previous research indicates that higher ranking employees are less likely to engage in OMB. This finding originated in studies pointing out that most higher ranking employees are committed to the organization and its aims, so it is reasonable to suppose that they will adopt and promote behavior perceived as beneficial to the organization. The explanation for their positive behavior lies in their function as supervisors, being in charge of the work of their subordinates, and their ensuing responsibility makes different demands on them than their subordinates, leading to differences in behavior patterns related to ranks in the hierarchy (Westman, 1992). The higher the job level of employees, the wider the scope of their decision making, resulting in an increase in feelings of responsibility and authority (Raelin, 1987).

However, we found no significant relationship between organizational level and most types of OMB except for minor misbehavior against property—supervisors reported a greater tendency by others to engage in OMB compared with reports by subordinates. If we assume that OMB as reported by others is congruent with that in self-reports, the relationship found may be explained by the built-in opportunities typical of managerial jobs. However, if this assumption is erroneous (i.e., if self-reporting about OMB and reporting about others describe two separate behaviors), other explanations may be offered, such as managerial responsibility to present trustworthy reports about their workers' behavior. The following are possible explanations.

Managers tend to engage in OMB more than their subordinates because, in their jobs, they are exposed to more built-in opportunities for deviance: Their own work is less supervised, they have more contact with elements outside the organization, and they have more information about the organization (Goldman, 1992). Recall that in the autonomy study we found some positive relationship between rank in the organization and OMB; managers reported more OMB than subordinates.

Another possible explanation is related to the local (e.g., organizational) definition of OMB. Several studies point out the differences of opinion between managers and subordinates as to what is perceived as OMB (Greenberg & Barling, 1996; Greenberg & Scott, 1996; Mars, 1974). Managers may take the liberty of behaving in a certain way, although it is formally forbidden, because they perceive the behavior as one of their rights as managers and not as OMB. This explanation was evident at the data-collection stage in the branches. In most of the branches (five of seven), the managers and people in charge of the shift did not hesitate to offer me a drink (without paying for it), although formally employees are not allowed to do so when acquaintances or relatives come to visit them. Moreover, a number of managers and those responsible for shifts had difficulty answering the questionnaire and frequently mentioned that some of the questions were irrelevant to them. For instance, one of the supervisors asked: "What do you mean by 'eating more than the permitted helping'? Who is going to tell me how much I am allowed to eat?" Another example is related to the item 'evades less pleasant work, such as cleaning.' A number of supervisors expressed surprise about this item and, while answering the questionnaire, replied: "Evading? Who's to tell me what to do?"

Higher level employees apparently perceive their job as allowing them to enjoy more privileges compared with their subordinates, and in their case they view OMB differently from that of the workers. While talking to the managers and workers, it became clear that if the supervisor is late for the shift, according to the organization's regulations it is not perceived as OMB, but they all agreed that it is undesirable. However, when a worker is habitually late, it is reason for dismissal. These examples illustrate that there are differences between managers and subordinates, and sometimes behavior by subordinates perceived as OMB is accepted as legitimate in the case of managers.

Job Subcultures

In this study too, the explanation of the differences between messengers' behavior and that of branch workers may lie in the fact that distinct subcultures have been established and that the subculture and general company value systems clash. According to Reimann and Wiener (1988) and Trice (1993), any complex organization consists of subunits of members who, in the course of time, develop cultural characteristics of their own that are different from the value systems of members of other units. Such value systems are in effect different subcultures. The main difference between organizational culture and organizational or occupational subculture is the emphasis on the organizational unit (department or section) or a shared group profile such as a particular job. In many cases, the influence of the group's culture on its members may be a stronger determinant of behavior than the organization's culture as a whole.

Discussions with messengers and branch workers revealed that each group of employees is apparently motivated by different organizational values and that their perceptions about their workplace differ. The messengers declared that they were motivated in their work by pay and benefits alone. In addition, most of the messengers were somewhat older than the branch workers, having completed their military service, and they considered the job a temporary one. Their commitment is strictly instrumental. When asked why he had chosen to work for Burger Farm, one messenger replied: "I am not like most of the workers at the branch, I am not interested in the parties they organize and in pleasing the boss. As soon as I've saved up enough money, I'll pack my bags and get on a plane." Another messenger observed: "We are different from the branch workers, we are not high school kids who are thinking of possible advancement here. . . . We are here temporarily, for a very definite purpose."

Further discussions with the various branch managers revealed that recruiting messengers and reducing their frequent turnover are quite difficult. The chain manager responsible for home deliveries explained: "Recruiting messengers is not a simple task, not to mention making sure they don't leave. Today almost every retail business offers home deliveries, not only food chains. There are plenty of these jobs around. So the delivery boys feel more secure. Branch managers are more dependent on them than on branch workes, and these guys often exploit that." Organizational values thus serve as principles guiding the collective behavior of the employees, and they comprise categories defining positive and negative behavior.

Branch employees often spoke about their workplace with pride and mentioned that they were considering staying there even after finishing school. One of the female employees emphasized the pleasant social relationships created at the branch, and she pointed out that one of the main factors motivating her to work is the feeling that the branch is like a family: "It's fun at work, especially because of the company. Many of the employees knew each other before coming here, because most of them were recruited through the 'bring a friend' program. There are even siblings among us, in short—a small family. Sometimes I feel that I am going out to meet my friends, rather than going to work. But you mustn't think that we aren't doing a serious job. Enjoying working with friends doesn't mean that you don't care about the place—on the contrary, it becomes even more important. . . . " Such obvious affect-based commitments may mitigate inclinations to engage in harmful behaviors.

Last, lack of identification with organizational values, especially those that advocate quality service and integrity, may lead to OMB. This could be exacerbated when values and practice are inconsistent as well. One of the more veteran messengers described such incongruency: "If there is something I can do that will affect my wages, like getting to the customer quickly for a bonus—which sometimes involves speeding or riding on the sidewalk—why not? You don't get fired for that. They only fire you for really serious things. They need us here. There's no problem in getting workers for the branch. They all want to bring their friends to work here. They also behave more like good kids, they do what they are told."

The findings are summarized as follows:

- Among messengers there was a greater tendency to engage in OMB compared with branch workers.
- Among branch employees there was a greater tendency to adopt positive organizational values compared with messengers.
- Managers were more likely to adopt positive organizational values than subordinates.
- An increase in the adherence to organizational values led to a decrease in OMB.
- Managers reported a greater tendency to engage in OMB against property compared with subordinates (when reporting about others).
- No moderating influence by organizational values was found on the relationship between organizational rank and OMB.

From this particular investigation, we may begin to draw some implications at least in terms of increased managerial awareness to job-level antecedents of OMB. To enable organizations to influence managers' and employees' intentions to engage in OMB, organizations must be aware of the following factors:

1. The differences between groups of workers and their differing perceptions of what is considered OMB.
2. The importance of organizational values in affecting the employees' behavior positively or negatively.
3. The possibility that conflict between core and subculture values may encourage adoption of certain patterns of OMB.
4. The need to maintain consistency between codes of behavior and managerial practice.

GROUP-LEVEL INFLUENCES

The Importance of Teams

Following the spirit of the previous analysis, this section (a) focuses on workers' tendency to avoid making a personal effort within a group framework, (b) identifies the various factors contributing to this phenomenon, and (c) raises some probable implications for management. Traditionally, the efficiency of most of the work process in organizations depends on the workers' willful collaboration (Porter et al., 1975). In an increasing number of organizations, planning and decision-making processes, as well as the actual work, are carried out by teams of workers. Obviously this work style has many advantages, both from workers' point of view and their job satisfaction, and can increase efficiency. For instance, in the past, managers were thought capable of efficiently supervising some 20 workers only. Today it is clear that they can oversee a large number as long as they delegate authority and make use of teamwork. Moreover, this style of management, enabling many groups to become self-managing, grants the team members greater autonomy and also opportunities to demonstrate their managerial and other skills. In addition, modern communication technology makes it possible to distribute the tasks among individual workers and teams as never before. Therefore, it is not surprising that most research studies dealing of teamwork emphasize these advantages. Managers of human resources and organizational consultants also stress the importance of teamwork in promoting solidarity among the workers, enhancing workers' productivity, and increasing their job satisfaction. (see West's, 2001, recent review on team dynamics).

Despite these important organizational benefits, organizations must be awarene of the difficulties arising within teams, which may constitute factors that are liable to be detrimental to the work processes. By definition, a *team* is characterized by ongoing interaction among its members to facilitate the attainment of a shared goal or execution of a collaborative project (Tziner & Vardi, 1982). Thus, the emphasis passes from individual work to interdependence, which calls for mutuality and full cooperation among the members, tolerance, and the overcoming of personal and professional differences of opinion. These questions arise: Are all team members willing and able to invest as much effort in the collective task as they would in an individual one? Will they feel committed to its success although they are not always rewarded accordingly? Are there not workers who exploit their participation in a team? The answers to these questions are not clear because, unlike in a primary group (e.g., a family) wherein the relations constitute its aim, the survival and successes of a team are greatly dependent on the individuals' belief that their participation in the group will be personally beneficial to them—more so than if they worked on their own. When this belief is lacking, the willingness of team members to contribute their relative share (and more than their share) to the success of the collective task diminishes.

The STEAL Motive (to Steal)

Greenberg (1997) offered an interesting insight into the role of groups in enhancing theft. This insight can be expanded to other forms of OMB as well, especially those classified as Type S. Through extensive research and grounding his theory in social psychology and group dynamics, Greenberg found that "employee theft is a behavior that is carefully regulated by organizational norms and work group norms and that stealing is an effective way of supporting these norms" (p. 89). This may sound quite surprising at first. However, this contention becomes quite clear when he explained the STEAL motive. STEAL stands for *Support, Thwart, Even the score,* and *ApprovaL,* which are four types of motives behind the act of theft. The two dimensions that produce them are (a) intention—whether the act is motivated by prosocial or antisocial considerations, and (b) target—whether the act targets the organization or coworkers.

Support is a prosocial behavior because the employee steals to adhere to his or her group, which condones the act. Thwart applies to the situation when the motive to steal assets from the employer is in defiance of the group. Stealing actual thwarts the group's attempts to control the employee's behavior. Stealing to even the score (as revenge or retaliation) occurs when an employee violates the emplyer's norms. In contrast, approval occurs when an employee steals to find favor by a supervisor known to condone such acts. Thus, from any vantage point, the group plays an extremely important role in either enhancing or limiting employee theft behavior (see detailed explanations in Greenberg, 1997).

Withholding Effort in Teams

As suggested in chapter 4, researchers have recently become more interested in team effects and have begun to wonder whether individuals working as a team experience full cooperation among its members for the attainment of collective aims. The social loafing literature suggests that members are actually preoccupied comparing their own efforts to those made by other participants. They often wonder whether it is worth making an effort because, as far as they can judge, the others are actually loafing. Kidwell and Bennett (1993) articulated a new construct that focuses on the propensity to withhold effort, denoting the probability that the individual will invest less than maximum effort in a group task connected to work. We follow their thinking and suggest a number of conditions that may facilitate the propensity to engage in loafing in work teams.

The Reward System. One of the effects of the economic approach to the issue of withholding individual effort within an organizational or team framework is the emphasis on a rewards system, which is considered likely to counteract this tendency. The most common point regarding the efficiency of this claim is that such benefits and the fear of losing them create motivation to refrain from counterproductive behavior and shirking (Chappell & Chauvin, 1991). This approach perceives the workers as rational thinkers who are preoccupied by their own interests, checking the costs against withholding effort. According to this approach, especially when there is widespread unemployment, workers are afraid they could be made redundant as a result of withholding effort, and therefore they desist from unproductive behavior. However, when the perceived cost of dismissal is low, such as in a full employment economy, team members are presumed to be more inclined to withhold effort. Thus, the tendency to withhold effort is more marked when the expected costs for the employee are perceived to be very low.

Group Size.   Interest in the productivity of the individual compared with the productivity of the whole group first appeared in the 19th-century research studies by Ringelmann, who found that when people work together as a group, their collective performance is lower than the expected sum total of their individual performances (cited in Kravitz & Martin, 1986). It was also found that the larger the group size, the corresponding individual contribution is less felt and the individual worker makes less effort. The larger the group, the greater the anonymity of the workers, and the possibility to supervise individual performance decreases. This, in turn, diminishes the transparency of individual effort. Such a situation appears to lead rational individuals to reduce their efforts because these are not sufficiently appreciated by the supervisors. In contrast, smaller groups may succeed in generating greater individual effort because they permit supervision of the individual's behavior, thereby promoting effort and collaboration. Moreover, in a small team, each member's contribution is more critical for the completion of the collective task than in a large group. Taken together the characteristics of the small team encourage the members to invest additional effort.

Turnover Rate.   Collaboration among team members may be influenced by long-term preservation of an accepted effort level. It is easier for team members to refuse to collaborate and withhold effort if their participation is temporary or if they are not well acquainted with other team members. Therefore, level of collaboration also depends on the replacement rate of the team member. When that rate is low, there is a good chance that the relations among the team members will be more personal and will involve deeper emotional ties (Granovetter, 1985), which may affect their willingness to invest effort. However, when the replacement rate is high, the workers' ties to the group are weak and temporary, and their motivation to collaborate and invest a great deal of effort is lower. Emotional ties, developing through sustained interaction and going beyond rational cost-effectiveness analysis, are therefore likely to affect individual effort. Therefore, we presume that, as the replacement rate rises, the team members will be less likely to invest individual effort in the collective task. However, the stability of the group may contribute to an increase in the investment of personal effort simply to avoid criticism by other members.

Length of Service.   A demographic variable that may play an important role in strengthening the emotional ties developing among the team members is the similarity of the team members' tenure or *homogeneous length of service,* which is defined as a group comprising people participating in the work of the team a similar length of time. Under certain conditions, individuals are likely to identify with their group, which promotes their collaboration and commitment to the group's obligations. The importance of this type of homogeneity lies in the socialization process the team members undergo; it may foster the development of stronger emotional ties among the members and create a close relationship. For example, when all the participants begin working together as a team at approximately the same time, have similar experiences, and arrive at shared perceptions of norms of satisfactory behavior, they are more likely to identify with the group and be committed to the attainment of its goals. Such solidarity may constitute an important factor affecting the decision of the team members to invest maximum effort, thus fulfilling their obligation to the other team members. Therefore, the longer time the team members spend together, the more likely they are to invest individual effort because of their feeling of mutual obligation and their commitment to the collective task. Conversely, heterogeneity in the length of service decreases the possibility of the group identity. Therefore, group members who have spent less time together or joined at different times are less likely to develop a sense of mutual obligation and more likely to withhold personal effort.

Contribution to Task.   What is the point of investing great effort if it is not duly acknowledged and appreciated? Apparently a necessary precondition for shirking is the lack of awareness and recognition of the workers' individual contributions by those in charge. The perception of transparency of performance is the workers' belief that their manager is aware of their personal efforts. Indeed the assumption underlying research on social loafing is that the larger the group size, the less motivated individuals are to invest effort, among other things, because they believe they can hide in the crowd or because they know that the person responsible can not identify their personal efforts and achievements. Thus, if workers believe that their manager encounters difficulties in supervising the task and identifying individual performance, they will be less willing to waste their efforts for nothing and tend to withhold them. Moreover, it is well known that in group tasks, based on complex technology, *interdependence* among the team members grows, supervision of performance decreases, and, as a result, workers' motivation to invest personal effort is low. However, when mutual dependence among team members is low and supervision is easier, the workers are more willing to invest personal effort during the performance of a collective task.

Social Norms.   Consensus within the group with regard to social norms may reduce the workers' individual, utilitarian self-interest. This means that if there is a social norms consensus in the team, most of the members will be willing to forego their personal gain and focus on the task and collective interest. It has already been shown that the individual is more influenced by the desire to act according to normative social standards than on the basis of cost-effectiveness. Obviously people may differ in this respect, but it is to be expected that, when the prevalent social norms emphasize investment of effort, team members will act accordingly even if it is not for their own benefit. Teams of volunteers provide a salient example of this phenomenon. Inversely, when individual loafing and withholding effort are the prevalent group norm, its members will join in and withhold individual effort even if such investment is likely to be of some personal benefit to them.

Perceived Fairness.   Do individuals reduce their personal effort because they expect their colleagues to slack and they wish to act in fairness to themselves? Indeed research revealed that the respondents preferred to reduce their efforts so as not to feel they are giving others *a free ride*. Workers' marked tendency to withhold effort is due to their being perturbed that others will withhold effort and enjoy their contribution to the task. However, this *sucker syndrome* is rejected by some researchers who maintain that individuals decide to withhold effort simply because they believe that other team members intend to do so. In any case, research reveals that under conditions of collective reward individuals decide on the amount of effort in line with their subjective perception of the situation's fairness. This means that, to the extent that workers believe that other team members invest equal effort, and that they are not the only suckers, they will invest personal efforts for the benefit of the collective task. However, if they feel that other team members receive the same reward for less effort, they will avoid investing any special effort in the collective task (Kidwell & Bennett, 1993).

Perceived Altruism.   *Altruism* is expressed in two types of assistance in an organization: (a) prosocial behavior—workers' behavior within or beyond their role, helping individuals, groups, or organizations, not necessarily profitable for the organization; and (b) good citizenship—an informal contribution that workers choose to make or withhold regardless of formal rewards and sanctions. Behaviors showing altruism in an organization, such as helping others with difficult tasks, instructing new workers, and helping those temporarily absent, may stem from inner moral principles or merely from friendliness or mutuality among colleagues involving empathy and sympathy for others. If workers feel that most team members behave in an altruistic way toward each other, their own motivation to help and invest effort may grow. However, to the extent that they feel that the behavior of others in the team is not altruistic, they will presumably tend to behave likewise and reduce their own individual effort.

Implications for Team Management

Many organizations today are engaged in establishing various teams of workers as a component of the modern perception of management, which entails a nonhierarchical organizational structure, delegation of authority, psychological empowerment of the workers, and their involvement in the decision-making processes. Terms such as *product development teams, marketing teams, self-managed teams, multidisciplinary teams, renewed planning teams,* and even *virtual team* are familiar to many managers and workers and have even become an inseparable part of the work process in organizations. The prevalent view governing organizations' activities is that teamwork is typified by mutual learning, coordination, and team members' collective contribution to brain storming and the completion of the final product. Moreover, most of the emphasis is placed on the investigation of the qualities of the team and its contribution to the enrichment of the workers' role. However, before deciding to set up work teams, managers must also consider the quality and quantity of the collective output. They should ask whether the team's final output is in fact greater than the sum of individual outputs of its members. Is the investment that group members are willing to contribute to the collective task smaller, identical, or greater than that which they would make if working on their own? Although the importance of inner needs, partly satisfied by teamwork, should not be underestimated, the output and organizational efficiency should also be taken into account.

As we have seen, many factors cause workers to withhold effort when they are working within the framework of a team. Such behavior can eventually lead to a decrease in the efficiency of the team and the organization as a whole. To improve the work of the team, managers may have to take a number of commonsense steps. First, before handing over the project to the team, managers should ensure that the task is challenging, complex, and perceived as important. The greater the importance ascribed to it by the team members and the more they identify with it, the greater will be their commitment to performing well on it, and their individual efforts will also increase accordingly. Moreover, the person in charge should identify individual effort and output so workers feel appreciated, leading them to invest personal effort. However, managers of human resources should be aware that the steps to be taken should not be merely instrumental; they should also take into account the norms developing in the team and possibly even assist in forging them. These norms may influence the willingness of each one of the team members to contribute to the collective effort. If a team has a tendency to behave fairly and altruistically, a sincere desire to collaborate, and the belief that all are contributing according to their ability, then their commitment to the task will increase, which may lead to greater individual effort. Therefore, the main role of managers of human resources is to establish such a work culture in the team. This is possible when the length of service is more homogeneous and there are long-term interactions among team members. However, mutuality and social ties established through less formal means have a decisive influence. In any case, a combination of these factors is beneficial and can reduce undesirable phenomena such as withholding individual effort within the team framework.

In the future, organizations will continue to rely on teamwork despite the growing awareness of the negative effects of this work style on organizational effectiveness. This question arises: will managers, particularly those in charge of human resources working extensively with groups, succeed in confronting such phenomena and taking preemptive steps before setting up a team to reduce misbehavior, such as the withholding of individual effort, and thereby increase collective effort?

8

Organization-Level
Antecedents

The principal assumption underlying most macrolevel writings on the management of OB (e.g., March & Simon, 1958; Weick, 1979) is that work organizations affect the particular ways their members choose to behave on the job. The classical organization theory writers have provided numerous frameworks designed to illustrate, explain, and provide the logic for these influences. Thus, we know that individual behavior is affected by a whole range of macrovariables such as the organization's environment (e.g., Aldrich, 1979; Katz & Kahn, 1978), the firm's strategy (e.g., Miles & Snow, 1978), the organization type (e.g., Etzioni, 1961), the organization design (Galbraith, 1977), the technology (e.g., Perrow, 1986; Thompson, 1967), the form and structure (Hall, 1976), and the organization's culture (Schein, 1985). Only recently have we begun to also explore organization-level effects on members' work-related misconduct (e.g., Ackryod & Thompson, 1999; Vaughan, 1998).

The goal in this chapter is to further this understanding through our OMB framework and to offer some evidence from field research. To that end, we focus on selected macrolevel (i.e., organization-level) characteristics that are, to a large extent, defined, designed, and managed by the organization: type and primary mission, culture and climate, and behavior control systems. Because these characteristics are accepted as important antecedents of members' work conduct

165

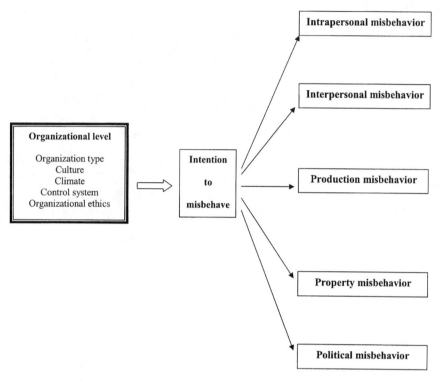

FIG. 8.1.   Organizational-level antecedents.

(e.g., Johnson & Gill, 1993; Kunda, 1992; Nadler & Tushman, 1980), we suggest that they may also be useful in predicting and managing patterns of OMB. This perspective is depicted in Fig. 8.1.

Before proceeding, we explain our point of view, noting that our main interest is in explaining individual work-related behavior. More precisely, we now identify macrolevel antecedents that may account for the formation of implicit intention to engage in OMB. Thus, we study the organization—a plausible antecedent for OMB. This approach differs from that of writers who choose to view misbehavior as an antecedent affecting the well-being of the organization as a whole. Consider, for example, the quite disturbing case-based book by Mitroff and Kilmann (1984) aptly entitled: *Corporate Tragedies: Product Tampering, Sabotage, and Other Catastrophes*. The authors discussed five types of organizational tragedies, some of which are caused by internal sabotage, others by external tampering with products, and yet others are basically an inevitable tragedy when products just malfunction. First, focus on the motive, not the consequences. Second, we pay more attention to sabotage and tampering by members of the organizations. We feel that it would be more useful for an organization to manage OMB perpetrated be members of the organization than to concentrate on external threats, some of which may be just plain *normal accidents,* to borrow Perrow's (1984) term.

ORGANIZATION TYPE

Work organizations are regarded by most theorists as formal social systems designed to produce goods and services through continuous exchange with their environments. In modern societies, they are formed, exist, and develop due to their relative advantage in effectively and efficiently utilizing resources, operating under various conditions of uncertainty, and handling large volumes of information processing to solve complex problems. Because of these capacities, work organizations come in different shapes and sizes representing countless possible combinations and interactions. It is useful to categorize them so that scientists can draw some generalizations and provide predictions as to how they might resolve their unique sets of problems in terms of both business strategy and human resource management (see general reviews in Hall, 1999; Scott, 1998; Usdiken & Leblebici, 2001).

Proposing organizational typologies is an important step in furthering our understanding of the complex social phenomena called *work organizations.* Unquestionably, the many typologies that have emerged over the past decades from this scientific effort and the specific classification criteria they have used allow for a large variety of theoretical explications of the organization–behavior relationship in which we are particularly interested. However, we focus on the high-technology organization, on the one hand, and the public-service organization, on the other. We examine the effects of organization type on misbehavior through the intervening role of positional and individual-level variables such as experience, autonomy, pressure, stress and burnout, and pay.

Hi-Tech

High-tech organizations employ, design, and/or manufacture software and hardware for advanced communications and computer technologies. Many of the firms devote their resources to technological advancement in the form of intensive research and development efforts. At times development of sophisticated technology may outpace the development of the hardware necessary for their application (Moore, 1995). The added value as an organization is the unique knowledge and novelty of the ideas their employees successfully generate. Because they face high levels of uncertainty, hi-tech organizations attempt to recruit and select competent individuals who can effectively operate under such conditions—people who can be creative, produce new concepts, break new grounds, raise substantial resources, and market their product on the highly competitive international market (Von Glinow, 1988).

One can identify the following core features that characterize hi-tech organizations.

Risk and Uncertainty. Hi-tech organizations, especially start-ups, operate in turbulent, high-risk, extremely competitive environments. Such external conditions are often reflected in internal work environments saturated with a high degree of pressure and stress to meet deadlines, internal interproject, interteam competitions, as well as extremely demanding and unstructured work schedules (Ganot, 1999; Reshef-Tamari, 1999).

Attitude Toward Time. Time is of the essence in any high-tech organization because the fast pace of product development often renders even new ideas obsolete as they enter the market. This is why time becomes such an important commodity and is constantly in short supply. Misuse of company time is considered extremely detrimental. Work is often not subject to normative time schedules—time zones in other parts of the world often govern local employee performance. Time pressure often results in less attention to strategic thinking and sometimes to product quality and safety.

Competitiveness. Hi-tech employees believe that a firm's success is directly tied to high-stake personal rewards and future options. This belief, in turn, leads to competitive behavior on the personal level and may lead to internal politicking and a jungle-fighting mentality at the firm level. Such beliefs, however, may contribute to a high attrition rate and burnout of many individuals.

Structural Flexibility. As a result of external turbulence, the internal designs of hi-tech organizations are agile and fluid. This environment is necessary for survival, and theorists have described this responsiveness with novel terms such as the *intelligent* (Arthur, Claman, & DeFillippi, 1995), *boundaryless* (Ashkenas, Ulrich, Jick, & Kerr, 1995), or *virtual* (Cooper & Rousseau, 1999) organizations. Although these terms hint at somewhat different organizational forms, all allude to work environments that are highly volatile, organic, and dynamic, with two related and distinct common denominators—uncertainty and pressure—directly impacting members' attitudes, behaviors, and careers.

Successful hi-tech firms, when they grow and reinvent themselves, expend considerable effort to attract managers and employees, assimilating them into a culture that encourages and rewards nonconformist and, at times, esoteric behaviors. At the extremes, such behaviors may also include phenomena such as bootlegging, subtle industrial espionage, and informal head and talent hunting. Indirectly, this employment culture rewards job hopping and high personal career commitment at the expense of the more traditional job or organizational loyalty. Kunda (1992) observed that, in this atmosphere, there is a constant tension between employees and management, which engineers the local culture as a control-enhancing mechanism. We believe that the manipulation of employees by means of such tacit strategies may backfire. Fimble and Burstein (1990), for example, found that in hi-tech organizations employee misconduct is indeed strongly related to such organizational strategies and traits. When employees receive a message from management that coming to market early is an important goal, they may release their product although they know full well it is not yet of proper quality—that it is not free from programming or hardware deficiencies.

Public Service Organizations

Although service organizations do not share the same features with hi-tech firms, both operate in highly stressful environments. Lovelock (1983) and Danet (1981) elaborated helpful methods for classifying service organizations. Lovelock's method lists the following lead questions:

Who or what is the direct receiver of service? Services can be aimed at people's bodies (e.g., health facilities), people's minds (e.g., education institutions), material and equipment (e.g., maintenance services), or nonphysical assets (e.g., financial services).

What kind of relationship exists between the customer and the organization? Some contacts can be permanent, such as the services given by an insurance company; others are per transaction, such as theater transcription rights. Some can be given regardless of any membership, such as police protection, whereas others require some type of affiliation, such as a community center or church. Some can be just a one-time contact, such as an international call serviced by a long-distance phone company.

What is the discretion given to the service provider? The major question here is the extent of leeway or degrees of freedom in responding professionally by matching appropriate responses to problems. For example, how much discretion is given by the organization to a team of experts in spending public resources on any given case?

What is the level of demand for the service relative to its supply? How do fluctuations in the demands for particular services relate to the organization's ability to provide services? In particular, the impact of limited resources on the quality of the service rendered may be worrisome.

What are the methods used in providing the services? Does the service require direct contacts with employees? Is the service to be delivered on-site or by means of remote communications? Is the service provided at the customer's location? Is the service concentrated in one locale or is it distributed?

In our studies of work-related misbehavior in public service organizations, we distinguished different organizations by the type of customer serviced (Danet, 1981): welfare agencies, general hospitals, schools, and postal services. These organizations trust their employees to provide customers with the quality service they are socially obligated to render. This is because, in most cases, service is delegated to individuals or groups that play the role of *boundary spanners*. That is, they represent the organization at the contact point with external clients or customers. Such are the roles of the nurses, welfare agents, and teachers whom we surveyed. Boundary spanners present problems for both the position holders and their employers. The primary problems are the direct encounter with customers and their expectations, the relative isolation in which the contact takes place, the duality of caring for the client while representing the organization, and working for bureaucratic systems, such as public social welfare agencies (Vardi & Weitz, 2002a). It is not surprising that these employees often feel pressured, suffer stress, and have higher degrees of burnout. In addition to being the good service providers they are trained to be, some tend to engage in various incidents of OMB. We attempt to propose some possible explanations for such contrasts in behavior from an interactional perspective.

Organization Type, Experienced Stress, and OMB

Both hi-tech and service organizations are stress-prone work environments (Brinner & Hockey, 1988). In hi-tech organizations, perceived stress may mostly result from the fast-paced, competitive, deadline-targeted atmosphere, whereas in the service environment, stress may result from the constant demand for ethical decisions, caring for the needy, and economic constraints limiting performance. Stress exists regardless of the specific source. In a study of the research and development (R&D) section of Rad, a large hi-tech firm, Ganot (1999) and Reshef-Tamari (1999) found some evidence that high levels of job ambiguity, job uncertainty, and a highly charged atmosphere (all considered components of stress) contributed to variance in production-related misconduct. They measured hi-tech misconduct by production deviance items found in Robinson and Bennett's (1995) questionnaire and additional items pertaining to computer-related misconduct, such as *cyber-loafing* (surfing through nonwork-related sites) or using the Internet for nonproject purposes on company time.

In public health services, work stress may bear negative influences on care-givers and thus hurt both their employing organizations and clients. In general, it may negatively affect the quality of service rendered to clientele Wolfgang (1988) suggested that continuous stress among health care workers decreases their level of concentration in solving problems and their obligation to provide high-level treatment. It may also increase incidence of substance abuse, as well as increase the likelihood of mental health problems, divorce, and even suicide. Ravid-Robbins (1999) investigated OMB among registered nurses in three Israeli hospitals. She identified stress as a major antecedent of both OMB *Types S* and *D*. In a similar vein, Levin (1989) and Kantor (1999) found that social workers who suffer work overload behave less professionally, their motivation to work with clients decreases, they become less empathetic and more apathetic, and they report some misbehavior toward their welfare agency as an employer.

Nurses occupy extremely vulnerable boundary-spanning positions in the hospital: They are in constant contact with patients who depend on their professionalism and compassion. Nurses working long shifts in intensive care units or emergency rooms are exposed to extremely tense work situations and must deal with doctors' demands and the pressures that come from worried family members as well. In many cases, they are also financially undercompensated. These inherent conflicts present additional stress (Gray-Toft & Anderson, 1981). Stressful work environments affect employee behavior because they may become the sources for frustration, annoyance, irritation, impatience, and intolerance. Such emotional states, in turn, may lead to various forms of improper conduct.

From this discussion, we draw the following general proposition with regard to the roles that organization type and character play in inducing employee misbehavior:

> *In both hi-tech and public service organizations, the higher the perceived stress in the work environment, the higher the extent of employee burnout, and the higher the probability for employees' intentions to engage in OMB Types S and D. Such intentions may be manifested in intra- and interpersonal, property, and production misconduct.*

The next section is devoted to research from the field. We report at some length a number of field studies conducted in different types of work organizations to explore antecedents of various measures of OMB. Although we emphasize macrolevel determinants, we also include variables that are customarily measured at the group and individual level, such as management style and organizational commitment.

Field Studies in Public Service and Hi-Tech Organizations

We conducted a series of four cross-sectional, exploratory, noncomparative studies in four organizations—a national utility company (Study 1), a group of hospitals (Study 2), a postal service unit (Study 3), and a hi-tech R&D unit (Study 4)—selected to represent a variety of work organizations and different sectors: private and public, utilities and health care, and mediating and intensive technologies. We explored a variety of organizations for cumulative rather than comparative purposes. We searched for statistically significant relationships between selected antecedent variables and perceived or reported expressions of misbehavior. Thus, we do not report a unified set of hypotheses and variables, but rather those to which these organizations gave us access due to the sensitive nature of the topic under investigation. In the first study, we posed three research questions: What is the relationship between the manner in which managers act (lead) and the misbehavior of their subordinates? Is the level of dissatisfaction at work reflected in reported misbehavior? Is misbehavior reported differently for the self and others (colleagues and peers)?

The interest in managerial leadership has traditionally tilted toward the search for effectiveness, with emphasis on positive work outcomes such as performance, organizational citizenship behavior, commitment, and attachment (House & Podsakoff, 1994), and managers' effects on subordinates' misconduct have been conspicuously neglected. Traditional research notwithstanding, it stands to reason that as much as managers influence normative behavior such as adequate level of work performance, managers' attitudes and behaviors should also influence subordinates' intentions to misbehave. For instance, Greenberg (1990a) demonstrated in a quasi-experimental study that the type of information managers provided their subordinates concerning change in pay is directly related to employee theft. Thus, we assumed that employees reciprocate considerate managerial behavior by refraining from damaging their manager, whereas a more restrictive style may lead to mistrust resulting in more revengeful intentions (Bies & Tripp, 1995). Thus, we hypothesized that OMB is related to leadership style: The more a manager employs a considerate style toward subordinates, the lower is the subordinates' misbehavior.

Based on previous findings of employee misconduct research (Hollinger & Clark, 1983; Mangione & Quinn, 1975), we suggested that feelings of frustration (Spector, 1997) and job dissatisfaction are important affective forces that should enhance people's intentions to engage in misconduct in much the same way that they enhance withdrawal behaviors such as tardiness and absenteeism. Therefore, we expect that the employee's level of job satisfaction is negatively related to OMB: The lower the level of job satisfaction, the higher the OMB.

The measurement of sensitive issues in organizations is cumbersome. It is certainly problematic when it comes to behaviors that are deemed by employers as unhelpful, counterproductive, or dysfunctional (Bennett & Robinson, 2000; Sackett & DeVore, 2001; Skarliki & Folger, 1997). To avoid making respondents uncomfortable and to lower the effect of social desirability, researchers may use nondirect language when asking individuals to report other's (rather than their own) misconduct. Based on attribution theory (Weiner, 1974), we expected that, as a rule, when reporting misbehavior both managers and employees tend to minimize their own misbehavior while perhaps exaggerating others'. Therefore, we argue that organization members tend to attribute more misbehavior to others than to themselves.

Work environments in general, and human service organizations in particular, often pose extremely demanding contexts for their employees. Such demands may be especially acute in jobs in which service providers directly interact with clients or customers (Schneider & Bowen, 1995). Although they attempt to provide quality service, we expect such settings to also enhance work-related misbehavior among their staff. Hospital nurses are a good example of workers who are subjected to such demanding organizational environments because of the crucial patient service they perform, their boundary-spanning role, and the inherent conflicts with other stakeholders (physicians, administrators, and patients' families). Their behavior (and misbehavior) is determined by their attitude toward the work, level of responsibility and authority, and manner in which they perceive organizational and professional obligations. Specifically, we expected nurses' misbehavior to be related to how they perceive their unit's service climate, their own attitude toward providing health care service, and the level of their job and professional commitments. For example, nurses in supervisory roles would relate to misbehavior differently than staff nurses. That is, OMB is negatively related to employee orientation toward service and perceived service climate, employee attitudes of organizational commitment and professional involvement, and level of job responsibility.

The traditional assertion posited in the mainstream OB literature has been that employment status (Archer, 1994) as well as the design of one's task (Hackman & Oldham, 1980) influence attitudes and behaviors toward both work and employing organization (Steers & Mowday, 1977). We now extend these assumptions and argue that these factors also bear on employee misbehavior. For example, in chapter 7 we addressed the issue of job design and OMB, suggesting that it may offer built-in opportunities to misbehave and thus be an important antecedent of OMB. Although job autonomy can enhance performance, it might also tempt employees to misbehave (Vardi & Weitz, 2001). Similarly, temporary employees can be expected to feel less attached to the organization and more inclined to engage in OMB than full-time, permanent employees.

The Israeli Postal Service was selected for Study 3 after some incidents of mail theft in several distribution centers were discovered and reported in the local media. This particular work environment is characterized by relatively lax controls and obvious temptations (employees handle mail containing goods, cash, and checks during the night shift), with full- and part-time employees performing similar work side by side. We agree with previous findings that temporary employees engage in OMB more than full-time permanent employees, and that job satisfaction, work commitment, and career opportunities moderate the relationship between employment status and OMB.

The possible effects of the work environment on OMB were investigated in study 4—a hi-tech setting. Typically, the hi-tech culture is characterized by extended work hours, extremely heavy workload, competitiveness, unrealistic deadlines, high levels of turnover, and pressure to excel. The work atmosphere is replete with underlying tensions between individualism and managerial controls (Kunda, 1992). Reports (e.g., Fimbel & Burstein, 1990) indicate that the hi-tech industry is replete with employee misconduct (e.g., concealing bugs in a software product from customers). We sought to identify some of the determinants of OMB (e.g., time wasting, Internet surfing, quality compromising, bootlegging, and substance abuse) in such a stressful work environment. Based on mainstream stress literature (e.g., McGrath, 1976; Shirom, 1982), we assumed that the subjective pressure that emanates from a job environment characterized by ambiguity, role conflict, and overload (Kahn, Wolfe, Quinn, Snoek, & Rosenthal, 1964) may not only enhance excellence, but OMB as well.

In hi-tech work environments, the intention to misbehave could be related to the employee's affective state, such as satisfaction drawn from work and the organization as a whole (Vardi & Wiener, 1996). Specifically, job satisfaction is postulated to play a mitigating role between the level of subjective pressure and misbehavior because for professionals pressure is not necessarily a negative motive (Meglino, 1977) and because positive affect toward the organization may inhibit thoughts of revenge or malice aimed at the work, colleagues, or the employer (Spector, 1997a). Therefore, we expect that there will be a positive relationship between OMB and perceived work-related job pressure (ambiguity, role conflict, and overload), and that job satisfaction moderates the relationship between stress and OMB.

Study 1: Public Service—Utilities

This investigation was conducted among employees of the Israeli National Electricity Company, Israel's largest and most powerful utility. From the 185 questionnaires distributed in the company, 162 employees at the nonsupervisory (26%), supervisory (34%), lower managerial (32%), and higher managerial (8%) levels responded (for an 88% response rate). The questionnaires were administered while the respondents attended various training sessions in the company's human resources development center. Most of the respondents were men (93%) with at least a high school education, and their average age was 40. They all considered their income as being above average (actually, they are among the highest paid employees in the Israeli public sector).

Study 2: Public Service—Health

Of 550 randomly selected nurses from three general hospitals (1,100 beds) located in the greater Tel Aviv metropolitan area and members of Israel's largest HMO, 318 returned usable questionnaires. Because of the common employer and the similarities among the three hospitals in mission, structure, and location, the participants were pooled into one sample comprised of 90.6% women, 23.9% practical nurses, 44.5% registered nurses, and 31.6% academic nurses; 15.8% held supervisory positions and 58% held full-time positions. The median length of service as a nurse was 8 years and in the hospital 6.5 years.

Study 3: Public Postal Services

This research was conducted in the central mail-sorting unit of the Israeli Post Office, a governmental agency similar to the U.S. Postal Service. We randomly selected 160 employees to represent full-time, permanent, and temporary employees and different types of jobs such as manual sorting clerks, mechanized sorting typists, bulk mail handlers, and third-shift workers. Following Analoui and Kakabadse's (1992) model for qualitative field research on employee misconduct, this study combined 11 months of participant observation by a graduate student who was also a personnel contractor for the unit, follow-up formal and informal interviews, and self-report questionnaires. The questionnaires were distributed at workstations during shift hours (morning, afternoon, and night), and 121 (61 temporary and 60 permanent employees) were individually collected after $\frac{1}{2}$ hr. The response rate was 75%.

Study 4: Hi-Tech

This study was conducted in the R&D section of one of Israel's leading hi-tech firms located in an industrial park in Tel Aviv. The company manufactures and markets data transmission and communication products for wide area and local area networks and employs 650 persons. All 200 members of the R&D section received questionnaires via interoffice mail. The cover letter explaining the study promised confidentiality and asked participants to return the completed questionnaires directly to the researchers. We received 95 complete and usable questionnaires (47.5%). The sample included 73 men and 22 women, with an average age of 31 ($SD = 6.09$); a majority (84.3%) were trained professionals in computers and electronics, 60% with a bachelor's degree and 11% with a master's; and the rest identified themselves as students. Most of them (67%) performed duties in the software area, and 30% held supervisory positions.

Measurement

Study 1. Employee perceptions about management leadership style, job satisfaction, and misbehavior were measured by a 105-item questionnaire. Also collected were some personal and organizational background data. OMB (by both self and others) was measured by 11 items adopted from three sources: (a) Hollinger and Clark's (1982) distinction between *property deviance* and *production deviance,* (b) Bateman and Organ's (1983) reversed items in their organizational citizenship scale (e.g., "I take undeserved breaks," and "Employees in the company waist material or damage property"), and (c) Robinson and Bennett's (1995) distinction between minor and serious acts of work-related deviance. Minor infringements include wasting time and work schedule activities. Major infringements include property-, equipment-, and material-related misconduct. Employees were asked to assess their immediate supervisor's management leadership style using an adapted version of Fleishman's (1953) Supervisory Behavior Descriptive Questionnaire consisting of 23 items for Initiating Structure (Cronbach's $\alpha = .88$) and 22 items for Consideration ($\alpha = .91$). Both styles (average scores) were recorded and used.

Employee job satisfaction was measured by the Job Description Index (JDI) (Smith, Kendall & Hulin, 1969) short version tapping three facets: Work ($\alpha = .76$), Supervision ($\alpha = .82$), and Pay ($\alpha = .82$). Overall satisfaction ($\alpha = .84$) was also calculated as an average of the three index scores. Personal and organizational background data included gender, year of birth, formal education, family status, number of children under 21, family income, position, and seniority.

Study 2.   OMB was measured with 25 Likert-type items translated from Robinson and Bennett (1995) and adapted to a hospital setting. A confirmatory (varimax rotation) factor analysis produced a four-factors structure that represented: (a) misbehavior toward patients (six items, $\alpha = .86$; e.g., "Talks impolitely to patient's family," and "Ignores patients calls"), (b) dishonesty on the job (eight items, $\alpha = .84$; e.g., "Submits incomplete reports on patients," and "Accepts presents from patients"), (c) improper intercolleague relationships (four items, $\alpha = .76$; e.g., "Insults another nurse in the department," and "Blames another nurse for own mistake"), and (d) unjustified absenteeism (six items, $\alpha = .79$; e.g., "Leaves position too early," and "Takes sick leave without really being sick"). The service climate perceptions items, originally designed by Schneider (1985) to assess service climates in banks, were adapted to Israeli hospitals to measure service climate. Using a factor analysis, two service climate facets were established: (a) role of head nurses in service (six items, $\alpha = .85$; e.g., "The head nurse regularly meets with nurses to discuss client service goals," "The head nurse establishes clear standards for good service to clients," and "The head nurse supports nurses when they raise new ideas for improving service"), and (b) role of equipment in service (five items, $\alpha = .65$; e.g., "The department always has adequate equipment to provide medical and nursing service," "Clients express high satisfaction from the equipment used," and "Instruments and equipment are well maintained and only rarely break down").

Attitudes toward service were measured with a 15 Likert-type items scale ($\alpha = .76$) asking the respondents the extent to which they agree or disagree with such statements as, "Even when we are overworked in the department, patients and their families deserve good service." Two variables concerning the nurses' level of commitment to work were measured. One was organizational commitment using Porter, Steers, Mowday, and Boulian's (1974) Hebrew version of the Organization Climate Questionnaire. The measure (15 items, $\alpha = .88$) taps nurses' beliefs in the values and goals of the organization, willingness to exert effort for the organization, and a desire to stay. The second was professional involvement employing a Hebrew translation of Ferris and Aranya's (1983) 14-item instrument ($\alpha = .89$) that measures the nurses' identification with, loyalty to, and pride in their profession.

Study 3.   The dependent variable—OMB—included two types of reported misconduct: OMB time (e.g., excessive absenteeism and tardiness and infringement of time-keeping rules, such as wasting time in idle discussions with peers or on the phone; $\alpha = .88$) and OMB reporting (infringement of set rules about reporting of work hours, mishandling of mail, and reporting sick when not; $\alpha = .69$). With the help of the graduate assistant who was familiar with the specific work setting, the items were especially worded for this study to best capture the local patterns of work behavior and language. Employment status (permanent vs. temporary) was the independent variable. Three moderating variables were measured as follows: (a) job satisfaction was measured by the JDI items pertaining to satisfaction with the work itself (five items, $\alpha = .85$); (b) work commitment was adopted from Wiener and Vardi (1980) and included measures of general ($\alpha = .75$), normative ($\alpha = .75$), and instrumental commitment ($\alpha = .62$); and (c) perceived career opportunities in the organization (three items pertaining to estimated chances to experience some career development in the Postal Service).

Study 4. Twenty three items adapted from Robinson and Bennett's (1995) list of statements denoting property and production deviance were adjusted to a hi-tech work environment in consultation with two company human resource specialists. The items were preceded by the following sentence: "The next statements will ask you whether someone in the department exhibits the following behaviors. Please circle the number that best reflects the extent to which this happens." The answers ranged from *never* (0) to *quite often* (4). Examples of items are "A worker misusing a computer program," "A manager firing an employee unjustifiably," "A worker sexually harassing another employee," and "Using company e-mail for purposes other than work." An analysis failed to support a two-factors simple structure, and thus we used the 23 items as a unified scale ($\alpha = .84$), and the score was a summation of all answers (range: 6–38, $M = 19$, $SD = 7$). For pressure, we used measures originating with the Kahn et al. (1964) typology of job stressors and used in previous studies in Israel. Role conflict ($\alpha = .78$) and role ambiguity ($\alpha = .70$) were measured by items adapted from House, Levanoni, and Schuler (1983), and role overload ($\alpha = .69$) was measured by items from Illgen, O'Driscoll, and Hildreth (1992). We also calculated a score for overall subjective stress. For job satisfaction, we made use of a Hebrew version of Schnake's (1983) instrument, which taps into affective reactions to one's work environment. It asks the subject to indicate on a 7-point Likert-type scale how satisfied he or she is regarding such aspects of the job as pay, workload, support, autonomy, peers, supervision, and promotion opportunities. For our measure, the interitem reliability was Cronbach's $\alpha = .85$.

Research Results

We expected that supervisory or leadership style is related to misbehavior in a way consistent with the notion that consideration by the leader will be reciprocated by good behavior, whereas initiating structure is conducive to misbehavior because it may be perceived as more controlling and invasive. However, both styles were

TABLE 8.1
Correlations Between Managers' Leadership Style and Reported OMB

Leadership	Other OMB Minor	Other OMB Serious	Other OMB Overall	Self-OMB Minor	Self-OMB Serious	Self-OMB Overall
Considerate	−0.09	0.05	−0.03	−0.19*	−0.02	−0.10
Initiating structure	−0.17*	−0.16*	−0.18*	−0.08	−0.08	−0.09

Note. $N = 162$.
$^*p < .05$.

correlated with OMB (albeit in a differential manner): Self-reported OMB Minor was negatively correlated ($r = -.19$, $p < .05$) with consideration and not related to initiating structure. Both Other OMB Minor and Serious were negatively correlated with initiating structure ($r = -.17$ and $-.16$, respectively, $p < .05$), but Self-OMB was unrelated both styles (see Table 8.1).

We also anticipated that the less satisfied (overall, as well as with work, superior, and pay) the employee, the more misbehavior experienced. The findings show that the relationships between satisfaction and OMB were varied: (a) all measures of OMB (self, other, minor, and serious) were negatively correlated with overall satisfaction, and (b) Self-OMB Minor was strongly related to satisfaction from work ($r = -.39$, $p < .001$) and from the manager ($r = -.30$, $p < .001$). Other OMB Minor was related to satisfaction from the manager ($r = -.26$, $p < .05$), but not correlated with satisfaction from work. None of the OMB measures was related to satisfaction with pay (see Table 8.2).

We tested assertion that people attribute more misbehavior to others than to themselves using two-tailed t tests for dependent groups and found this to be true (2.18 vs. 1.60, $t = 7.75$, $p < .001$, $df = 161$) for Serious OMB as well as for Minor OMB (3.13 vs. 2.28, $t = 9.31$, $p < .001$); (see Table 8.3).

Our expectation that OMB could be predicted by employee work and organization-oriented variables was tested with a multiple regression analysis. Results are shown in Table 8.4. About 20% of the variance in overall OMB reported by the respondents was accounted for by the variables of service climate, organizational commitment, professional involvement, and rank ($F = 13.891$, $p < .001$, $N = 318$). Overall OMB committed here was negatively related to service climate perceptions and to organizational commitment ($r = -.355$ and $r = -.293$, respectively), but unrelated to professional involvement and service orientation, partially supporting our hypotheses. In addition, it was positively related to rank and level of formal education. That is, supervisors and academic nurses reported more OMB than others (see Table 8.5).

TABLE 8.2
Correlations Between Satisfaction and OMB

Satisfaction	Other OMB Minor	Other OMB Serious	Other OMB Overall	Self-OMB Minor	Self-OMB Serious	Self-OMB Overall
Work	−0.13	−0.16*	−0.16*	−0.39***	−0.30***	−0.37***
Manager	−0.26**	−0.11	−0.21**	−0.30***	−0.19**	−0.25***
Pay	−0.02	−0.06	−0.04	−0.13	−0.12	−0.13
Overall	−0.21**	−0.16*	−0.20**	−0.38***	−0.28***	−0.35***

Note. $N = 162$.
*$p < .05$.
**$p < .01$.
***$p < .001$.

TABLE 8.3
Differences Between Self- and Others Attribution to OMB

OMB		M	SD	t
OMB	Other	2.70	1.11	11.4*
Total	Self	1.85	0.90	
OMB	Other	2.18	1.10	7.75*
Major	Self	1.60	0.92	
OMB	Other	3.13	1.22	9.31*
Minor	Self	2.28	1.06	

Note. $df = 161$.
*$p < .001$.

As expected, on all attitudinal measures, permanent postal workers scored significantly higher than temporary employees. We found that employment status and satisfaction were positively correlated ($r = .31, p < .05$), and the permanent workers are significantly more satisfied than temporary workers ($t = 2.01; p < .05$). The overall commitment of the permanent workers was significantly higher ($M = .30$) than temporary workers ($M = −.30, t = −6.25; p < .05$); the normative commitment among permanent employees was also significantly higher ($M = 3.40$) than that found among temporary employees ($M = 2.82, t = −3.56, p < .01$). Perceived career opportunities in the organization indicate that permanent

TABLE 8.4
Results of Regression Analysis for OMB

Predicted Variables	OMB			
	b	$SE B$	β	t
Service orientation	0.03	0.51	0.03	0.56
Service climate Perception	−0.23	0.47	−0.29	−4.95**
Organizational Commitment	−0.25	0.56	−0.33	−4.52**
Occupational Commitment	0.13	0.50	0.18	2.68*
Position	0.23	0.69	0.18	3.35**
Education	0.03	0.61	0.03	0.49
R	0.47			
R^2	0.22			
Adjusted R^2	0.20			
F	13.9			
Overall	.000			

*$p < .01$.
**$p < .001$.

TABLE 8.5
Means, Standard Deviations, and Correlations Among Research Variables

Variable	M	SD	1	2	3	4
1. OMB	0.93	0.46				
2. Service orientation	3.30	0.53	−0.04			
3. Service climate perception	3.57	0.58	−0.35*	0.25*		
4. Organizational commitment	3.83	0.62	−0.29*	0.35*	0.47*	
5. Occupational commitment	3.56	0.61	−0.06	0.34*	0.28*	0.61*

*$p < .001$.

workers perceive their opportunities as significantly ($p < .01$) higher ($M = 3.13$) than temporary ($M = 2.56$) workers. However, contrary to the main hypothesis, there was no difference in either observed or reported misconduct between temporary and permanent employees.

The overall self-reported OMB Time was 2.10 for permanent employees and 1.96 for temporary employees (on a 5-point scale). OMB Reporting was 1.78 for the temporary employees and 1.66 for the permanent ones. The most frequently observed misconduct in both groups was wasting time or loafing, with averages of 2.55 for permanent and 2.40 for temporary workers. Using a moderated regression analysis controlling for employee status (permanent or temporary), misconduct for the temporary group was best explained by low organizational commitment, low perceived career opportunities, and high supervisory control. For the permanent employees misconduct (OMB Reporting) was best explained by low satisfaction, low challenge at work, and high supervisory control. Note that the groups also differed on several human capital characteristics, with the permanent employee being older, less educated, and less skilled than the temporary employees, many of whom were college students. Thus, for the two groups, we can detect different sets of forces that influenced their propensity to engage in or refrain from acts of misconduct.

OMB was found to be positively related to overall subjective pressure ($r = .24$, $p < .05$) and more strongly to one of its dimensions—job ambiguity ($r = .28$, $p < .01$)—but it was not related to either job satisfaction or the other dimensions of subjective pressure: role overload and role conflict. However, as anticipated, satisfaction and pressure were interrelated ($r = -.30$, $p < .01$) especially due to the strong relationship with role ambiguity ($r = -.39$, $p < .001$). When we regressed OMB on the independent variables, almost 12% of the variance was explained ($F = 2.869$, $p < .05$), with ambiguity again showing the most significant effect ($\beta = .357$, $p < .001$). A regression analysis failed to provide adequate support for the role of satisfaction as a moderating variable.

Conclusions From the Four Studies

The four studies should be evaluated both separately and integratively. They are exploratory in nature and begin to converge toward a systematic conception of the antecedents of OMB. Thus, we discuss the results and their empirical and practical implications from both perspectives. Undoubtedly, further research on OMB should be of a more comparative nature and should utilize both qualitative and quantitative methods to encompass and account for more of the variance.

The results of Study 1 suggest that there is a significant negative correlation between considerate leadership style and self-reporting of OMB. We can ascribe this finding to the influence managers have on their subordinates' attitudes and behavior, which can either enhance normal conduct, good citizenship behavior (Pillai et al., 1999), or misbehavior. This finding provides additional verification of studies that report negative correlations between considerate leadership style and physical withdrawal from work (e.g., turnover and absenteeism). However, consideration could be interpreted by subordinates in a variety of ways. Although most employees take it for what it is—considerate treatment—some view such style as a sign of weakness and may take advantage of a lax manager. However, many interpret consideration as an expression of trust and reciprocate by abstaining from misconduct.

Our data also indicate that there is a negative correlation between initiating structure leadership style and OMB. This finding is contradictory to our initial assertion, which was based on the literature that establishes a positive correlation between this kind of leadership style and employee grievances and turnover rate (Fleishman & Harris, 1962). This may be explained by the fact that when managers provide stricter and less ambiguous supervision, there is actually less built-in opportunity to misbehave (Vardi & Wiener, 1996). Alternatively, although some withdrawal behavior may be related to a more strict control, it does not necessarily lead to actual willful misconduct.

The relationship between work satisfaction and misbehavior is more complex than the straightforward negative correlation we expected. For example, satisfaction with the work and satisfaction with the supervisor were more strongly related with Self-OMB than with Other OMB. This finding supports Locke's (1968) contention that job-related satisfaction, perceptions, and behaviors are interconnected in significant and often instrumental (and perhaps even causal) ways. However, we failed to find empirical support for the claim that misbehavior is related to dissatisfaction with pay. Again we may conclude that such a relationship is not a simple one. It may be mitigated by both internal and external factors. Kraut (1975), for example, failed to show that changes in pay satisfaction and voluntary withdrawal behavior were related, whereas Greenberg (1990a) demonstrated that dissatisfaction with company pay policy was related to theft.

We found significant differences between Other-OMB and Self-OMB reporting, for both minor and major misbehaviors. Minor misbehaviors were more frequently reported than major ones. This is consistent with Hollinger and Clark's (1982) findings that more than one half of the subjects who participated in their research reported that they were involved in production deviance (considered minor), but only one third reported property (major) deviance. The reason for this pattern may be that minor misbehaviors are perceived as less critical to the organization's well-being than major misbehaviors.

Caregivers such as hospital nurses (Study 2) are expected not only to demonstrate compassion and empathy, but also to perform their duties professionally and efficiently. In carrying out their demanding work, they may earn a patient's gratitude, but they are also held accountable for mistakes that may be costly as well as fatal. Yet quite often nurses find themselves between a rock and a hard place because of their relatively low professional status and their boundary-spanning employee–client role. In many cases, their level of responsibility far exceeds their level of authority. Thus, nurses have been shown to be prime candidates for occupational stress and burnout (Pines & Kanner, 1982). When coupled with the highly intense 24-hr work environment and the continuous sense of emergency, such conditions may also trigger misbehaviors that run counter to organizational and professional codes of proper conduct.

Reports on OMB also differed by rank and formal education. Nurses with academic backgrounds reported more misbehavior, as did nurses who held supervisory positions. This may be related to a major limitation of this study. Originally, we designed the OMB measure to inquire about personal engagement in such activities as proposed by Robinson and Bennett (1995), but this was vetoed by the HMO's director of human resources. The questionnaire was perceived to be too intrusive and politically explosive. Only a nondirect approach was approved. Thus, the data may be contaminated by the participant's position and responsibility to report as well as by social desirability. These limitations notwithstanding, this study may still imply that instilling a service orientation, creating and maintaining a quality-service atmosphere, as well as encouraging personal identification with the hospital may help in two complementary ways: enhance service and its gains, and reduce misconduct and its costs.

We assumed that temporary employees would identify less with the organization and therefore be more inclined to engage in OMB than permanent employees. In fact, the results of Study 3 reveal some differences between the two groups. As expected, permanent postal workers scored significantly higher than the temporary ones on all attitudinal measures (satisfaction, commitment, and perceived opportunities). The groups also differed on several human capital characteristics—the permanent employees were older, less educated, and less skilled than the temporary employees, many of whom were college students. However, contrary to the main hypothesis, there was no difference in both observed and reported misconduct between temporary and permanent employees.

Among the R&D professionals participating in Study 4, reported misbehaviors were positively related to stress, whereas stress was negatively related to job satisfaction. Stress was also positively related to important job attributes such as seniority and rank. However, contrary to our expectations, misbehavior was unrelated to both these attributes and job satisfaction. Of the three dimensions of perceived stress regressed on OMB—overload, conflict, and ambiguity—only the latter contributed significantly to the variance explained in the OMB dependent measure. Such a result may allude to the complexity of the hi-tech experience for individual employees.

In intensive hi-tech environments such as competitive R&D units, employees are exposed to high levels of stress that emanate from high job demands, expectations to innovate and solve nonroutine problems, and expectations for quick solutions. Thus, both role overload and role conflicts are prevalent. In fact, new R&D employees are selected for their ability to withstand both work attributes. Moreover, employees are probably attracted to this work environment because they find it not only nonthreatening, but actually challenging. This type of self-selection into specific organizational environments was discussed by Schneider (1987) and articulated as an attraction–selection–attrition process. Thus, for our subjects, overload and conflict may not be stressors at all. However, role ambiguity appears to be a stressor because it primarily manifests itself in uncertainty about resource availability. If such ambivalence causes frustration (Spector, 1997), it may lead to misbehavior on the job.

ORGANIZATION CULTURE AND CLIMATE

Culture has been a central research topic in sociology and anthropology and was gradually integrated into organization analysis during the past five decades. Its inclusion in organization theory has broadened the scope and depth of our understanding of organizational dynamics. It has made our perception more holistic and articulate. Adopting organizational culture as a key construct has brought researchers closer to understanding the intricacies of the human condition in formal systems and allowed for legitimizing ethnographic methodology as a viable research approach (see a thorough review by Ashkanasy & Jackson, 2001). We now know that members of organizations are not only reacting to the complexity of specialized formal arrangements that make up the organization's structure, but also to the softer attributes of values, codes, language, cues, symbols, and so on (Trice & Beyer, 1993; Wiener, 1988). Our ability to study organizational culture has made it possible to understand how members comprehend their organization and how, for instance, they develop, assimilate, and adjust their organizational identity (Ailon-Souday, 2001; Kunda, 1992).

Schein's (1985) organizational culture model elegantly captures this conception. He viewed organization culture as the pattern of common fundamental assumptions that helps members cope with both internal and external problems. Schein (1985) defined *organizational culture* as "a pattern of basic assumptions—invented, discovered, or developed by a given group as it learns to cope with its problems of external adaptation and internal integration—that has worked well enough to be considered valid and, therefore, to be taught to members as the correct way to perceive, think, and feel in relation to those problems" (p. 9). He identified culture at three levels: artifacts, espoused values, and basic underlying assumptions. As behavior, patterns of OMB are such artifacts, but they are rooted in the espoused values and basic paradigms underlying cultural precepts. By communicating expectations and role modeling, managers transmit these cultural precepts to members in regard to desirable and acceptable behavior, as well as to misbehavior.

Others view organizational culture more narrowly, emphasizing its function as a bonding mechanism holding the organization together (Tichy, 1982)—a local value system crystallizing the core beliefs of the organization's founders, owners, or principal stakeholders (Wiener, 1988). Daft (1995) added the notion that culture represents the emotional, less definable, less discernible portions of the organization.

Often culture is taken for granted because it is unobtrusive by nature. Its presence is subtle. It may become prominent when change takes place: when one enters a new organization, when strategic shifts are planned, and when mergers and acquisitions become a reality. Then culture takes a unique meaning—a unique sense-making role.

Some distinguish between weak and strong cultures by the strength of members' normative commitment toward the organization (e.g., Wiener 1988). In organizations with strong cultures, employees feel a deep sense of normative commitment the more they identify with their goals. Moreover, in these environments there is a strong and clear relationship between goals and means, missions and strategies, and aims and actions. This type of coherence between intentions and deeds makes people highly committed to both. According to Wiener, such systemic congruence enhances employees' duty and loyalty, as well as their willingness to sacrifice their own interests for the organization. In a similar vein, Meglino, Ravlin, and Adkins (1989, 1991) defined *strong culture* by the high level of unity among members in terms of common beliefs, values, and norms. For them this sense of unity is the very source of positive motivational, affective, and behavioral outcomes at work. Wiener and Vardi (1992) and Kunda (1992) also suggested that under such cultural influences employees' motivation and performance may be positively charged and observed in increased efforts on behalf of the organization. However, such efforts, we argue, may not only manifest themselves in positive energy (e.g., extrarole citizenship behaviors of not-for-reward contribution), but also in negative, potentially destructive energy (manifested in OMB Type O) or in cases of blind loyalty (Wiener, 1988).

We now present another field study conducted in an Israeli company designed especially to ascertain our proposition that organizational culture and climate are contextual variables, that are closely tied to OMB. The study nicely demonstrates the empirical usefulness of an integrative approach to the observation of OMB patterns.

Effects of Organizational Climate on OMB

OMB is a product of the interaction between factors at the individual and organization levels; its frequency and intensity vary under different contextual circumstances. Initially, Vardi and Wiener (1992) proposed a motivational framework for OMB, which delineates individual and organizational antecedents of the intention to misbehave. At the individual level, they included personality, person–organization value congruence, generalized values of loyalty and duty, personal circumstances, and lack of satisfaction of personal needs. The organizational level included such factors as built-in opportunities to misbehave, control systems, goals, culture, and cohesiveness. Several other scholars also emphasized the effects that organizational factors have on employee misconduct in work organizations. Some of the factors suggested were organization values (Kemper, 1966), organization culture and climate (Boye & Jones, 1997; Hollinger & Clark, 1983; Kemper, 1966; Trevino, 1986), organizational socialization (Kemper, 1966), ethical climate (Carr, 1968; Jones, 1991), and built-in opportunity (Hollinger & Clark, 1983; Kemper, 1966; Trevino, 1986). In line with these observations, we chose to further examine the role that specific climate perceptions (i.e., ethical climate) may play in affecting reported incidents of OMB in a given organization.

The Ethical Climate Study

The study was conducted in a metal products company in northern Israel that em- ploys 150 persons, of whom 138 worked at that particular location. They belonged to four departments: production, production services, administration, and market- ing. From the 138 individuals contacted, 97 returned the research questionnaire (for a 70% response rate) distributed on an individual basis at the workstation or office. The sample included 81% men with an average of 11 years of work experience. Their ages ranged from 24 to 60 years, and the average level of for- mal education was 12 years. Twenty-five individuals were classified as managers and all others (74%) as subordinates. Due to the sensitive subject matter, partici- pants were promised full confidentiality and anonymity. No raw data were made available to the company, and feedback was given only at an aggregrate level.

This study was designed to test the proposition that OMB is in large measure in- fluenced by perceptions related to organization-wide and/or unit-specific climates. It follows a line of conceptual and empirical research that has established the role of organizational climate as an antecedent of employee unethical behavior (Vic- tor & Cullen, 1987, 1988). The principal tenet underlying this line of research is twofold: (a) climate perceptions reflect some commonality in or sharing of some core impressions about the organization and its components, such as the human resource systems; and (b) such shared beliefs are espoused by members indepen- dently of individual attitudes and intentions. Thus, climate perceptions may be viewed as correlates (antecedents or outcomes) of other role- and organization- related variables. For example, Victor and Cullen (1988) posited the following claims: (a) organizations and subgroups within organizations develop different normative systems; (b) although these are not necessarily monolithic or homoge- neous, members know them well enough to be perceived as work climate; and (c) these perceptions differ from affective evaluations of the work environment. This line of research originates from Schneider's (1980) suggestion that various types and facets of climates are embedded in perception of an overall organizational climate.

In our view, ethical climates are embedded in an organizational climate, which in turn is part of the organizational culture. We believe the difference lies in the level of specificity of the observed criterion. Organizational culture pertains mostly to overall shared values (Wiener, 1988), climate relates to systems and subsystems (Schneider, 1975), and ethical climate reflects local constraints and guidelines of individual decisions and behavior. This assumption merits further investigation using a multilevel, multicompany research design—a design that was unfortunately beyond the scope of this study.

Organizational culture, as suggested earlier, is one of the principal factors affecting individual motivation and behavior in general (Kunda, 1992; Wiener & Vardi, 1990) and misconduct in particular (Hollinger & Clark, 1983; Kemper, 1966; Trevino, 1986; Vardi & Wiener, 1992). Organizational culture plays an important role in affecting motivation at work. In an organization with a strong culture, one in which the values and norms are directed toward deviance, OMB becomes normative and may endanger the organization's existence. Trevino (1986) also indicated that the organization's culture provides the collective norms that guide behavior. Those norms about what is and what is not appropriate behavior are shared and used to guide behavior. In a weak culture, the values, goals, purposes, and beliefs of the total organization are not clear, and therefore diverse subcultures are likely to emerge (Trice, 1993; Trice & Beyer, 1993). Members' behaviors are then likely to rely on norms generated by their referent groups or relevant subcultures (Schein, 1984). Hence, exploring the role of subcultures in an organization may be important in creating different value systems with regard to both normative and non-normative behavior.

Ashforth (1985) and Moran and Volkwein (1992) demonstrated the relationship between organizational culture and organizational climate. Whereas culture is conceptualized in terms of shared and therefore implicit values, climate expresses those perceptions shared by organization members that reflect the way they comprehend and describe their organizational environment (Hellriegel & Slocum, 1974). Climate is often regarded as the shared perception of "the way things are done around here." Reichers and Schneider (1990) proposed a more precise definition: "Climate is shared perceptions of organizational policies, practices, and procedures, both formal and informal" (p. 22). Climate is thus the perceived representation of the organization's goals and the means and ways adopted for goal attainment. Because members also attach symbolic meanings to such factors (Bruner, 1964) and such meanings influence intentions, climate too is regarded as an important determinant of work behavior (e.g., Litwin & Stringer, 1968; Schneider, 1975, 1980; Turnispeed, 1988).

Schneider and Rentsch (1988) defined *organizational climate* as a multifaceted construct reflecting key organizational functions or goals, such as safety or service climate. In the same vein, organizations are also believed to have ethical climates (Victor & Cullen, 1988) that reflect common perceptions and beliefs concerning organizational expectations of proper conduct. Albeit "in the eye of the beholder," climates are considered as more discernible, measurable organizational attributes than cultures. Such beliefs are considered more manageable because a specific climate (e.g., service climate) is closely related to manager–employee interactions, performance, and effectiveness (see Isaac, 1993). In addition, the promotion and management of ethical climates has received considerable empirical attention (e.g.,

Cullen, Stephens & Victor, 1989; Petrick & Manning, 1990), emphasizing their importance.

Researchers have claimed that people tend to accept and internalize the climate of the organization in which they work, and that the perception of climate has an important impact on their behavior (Friedlander & Greenberg, 1971; Hellriegel & Slocum, 1974; Litwin & Stringer, 1968; Pritchard & Karasick, 1973; Schneider, 1975; Schneider & Hall, 1972; Steers & Porter, 1979). For instance, perceptions of a positive organizational climate were significantly related to job satisfaction in work organizations (Friedlander & Margulis, 1969; Litwin & Stringer, 1968; Pritchard & Karasick, 1973), unit effectiveness in a military setting (Weitzman, 1985), and employee performance in a large print shop (Landau, 1981). Therefore, we expected that the more the overall organizational climate is perceived as positive, the lower will be the level of reported intentional OMB.

Researchers have agreed that such organizational climates have a positive impact on work attitudes and behaviors, as well as on organizational performance (Friedlander & Greenberg, 1971; Pritchard & Karasick, 1973). One explanation for this is the view that organizational climate is the extent to which employee expectations from the organization are being met (Isaac, 1993). When people's expectations for receiving support for their performance are perceived to be met, they feel positive about the organization's climate and effectively perform their tasks. Steers and Porter (1979) argued that when the climate is worker oriented, the employee would adapt his or her behavior to attain organization goals. In contrast, when the climate is mainly directed toward obtaining organization goals, individual job performance may decrease. Positive work conditions such as warmth, differential reward system, care for the new worker, supportive monitoring, information about what is going on in the organization, varied job, autonomy, cooperation, high and clear standards, and authenticity are all conducive to enhanced work behavior (Rahamim, 1979). Such a work environment generates more positive than negative work behaviors (Vardi & Wiener, 1996). Hence, we expected that the more the organizational climate is perceived as socially and emotionally supportive, the lower will be the level of OMB.

Results

We found OMB to correlate with Reward Climate ($r = -.24$, $p < .05$) and Support Climate ($r = -.24$, $p < .05$). Thus, the more positively organizational climate is viewed, the less the reported misbehavior. We argued that managers view the organizational climate as being more positive than their subordinates. Supporting this hypothesis, for managers the mean was 3.08 ($SD = 0.28$) and for workers 2.91 ($SD = .27$; $t = 2.26$, $p < .01$).

Conclusions

As opposed to many studies that used data from random individuals from different organizations and industries, this study was conducted onsite. The sample represented the behaviors and perceptions of the workforce of this particular company; it reflected both managerial and rank-and-files employees and the functional structure of the company. Thus, we believe that, given certain field research limitations, the data present an authentic assessment of both climates and misbehaviors in the plant. We found that there was a significant negative relationship between organizational climate and OMB and between the organizational climate dimensions (Warmth and Support, and Reward) and OMB. This supports the theoretical supposition that climate has both a positive and negative effect on members' intentions to behave on the job. The overriding implication for management is that it must be aware of the differential impact of climate dimensions on employee attitudes and behavior. More important, certain climates may encourage patterns of misbehavior.

BEHAVIOR CONTROL SYSTEMS

The case of Ms. Eti Alon—the Commerce Bank manager who admitted to the embezzlement of almost $50 million, which we present in chapter 9—raises the inevitable question the Israeli media adamantly posed to the bank officials: How is it possible that such large-scale, long-term misconduct goes unnoticed in a system based on integrity and accountability as a commercial bank? In other words, how does this damaging activity go on undetected by any number of control mechanisms and functions this organization had in place? This obviously is a question of organizational and behavioral control. We refer to both physical means used for control and surveillance (e.g., closed-circuit television) as well managerial tools (e.g., rules and regulations, auditing, and disciplinary means) whose aim is to monitor, detect, penalize, and eventually decrease improper conduct. In the following section, we discuss the role of management control systems in monitoring OB and OMB.

Johnson and Gill (1993) entitled their book *Management Control and Organizational Behavior* to denote the importance they explicitly attached to control as the quintessential task of management. In their words: "Control means making potential labour power real, and it also entails controlling and manipulating the non-human resources that make this power possible" (p. viii). Furthermore, they suggested that if managerial work is concerned with controlling human resources, all managers must cope with the vagaries of OB. This includes understanding and predicting both pronormative and counternormative behaviors (i.e., both standard and expected modes of conduct and misbehavior).

According to Sewell (1998), the use of control systems has diffused in many work organizations since World War II, when the concepts of command and control were tested and implemented by the huge military organizations that took part in the war. These concepts pertain to managerial functions that monitor the execution of plans, evaluation of their success, and feedback needed for taking corrective measures for failures. Despite the popularity of these concepts among managers, it appears that it is difficult to ascertain the effectiveness of organizational control systems.

This may be due to the view of many organizations that publicizing data about their control systems may be construed as an admission to the existence of counter-productive and damaging activities within their boundaries. Although from a public scrutiny perspective such information should be desirable and welcome, from a business perspective it might be considered a target for offensive by competitors (cf. Rosenbaum & Baumer, 1984; Sackett & DeVore, 2001).

The current integrative view of organizational control, to which we too sub-scribe, has its roots in the early (1950s) psychological approach described by Argyris (1957) and the classical organizational sociology works of Gouldner (1954), Merton (1953), and Selznik (1957). Argyris studied how budgets affect organization members' behavior from an individual, psychological perspective. His sociological counterparts showed that members react to hierarchical control systems both favorably (demonstrating compliant behavior or, in their language, anticipated consequences) and unfavorably (unanticipated consequences). From a sociological view point, these nonconformist reactions by organizational mem-bers were interpreted as people's natural resistance to formal control means, on the one hand, and the inability of managers to mobilize members' motivations and commitments, on the other hand.

An example of a formalistic approach to management control that has ignored the human side was the Management Accounting School at Harvard University advanced by Anthony and Dearden (1976). This highly technical approach to con-trol puts the burden on managers because it holds them accountable for executing plans on a daily basis. For them control is proper and necessary. However, such a conception of organization control, although elegant and appealing, is too narrow because it tends to ignore the complexities and uncertainties in explaining OB. We add that accounting alone cannot justify many of the darker side realities discussed so far in this book. Hence, we agree with Johnson and Gill's (1993) framework because they too viewed control as an organization process that is ongoing and in-cludes various facets of managing human OB such as the effects of organizational socialization, the deliberate manipulation of culture, and the effects of different management styles.

Such an approach was taken by Leatherwood and Spector (1991) in their study of employee misconduct. The researchers integrated two theoretical models (organizational control and agent theory) to explain misuse of company resources such as taking kickbacks, vandalizing equipment, unauthorized markdowns, and theft of cash, merchandise, and time. Such deliberate misconduct is referred to as *moral hazard* (traditionally associated with more benign misbehaviors such as free riding, social loafing, and shirking) because it threatens the implicit delicate contractual relationship between organizations and members. The two models (see Eisenhardt, 1985, 1989) suggest that there are two main conditions that enhance misbehavior. One is the existence of significant divergence in preferences between agents and their principals (agent theory). The second is the existence of concrete opportunities to pursue self-interest (control theory). Thus, when opportunities to engage in misconduct are constrained (controlled) or when interests are better aligned, misbehavior decreases. To constrain agents' opportunity to engage in misbehavior, we can use inducements to participate in proper and desirable (i.e., aligned) modes of performance by offering incentives, stock options, and competitive packages of pay, profit sharing, and bonuses. Such privileges must be contingent on proper conduct. We can also use enforcements designed to constrain opportunities like forming a policy or method to thwart probable misconduct: inventory control, internal and external auditing, and monitoring and disciplining improper activity.

The Role of Punishment

In addition to monitoring and deterrence functions, organizational control mechanisms provide management with specific information necessary to activate disciplinary action when warranted. This leads us to the role of punishment in the management of OB. Punishment is no easy task because our cultural upbringing immediately conjures up images of corporal and physical modes of discipline, which by and large are viewed negatively and are prohibited. It also brings up images of totalitarianism or coercion (Goffman, 1959), in which compliance is, in principle, based on strict adherence to institutional rules and regulations, and where any deviance is punishable. Indeed, in many non-Western societies and in some religions, refraining from harshly disciplining a naughty child, deviant citizen, or straying believer would be considered a weakness and bad control strategy. Furthermore, in organizations, punishment is typically discouraged because quite often it may actually generate undesirable affective, attitudinal, and behavioral reactions that could outweigh the intended benefits (e.g., Luthans & Kreitner, 1985).

Some form of disciplinary systems must exist in any organized social endeavor, both within and outside formal organizations (family, community centers, work teams, and departments). It is necessary because most social entities are predicated on implicit trust; when trust is breached, they must react to restore authority and accountability and, in turn, restore trust. Moreover, discipline is certainly essential in the dyadic (one-on-one) work relationship between authority figures such as teachers, commanders, and supervisors and their students, soldiers, or subordinates. Following Trevino's (1992) justice perspective of punishment in organizations, we also suggest that the value of maintaining a viable and relevant disciplinary system lies in the effects it should have on the observers (third-party organization members), not only the penalized perpetrator of misbehavior.

According to Trevino (1992), "punishment is defined as the manager's application of a negative consequence or the withdrawal of a positive consequence from someone under his or her supervision" (p. 649). Punishment follows acts of misbehavior or misconduct viewed as such from the agent's (i.e., the manager's) perspective. It is likely to be witnessed, observed, or at least heard of by observers in the immediate work environment. Thus, *misconduct* is defined as "behavior that falls short of the agent's moral or technical (work) standards" (p. 648). It would almost invariably include instances of employee theft, harassment and bullying, unjustified absence, insubordination, vandalism, and purposeful substandard performance. Arguably in most work environments, there is reasonable agreement between agents and observers that such behaviors are not condoned by either side, are unacceptable, and thus are punishable. In this case, we can expect a direct and positive effect of the punishment event on the observers. Namely, because of social learning processes, observers of credible punishment are likely to learn from it and be deterred from engaging in similar acts. At the same time, failure to punish may result in increased misbehavior. Whether the punishment is effective in reducing future misbehavior also depends on people's perceptions of the events and their evaluations of whether justice was done. More specifically, the model suggests punishment will affect third-party members when they evaluate it positively in terms of retributive, distributive, and procedural justice.

Retributive justice is a fundamental social belief in the function of punishment and its necessity for the maintenance of social order (Blau, 1964). In organizations it may translate into the notion that "here people get what they deserve" when they misbehave. Perhaps even more important is the notion that punishment is required to "hold the organization together." Thus, Trevino (1992) developed the following proposition: When observers agree with the supervisor's definition of a coworker's behavior as misconduct, they expect and desire punishment and evaluate it as just. To stress the point, she also suggested that when observers agree with the supervisor's definition of a coworker's behavior as misconduct, they evaluate management's failure to punish the individual as unjust.

Because this has to do with other work-related outcomes, it is certainly related to two other types of organizational justice: distributive and procedural (see chap. 3 for a discussion of organizational justice in the context of the influence of employee personality on OMB). To quickly recap: Distributive justice (e.g., Deutsch, 1985) taps the process of subjectively evaluating the fairness with which organizational resources are allocated to different members. Procedural justice (e.g., Lind & Tyler, 1988), in contrast, concerns the perceived process of allocating the resources (policy, decisions, and implementation). Hence, researchers proposed that these fairness perceptions are essential in making any reward and punishment system effective as an antecedent of actual work behavior. For example, Trevino (1992) suggested the following: Observers' attitudes such as commitment, loyalty, satisfaction, trust, and, consequently, work performance are associated with their evaluations of the punishment as just and fair. Undoubtedly, such a proposition can be expanded to include predictions about OMB. For example, we argue that observers' OMB Types S and D increase when they perceive the organization's as unjustly and unfairly treating coworkers who are blamed for some form of OMB. One viable explanation would be that this increase demonstrates a retaliatory or revenge behavior on behalf on the perpetrators who, by the justice perceptions of their observing peers, were wrongly treated by management. This would be the case when some are more harshly punished than others for committing the same type of misbehavior under similar circumstances.

III

IMPLICATIONS FOR RESEARCH AND MANAGEMENT

9

Managerial Ethics:
An OMB Perspective

PROLOGUE

Ms. Eti Alon called her lawyer and asked him to accompany her to the Tel Aviv police headquarters. The next day, April 20, 2002, they approached the policeman at the desk and asked to see the officer in charge. When he arrived, the 35-year-old Ms. Alon presented herself as the deputy manager of investments at the Commerce Bank and formally confessed to major embezzlement from the bank, and a major one it was: The manager admitted stealing about 250 million Israeli shekels (close to $50 million American) from clients' accounts over the past 5 years. When asked for her motive, she simply said that her brother, a habitual gambler, had asked her to help him out with some cash. She was arrested and an immediate interrogation ensued. The brother was eventually arrested in Romania and extradited to Israel.

Allegedly the deputy manager had devised a clever method of fraud whereby she misused her clients' accounts by creating fake loans. The money was secretly channeled to certain accounts in other banks without appearing on regular bank statements. To avoid detection, Ms. Alon, through a special arrangement with the human resources department, declined to take vacations or utilize sick leave privileges during the past few years so that no one would replace her. As the interrogation widened, it became clear that there was more to this case than met the eye. A whole network of shady individuals who deal in money lending and laundering schemes, as well as traces of organized and international crime and major gambling scams, began to surface.

Now was Eti Alon a smooth operator? A big-time crook? A greedy and unethical manager? A victim of extortion? A naive altruist? To pass judgment, we will have to wait for the police to finish its investigation, for the case to go court, and for the judge to render a verdict. Yet the business community cannot wait. The Commerce Bank collapsed. It shut its doors to a wide range of clients and was unable to give them access to their hard-earned savings. Only partial government guarantees for the return of the money were given to the customers, who therefore are likely to lose their savings. When asked about his indirect responsibility for this affair, the head of the banking security unit at the Bank of Israel, Israel's central bank responsible for overseeing the country's banking institutions, replied that it was his mandate to monitor banks for internal thefts. His boss, the bank's chief, incredibly blamed the customers for not checking their bank statements and for risking their money by investing it in small, albeit private, banks. "We are not responsible," claimed Dr. Klein, head of the Bank of Israel, because the collapsed bank had supervisors, managers, directors, accountants, and auditors just for this purpose. On May 12, 2002, in its weekly meeting, the government decided to guarantee a full refund for up to $1 million per account. Prime Minister Sharon bluntly scolded the Bank of Israel for failing to detect the huge fraud. Just 1½ months later, U.S. President George W. Bush publicly admonished the failed telecommunication giant WorldCom for an unprecedented accounting scandal and angrily vowed to "hold people accountable."

Organizational and managerial ethics have evolved into a relatively well-developed body of knowledge with a significant theory base and a specialized body of literature as well as some well-documented cases. Managerial ethics is an extremely important and controversial field because of the organizational and public impact such behaviors can have on our lives (see Maidment & Eldridge, 2000). A number of academic publications such as the *Journal of Business Ethics* and the *Business Ethics Quarterly* are devoted to this area, and recent management textbooks have begun to include special chapters on ethics (e.g., Daft & Marcic, 2004; Hellriegel et al, 2001). Books devoted to morality in business and management have also become mandatory reading in business and management schools (e.g., Maclagan, 1998; Shaw & Barry, 1995).

As stakeholders we are led to believe that managers, because of their training and responsibility, make decisions that are not only correct and proper from the business perspective, but they are also moral and ethical. Thus, must trust managers to handle our economy and finances for us. As OB students, we want to understand unethical managerial decisions and misbehaviors not just because they are complex and interesting to study, but because they are extremely consequential for organizations, their members, their environment, and society at large.

We devote this chapter to unethical managerial decision making and managerial misbehavior, which we consider a special case of OMB. First, we present a general framework for unethical managerial behavior as a form of OMB, and then we apply it to two well-known cases, one in Israel and one in the United States: the 1983 Israeli banks share fiasco and the recent Enron collapse. In both cases, unethical decisions by top managers led to economic disasters with major consequences to employees, the business community, and the public at large. In both cases, the watchdogs were sound asleep.

A FRAMEWORK FOR UNETHICAL MANAGERIAL BEHAVIOR

Traditionally, researchers have two opposing views in their attempts to understand and explain unethical managerial conduct (see Trevino & Youngblood, 1990). The *bad apples* approach posits that unethical behavior is committed by seedy individuals—managers who typically score low on scales of moral development, values, self-worth, and the like and score high on Machiavellianism, self-interest, and blind loyalty. The *bad barrel* approach assumes that unethical conduct is a result of the shortcomings of the situation in which managers operate: unfair competition, unreasonable pressure for results, limited resources, poor modeling by superiors, and so on. More balanced models (e.g., Jones, 1991; Trevino, 1986; Vardi & Weitz, 2002; Weber, 1996) posit an integrative schema in which individual and organizational factors explain both job- related misconduct and unethical decision making in organizations.

The ethical dilemmas facing managers are well elucidated by Ferrell and Fraedrich (1994). They viewed ethical dilemmas as situations, problems, or opportunities that demand that the manager choose among alternatives evaluated in moral terms of good or bad and correct or wrong. Hosmer (1991) viewed the conflict between economic goals and human concerns as ethical dilemmas, and Trevino and Nelson (1994) focused on conflicts among basic values as the source of ethical dilemmas. According to Toffler (1986), managers face three major issues that create moral dilemmas for them: Human resource issues make up 67% of these dilemmas, 27% are related to suppliers and customers, and, to a much lesser degree, 6% are pressures from superiors to act in ways that are contrary to one's personal values.

In many cases, managers must choose between different of modes of operation. Sometimes the choice is between ethical and unethical solutions. If the choice is clear-cut from a moral standpoint, there may not be an ethical dilemma. A manager faces a real dilemma when he or she is confronted by two ethically acceptable solutions—when the implementation of one could benefit some but cause harm to others. This type of dilemma is surely exacerbated when the needs of varied stakeholders are in conflict. For example, managers who debate whether they should divulge information concerning certain shortcomings of a product may be pressured by their own values (concern for the safety of the public), on the one hand, and by the interests of the stockholders or other managers in the company (dividends, profit, and market share), on the other.

Trevino and Nelson (1994) defined *business ethics* as behavior based on principles, norms, and business standards about which society is in agreement. Brummer (1985) viewed the discussion of ethics at two levels. Dilemmas on the microlevel focus on conflicts between the person's job demands and the person's moral judgment and values—workers' loyalty to the organization and management versus their conscience, values, and principles. At the macrolevel, most dilemmas pertain to matters of strategy and organization policy. Petrick, Wagly, and Thomas (1991) also dealt with the concept of ethics in business. They suggested introducing the philosophical level in addition to the micro- and macrolevels. The microlevel deals with individual and interpersonal issues regarding ethical dilemmas whereas macrolevel are issues involving businesses, markets, and publics. Such issues as the definition and dimensions of morality and moral principles are debated at the metaphilosophical level.

Three historical approaches to the business ethics relationship were reviewed by Bowie and Dunska (1990). The early approach (e.g., Carr, 1968) argues that there is no such thing as business ethics—business profit is clearly the name of the game, moral standards are immaterial. The second approach (e.g., Carroll, 1978; Friedman, 1970) argues that, although the ultimate goal of a business organization is profit maximization, the firm must go about its business ethically and morally. In fact the good of society and the good of business are not in conflict, but ultimately go hand in hand. Thus, managers should exercise ethical judgment when making organizational decisions, taking into account the needs of the firm and the public as well. A more recent approach—the stakeholder approach—goes one step further (see Freeman & Gilbert, 1988), arguing that the consideration is not only sufficient, but a necessary condition for business success. For instance, Allinson (1998) suggested that ethics and ethical considerations are an integral element of business. They should be regarded as a contributing rather than a constraining factor ("Ethics is good business"). Therefore, this approach puts ethics at the core of management and managerial decision-making processes (Green, 1994; Welch, 1997).

MODELS OF ETHICAL DECISION MAKING

Making strategic and tactical decisions is the primary and most significant activity conducted by managers in all types of organizations and at all levels of management. It is the prototypical function of managers, and it distinguishes between them and nonsupervisory employees. Not surprising, the importance attributed to ethical and unethical decision making in management is reflected by the extensive literature dealing with ethical decision making in business and the various models developed by researchers, each focusing on different analytical framework and variables. In many ways, the extensive literature on the topic reflects the many dilemmas routinely facing managers and the variables likely to affect their decision-making processes.

Ferrell, Gresham, and Fraedrich (1989) presented an integrative model of ethical decision making in business, creating a synthesis of the three historical approaches described earlier. Their integrative model relates to both cognitive influences and social learning. The cognitive model comprises five stages: the first stage is the identification of the moral dilemma by the individual; the second relates to the effect of the individual's moral development on the decision-making process; the third deals with the cognitive stage and the individual's moral assessment, his or her perception of the situation, affecting his or her judgment. The individual's moral judgment then affects the willingness to engage in a certain behavior or make a decision on the basis of the preliminary decision, which is the fourth stage. The decision leads the person to the fifth and last stage—executing the decision, which can be perceived as either ethical or unethical.

Ethical decision making, as Rest (1986) showed, is comprised of a number of elements: awareness of the existence of a moral problem, enactment of moral judgment, establishment of a moral intention, and carrying out a moral action. Based on Rest's findings, Jones (1991) proposed a model based on two external variables affecting the decision-making process. The first variable relates to organizational factors, including group dynamics, group cohesion, authority structure, and socialization processes. The second variable is the moral strength of the decision assessed on six dimensions: significance of the outcome, social consensus, likelihood of outcome, frequency, closeness to decision, and concentration of results.

A breakthrough was made by Trevino (1986), who developed an interactional model of managerial decision making. Her model posits that ethical decisions in organizations can be explained by the interaction of individual- and situation-level variables. Trevino drew on Kohlberg's (1969) model of cognitive moral development and argued that the individual's stage of moral development affects his or her perception of the moral dilemma and determines the decision-making process regarding what is right or wrong in a certain situation. The perception of right and wrong cannot adequately explain ethical decision making because moral judgments occur within a social context and may be affected by both situational and personality variables. The situational variables that may influence the process are job context, cultural orientation, and organizational context. Personality variables—ego strength, field dependence, and locus of control—also affect the likelihood of distinguishing between right and wrong. Trevino's model provides a theoretical and practical basis for understanding managers' way of thinking when faced with moral dilemmas, and it shows that unethical managerial behavior is affected by factors at the individual, organizational, and environmental levels.

A cognitive model of ethical and unethical decision making by managers relates to two main variables—individual characteristics and influence of the environment—affecting the decision-making process. It does this by way of the individual's decision-making process, which is affected by variables such as available information, whether the information contains hard quantitiable or soft variables, individual attributes, managers' cognitive ability, perception of the results, risk inherent in the decision, and value or effectiveness they attribute to the outcome. The individual attributes are the level of moral development according to Kohlberg's model; personality traits such as locus of control, authoritativeness, and neuroticism; demographic variables such as gender, age, and education; motivation (self-esteem and confidence); personal goals; values; and additional variables such as life experience and intelligence. The situational variable is the five different social contexts: the personal environment, comprising family, peer group, and professional environment, reflecting codes of behavior; the work environment, presenting an explicit policy, collective culture, and influence of shared goals; the governmental and judicial environments, including laws, administrative offices, and the judicial system; and the social environment, including the religious, humanistic, cultural, and social values of the individual in the process of making ethical and unethical decisions (Bommer, Gratto, Gravander, & Tuttle 1987).

Dubinsky and Loken (1989) developed a model based on the theory of the reasoned action (Fishbein & Ajzen, 1975; reviewed in chap. 6). Their model describes four stages in ethical and unethical decision making. The first stage relates to four concepts: beliefs about behavior, assessment of the outcomes, normative beliefs, and motivation to comply. The next stage includes two variables: attitude toward the behavior, affected by beliefs about behavior, and assessment of the outcomes and subjective norms relating to ethical and unethical behavior, affected by normative beliefs and motivation to comply. The third stage is influenced by the last two variables—intentions to behave in an ethical or unethical way. These intentions determine the fourth (final) stage—the actual ethical or unethical behavior.

Focusing on managers, Izraeli (1994) developed a model of stakeholders circles, which situates the manager within five spheres of environmental factors: social, business, professional, intraorganizational, and personal. The first four circles include factors of the organization, whereas the fifth is indirectly affected through the managers' interactions with their personal environment. Each circle includes varied types of stakeholders who influence the organization and are influenced by it. Thus, Izraeli's model assumes that the behavior of senior managers, who are affected by all five spheres, is influenced (because they represent the organization and liaise between it and the environment) by the social, cultural, and political constraints of their environment and the value system and cultural norms derived from it, as well as by the economic constraints (the state of the market, the competitors, and the company's financial balance), which are in fact the sources of legitimization and the motivation for their ethical or unethical behavior. At the same time, they are influenced by the specific characteristics of their organizational environment: the role structure that gives them broad autonomy in decision making, and the ability to influence many stakeholders in their organization and immediate environment.

Finally, Schminke (1998) developed a nonrational model of ethical decision making based on the classic garbage can model (Cohen, March, & Olsen, 1972) called the *magic of the punch bowl*. The underlying idea is that four components—problems, solutions, participants, and choices—are constantly mixed and circulated in management's proverbial punch bowl. For an organizational decision to be ethical, all four components must somehow come together. This model highlights the fact that the decision-making process in organizations is almost never orderly, rational, and linear as we sometimes imagine it to be, but rather an outcome strongly influenced by human limitations, bounded rationality, error, hidden individual and group agendas, and organizational politics (cf. Allison, 1971). Like the punch we sometimes drink, the quality is not only a function of the caliber of its components, but of the unique way the ingredients are prepared and mixed.

AN OMB PERSPECTIVE OF UNETHICAL DECISIONS

We chose Trevino's (1986) interactional model of unethical managerial decisions to serve as a conceptual basis for further theoretical developments. Her model aptly combines antecedents of decisions that represent the wide range of influences beginning from personality traits through positional characteristics to critical organizational constraints. In addition to being comprehensive, the model and its propositions offer an interactional thinking aspect that we find useful. This does not mean that other models (e.g., Bommer, Gratto, Gravander, & Tuttle, 1987; Ferrell & Gresham, 1985; Hosmer, 1987; Jones, 1991; Schminke, 1998) are less valuable or that they should not be consulted as well.

Trevino (1986) maintained that ethical issues are ever present in the uncertain environment in which modern organizations exist—with their varied stakeholders, conflicting interests, and values. Sometimes they may collide. Because their decisions affect the lives and well-being of others, managers, engage in discretionary decision-making behavior that often involves ethical choices: "Their decisions and acts can produce tremendous social consequences, particularly in the realms of health, safety, and welfare of consumers, employees, and the community" (p. 601). Her model posits that ethical and unethical decision making in organizations is explained by the interaction of individual and organizational components, not by a single dominant characteristic of either the manager or company. Any such decision stems from the need to personally resolve an ethical dilemma and act on it. What mediates the dilemma–decision linkage is the person's moral development. The manager reacts to the dilemma with personal cognitions determined first and foremost by his or her moral development stage. Kohlberg's (1969) notion of cognitive development was deemed relevant because it proposes that the person's level of cognitive moral development strongly influences the decision of what is right and wrong as well as the rights of the relevant others—duties and obligations presented by the particular dilemma the person is facing. That is, it is a useful conceptual tool for explaining how managers think about ethical dilemmas and what additional factors influence how they decide what the right thing to do is in a particular organizational situation (for a detailed presentation of the model, see Trevino, 1986).

Ethical judgment and reasoning at work are principally predicated on a person's moral development, which involves the individual's orderly passage through developmental stages. At the early, preconventional stage, the individual is preoccupied with personal interests and the actual consequences of his or her deeds. At the conventional level, the individual is guided by expectations of others—society at large or closer affiliation groups including peer and family groups. At the principled stage, the individual upholds values and higher order principles, including social contracts, ideologies, and religious beliefs. For example, Manning (1981) used the model to explain how different managers reacted to decreases in productivity among salespersons who had experienced emotional problems. It was suggested that a principle stage manager, when appraising such performance records, would consider the mutual obligations that the organization and employees hold. For example, he or she would recommend that professional help be given in light of a previous good record. However, a pre-conventional manager would focus on his or her own job, reasoning that failing to penalize the employees would harm his or her own position and career.

Obviously managers enter the organization with a previously determined level of moral development. Over time and with increased experience, they may continue to develop morally. Moreover, organizational characteristics and processes, such as technology and culture, also influence moral judgment. At any time, decisions are not only a function of personality traits (e.g., locus of control and ego strength) and the specific stage the person is in, but of their interaction with situational attributes such as normative and authority structures characteristic of the organization's culture. Thus, unethical decisions, which by definition are intentional and purposeful choices, may be explained by self-benefiting considerations (OMB Type S), organization benefiting motives (OMB Type O), or destructive consideration (OMB Type S). How, under different conditions, specific internal and external forces that affect such considerations are formed remains an empirical question.

In the next section, we present and analyze two cases of unethical behavior by high-echelon managers using an interactional perspective of OMB that puts such behavior in the context into which it unfolds. The general conclusions drawn from these two incidents are then presented in the form of general propositions, which should lead to further research. These cases (a banking system in Israel and a huge energy corporation in the United States) were chosen to represent two cultures, two different periods, and different types of work organizations.

THE ISRAELI BANK SHARES REGULATION AFFAIR

The Bank-Shares Regulation Affair, which came to light with the Israeli stock market collapse in October 1983, is regarded as one of the gravest cases to date in terms of its results and implications for Israel's economic history. Its investigation by a national inquiry commission, headed by Judge M. Bejsky, exposed not only the flawed structure of norms and values that became entrenched in major parts of the Israeli governmental system, but also the deep economic implications of the government's involvement in capital markets (De Vries & Vardi, 2002). We focus here on managers who played a major role in the affair.

For 6 years—from 1977 to 1983—the highest echelons of Israel's banking system behaved fraudulently to draw in as many investors as possible while exploiting their power in the economy in general and its institutions in particular. The scheme was put in place to maintain the banks' profitability and stability, threatened by rising inflation and competition with government-issued bonds. The regulation affair involved the banks' intervention in the prices of their shares. Through artificial regulation, the banks sought to mobilize capital from the public to enable them to issue shares independent of supply and demand constraints and without regard to the shares' actual financial value. The bank managers used various techniques to effect a change in the way the free market works, a market in which supply and demand determined the shares' value. Throughout the regulation period, the banks were able to grant their shareholders real positive returns at a higher rate than the capital markets' financial instruments (the Local Resident Foreign Currency Account and the Government Loan Stocks). The regulated share became a unique financial good—a share whose price rose constantly regardless of the state of the market.

Apart from the banks' need to constantly raise capital, there was also legal difficulty. Clause 139a of Israel's Company Ordinance states that a company cannot directly or indirectly give any person financial assistance—in the form of a loan, bond, guarantee, or in any other way—for the purpose of purchasing its shares or in connection with such purchase that has been made or is about to be made. Because a company that acquires its own shares in fact reduces its capital, and as reduction of capital is permitted only by a special court order, the bank managers overcame this difficulty by ensuring that shares would not be acquired directly. Therefore, they set up straw companies in countries where business was exempt from taxes and used seemingly external companies, which were engaged in manipulating bank stocks and other shares associated with it. These companies were, in fact, connected with banks, acted according to their instructions, and served as the main organs that acquired the bank shares during the regulation period. In this way, the banks' direct involvement was concealed. The assumption was that if the demands for shares were scattered among many companies, it would be easier to hide them from the state's supervisory authorities. These companies were in fact means through which the money was channeled. However, they successfully swayed the trends and leveled the shares by systematically exploiting the stock market trading method, the leader system, in which orders for the purchase or sale of the various shares were given before trade had opened. This was done in breach of Clause 54a (2) of Israel's Securities Act, which determines that anyone who fraudulently influences fluctuations in rates of securities contravenes the law.

Technically, this price regulation was achieved by introducing fictitious demands in the leader, which is the daily sum of all the purchase and sale orders that reach the offices of a member of the stock exchange up to a set hour before the beginning of trade. Because the leaders of the large banks constituted a large part of the stock market activity, they provided an indication as to what was expected in trading in the various shares that day. Therefore, the leader allowed hiding the real situation of the stock market. The banks acted simultaneously as a leader that pooled together demand and supply, as a financial institution with (ostensibly unlimited) means, and as a member of the stock exchange that could give instructions to buy and sell during trading. This allowed the banks to easily channel demands or supply to the leader as they wished; thus, these actions were a gross violation of the previously mentioned Securities Act.

By using leaders, scattering demands through separate bodies under their control, and making a significant proportion of their transactions outside the stock exchange, the banks were able to hide the shares regulation from the public and supervisory authorities. The prospectus (yearly reports) published by the banks up to mid-1979 contained no mention of the regulatory actions taken. However, at the end of 1980, in view of the many findings on the scope of their intervention in the stock regulation, the banks were compelled to publish their activities in the prospectus, but bank managers asked the authorities to exempt them from giving information. As the process went on, the bankers did not hesitate to ignore the regulations, issuing incomplete reports and failing to report on ways of financing the purchase of shares or the real quantity of shares in the regulating companies, in provident funds and trust funds. Thus, the bankers knowingly violated Israel's Securities Act 20 (which requires those issuing shares to include in the projection all the information that is important to the investor and to faithfully describe all that is presented in the prospectus). The purpose of this transgression was to reinforce and enhance the banks' status. In the end, however, it put their stability in jeopardy. Furthermore, the banks made every effort to present to the public only the advantages and prospects of the regulated bank shares while deliberately hiding the risk involved in holding them. For this purpose, they presented a misleading display of the shares' characteristics using the bank's consultation system. Employees, financial consultants, and managers were recruited for aggressive share sales campaigns, creating expectations that this was a secure, blue chip stock that bore a positive long-term yield. Their status as a professional authority gave them a broad scope for manipulating and exploiting the trust placed in them by their clients.

The bank-shares crisis began in September 1983. Following rumors of imminent devaluation, many shareholders preferred to acquire foreign currency and sell their stocks. Facing this excess of supply, the banks began unprecedented purchases of their own shares and had no choice but to request further credit from the Bank of Israel to finance the share purchase. The bankers' urgent attempts to find a solution that would extricate them from the crisis proved futile. On September 6, the Israeli banking system was on the verge of collapse. The banks, as described by the Bejsky Commission (1986), had on that day reached the end of their tether. It was clear to both bankers and authorities that without immediate help from the government and the Bank of Israel they would not be able to continue buying the vast amounts of shares the public so desperately wanted to sell. The liquidity problems that developed threatened their existence and Israel's very financial stability. Consequently, the government decided to take the bank shares under its wings and both protect and compensate the shareholders. This Bank-Shares Settlement eventually cost the state coffers 7 billion.

Bank managers' (mis)behavior had far-reaching implications. In the short term, it led to the collapse of firms, organizations, and individuals who had invested in their shares. In the long term, it caused a loss of public faith in the banking system, injured the image of Israeli banking in the world, and placed a heavy burden on the state budget due to the financial commitments undertaken by the government. The process that was expected to expand the banks' capital basis and their financial power in fact caused them to suffer huge losses, placed them in danger of collapse, and finally turned them into government-controlled corporations.

As suggested, the impact of the social, cultural, and financial systems on managerial behavior was crucial as a source of legitimization and motivation for the bankers' misbehavior. However, organizational factors and processes were no less influential. The behavior of employees is influenced by elements in the organizational environment, among them the organizational culture, the senior manager's opportunity structure, and the influence of colleagues on the manager's behavior. In this sense, the shaping of the organizational culture and its assimilation by the members of the organization (staff and management) affected the entire bank-shares regulation process.

Organizational culture (see chap. 5) influences employees' behavior in that it also represents the shared ethical values of the organization. Corporate ethical values are those common to the members of a group or corporation; they dictate the ethical norms according to which it is appropriate or forbidden to behave in the framework of the organization and on its behalf. Because leadership norms are expressed by the goals and priorities of the organization, senior managers in the organization have a strong influence over individuals' ethical decisions. Hence, the organization's ethical conduct clearly depends on the values of its leaders. Moreover, in a strong organizational culture, characterized by conformity to norms set by the top echelon of the organization, the management can (mis)use its power to engender unethical behavior in the entire system.

Top management shapes the norms of what is considered acceptable and appropriate behavior. The employees' and junior managers' commitment to fulfill the expectations of the top management, and the latter's power to label or 'legitimize' even unethical behavior as acceptable, motivates employees to cooperate. In addition, the individual's behavior is influenced by the values and beliefs of his or her social reference group, sometimes referred to as *significant others* or *referent others.* Managers and colleagues in work environments are, in fact, agents who influence the employees' moral decisions and behaviors. When the top management, which serves as significant others , behaves according to a certain norm, the entire body of employees may be influenced to conform to the same norms. Thus, through social learning and molding, it is possible to transmit unethical norms of functioning to the employee.

In light of this, we may determine how the bank managers' explicit philosophy became not just a guide for employee behavior, but an exclusive criterion for determining the acceptable and moral organizational culture. This philosophy was expressed in the setting of priorities for the organization—namely, massive sales of shares to the public. Bank managers personally contacted clerks and instructed them to raise the issue of purchasing shares while working with the clients. As claimed in the Bejsky hearings, (1986) "Promoting the rates of shares will continue to be our central interest." "It is our duty to aim for every client of the bank to acquire shares, not just those who possess securities." Circulars distributed to branch managers said,"Distribution of our bank's shares is our primary interest. We attach great importance to the number of orders processed by each branch."

Bank managers created a feeling among their employees that they were partners in achieving an important moral goal, and thus they were in a position to guide their behavior. The following citation emphasizes the method by which managers influenced employee misbehavior: "We are happy to note that a considerable number of branches have attained good results, but on the other hand, in many other branches there is a significant decline in stock holdings. We are sure that those branches that did not manage to increase the distribution of the bank-shares during this period will make every effort to succeed in the future."

Furthermore, when top management and staff behave according to the same code, it strengthens the feeling that it is the right and proper way to behave even if it contradicted some individuals wishes. The emphasis on personnel's commitment to meet management's expectations was translated into quantitative measures, which made it easier for bank managers to see which employees and managers contributed and saw themselves as committed in practice. Sales targets were set for the branches and translated into daily quotas. Branch managers were required to initiate telephone contacts with various clients to fill the quotas required of them. Managers aroused a feeling among their employees that they were in a constant race to achieve a very important goal for top management. Monthly charts were sent to branch managers to help them estimate their own part in distributing the bank shares. Branches that excelled in selling shares received rewards and recognition. Their managers were considered for promotion. Managers ensured that the organizational norms they set would not only be adopted by branch managers, but that each and every employee would feel that top management evaluated his or her behavior. Client consultation became a tool—a method to exploit the naivety of small investors to persuade them to act according to the bank's interest. In fact the consultants were directed, verbally and in writing, to deliver certain messages to draw in as many investors as possible.

Bankers at all levels accepted this goal leading to the feeling that their actions were normative and acceptable. A situation developed whereby non-normative actions, such as cheating the clients, coincided with normative organizational actions, such as evaluation and reward of personnel. Through this tactic, they reinforced neutralization and blurred the perceptions of proper and improper behavior. The socialization process that takes place in an organization acquaints employees not only with standard norms of performance, but also with unethical behavioral norms. Therefore, it becomes clear how the shaping and development of the organizational culture virtually give managers control over their employees. Such control is liable to lead many to misbehave. From an organizational culture perspective, the planning, implementation, and maintenance of the stock regulation mechanisms in the banking system may be seen as a kind of socializing experience shared by all parties: top officials, clerks, customers, and even stakeholders.

Certainly, intent and lack of moral standards cannot materialize into unethical deeds without the opportunity to actually engage in them. Hence, the opportunity structure of senior management is an essential factor that facilitates easy access to unethical behavior without punishment. The higher the level of managers in the organization, the more they are exposed to a structure of opportunities convenient for deviation. Similarly, the closer the managerial position or job is to sources of knowledge and crucial resources, the better the opportunity. This is due to the amount of information they are exposed to, the extensive contacts they establish, the absence of supervision and control over their activities, and the degree of autonomy at their disposal. For example, as shown in chapter 7, the opportunity structure inherent in the organizational system is one of the causes of OMB Type O. Such opportunities for organization-level factors create conditions for unethical behavior.

These conditions may result from the lack of corporate policy clearly defining what is allowed and what is forbidden, and from a defective and permissive control system that gives rise to a normative code, whereby those who deviate receive backing if their action was for the organization's benefit. Indeed managers tend to behave unethically when the potential results of their behavior are moderate and the risk of punishment is small, compared with the chance of increasing the organization's profits. Managers' unethical behavior can originate in an implicit assumption that they will not be caught and, if they were caught, they would not be sanctioned. That is, corporate policy that does not clearly define what is expected and permitted and what is not allowed provides a breeding ground for deviation. Theoretically, it may be argued that bank managers' unquestioned control of their organizations, power, and status in the business and political community created a convenient opportunity structure for deviation. The absence, at the time, of regulations in the stock exchange distinguishing between permissible regulation (limited to establishing random fluctuations in rates) and manipulation (also called *regulation*) made it easy for the bankers to present their actions as legitimate and served as an excuse for the Securities Exchange and other authorities to not intervene in the bankers' actions. In fact the matter was not dealt with in any practical way until October 1983, following the outbreak of the stock crisis. In this situation, when the field is wide open in terms of the law, rules, and regulations, the risk of punishment was negligible compared with the prospect of increasing the organization's profits.

In fact it was only in 1981 that bank managers and directors learned of the regulation—after it became obligatory to publish it in the banks' annual reports. Even auditors of the major banks testified that the term *regulation* did not appear in the books or minutes and their information about it came from the press. Although positioned as inspectors of the banking system, they were not able to perform their role satisfactorily in face of the bankers' power. Therefore, they appealed to the banks' supervisor to use its formal authority and force the bankers to reveal matters openly in their prospectus. The mechanisms that were in place during the regulation period did not work properly and did not serve their intended function. In addition, those involved in operations did not feel that it was part of their job to criticize or question the actions of the most senior ranks in the bank. The result was that the management ruled absolutely, freeing itself of any accountability and any form of internal inspection. This is how bank managers' unethical behavior in the regulation affair became possible.

This was not the case of just a single bank manager who found himself in trouble because of his actions; the affair involved most of the top bankers—and the most prominent of them—in Israel. In fact the decision of all the managers of the major banks to enter into the regulation process was made at the same time—the end of 1977 (when they had to decide whether they wanted to continue issuing stock regardless of the fluctuations of supply and demand in the capital market to expand their capital base). All the banks maintained the Bejsky Commission unanimously decided on an identical share-issuing policy that would be independent of the state of the market. The evidence shows that in the second half of 1978 the three main banks issued more shares than they had issued between 1971 and 1976.

Any significant action that was done in one of the banks immediately influenced the acts and misdeeds of the others. For example, when Bank Leumi in early 1979 stopped intervening in its shares' prices (intending to moderate the regulation, not stop it), the other banks asked it to return to its previous policy. Similarly, as the bankers prepared to implement the regulation, they found sources of funding by identical means: establishing straw corporations abroad through which the demands were channeled. This was also the case with regard to the methods of persuasion they chose—using a market leader and exploiting the bank's financial consultation system for the purposes of regulation. Thus, imitation and mutual adoption of operating methods became a matter of routine. In early September 1978, Bank HaPoalim launched a share sales campaign based on what was called a *triangular deal:* The bank offered its clients a loan on easy terms, the sum of the loan was used to purchase bank shares, and the shares were mortgaged as collateral for the loan. Within a short time, Bank Leumi adopted the same method, and it appears that Bank Mizrachi also conducted the same kind of transactions. As mentioned, this clearly ran counter to existing rules and regulations.

The bankers formed a *social network.* The network members helped each other hide the manipulations entailed by the regulation. On the eve of announcing the financial balance reports, for example, the bank managers conducted one-sided deals: the sale of shares by one bank to another and repurchase of those shares after publishing the balance—all to avoid showing the decrease of capital. In these cases, Bank Leumi passed its shares from Leumi Cayman to Bank Discount and repurchased them after the date of the balance sheet report. The same kinds of deals were conducted with securities, which were at the banks' disposal.

The bankers' approach to the resolution of the crisis in which they found themselves was identical. In meetings with the government authorities—the chairman of the stock exchange, the banks' supervisor, the top echelons of the treasury, and Israel's central bank—the bankers presented a united front, opposing any real restrictions on themselves and the banks they managed. Paradoxically, the fact that it was not a matter of one single bank manager, but the overwhelming majority of leading bankers in Israel, strengthened their hand. This false sense of cohesiveness and the influence of their significant others guided the managers' decisions and their functioning in the regulation affair.

THE ENRON AFFAIR

Enron, one of the seven largest American corporations, is about to earn the dubious distinction of being the largest bankruptcy in business history. Enron began as a pipeline company in Houston in 1985. It profited by promising to deliver gas to a particular utility or business on a particular day at a specified price. Enron turned from an infrastructure company for the transfer of oil and natural gas into a company whose principal activity is the provision of products and services related to natural gas, electricity, and communications to wholesale and retail customers through subsidiaries and affiliates. During its heyday, it operated in the United States, Canada, Europe, Japan, Australia, South America, and India. In 1995, it became the largest company purchasing natural gas in North America. Enron became a giant middleman that worked like a hybrid of traditional exchanges. Instead of simply bringing buyers and sellers together, Enron entered the contract with the seller and signed a contract with the buyer, making money on the difference between the selling price and buying price. Enron kept its books closed, making it the only party that knew both prices. Over time, Enron began to design increasingly varied and complex contracts. In a bold stroke, Enron moved its gas and electricity trading online. Going far beyond the energy market, Enron created a yet unheard of commodities bazaar, even offering weather derivatives—contracts that gave businesses financial protection against the costs of heat waves or blizzards.

Enron's complicated accounting practices, audited by Arthur Andersen, began to unravel in late 2001 when the Securities and Exchange Commission (SEC) announced an investigation into the company's partnerships. Soon after Enron revealed that it had overstated earnings for the past 4 years by $586 million and that it was responsible for up to $3 billion in obligations to various partnerships. A $23 billion merger offer from a rival was dropped after lenders downgraded Enron's debt to junk-bond status. Enron's share price plunged, and the company temporarily barred employee stock sales. In the interim, billions of dollars in market value were erased, and the stock was eventually delisted from the New York Stock Exchange. Enron was also forced to declare bankruptcy. As a result of the company's collapse, thousands of Enron employees were left jobless with nothing left in their 401(k) retirement accounts.

Enron executives and Arthur Andersen had warnings. According to a February 6, 2001, e-mail, Andersen considered dropping Enron as a client. In August 2001, Enron executive Sharon Watkins wrote an anonymous memo to former Chairman Kenneth L. Lay detailing reasons she thought Enron "might implode in a wave of accounting scandals." Enron now faces many civil and federal investigations and lawsuits. Also federal regulators are pushing for changes in the way corporations record financial transactions, including a move to have chief executives personally vouch for the correctness and completeness of information in their reports to investors. Enron's top executives were directly involved in the overstatement of profit. They sponsored and approved accounting and tax gimmicks with private partnerships and funds that contributed billions in improper or questionable earnings. Those deals helped elevate Enron's stock price during the market's boom in the 1990s. Enron executives and directors sold $1 billion worth of privately held shares in the 3 years before the company collapsed.

Enron declared 2000 as an exceptionally successful year with $101 billion in revenue, more than double that of the year before, putting it at Number 7 on the list of largest U.S. corporations. Senior management and directors signed the

2000 financial statements, declaring them to be a true picture on which investors could rely. The numbers were a facade, and the portrait was a fake. Enron's profits were nothing but a fleeting mirage and a subterfuge.

The company claimed that it earned $979 million in 2000, but $630 million of that came from improper accounting involving shady partnerships, investigators for the company's board concluded. Another $296 million of profits came from hidden tax-cutting transactions, not normal business operations. Without the accounting wizardry, the company was making little profit, if any. Enron persuaded federal regulators to let them use a market-to-market accounting system—a mechanism that allowed Enron to calculate revenue from long-term contracts and count much of it as immediate profit, although the money would not be recouped for years if ever. In the 1990s, banks and law firms began aggressively marketing structured finance deals in which companies set up separate affiliates or partnerships to help generate tax deductions or remove assets and debts at the mere stroke of a pen. It worked well for the short term when Enron needed a quick boost for its quarterly earnings. Yet as Enron's trading expanded, its other businesses underperformed. Its debt and cash needs kept growing, so the company needed to make more and bigger structured transactions to keep the game going—pledging increasing amounts of stock. Enron turned itself into a factory for financial deals that would pump up profit, protect its credit rating, and drive up its stock price. Enron used the bewildering complexity of its finances to hide its true nature. Some people had nagging suspicions. Yet as in the children's story, few questioned the emperor's new clothes.

The culture at Enron was, unsurprisingly, all about money. To determine why managers act in a given way and their real interests and agendas, common Enron wisdom was to first study their compensation deal. Top executives' remuneration packages were directly tied to performance. For example, they benefited greatly when Enron's book value skyrocketed as a result of the SEC approval of the market-to-market accounting scheme.

Enron's board twice waived the company's code of ethics to allow top executives to operate in areas of conflicting interest. It could have asked tough questions, but it did not. Board members later said they were misled by Enron executives. The board set up an elaborate monitoring system, but board members put little energy into it, repeatedly failing to ask pointed questions, a Senate subcommittee later concluded. Enron's top executives were also supposed to be corporate watchdogs, but they personally profited from the corporate malfeasance. Even secretaries became paper millionaires. Many had fancy cars and mansions in high-class neighborhoods. The Enron people were living the good life, and pretty much everyone went along.

Enron's slide toward scandal and bankruptcy exposed the failure of watchdogs at every level. Its board defaulted on its oversight duties. Outside accountants ceded their independence and violated their profession's rules and ethical standards. Outside lawyers approved misleading deals and partnerships and failed to vigorously pursue a crucial allegation of accounting misdeeds. Wall Street analysts led a cheer-leading section while their firms collected enormous banking fees from the company. Regulators were overwhelmed by Enron's complexity. The media were blinded by the illusion of success.

Were Enron stockholders swindled? Its employees defrauded? Were regulators deceived? Did accountants at Arthur Andersen knowingly create a false picture of company health? Based on what is currently known, the answer to all of these questions is an unfortunate and resounding "yes". Enron and its top officials are now facing myriad investigations. Arthur Andersen was convicted on federal obstruction of justice charges for shredding Enron documents amid an SEC investigation, and the firm will no longer perform audit work. Its future is tenuous.

Enron management devised complex partnerships initiated and managed by the highest echelons in the company as an ingenious maneuver to cover up debts of billions of dollars and conceal other financial problems, thus enabling Enron to continue to receive cash and credit for doing business. The function of the external entities was to serve the needs of the parent corporation, assume risks and debts, absorb losses, and serve as a conduit for distribution of substantial dividends to its principals. Above all, no hints or trace would appear on Enron's financial reports. Thus, one of the most promising ventures on the American market collapsed after the exposure of serious accounting irregularities and illegal financial transfers.

The Enron affair was a severe blow to the U.S. energy market; to Enron employees, who, at management's behest, invested their retirement funds in Enron stock; to Enron's shareholders who lost billions of dollars; and to financial institutions throughout the world. These banking institutions will have to absorb unprecedented losses due to severe Enron debts.

Enron management was not honest with its investors; even more reprehensible was their ill treatment of their own employees. Although some of the investors were able to change their position and dump Enron equity, the employees were not permitted to sell shares, which were part of their pension plan program. Thousands of hard-working Enron employees, representing middle America, not only lost their jobs, but also lost what their retirement funds. Top management, in contrast, left in time, and some even sold their stock at a profit.

The FBI is investigating whether Kenneth Lay, former president of Enron, sold shares illegally after realizing that his company's financial state had begun to flounder. It seems that he sold a $100 million worth of Enron stocks between February 1999 and July 2001. Lay is also accused of selling shares immediately after his meeting in August 2001 with Sharon Watkins, the senior Enron employee who warned him that the game had ended and that the shady practices were threatening to drown the company in a flood of scandals.

Sharing in the deception was Arthur Andersen, one of the Big Five accounting firms. Apparently during the last months preceding the exposure of the Enron affair, employees were busily shredding and systematically destroying thousands of documents related to the affair. David Deacon, a senior Andersen partner, admitted to his role in concealing evidence in the Enron affair. "I did so intentionally, dishonestly, and fully aware that these actions will suppress information needed in the investigation by the authorities" (The Marker, April, 2002). Clifford Baxter, an Enron senior manager, was found dead in his car. According to the local police, Baxter apparently committed suicide. Baxter is thought to be a person who opposed the method of secret reporting and external partnerships, which concealed debts amounting to hundreds of millions of dollars.

At the very least, it is ironic that Kenneth Lay, whose signature is on the Enron annual reports, wrote about Enron's corporate responsibility and even referred the reader to Enron's code of ethics. He refused to testify before the Senate committee investigating the affair. The person who emblazoned honesty on Enron's flag of values went so far as to express doubt regarding the integrity of the congressional committee investigating Enron and his own conduct. President George W. Bush signed into law a sweeping corporate fraud bill with central provisions aimed at improving the transparency of corporate financial reports and designed to hold both senior management and outside accountants personally responsible for them. Vowing stiff punishment for corporate wrongdoers, president. Bush bluntly threatened, "No more easy money for corporate criminals, just hard time." He called the legislation "the most far-reaching reforms of American business practices since the time of Franklin Delano Roosevelt."

COMMENTARY—THE ORGANIZATIONTHINK PHENOMENON

The Israeli bank-shares fiasco, the Enron affair, and, in its wake now, the World-Com and Tyco scandals clearly demonstrate that unethical managers are a liability not only to their own organizations, but to the general public. The problem is that the formulation and publication of codes of ethics alone do not guarantee that managers and employees will behave ethically. Moreover, it is evident that managerial ethical behavior has a great deal of influence on the ethical climate and culture of the organization. Walking the talk is the name of the game—managers must not only be familiar with the ethical culture and accept it, but must serve as examples to the rest of the corporation. Any disparity between the declared ideology of the organization and managers' behavior has a deleterious effect. To establish a reputation of ethical leadership, managers must adhere to a high moral ground and ensure that their actions are perceived to be ethical. However, according to Trevino, Hartman, and Brown (2000), the two aspects are not always congruent.

When ethical dilemmas are not confronted and when ethical aspects of daily managerial life are ignored, employees quickly perceive that ethical considerations do not constitute an integral component of the organization. They may rightly observe that bottom line and profits, not integrity and accountability, are core values. Consequently, when employees are faced with an ethical dilemma, the almighty dollar is most likely to rule the day.

Wiener (1988) predicted the emergence of this type of corporate mentality. He defined *organizational culture* in terms of shared values: "When a number of key or pivotal values concerning organizational-related behaviors and state of affairs are shared—across units and levels—by members of an organization, a central value system is said to exist" (p. 535). The sources of shared values are tradition and leadership. Such core values outlive members because they are independent of the potential influence of individuals and situations. Wiener offered a classification of value systems based on two dimensions: the focus of values (traditional vs. functional) and the source and anchoring of values (organization tradition vs. charismatic leadership). A Type I organization has a functional–traditional culture. This type of solid values system encourages a policy of coherence and supports integrity and rewards efficiency and goal achievement. This is a culture of hard, honest work. A Type II organization has a functional–charismatic culture. This is usually a transitional stage when strong leadership begins to institutionalize norms and codes of performance. It all depends on the kind of values such powerful leadership espouses. A Type III organization has a elitist–traditional culture. This organizational culture sustains a long-term elitist reputation and status. It lives up to its good name, and it is geared toward producing quality and exclusive products. Such would be some big-name accounting firms. A Type IV organization has a elitist–charismatic value system. Such systems are the least likely to result in long-term organizational success. In fact, this is where *Organizationthink* (the aggregate of Janis', 1982, term *Groupthink*) takes hold of the organization. The symptoms are familiar: invulnerability, self-righteousness, stereotyping, being above the law, censoring internal criticism, and so on.

Our analysis of the two cases leads us to believe that the banks moved from a traditional–functional systems a functional–charismatic one. The trouble was that influential and charismatic executives such as Bank Leumi's Ernst Yeffet adopted unethical norms of behavior and used a strong culture to instill it without internal opposition. Enron is the prototype of the elitist–charismatic system. Young, exceptionally bright, ambitious, and financially motivated entrepreneurs rewriting the book on corporate success swept employees and investors, by sheer conviction and charisma, along with them. Thus, when Enron's ambition was not properly monitored by its mechanisms of control and supervision, such as its board of directors and elitist–traditional accounting firm, the eventual collapse was in the making.

As we showed, although the ethical climate is important, the organization's rules and procedures are vital. Management's enforcement of the ethical behavior is of utmost importance. Organizations interested in fostering consistent ethical behavior and moral judgment must develop a structure that encourages managers to take personal and public responsibility for their actions and decisions. If employees perceive that the organization is unable to control (mis)behavior and enforce an ethical policy, corruption and unethical behavior by members at all levels become widespread (Trevino, 1986).

In the bank-shares affair, we detected a noxious combination of instrumental motivation (i.e., corporate greed) with a strong culture capable of controlling and directing the thoughts and feelings of both managers and employees. Top-level managers acted unethically because of their desire to increase the organization's profits (OMB Type O) and considered the likelihood of sanctions being applied to be minimal. Bank executives fostered among employees a feeling that the operation in which they were participating had a legitimate cause. To direct them toward the attainment of their goals, bank managers emphasized the importance of organizational goals and created a new organizational ideology around the issue. Thus, the bank executives used both enticing instrumental rewards and normative control to forge a commitment among the workers and rally them to participate in striving to reach the banks' financial goals while violating codes of ethics they had espoused in the past. Some of the key executives quite cynically made the employees feel they were participating in an important transaction. In one of the banks, this message was circulated:

> We are pleased to note that a considerable number of branches have shown commendable success, while in many other branches there has been a significant backtracking in holdings. We are confident that the branches that did not succeed in selling the bank shares during the above period will make every effort to succeed in doing so in future. (Bejsky, 1986, p. 143)

In both cases, social networks and assumed autonomy served as energizing factors. Such was the exploitation by Enron top managements of their network of personal relationships and their incredible independence from external controls. Chief executives offered banks, insurance companies, and Wall Street information about Enron and about the external holdings feeding them—information not released, as required, to the shareholders in the company. An internal investigation revealed that top management concealed from the shareholders the existence of business partnerships, which enabled Enron to hide from investors losses of at least $1 billion, which eventually led to the collapse of the company. We see this as OMB types O and S. Unethical behavior aimed at benefiting and protecting the organization can also be detected among the chief executives of the Arthur Andersen accounting firm when the managers hastened to destroy potentially incriminating documents before FBI agents presented them with a search warrant.

The Enron affair also has implications for the way corruption and deception should be confronted. Evidently it is mandatory to deal with the rewards and punishments system. Because of the Enron and similar financial corporate scandals, President George W. Bush and the SEC signed into law a program aimed at making the financial reports more transparent and to make top management and accountants acting on its behalf legally responsible for their actions and the well-being of the firm.

In summary, this chapter described and explained the behavior of top management teams in the bank-shares affair and the Enron debacle. One of the salient organizational characteristics is top managements' power and ability to shape the organizational culture and determine its priorities (Kunda, 1992). This power evidently can be misused, turning well-meaning and loyal organizational members into victims. For example, we found that the lack of resolve of environmental stakeholders as well as controlling bodies contributed to the development of a serious managerial malfeasance. Using their power and professional authority, executives unfortunately made their unethical behavior normative. Paradoxically, in both cases, the bankers and executives succeeded in shaping a strong culture characterized by conformity to norms of immorality and, to a large extent, illegality. Warning signs were visible, be they internal to the organizations or external, but neither the complaints of citizens nor the reports of observers, on behalf of relevant authorities were heeded.

GENERAL PROPOSITIONS ON MANAGERIAL ETHICS

In summary we offer the following propositions regarding managerial ethics:

* The higher the managers' level of moral development, the greater the likelihood that they will make ethical decisions.
* The less aware managers are of potential damage and the effect of the negative consequences of their decisions, the more likely it is that their decisions will be unethical.
* The more familiar managers are with organizations' codes of ethics and accept them, the more likely it is that they will make ethical decisions.
* The more the organization encourages managers to take personal responsibility for their actions and participate in decision making, the more likely it is that their decisions will be ethical.
* The clearer the definition of the activities to be rewarded and those to be sanctioned, the less likely it is that managers will engage in unethical behavior.
* The more serious the potential outcomes of unethical behavior is perceived by managers, the less likely they are to behave unethically and vice versa.
* The decisions of managers confronting complex dilemmas will tend to be less ethical than those of managers dealing with routine problems.

- The higher the managers are in the organizational hierarchy, the broader the structure of opportunities and the greater their freedom of action, the more likely it is that they might engage in unethical behavior.
- The higher managers are in the organizational hierarchy, the greater their influence on the ethical climate of the organization.
- The more significant and tight the social network, the greater its influence on the unethical behavior of its leading members.
- The greater the pressure on managers to produce short-term, bottom-line results, the more likely they are to engage in unethical behavior.
- Viable internal and external systems of control will reduce managers' unethical behavior.

A SAD EPILOGUE

As we were putting the finishing touches on this chapter, the news broke out. On June 26, 2002, WorldCom, the giant communications company, publicly admitted to the biggest business fraud in American history—and perhaps in the world. The next day, Wall Street reacted sharply. Share prices dose to virtually zero. The company admitted to overstating its cash flow by close to $4 billion. Instead of the 2001 reported profit of $1.4 billion, the company declared that it was actually losing money. How was this possible? Clever bookkeeping coupled with lax controls (once again the external auditor is Arthur Andersen, the same accounting firm involved in the Enron debacle). The fired chief financial officer, Scott Sullivan, apparently devised a system in which operating costs such as basic network maintenance had been booked as capital investments—"an accounting gimmick that enabled WorldCom to hide expenses, inflate its cash flow and report profits instead of losses" (*The New York Times,* 6.26.02). Following Enron and Global Crossing, WorldCom demonstrated again how unethical, powerful executives create havoc in the world economy and labor markets. Why do they do it? Partly, we believe, because of just plain personal immorality, partly, overidentification with their organization (OMB Type O) and partly sheer greed (OMB Type S).

We received an e-mail from Professor Michael Lissak addressed to business professors around the globe on June 28, 2002. It was loud and clear: WorldCom, Andersen, Merrill Lynch, Enron. . . . The list goes on and on. American confidence in our largest corporations is at an all-time low. Media pundits speak of ethics and lack of standards. Yet there is a source of ethics and standards common to all these cases—business schools and suppliers of masters degrees in business administration (MBA's). What kind of standards were Jeff Skilling and the Wall Street analysts taught when getting their MBA's? What kind of ethics? Is it that money was the measure of success—that it is standard to focus on maximizing shareholder wealth? That present value matters more than long-term anything, including responsibility? That you "are a team of one" so focus on self (and maximize those stock options)? The responsibility is the market's not ours—and, anyhow, no one like us ever go to jail.

Bad apples or bad barrels? Apparently both. This chapter shed some light on certain darker areas of management behavior, raising some tough questions about ethics and morality in today's organizational world of business and service. Do we have a problem in the way managers are socialized into the profession? Maybe we do. Have we created organizational cultures that tolerate such behaviors? We most probably have. Should we know more about managerial OMB? Certainly. Thus, we shift our attention to the two concluding issues: How do we deal with the measurement of OMB (chap. 10), and how do we manage and cope with OMB (chap. 11)?

10

Measurement Dilemmas in OMB Research

For over 100 years, the behavior of people in organizational settings has been the subject of some of the most interesting research published by sociologists, anthropologists, and occupation and organization scientists. Undoubtedly, what makes this research both challenging and frustrating is the absence of the single unique formula that would provide a perfect solution to problems arising in organizations (Porter, Lawler, & Hackman, 1975). Each academic discipline focuses on different aspects of behavior and implements various measurement strategies; almost all of them are valuable and contribute to the growing body of knowledge commonly known as *organizational behavior* (see chap. 1). Yet as Daft (1980) argued, the various methods of research use & create a limited view of reality and an incomplete description of the phenomena of interest. Both the organizational world and human behavior are complex. Furthermore, as already shown, turning our research agenda to work- and job-related misbehaviors makes our investigation of organizations even more complex and challenging. Our challenge then is not to decide which approach is the best, but rather to eclectically and by design incorporate a variety of methods, tapping and reflecting such complex realities (Jick, 1979).

   This chapter highlights the main dilemmas inherent in the current investigation of OMB that runs, as demonstrated throughout this book, a whole spectrum of actions from relatively minor misbehavior (minor incivilities, ignoring rules, and undermining behavior) to the most serious (theft, violence, harassment, and destruction). Certainly, no specific approach is perfectly suited for such variety and complexity; the choice of strategy mainly depends on the goals of the study, the particular research population, the site and setting constraints, and the researcher's training and preferences. As with all social and behavioral research, identifying the pertinent dilemmas facing the researcher is a good starting point. In the following sections, we characterize various research methods and review strategies for the study of OMB.

DILEMMAS PERTAINING TO MEASUREMENT STRATEGY

When embarking on the study of the behavior of people working in organizations, a strategy must be adopted. We organize the dilemmas facing the researcher following the logic of the now classic bipolar scheme proposed by Porter et al. (1975). To illustrate each dilemma, we refer to research mentioned in earlier chapters.

Theoretical Versus Empirical

The first dilemma, relevant to any scientific endeavor is the choice between an empirical and a theoretical approach. In OB, the tendency has been to focus on empirical research rather than theoretical issues. Perhaps one of the reasons for the emphasis on empirical research is that this field has its roots in industrial psychology (Porter et al., 1975; *Annual Review of Psychology's* OB reviews, 1979–1997 see Table 1.1). Industrial psychologists focused mainly on empirical testing aimed at developing instruments to be used in the selection of employees; they tended to deal thoroughly with research methodology. Organizational psychology—the apparent heir of industrial psychology—still emphasizes rigorous measurement because of practicing psychologist's need to rely on precise data to make decisions about their clients (Aguinis, Henle, & Ostroff, 2001). Nonetheless, the importance of developing conceptual frameworks for OB has been widely recognized, as evidenced by the status a theory-oriented and hypothesis-testing periodicals such as the *Academy of Management Review* and the *Academy of Management Journal* have achieved during the past two decades.

In their survey of the literature, Randel and Gibson (1990) found that of 94 empirical studies examining the beliefs and ethical behaviors of employees, 64% did not present any theoretical framework serving as a basis for their research, and 75% of the studies did not propose any hypothesis to be examined. Therefore, they called for special efforts to improve the research methodology. A solid theoretical basis enables us to (a) predict the types of behaviors we may expect under different conditions, (b) develop a logical research design to examine our assumptions and/or the predictions, and (c) interpret the findings in the light of the specific theory. If the need arises, the theory can reformulated. Indeed some important insights regarding organizations may be obtained when predictions based on a theory are rejected. The following points should be considered when developing a useful OB theory:

- A strong OB theory is interdisciplinary, combining both micro and macro levels of analysis (Rousseau, 1997). Daft and Lewin (1993) shared this view and maintained that the science of OB must develop and maintain inter-disciplinary research. They pointed out that environmental, technological, and economic changes create new organizational realities to which previous explanations may not be relevant. Thus, continuous theory construction is required if we are to better comprehend such realities.
- Collecting empirical data is critical for the evaluation of a specific theory's validity. A specific theory indicates what is supposed to be taking place, and empirical information demonstrates to what extent these relationships do in fact exist (Porter et al., 1975). According to Bacharach (1989), one of the critical criteria for evaluating theory building is *empirical adequacy:* "If a theory is operationalized in such a way as to preclude disconfirmation, then it is clearly not falsifiable" (p. 506). Therefore, for the measurement to be valid, it is essential that the instrument used be based on at least a tentative theoretical model guiding the development of the measurement scale (Bennett & Robinson, 2000). Yet without proper measurement, we cannot accept or reject a theoretical interpretation of the phenomenon.
- Premature adoption of a theory should be avoided (Spector, 2001). That is, a theory may be a useful tool; but to be a truly efficient one, it must be solid, and based on conceptual and empirical studies. These studies invariably supply the best raw materials for the construction of a theory. Daft (1980) maintained that one of the main problems of the models in the field is the dearth of adequate terminology. In his study of the complexity of organizational models and the lexis and language used to report the observations conducted in organizations, a low variance in the terminology was revealed, leading him to conclude that only simple, quantifiable relationships had been examined. He also pointed out the need for a greater variety and specificity of the terminology used for the definition of phenomena to enable researchers to analyze more complex organizational models. More variables should be incorporated in OB research to create more complex models. This change must be accompanied by a significant modification of the models, such as the conversion of static relationships into dynamic ones and the use of specific human attributes rather than general terminology.

Similarly, a solid theoretical base and sound empirical research are of critical importance for the development of the scholarly study of OMB. Although misbehaviors constitute an integral component of the variety of behaviors in the workplace, the science of OB lags behind with regard to the collection of empirical data and the development of a broad theoretical framework. Both are necessary to further the understanding of the phenomenon and to pave the way for future research and theory building. Bennett and Robinson (2000) convincingly drew our attention to the *conceptual confusion* we face when we use the terms *deviance, antisocial behavior*, and *aggression*. In addition and perhaps related to this confusion, the measurement of misbehavior is rather difficult (Slora, 1989). First, the commonly used instruments cannot adequately capture manifestations of invisible misbehavior, such as loafing or making negative impressions. Second, the measurement may not reflect the actual frequency of phenomena such as theft by employees (e.g., inventory shortages may be due to either to errors made purposely or theft). Third, determining the degree of employee theft by the number of employees caught stealing or by those who willingly admit stealing does not reflect the full extent of the phenomenon. It is always difficult to determine the ratio of those whose misbehavior remains unreported.

During the last decade, we witnessed a significant development in the knowledge about OMB—in both theoretical and empirical terms. A number of researchers have developed theoretical frameworks with different emphases. For example, Griffin et al. (1998b) proposed a process model for describing dysfunctional workplace behavior; Vardi and Wiener (1996) proposed a motivational approach to misbehavior using a deductive approach (building on previous theories and constructs); Robinson and Bennett (1995), using an inductive methodology, generated an influential typology of employee deviance; and Sackett and DeVore (2001) reviewed the emerging knowledge and developed a comprehensive framework for the understanding of counterproductive work behavior. Following their 1995 model, Bennett and Robinson (2000) developed a research instrument measuring OMB. They maintained that, despite the phenomenon's pervasiveness and cost, our current understanding of misbehaviors is still limited, and there is a need for extensive empirical research. Such research is possible only if a valid measure of deviance in the workplace is available. They provided an instrument of great importance for future studies in the field (this and other instruments are discussed later in this chapter).

On the empirical side, studies have attempted to assess OMB and account for the variance. We present a random sample: Greenberg (1990a) examined the relationship between employees' sense of having been treated unfairly and thefts in the workplace, Ashton (1998) related misconduct to personality traits, Biran (1999) studied the relationship between job autonomy and misbehavior, Kurland (1995) and Vardi and Weitz (2002c) used the model of reasoned action for the prediction of misbehaviors, Raelin (1994) examined the difference between deviant and adaptive behavior among professional, and Baron and Neuman (1996) studied aggressive behavior.

Descriptive Versus Prescriptive Studies

The second dilemma facing the researcher is whether to undertake a descriptive or prescriptive study. In reality, the relationship between description and prescription can be symbiotic (Porter et al., 1975). In fact both approaches are essential for an in-depth analysis of organizational life. Those who formulate prescriptions are in need of insights and information gleaned from descriptive studies (i.e., adequate descriptions that provide the basis for any prescription). OB researchers are greatly tempted to move from describing the phenomenon to prescribing to an organization what is best for it and its employees. We are often quick to assert how much better it would be "if the employee had more autonomy" or "if only supervisors were more considerate." Although it is usually quite easy to arrive at a consensus regarding how things should be, we believe ready-made prescriptions should be avoided. For instance, we found that both consideration and autonomy might actually increase the intention to misbehave (Vardi & Weitz, 2001, 2002b). When solid theoretical grounding is lacking, recommending interventions may be premature and, at times, risky. Moreover, even after conducting an empirical study that has applicable elements, recommendations based on such findings must be given with utmost caution and awareness of the limitations.

Our preference for a prescriptive approach stems from the congruence paradigm described in the beginning of the book: (a) on the subjective level—the model of psychological contract (Kotter, 1973). Kotter maintained that the manager has three objectives vis-à-vis the employee: attachment, satisfaction, and performance. These are attained by the management of OB if there is greater congruence between the expectations of both parties. Congruence leads to outcomes desirable for the organization. (b) On the job level—Hackman and Oldham (1976) argued that a well-designed job produces positive outcomes (i.e., motivation, satisfaction, and long-term employee commitment to his or her work and organization). The importance and understanding of the results and responsibility for them lead to the expected outcomes. (c) On the occupational level—Holland's (1985) model presents states of congruence between the occupational environment chosen by individuals and their personality traits. There are six basic personality types, and it is possible to match each one of them to a different occupational environment that is the most suitable and in which individuals can fulfill their potential and find satisfaction. (d) On the career level—Schein (1971) proposed that individuals and organization's are two entities with different sets of needs. The individual needs to develop and feel secure, whereas the organization has the need and resources to meet those needs. If an organizational career incorporates the individual and his or her needs and the organization and its needs, the results will be positive—development, success, and high morale. According to Schein, congruence between the two entities constitutes the ideal, desirable situation. (e) On the organizational level—Nadler and Tushman (1980) posited that the most successful organization is one that displays congruence among its organizational components; the greater the degree of congruence, the better the organization functions.

Models and conceptual frameworks such as these should raise several important questions with regard to the sole desirability of states of congruence: Are they indeed functional for the organization? Are states of incongruence necessarily dysfunctional for the organization? Will states of congruence necessarily lead to functional behavior? Researchers of OMB should assume that both *congruence* and *incongruence* may lead to proper behavior *and* misbehaviors. Think about how unchallenging a job that fits perfectly could be, and how creative employees can become when some friction and uncertainty exist on their job. Furthermore, before offering sweeping recommendations, we need to ascertain that misbehaviors we wish to control are indeed dysfunctional for the organization and its members.

Macro-level Versus Micro-level

The third dilemma facing researchers is whether to focus on the macro or micro levels (Porter et al., 1975). The macro-level of OB has its origins in sociology, political science, and economics; it deals with organizational structures, planning, and activity within the general social context. The microlevel has its origins in psychology and social psychology; and it deals with individuals and groups and how they affect and are affected by the organizational system (O'Reilly, 1991; Staw, 1984). Macro level researchers are interested in broad theories explaining the functioning of systems and the common alities and differences among organizations. They often use descriptive empirical studies and pay relatively little attention to practical implications and application. Micro-level studies mostly ascertain commonalities and differences among individuals and groups using survey and experimental methods for precise hypothesis testing (O'Reilly, 1991). In this book, we discussed antecedents of misbehavior and the distinguished between levels of conceptualization and measurement: organization at the macro-level and group, task, and individual at the micro-level. A similar classification of antecedents was proposed by Sackett and DeVore (2001) with regard to counterproductive behavior. We recommend that researchers of OMB utilize multilevel, interactive designs when data fitting such designs are available. This allows for better control of demographic background and organization setting characteristics in a multivariate analysis.

Structure Versus Process

The fourth dilemma facing researchers is whether to adopt structural or process perspectives. Structure comprises the type of arrangements among the various components of the organization and their relationships. Because formal organizations may be viewed as structured social systems, clearly their structure is man made and is not inherent in a certain set of circumstances; structures are a matter of choice and may therefore be changed. A study with emphasis on structure typically deals with the way the various components form part of a coherent framework and how they affect individual and group behavior. Emphasis on process aspects is found in studies focusing on dynamics and activities such as socialization, communication, leadership, and careers. From an analytical point of view, it is essential to emphasize structure as opposed to function. An approach combining the two generally provides the best explanation of OB.

Our research on organizational structures and their effects on misbehavior has dealt with questions concerning the relationship between employment status (temporary and permanent) and misbehavior (Galmor, 1996), the role of organizational climate (Vardi, 2001), and the influence of job autonomy on misbehavior (Vardi & Weitz, 2001). Using a macrohistorical perspective, DeVries and Vardi (2002) examined the bank-stocks regulation affair in Israel utilizing system and organizational levels of description and analysis. The system level of analysis dealt with the contribution of mechanisms and processes pertaining to the social, cultural, political, and economic environments. The organizational level examined the influence of structure and culture on the misconduct patterns of the bankers and managers involved. A process perspective on misbehavior can best be exemplified by Andersson and Pearson's (1999) work on incivility at work. They posited a spiraling effect of uncivil OB and maintained that, although an accidental expression of incivility may not strongly affect what goes on in the organization, a spiraling process may lead to significant manifestations of aggressiveness.

Formal Versus Informal

The fifth dilemma involves the decision of whether to focus on the formal or informal aspects of organizational life (Porter et al., 1975). Complex organizations involving people at work constitute structured social systems that are usually called formal organizations because they include specific and well-defined relationships and functions. However, any formal organizational system generates an informal system of behaviors and relationships that reflects the dynamics emerging as a result of the social and interpersonal interactions among members. Metaphorically, one can view the formal aspects of an organization such as size, form, and rules as the observable tip of an iceberg and the informal relationships, value systems, interactions, and dependencies as the voluminous unseen part below the water.

In the past, OB studies tended to focus on the formal organizational structure. They mostly dealt with ways the organizational structure can be made more efficient and rational. In the 1930s, researchers noted that focusing on the formal organizational structure is not the only means to explain OB or change it. The now famous Hawthorne studies were the first to incorporate the informal dimension into organizational research, including group influence, social status, informal communication, norms, and so on. Since then, there has been an increasing tendency to focus on the informal features of work life. OB researchers encounter a variety of structures, relationships, and actions requiring research that combines both formal and informal facets. OMB researchers should examine formal codes of ethics, rules and regulations, and management control systems, on the one hand, and the dynamics of behavior, such as social loafing, impression management, retaliation, or undermining, on the other hand. Eventually, we should be able to combine both perspectives to form more viable accounts of why individuals misbehave.

Objective Versus Subjective

The choice between a subjective and an objective observation is our sixth dilemma (Porter et al., 1975). Researchers go to great lengths to produce reliable and sound data that can be validated and expanded. Although to many science strives to be as objective as possible, this does not reduce the importance of subjectivity as a source of valid information. After all the OB of individuals stems, to a significant degree, from the subjective world from which it is formed by perceptions, intellect, values, predispositions, and attitudes. Our OMB perspective and research originated from the idea that misbehavior is internally motivated by both cognitive and affective subjective processes (Vardi & Weitz, 2002c). The so-called *real features* of the situation are not those that influence the specific behavior; it is the way we see, interpret, and are influenced by them that lead us to action. In fact this very gap between objective circumstances and individuals' perception of that reality is an important source of unexpected behaviors. Take, for example, the notion of *stress*. In many types of organizations (e.g., hi-tech, hospitals, and law firms), work, objectively speaking, is loaded with stressful elements. Yet individuals working under such conditions perceive them differently. For some these are considered challenges and opportunities (e.g., Type As and workaholics); for others they are a source of personal tedium, anguish, and strain that affects their personal well-being (e.g., burnout, and physical symptoms). To truly comprehend misbehavior, we need both phenomenological observations and hard objective data. Conclusions based on just one or the other are bound to lead to erroneous and lopsided conclusions.

Cognitive Versus Affective

The seventh dilemma is the choice between cognitive- and affective-focused research (Porter et al., 1975). Cognition relates to the individual's thought processes, such as decision and choice making, whereas affect refers to the individual's emotional world. People express both thought and emotion at work. For example, when things seem under control or have little direct effect on the individual, he or she might rely on cognitive, rational processes. Yet when the individual senses pressure or is directly affected by the events, he or she will have more affective reactions. Behavior is the result of cognition, affect, or both. Unquestionably, OMB researchers must account for both. We showed that OB literature presents promising cognitive and affective models that can be utilized in OMB research (e.g., see Fishbein & Ajzen, 1975, for a cognitive model; Weiss & Cropanzano, 1996, for an affective model). Certainly models that include both cognitive and affective variables will offer better explanations of misbehavior variance than either model separately.

Direct Versus Indirect

Our eighth research dilemma is the choice between direct and indirect measurement. The ideal way is to measure every form of misbehavior objectively, but this type of research necessitates the existence of visible, easily measurable behaviors, such as absences, as opposed to a variety of concealed behaviors that employees (and management) may not wish to reveal, such as theft and sexual harassment. Basically, the instruments at our disposal are either direct, such as self-reports, or indirect, such as reports about others. There are difficulties in interpreting both direct and indirect reports. For example, the data in self-reports may be biased due to the effect of social desirability, and ranking by superiors may be affected by the halo effect. Both of these problems are discussed in detail later; here we merely point out that these strategies are not ideal.

Although there is evidence supporting the validity of self-reports in general, and although they provide accurate assessments of deviant behavior in particular, this method has limitations. First respondents tend to create a more positive impression of themselves, possibly distorting the results. However, a meta-analytical study by Ones, Viswesvaran, and Schmidt (1993) showed that self-reports provide more valid results than external measures of deviance. They explained this by the fact that many deviant behaviors are concealed; therefore, external measurement is ineffective. Second, there is significant evidence that the correlation between admission of the misbehavior and the actual behavior is high. Therefore, researchers believe that self-reports can serve as a valid instrument for the assessment of a great variety of misbehaviors in the workplace, especially when the respondents' anonymity is ensured. Slora (1989) designed a study to determine the rate of employee deviance based on Hollinger and Clark's (1983) typology and concluded that the use of anonymous surveys may be efficient in determining the base rate of deviance. The high response rate to the surveys and frequency of admitting misbehavior revealed that employees are willing to report their own deviant actions.

Similarly, Fox and Spector (1999) argued that if the research objective is to understand what employees feel and perceive, and how they respond, the method of self-reports may be effective. This conclusion stems from the difficulty in obtaining solid and objective data on criteria such as delinquent behavior, theft, and damaging organization's property while the respondents are employed by the organization (Hogan & Hogan, 1989).

Despite the advantages of self-reports, most researchers emphasize their limitations. Lee (1993) pointed out that this method leads to incomplete data . The respondents' tendency to report less misbehavior than that which actually occur's may stem from their fear of being discovered and may result from social desirability. Distorted responses may also result from research reports of false relationships among variables (Zerbe & Paulhus, 1987). This may have a significant effect on research because incomplete reports may reduce the range of the variable and weaken the correlation of the relationship examined. According to Lehman and Simpson (1992), these shortcomings of self-reports questionnaires. may have a detrimental effect on the reliability of the information obtained.

The second strategy aimed at determining the level OMB relies on information obtained from relevant others in the organization, those responsible for the work, or co-workers. Utilizing an indirect strategy, Hunt (1996) conducted a large scale study and obtained data for over 18,000 employees in 36 firms. From those, 5 types of misbehaviors were effectively derived: absence, misbehavior while on task (unauthorized breaks, and conducting personal affairs during work hours), unruly behavior, theft, and substance abuse. Thus—projective questionnaires, ones that ask about others' behavior—may reduce the lack of reliability typical of direct reports, particularly when dealing with unconventional organizational behavior (see OMB questionnaire in Appendix 1). Social projection (Allport, 1924) denotes the projection of individuals' personal attitudes onto others around them. This method is based on the (somewhat naive) assumption that others feel or respond the same way as we do. Ross, Greene, and House (1977) maintained that individuals tend to (a) be affected in their thinking by false consensus, (b) perceive their own judgment and behavior as common to everyone, and therefore (c) reject alternative answers that may seem atypical. People tend to deem their own behavior as acceptable and widespread, otherwise it would be deviant. We used both direct and projective questionnaires to obtain data on OMB (Vardi & Weitz, 2001, 2002a, 2002b, 2002c). As a rule the measures are intercorrelated, because the average correlation in four different studies was 0.35, it is methodologically justified to employ different methods.

Quantitative Versus Qualitative Research

The final dilemma concerns the choice between qualitative and quantitative methods. Quantitative measurement is the assignment of numbers to qualities or properties of people, objects, or events based on a given set of rules (Stevens, 1968). Spector (2001) posited that the field of I/O psychology tends to be a statistical science (i.e., the type of data gathered makes possible the use of statistical methods). When hundreds and sometimes thousands of observations take place, there is a need for a variety of statistical methods and tests to draw sensible conclusions (e.g., Hollinger & Clark, 1982). These tests make it possible to determine whether variables are related and, in some cases (e.g., a strong theoretical basis and a longitudinal design) infer causality.

There is a multitude of statistical tests (e.g., Kanji, 1999), but only a few are commonly used in the OB field. As in other scientific disciplines, at times tests are misused. Frequently, a particular statistical method becomes fashionable and is used because it increases the prospect of the study's publication, rather than being chosen as a result of a careful examination of its appropriateness as the best tool to provide answers to the research question. Moreover, there is a tendency toward excessive reliance on the analysis of complex data as a means to overcome a weak research design, which sometimes leads to erroneous interpretations of complex statistical findings, whereas the use of a simple approach would provide a clear answer to the research question. The statistical methods commonly used in the OB field include correlational analysis, multiple regression, various analyses of variance, and factor analysis (see Aguinis et al., 2001).

Van Maanen (1979) argued that qualitative research is more suitable than quantitative for the description and analysis of social processes, whereas the quantitative approach is more appropriate for the analysis of a situation and social structures. The qualitative approach is better able to analyze a complex event. He maintained that the quantification of measures and analysis of the relationships between variables may shed light on only a small part of the overall picture because the picture is greater than the sum of the elements composing it. Social relationships have deep underlying structures, which may elude research using the analytical method.

Qualitative research methods include use of participant observation, nonparticipant observation, interviews, and archival research (Analoui & Kakabadse, 1992). Qualitative measurement has also been applied for the observation of OMB. Dabney and Hollinger (1999) used interviews in a study on pharmacists, illegal use of drugs. The data were collected by means of interviews with 50 pharmacists recovering from the misuse of drugs. The information was recorded, and a thematic analysis was carried out. Results reveal that the face-to-face interviews, planned to examine the personal histories of a random sample of pharmacists, provide firsthand information about the attitudes and behaviors of pharmacists using drugs. Yanai (1998) investigated sexual harassment in the workplace by means of in-depth interviews with 18 working women. She obtained rich information about intimate experiences, feelings, personal interpretations, and retrospective rationalizations.

Another method used in qualitative research is unobtrusive observations of individuals going about their normal practice. Typically, one or more observers are instructed on how and what to look for in the workplace setting, or the observations may be completely unstructured (Ailon-Souday, 2001). An alternative method is participative observation—facilitating the documentation of behavior in the most natural setting possible (Analoui & Kakabadse, 1992). Although ethnographic methods are used more in anthropological research, this method can also be used in OB research to assess employees' behavior without the observer's presence affecting the subjects' behavior (see Kunda, 1992). Because of ethical considerations and the need to safeguard the rights of the individual employees, the use of this method is mostly limited to behavior in public research sites.

When the researcher's goal is to examine the underlying processes leading to sensitive and controversial misbehavior, the participative–observation approach offers appropriate tools and techniques that may yield explanatory insights. Using such methods, whether overtly or under cover, has the potential to generate rich, firsthand impressions. Analoui and Kakabadse (1992) implemented a qualitative, long-term research design using direct observations in a particular service organization. They emphasized the great importance of choosing the method and instruments of data collection. They posited that subtle forms of unconventional behavior, such as when subordinates are dishonest with their supervisior, cannot be studied the same way as behaviors such as unauthorized strikes and absences. The dilemma is this: Any attempt to question the participants or ask them to describe and explain their motives by means of common research methods, such as questionnaires and structured interviews, will actually call for less than honest replies. The simple labeling of certain behaviors as *unconventional* or *deviant* would make sharing innermost thoughts with an outsider undesirable. Therefore, Analoui and Kakabadse, opted for participative observation, one of the researchers spent about 6 years posing as a regular employee while taking notes about incidents in which he judged some misconduct was involved. This procedure enabled them to overcome problems of physical access to information with no disruptions in the work environment. The collected data—about rank-and-file as well as supervisory personnel—were then carefully analyzed, and theories to explain them were proposed.

Historical archival research is another type of qualitative, unobtrusive study. Historical analysis is clearly an important method of investigation of organizational misconduct at both the individual and organizational levels (DeVries & Vardi, 2002). In such studies, questions on past phenomena are answered by means-selected facts and organized in explanatory patterns that emerge from the data. Obviously a historical perspective attempts to view the past through the eyes and representations of those who lived and acted at the time. Thus, it depends on the quality and extent of evidence left behind. One advantage of a historical investigation lies in the ability of the social scientist to anchor the observations in a larger picture—the social, cultural, and economic conditions prevailing at the time. Another advantage lies in the possibility of examining and analyzing behavioral processes and phenomena without relying on the faulty memory of subjects or their tendency to tell what they want you to know.

Unquestionably, the conclusions drawn from the qualitative material collected by means of interviews, observations, historical records, and case studies depend on how well they are analyzed. Content analysis is a technique aimed at drawing inferences by means of systematic and objective identification of defined attributes and messages embedded in written material (Holsty, 1968). Berelson (1971) defined *content analysis* as a research method aimed at describing objectively, systematically, and quantitatively the contents of communications. The objectivity emphasized in both definitions relates to analysis carried out on the basis of explicit rules, enabling, in principle, other researchers to replicate the analysis. Content analysis enables us to logically interpret large volumes of data derived from archival records and documents, letters, diaries, newspaper articles, protocols of meetings, and so on. Although tedious, such effort often yields fascinating depictions of intricate relationships and trends. These qualitative methods were recently employed by Sukenik (2001) to learn about airline pilots' safety culture and by Turgeman Goldschmidt (2001) to delve into the world of computer hacking.

In summary we propose that OMB researchers consider the following. First, due to the sensitive nature of OMB, the unwillingness of management to let academicians research the phenomenon, and the reluctance of employees to divulge information regarding it, we recommend the use of both direct and indirect measurement methods. Integrating both methods within one study is frequently invaluable—it contributes to both construct validity and reliability of the data. Second, one of the most effective methods for the study of OMB is the implementation of qualitative research by means of systematic observations. Participative observation is efficient because it reveals behaviors people usually prefer not to report. Being just another member of the organization, the researcher has a far better chance to identify manifestations of misbehavior without encountering apprehension or attempts to conceal or distort them. Third, experimental research designs and longitudinal studies may reveal causal relationships. The more commonly used non-experimental, cross-sectional research designs, although providing higher external validity, usually lack internal validity, tend to produce limited variance data, and do not allow for straightforward tests of causality.

PROBLEMS AFFECTING THE MEASUREMENT OF OMB

The difficulties in measuring OMB may be roughly classified from the most general to very specific problems. The most general problems are related to the macrolevel of measurement, including difficulties stemming from cross-cultural data, effects of the measurement technology and the measurement of low base rates, and limited variance behaviors. Specific microlevel problems pertain to the respondents and include issues of social desirability, impression management, halo effect, and cognitive dissonance. In this section, we discuss microlevel problems first and follow with macrolevel problems.

Social Desirability

Social desirability is defined as respondents' tendency to wish to appear in a favorable light, whatever their feelings, opinions, or behaviors may be in a particular context (Crowne & Marlowe, 1960). To be perceived in a positive way, subjects tend to reply in a way they assume is preferred by the researcher even if their answers may not reflect their real opinions. Thus, correlations resulting from self-report questionnaires may be exaggerated and should be interpreted with coution.

The contaminating effects of questionnaire answers in the OB field are evident in the work of Golembiewski and Munzenrider (1975). They were especially concerned with the influence of social desirability because high grades on the scale measuring social reliability suggest that respondents faked their answers to appear in a favorable light. Any such distortion of the answers may lead to the appearance of a false, nonexistent relationship between variables (Zerbe & Paulhus, 1987) or the omission of sensitive behaviors, attitudes, or feelings untapped by the range of actual answers. Lehman and Simpson (1992) strongly argued that these limitations raise doubts as to the reliability of information obtained by means of self-report questionnaires. Moorman and Podaskoff (1992) examined how social desirability had been researched in the OB field, and how it had affected the research results based on the collection of data by means of self-reports. By use of meta-analysis, they analyzed 33 studies that examined the relationships between patterns of social desirability responses and OB variables. They found social desirability to be significantly related to commonly used variables such as locus of control, overall job satisfaction, role conflict, role ambiguity, and organizational commitment.

Social desirability creates methodological difficulties when attempting to expose misbehaviors, as evidenced in empirical studies. Our survey reveals that almost all OMB research focused on the less severe aspects of misbehavior. Most of the relationships found dealt with relatively minor behaviors such as faking illness, arriving late and leaving early, attending to personal matters at work, and so on. When it comes to more serious misbehaviors (e.g., interpersonal aggressiveness, verbal abuse, and sexual harassment), the range of the variables examined is often limited, precluding it from rigorous statistical analysis. We may certainly attribute some of this restriction of variance and data skewness to the effects of social desirability.

Impression Management

This concept is commonly defined as any behavior designed to reinforce a person's image in the eyes of another with the intention of attaining personally valuable goals (Villanova & Bernardin, 1989). Zerbe and Paulhus (1987) viewed impression management as a subcategory of social desirability responses. Such behavior is geared toward the control of the perceptions of others regarding one's behavior, both in a positive and negative way (Becker & Martin, 1995; Wayne & Kacmar, 1991). Because individuals in an organization are naturally reluctant to admit to having participated in OMB due to its often sensitive nature and the fear of being branded as deviants, they may choose to create a positive impression, averting the need to divulge true behaviors. However, as suggested, impression management may not be necessarily due to a desire to please the researchers or interested party (Zerbe & Paulhus 1987). For different reasons, employees may, want to make bad impressions as well. For instance, they may want to avoid extra responsibility, be left alone, withdraw into more passive positions, and so on (Becker & Martin, 1995). It stands to reason that such tendencies may also be reflected in research surveys especially when subjects suspect research results will be reported to superiors on whom they wish to make a bad impression.

Halo Effect

This bias is defined as the tendency of a general impression of a person to affect the way specific traits are evaluated (Greenberg & Baron, 1997). A positive impression leads to the appraisal of additional positive traits, and a negative impression results in the assessment of additional negative traits. The underlying assumption is that individuals construct a specific image of one's personality on the basis of a presumed relationship between traits. Thus, if a person is perceived as diligent, he or she is also considered thorough and meticulous and is perceived as one who invests a good deal of effort in carrying out work-related tasks even if there are no compelling reasons to make such attributions. Halo effect most certainly impacts the measurement of reported OMB, especially when the scales are based on reports about others (coworkers, subordinates, or superiors). For example, when superiors evaluate and report the work performance of subordinates whom they consider efficient, this initial opinion will deter their attribution of misbehaviors to these subordinates. Conversely, we found that managers tend to report higher levels of OMB about subordinates who also had lower levels of organizational commitment and job satisfaction. We interpreted this finding as a possible result of the influence of negative halo effect on managers' assessments.

Cognitive Dissonance

Almost 50 years ago, Festinger (1957) defined *cognitive dissonance* as the state in which two conflicting positions are simultaneously held by an individual. Apparently holding contradictory cognitions causes some psychological tension and discomfort. The individual naturally seeks to reduce this uneasiness and resolve the dissonance. For example, the sense of dissonance leads the person to justify behaviors devoid of any obvious logical basis and to find reasons reinforcing choices made in the past (known as *postdecision dissonance*). Hence, once an individual has chosen to behave in a certain way, he or she will seek to justify and endorse the decision. If the decision appears justified, a state of dissonance will not ensue; if the justification does not appear satisfactory, a feeling of dissonance will develop and the person will attempt to reduce it. Therefore, when observing OMB, we should take into consideration the respondents' tendency to reduce the feeling of cognitive dissonance if it exists. Because OMB is intentional and involves the violation of acceptable norms, it is quite natural for individuals engaging in such conduct to experience dissonance. To cope with dissonance, they may rationalize their choice, deny it, or use neutralizing tactics (Sykes & Matza, 1957).

Impression management may be considered to be a specific behavioral manifestation of dealing with cognitive dissonance (Tedeschi et al., 1971). That is, instead of perceiving cognitive dissonance as the result of two conflicting positions held by one individual, we may consider an individual's two conflicting behaviors as the unit of analysis. Tedeschi et al. maintained that the reduction of the feeling of dissonance is actually connected to the person's attempt to create a consistent impression in relating to significant others. That is, the person's desire is to appear trustworthy, which is valued socially. When people behave in a harmful way inconsistent with their previous behaviors, they find it difficult to explain it rationally without detracting from their trustworthiness. Therefore, they may justify these behaviors as stemming from emotions not under their control. In general terms, OB researchers need to be aware of such situations; otherwise they will not be in a position to draw realistic conclusions about the respondents' genuine beliefs. We believe this caveat is especially relevant in the study of sensitive issues such the ones explored throughout this book. We now to some macrolevel research problems.

Low Base Rate Behaviors

Although OMB is a widespread and costly phenomenon, researchers need to be aware that they deal with what is known as *low base rate behaviors*. In relative terms, OMB (like its counterpart organizational citizenship behavior (OCB)) is still the exception, not the rule, in our everyday work-life experience. Although serious misbehaviors such as sabotage or sexual harassment do occur, at any given time in any given sample they may be relatively infrequent, and therefore not every respondent may be in a position to provide the information required. As Roznowski and Hulin (1992) argued, the problem in the study of low base rate behaviors is particularly evident when we research an isolated behavioral manifestation of a widespread phenomenon (e.g., theft). The low base rate of an isolated binary variable creates an abnormal distribution, and therefore relating to such distributions as if they were normal is problematic. An attempt to turn a distribution into a normal one by collecting data over a longer period of time or generalizing individual rating to the group level may be only partially successful at best.

To cope with the problem of low base rate behaviors, a wide conceptual framework should be developed encompassing clusters of misbehaviors (Roznowski & Hulin, 1992). However, Robinson and Greenberg (1998) maintained that one of the improper ways to cope with this phenomenon is to create a wide and sometimes unsuitable conceptual framework encompassing a number of deviant behaviors, thereby raising their overall rate. This method replaces one problem with another—an unreliable measurement with a more fundamental problem, the degree of construct validity. We do know from our own research that dealing honestly and ethically with the concerns of management and guaranteeing strict anonymity and confidentiality usually improves the chances of gaining access, obtaining truthful answers, and receiving reports of sensitive attitudes and behaviors.

Measurement in Different Cultural Settings

Such measurement involves two main problems. First, due to rapid globalization and the creation of a world economy, there is a growing interest in extending the research base from a limited number of English-speaking countries to other parts of the world (Spector, 2001). Second, as the scope of research widens to include many nations and cultures, the problem of transfering research instruments from one culture to another (and the comparisons among cultures) becomes more acute (Aguinis et al., 2001; Riordan & Vandenberg, 1994). Cultural differences raise the issue of the actual components of deviant behavior: employees' behaviors breaching multinational norms, or organizational norms breaching those prevalent in specific societies in which they operate (Bamberger & Sonnenstuhl, 1998).

The main methodological problem, of course, is the transfer of measures from one culture to another without first adjusting them to suit existing cultural differences. Many researchers have wondered whether what has been developed and learned within the framework of one culture may be used effectively in another (Hofstede, 1993). Consider what may happen to the validity and reliability of measures of aggressive behavior originally developed in the United States in English when employeded in countries where English is not the native language (Spector, 2001). It is necessary to determine to what extent an instrument developed in one culture is valid in another, before applying it, to ensure that the conclusions drawn from it are indeed valid. This may necessitate extra steps such as the provision of additional explanations and instructions, adequate presentation of the items, and training programs for supervisors and local representatives (Aguinis et al., 2001).

The first step in transferring instruments to other cultures is to translate them to the target language and then translate them back into the source language to asses the identity of the significance of the wording. This common method of *retranslation* can ensure that the two versions of the instrument are well matched (Spector, 2001). Considering that many words in one language have additional meanings and connotations—different from those intended in the original—meaning one person translates the instrument into the target language and another, who has not seen the source, translates it back. The second version of the instrument is compared with the original one, and any mismatch is discussed and dealt with promptly. The discrepancies between the two versions may be removed by a reformulation of the item in the target language and reexamination of the match. This process, as thorough as it may be, does not ensure that the transfer of an instrument to another culture will be completely valid. Yet such systematic steps may increase its validity.

Computerized Measurement

Improvements due to technological advances greatly affect research measurement. Interactive computerized employee assessment programs signal the transition from static methods of measurement to dynamic methods adaptive to respondents' abilities (Bartram, 1994). Moreover, computers and the Internet provide new methods to assess personal attributes, the data banks may be available online, and scoring and ranking may be done immediately. Despite the cost of the technology, the advantages of computerized measurement are likely to compensate for the initial capital outlay. Computers facilitate data management and offer speedy data collection, analysis, and the efficient storage of results. They also reduce errors and eliminate unnecessary duplication. However, we should be aware of the downside of computerized assessment. First, it makes the data collection devoid of the human touch. Although this may be effective in other disciplines, the measurement of human behavior requires the involvement and judgment of experts. Second, as discussed, there are new-age problems emanating from the availability of data on the Internet. If research data are compromised, human rights—privacy and protection—may be violated.

The measurement of OMB can also be done via the Internet. It is probably cheaper and less time-consuming compared with conventional methods (Schmidt, 1997). The measures can be sent to the target population by e-mail, or the questionnaire may be presented on a special Web site. Access to the instrument may be open or controlled electronically. Despite the advantages of using the computer for measurement, the inherent disadvantages should not be ignored. A major shortcoming lies of the difficulty of obtaining a representative sample. For instance, the Internet may attract more men, young professionals, or more computer savvy respondents (Aguinis et al., 2001). Although a computerized measurement instrument may facilitate a speedy and more efficient collection of information, it may also alter the significance of the results. Respondents' responses may be rated differently than the conventional method because a different format is used. Mazzeo and Harvey (1988) claimed that the differences may stem from the differential speed of the measurement, the graphics, and so on. Moreover, because of the seeming anonymity, it appears that respondents using the computerized version have a tendency to present themselves in a more positive light (Aguinis et al., 2001).

In conclusion, despite the advantages of computerized measurement, techno- logical advances leave several issues open. First, measures transferred from written assessment to the computer may not be identical and may not measure the same factors. Second, measurement via the Internet may yield an unrepresentative sam- ple. Third, although computers and the Internet are more readily available today and more people make use of them, they are more prevalent is some countries and cultures than in others. Computerized assessment may overlook certain popula- tions and increase anxiety among those not well versed in the medium. Fourth, because of the relative ease of computerized measurement, there is a tendency to measure anything and everything. The American Psychological Association (APA, 1996) issued a report recommending that the research questions be framed care- fully and the data collection be limited to what is absolutely necessary. The APA also recommended that the analyses obtained via sophisticated computer software be carefully monitored and checked.

HOW TO MEASURE OMB

To measure OMB, it is first necessary to define precisely what it is we wish to measure. Appendixes 2 and 3 enumerate the variety of behaviors and various definitions the literature provides. Although this wealth of information might be a discouraging factor to some, we prefer to look at its positive aspect—many more options may become available as we search and explore. Whatever method we choose in view of the dilemmas presented earlier—whether a theoretical or an empirical study, qualitative or quantitative research, direct or indirect reports— we must take into account the problems existing on the micro and macro-levels because these determine our choice of instrument. The final choice of definition will have a critical and decisive effect on the selection of the instrument to be used, the items to be included, and the way the results are interpreted. Furthermore, when using self-report scales to elicit evidence of personal misbehavior, we have to include a measure of social desirability to partial out its influence on the way respondents report their behavior.

Now that we have presented the dilemmas associated with measuring OMB, we demonstrate that sound and rigorous research is possible. First, it is necessary to properly define what it is we wish to measure. Second, we need to search for instruments designed to measure it. The chosen scale must serve the defined re- search question and encompass the various behaviors we wish to tap. For example, consider the measures of production and property-oriented misbehavior.

The first instrument we may consider is Hollinger and Clark's (1982) scale of workplace deviance. It includes a list of misbehaviors that are divided them into two categories: property deviance, including damage to tangible property or the organization's assets; and production deviance, including breach of the norms set for the performance of the work, detrimental to the quality and the quantity of the output. Its empirical advantage is twofold. First, it distinguishes property deviance items from production deviance items. Second, it allows for sector differences (retail, manufacturing, and hospitals). Property deviance includes such items as misusing discount privileges, damaging merchandise, taking store merchandise (retail); taking precious metals, taking raw material, taking finished products (manufacturing); taking hospital supplies, and taking or using medications (hospitals). Production deviance consists of items such as taking long lunch or coffee breaks, being under the influence of alcohol or drugs, and taking unjustified sick time.

Bennett and Robinson (2000) developed an instrument for measuring workplace deviance. They described in detail the theoretical basis for the instrument and the specific steps they took in deriving the items from different groups, the item-selection processes, and the construct validity study they conducted to test the instrument's theoretical rigor. Based on Vardi and Wiener (1992) and on their previous work (Robinson & Bennett, 1995), they defined *workplace deviance* "as voluntary behavior that violates significant organizational norms and, in so doing, threatens the well-being of the organization or its members, or both" (p. 349). They proposed that workplace deviance can be captured by two general variables: interpersonal and organizational, each ranging from very minor to severe deviance.

Factor analyzing a pool of 28 items generated from the different studies yielded, as expected, two meaningful factors (interpersonal and organizational deviant behavior). To demonstrate the convergence validity of the scale, measures conceptually similar to these dimensions were correlated with them. As hypothesized, organizational deviance was more strongly related to both production and property than to interpersonal deviance (e.g., for Hollinger & Clark's, 1982, production deviance measure and interpersonal deviance, $r = .39$, $p < .01$; for production deviance and organizational deviance, $r = .70$, $p < .01$). Similar correlations were established between the deviance scores and Lehman and Simpson's (1992) measures of physical withdrawal, psychological withdrawal, and antagonistic work behavior. Both interpersonal and organizational deviant behaviors were negatively related to conscientiousness and justice measures (see the discussion in chap. 6).

Other ways to measure misbehaviors were developed. Griffin et al. (1998a, 1998b) mapped various dysfunctional organizational behaviors. They maintained that the mapping of behaviors is important to place them on the research agenda. The scale they proposed distinguishes between behaviors detrimental to the well-being of the self and those harming the organization. Moreover, they emphasized the importance of measuring outcome variables. They distinguished between outcome variables resulting in a specific cost (absences, theft, and sabotage) and those with general consequences (impression management and political behavior). They maintained that research is more productive if it is not limited to variables such as satisfaction, but can be widened to include a wide range of functional and dysfunctional behaviors.

Skarlicki and Folger (1997) developed an instrument to measure organizational retaliatory behaviors; they maintained that such behavior increases in response to injustice and unfairness. They treated misbehavior as a reaction to critical events; they did not perceive deviant behavior as an inherent personality trait of individuals. The items pertain to various OMB manifestations, such as damaging equipment, wasting company materials, disobedience, making a bad impression at work, gossiping, spreading rumors, giving the "silent treatment", and working slow.

We therefore recommend the following:

- When measuring misbehaviors as an overall phenomenon, a comprehensive instrument should be used to measure a variety of (mis)behaviors defined by the researcher.
- To ensure efficient measurement of OMB, a combination of methods should be used. Triangulating questionnaire data with observations, interviews, and organizational documentation is recommended.
- When using an instrument originally formulated in a different language, an accurate translation that is faithful to the origin and culturally relevant is necessary for both validation and comparison.

Whether we chose to measure OMB as an overall phenomenon or a specific cluster of misbehavior, it is crucial to ensure that the instrument is appropriate for the population under study. Some of the items may not be relevant, and other items may have to be added to obtain a more comprehensive view of the target behaviors. Thus, when Runcie (1988) examined a series of behaviors of production line workers, he found manifestations of misbehavior such as workers' exchanging tasks without permission or one person taking on two tasks to enable a coworker to rest. These are rule-breaking behaviors and may be considered deviant. However, the researcher found that the employees and their supervisors viewed these behaviors as acceptable means of coping with routine and tedious assembly line jobs, thereby indirectly contributing to organizational effectiveness. Therefore, Runcie defined behavior as deviant only when it was actually considered harmful to other workers or actual production.

We therefore recommend the following:

- When studying misbehavior, an extensive pretest must first be conducted to identify the misbehaviors specific to the research population. A pretest is also necessary even when the instrument appears to be a perfect fit. This facilitates and ensures the construction of an appropriate instrument that is intelligible and relevant to the research population.

We have already dealt with the question of direct as opposed to indirect measurement of misbehavior. Direct measurement is carried out by means of self-report questionnaires whereas in indirect measurement we are looking for the respondents to project onto others what they would rather not report on themselves. Although researchers prefer to measure misbehaviors at the source, they should remember that self-report is typically incomplete because of a natural reluctance to admit to participation in such behavior. Cohen (1999) examined the relationship between types of commitment to the job and misbehavior, using both self-report and reports about others. She stressed that reporting about others is meant to increase the reliability of the measurement, because self-report may distort the data because of social desirability. In fact one of her research hypotheses was that there would be differences between misbehavior scores obtained via self-reports and those obtained from reports about others. She found that Other OMB means were significantly higher than Self-OMB. She also found the two measures to be positively correlated.

We therefore recommend the following:

To ensure efficient and comprehensive measurement of OMB, it is advisable to include direct (self-) and indirect (projective) techniques. This helps respondents overcome inhibitions and reluctance to report about behaviors they may initially prefer to keep to themselves.

Direct and indirect reports provide a partial solution to the problem of social desirability. To examine whether social desirability is a determining factor and how far it affects direct reports, a scale that measures social desirability should be included. Lichtenstein (2000) studied the effect of envy and jealousy at work on self-reported OMB. Because both variables pertain to sensitive issues, she included an instrument measuring social desirability. The assumption was that the greater the respondent's tendency toward social desirability, the lower the level of misbehavior divulged by means of self-report questionnaires. As hypothesized, she found a significant positive correlation between envy and OMB with social desirability partialled out. This finding underscores the importance of controlling for this variable in the assessment of sensitive behaviors, attitudes, and affects.

A survey of the literature by Moorman and Podaskoff (1992) shows that over 90% of the studies that included a measure of social desirability in the research design used the Crowne and Marlowe (1960) instrument. However, this measure is not without its limitations. Zerbe and Paulhus (1987) cautioned that it is problematic not only because of respondents' tendency toward impression management, but also their propensity for self-deception (an unconscious proneness to see oneself in a positive light). Because of such problems, correlations found in many studies do not conclusively reflect the degree to which social desirability really affects the results.

We therefore recommend the following:

Measurement by means of direct reports of misbehaviors should include a valid and reliable instrument measuring social reliability.

Mainstream OB researchers tend to assume that misbehavior is the opposite of good citizenship behavior. Whereas good citizenship is assumed to increase the efficiency of the organization, misbehavior is deemed harmful. Thus, some studies used reversed items of OCB to measure OMB. In fact Bateman and Organ's (1983) measure of OCB includes such items as acts impulsively, on the spur of the moment, tries to look busy when doing nothing, and purposefully interferes with someone else doing their job. Similarly, does a person not exhibiting good citizenship behaviors necessarily misbehave? We suspect that the assumption that OCB and OMB are similar is false. We posit that the two are separate phenomena independent of each other. An employee can exhibit positive extrarole behaviors and also engage in some misbehavior. Thus, we should deem OMB and OCB as independent variables. Sackett and DeVore (2001) supported this contention in their discussion about the relationship between prosocial (OCB) and counterproductive work behavior (OMB). We can think of many examples of highly esteemed employees who, besides being highly motivated and involved, participate to a considerable extent in various counterproductive activities.

We therefore recommend the following:

Using both OMB and OCB scales increases our understanding of the full extent of work-related behavior. An individual may be involved in both types of behavior.

The use of both scales to measure behaviors by reverse grading may impair the data and conclusions drawn from them.

Our own research and the extensive review of other studies enhanced our initial thinking that the dark side of any organization is indeed fascinating and in need of further exploration. The search has only begun, and this book and others like it may serve as stepping stones toward this scientific journey. That said, we are also convinced that this knowledge may have practical as well as intellectual value. As we become more aware of the antecedents and manifestations of OMB and of how they relate under different circumstances, we are in a position to think about strategies for managing these behaviors better. Our next and concluding chapter develops a comprehensive framework for the management of OMB.

11

A Model of OMB
Management

In recent years, the study of OMB has emerged as an important field of inquiry within OB. Yet based on our experience and numerous discussions with practitioners, it remains an uncharted territory for most managers. Hence, this chapter has two main goals: to propose a general integrative framework for the management of OMB and to draw managers' attention to the phenomenon, its social consequences, and steep financial costs. The model we present deals with the key question of why employees misbehave: It describes the varied processes, at different levels, that lead employees to engage in different kinds of OMB and suggests guidelines for OMB management.

Recall that we define organizational misbehavior as any intentional action by members of organizations that defies and violates the shared organizational norms and expectations and/or core societal values, mores, and standards of proper conduct. It is a motivational process in which the intention to misbehave mediates the relationship between its antecedents and expressions. The intention to misbehave and the decision as to which form of misbehavior one will engaged in is assumed to be influenced by two independent, yet possibly intertwined, forces: an instrumental force reflecting beliefs about personal interests, and a normative force reflecting internalized organizational expectations. These two forces are a function of one or more antecedents acting collectively or separately at varied organizational levels: individual, task/position, group, and organization. In other words, OMB comes with a hefty price tag (financial, social, or both), and these costs determine, to a large extent, the type, timing, and scope of the intervention to be used by management.

The integrative model of OMB posits four key points of intervention along the OMB process through which the organization may act to lower the probability of OMB occurring (thus minimizing costs and other negative consequences). These four action levers differ with respect to their focus and, hence, call for different kinds of interventions. One important implication derived from this perspective is that we should think of OMB management not as a linear, but as an iterative process (i.e., dynamic, repetitive, and ongoing). Furthermore, the organization may apply a preventive strategy or responsive strategy (react to identifiable OMB). The key issue is to what extent the intervention succeeds in lowering the level and frequency of the misbehavior. In other words, do the interventions succeed in altering the behavioral patterns of its target population so that the frequency and severity of OMB are decreased? (see Figure 11.1)

To cope with OMB, one must be familiar with the dynamics of this phenomenon. That is, management needs to understand why employees intend to misbehave (i.e., be aware of different processes, in varied levels and settings, that lead certain individuals to engage in specific forms of OMB). Management should also be aware of the forces that influence (increase or decrease) the intention to misbehave, and what possible expressions and costs are to be expected. However, keep in mind that there are possible beneficial as well as adverse consequences of the intervention(s) designed to control these behaviors.

We do not intend to provide the reader with a complete one-size-fits-all remedy to OMB. This is primarily because, as is demonstrated later, such a panacea is beyond our reach. After all, work organizations have different goals, values, culture, rules, norms, and design, as well as control systems and the built-in opportunities to misbehave. Similarly, employees have different personality traits, personal needs, attitudes, intentions, and desires. Thus, the varieties of possible forms of misbehavior, as well as the ways to confront them, make it impossible to encompass the whole range of probable antecedents and expressions of OMB and to develop and implement a generic solution. Rather, we offer some assistance for the decision makers and organization development practitioners in their attempt to cope with the problem, and we present the reader with a guideline for dealing with the relevant issues and devising proper alternatives for action. A word of caution: Interventions designed to prevent OMB may have an adverse impact on the level of OMB if not designed and implemented carefully and sensitively.

TOWARD OMB MANAGEMENT:
PREVENTION VERSUS RESPONSE

Researchers debate whether organizations should focus its efforts on preventive activities (e.g., use selection procedures to screen potential troublemakers, and design the job a priori so it does not allow autonomy-related misbehavior) or responsive activities (e.g., termination of employees caught stealing). Several models (e.g., Neuman & Baron, 1997; O'Leary-Kelly et al., 1996; Trevino, 1986; Vardi & Wiener, 1996) pointed to the relationship between personality traits and OMB, suggesting that thorough selection scanning procedures to address these characteristics prior to actual hiring (i.e., applying selection as a prevention strategy) may help reduce the possibility of OMB occurring. Denenberg and Braverman (1999) argued that trying to identify the cause of violence (and, for that matter, any form of OMB) makes less practical sense than examining the organization's capacity to respond to the signs of stress or potential danger, whatever their origin. Prevention, they argued, lies in recognizing the need for a prompt and effective response as soon as early signs (e.g., distress) appear. Hence, a more significant question, they claimed, is not what causes organizational misbehavior, but rather how well (i.e., quickly and efficiently) the system responds to misbehavior (irrespective of the cause).

A combined approach, suggesting that counterproductive job behavior can be controlled through the prevention of dysfunctional activities, maintenance of functional work behavior, and discharge of counterproductive employees was proposed by Collins and Griffin (1998). Prevention, they claimed, begins with personnel selection and screening using cognitive ability (e.g., critical reasoning, and interpersonal problem solving) and personality (e.g., reliability) tests designed to predict both productive and counterproductive job performance. Maintenance involves the integration of the newly hired employee into the organization through regulated practices, procedures, and culture. Following Sonnenstuhl and Trice (1991), they suggested that supervision, the degree of prominence and visibility of job performance, and work roles may serve to better integrate the new employee into the organization. That is, engaging in counterproductive job performance becomes more difficult for work roles that are well supervised and interdependent of other tasks and where performance is visible, there is limited geographical mobility, and changes among fellow workers and supervision are infrequent. Hence, discharge implies violating effective control mechanisms that have been put into place.

Similarly, the organization might act to mitigate organizational-motivated violence (OMV) in two ways. First, it may intervene before aggressive action leads to violence by use of control mechanisms such as security measures. Second, it may mitigate OMV by altering either individual or organizational characteristics that prompt aggressive behavior before (i.e., prevention) or after (i.e., response) violence has occurred (O'Leary-Kelly et al., 1996). Neuman and Baron (1997) also suggested that some tactics such as the use of personnel selection procedures designed to screen for potentially aggressive employees, sanctions to discourage aggressive acts, strategies designed to reduce feelings or perceptions of injustice and inequity, and implementation of training programs (to provide individuals with improved social skills, coping strategies, and behavioral alternatives to aggression) may prove useful in preventing and controlling OMB.

Finally, management may choose to deal with OMB at both ends of the process. That is, it may choose to act both with the antecedents as well as the outcomes. For OMB management to be effective, it should be proactive as well as reactive.

THE RATIONALE FOR OMB MANAGEMENT

OMB may have nefarious effects (Vardi & Weitz, 2002b), economically (e.g., productivity loss and liability compensation) and socially (e.g., mental and physical injuries, psychological withdraw, and decreased job satisfaction). A closer look at some recent findings regarding the cost of three of the more pernicious forms of OMB—theft, substance abuse, and violence—reveals a stark picture.

Costs of Theft

A recent study of 745,000 businesses found that dishonest employees steal an average of $779 each year. This figure increases every year (Towler, 2001a). A study of 30 major companies with 10,663 stores and 1.9 million employees across all retail sectors in the United States reveals that 1 of every 22.4 employees was caught stealing from his or her employer in 2000. Moreover, 2000 was the seventh consecutive year that this number was on the rise. In 6 of those past 7 years, the rate of increase had been in the double digits (Egozi, 2002). According to Neven (2001), shrinkage costs retailers $25.35 billion per year, and more than half of that shrinkage is attributable to theft by a company's workforce. A staggering 75% of all employees have stolen from their employer at least once (Robinson & Greenberg, 1998), and Greenberg (1997) estimated the economic costs of employee theft to run as high as $200 billion annually in the United States alone.

Costs of Substance Abuse

The U.S. Department of Health and Human Services, Substance Abuse and Mental Health Services Administration (2000) reported that an estimated 6.5% of full-time and 8.6% of part-time workers in the United States are current illicit substance users. Alcohol is the most widely abused substance among working adults: An estimated 6.2% of adults working full time are heavy drinkers (five or more drinks on 5 or more days in the past month). The U.S. Department of Labor reports that 73% of all current substance abusers were employed in 1997, and more than 14% of workers report heavy drinking. Given alcohol's tendency to impair motor skills, it is not surprising that alcohol consumption leads to reduced safety in the workplace: Of all accidents on the job, 65% are related to substance abuse (Rosen, 2001a, 2001b). Up to 40% of industrial deaths and 47% of industrial injuries are linked to alcohol consumption; 21% of workers have reported being injured, put in danger, having to redo work, or needing to work harder due to coworkers, alcohol use (Akeroyd-Lear, 2000).

In 1992, substance abuse cost U.S. companies $100 billion in lost productivity (McGarvey, 1992). Almost a decade later, the figure has doubled to a staggering $200 billion in lost productivity (Akeroyd-Lear, 2000). One survey of CEOs reported that use of alcohol and drugs costs their organizations from 1% to 10% of their total payroll (Akeroyd-Lear, 2000). The U.S. Department of Labor estimates that substance abuse in the workplace costs employers $75 billion to $100 billion annually in lost time, accidents, health care, and workers' compensation.

Costs of Violence

Workplace violence became a major organizational problem in the 1980s, making homicide the second leading cause of work-related deaths by 1990. For example, 6,965 work-related homicides occurred between 1980 and 1988 in the United States, accounting for as much as 17% of all deaths in the workplace (Denenberg & Braverman, 1999). The number of violent acts in the workplace increased by 300% during the 1990s alone. Currently an average of 20 people per week are murdered while at work in the United States, 18,000 are assaulted each week, and more than 1,000 workplace homicides take place every year, making it the fastest growing form of murder in the United States (Towler, 2001b). When it comes to violence, human resource managers are commonly victims (Kurland, 1993), and women, for whom homicide is the leading cause of death in the workplace (Nomani, 1995), are particularly likely to be targeted (Women's Bureau, U.S. Department of Labor, 1994).

A 1993 survey conducted by Northwestern National Life Insurance Company found that one of four workers reported being harassed, threatened, or physically attacked on the job during the previous 12 months. A survey of 500 human resource managers by the American Management Association showed that more than half of the survey participants reported incidents of threats of violence in the previous 4 years. Thirty percent of the managers reported multiple occurrences (see Chappell & DiMartino, 1998). The International Labor Organization concluded that workplace violence was a worldwide phenomenon—that one that transcends the boundaries of a particular country, work setting or occupational group (Chappell & DiMartino, 1998).

Workplace violence, apart from inflicting direct damage, bears some dire indirect consequences as well: Employees who witness and have firsthand knowledge about violent acts tend to suffer from increased stress, lower morale, psychological withdrawal, a growing sense of insecurity, physical injuries, decreased productivity, and increased absenteeism and turnover (Denenberg & Braverman, 1999; Lehman & Simpson, 1992; Towler, 2001b). In 1997 alone, this translated into 876,000 lost workdays and $16 billion in lost wages (Towler, 2001b). In addition, survivors of workplace violence, families of the victims, and even the violent offenders can and do sue employers, adding substantial liability costs to those already mentioned. For example, Towler (2001b) reported a supermarket chain found liable for the actions of an employee who attacked a boy urinating on the building. The child was awarded $150,000. In another case, the family of a female employee who was stalked and killed by a fellow worker sued the company for negligent hiring and retention of the killer. Overall, the cost of lost productivity and lawsuits due to organizational violence is estimated to reach $4.2 billion in 1992, and the total cost of workplace violence in the United States is $4 to $6 billion per year (Towler, 2001b).

The economics of OMB are indeed staggering, and the price tag increases when the costs of misbehaviors such as fraud, sabotage, industrial espionage, and so on are factored into the equation. In addition, from a wider perspective, it becomes clear that employees engaging in OMB may negatively influence investors' decisions, influence customers' intentions not to return or avoid purchasing the company's products, manipulate suppliers to break contracts, and sway coworkers to be less satisfied and even leave their positions. Obviously such costs affect bottom line performance and productivity and may even pose a threat to the organization's survival (Analoui & Kakabadse, 1992). Despite that such costs may be offset by the benefits that often follow organizational improvements due to misbehaviors, such as whistle blowing, bootlegging, or new quality and monitoring regulations and practices, it can be easily understood why OMB may have such insidious effects on the organization and its stakeholders.

That OMB may have negative effects is clear. The dollar costs of OMB may be high. That alone may give sufficient reason for management to attempt to control it. There is the legal aspect to consider as well: Many forms of OMB (e.g., theft, homicide, fraud, sexual harassment, and discrimination) are legally forbidden by state regulations that employers are obliged to enforce. Moreover, companies are typically considered liable for their employees' actions even when these actions are not in accordance with company policies, and firms can be held responsible for employees' OMB (Towler, 2001a, 2001b). For example, employers may be held liable of negligent hiring or negligent retention of employees with a known propensity for violence (Amernic, 2001; Rosen, 2001b; Towler, 2001a, 2001b).

In summary, the wide range of recorded manifestations (see Appendix 2) and the heavy socioeconomic price tag they bear clearly indicate that OMB cannot be perceived as a marginal aspect of the organizational life and it cannot be overlooked. Managers should be aware of the phenomenon, its negative consequences to the organization and its stakeholders, and their need to alleviate the problem. The next section presents an integrative model of OMB management designed to assist managers, Organization Development (OD) practitioners, and management researchers.

AN INTEGRATIVE MODEL OF OMB MANAGEMENT

Figure 11.1 presents a revised integrative model of OMB management following and expanding the model depicted in Fig. 2.1 (see chap. 2). In addition to the assertion that the intention to misbehave is assumed to mediate the relationship between the antecedents and expressions of OMB, the model further posits that OMB and OMB management is a dynamic and intentional ongoing process, in which the costs associated determine to a large extent the type, timing, scope, and severity of the intervention(s) designed to cope with the counternormative act. The model identifies four phases of intervention designed to decrease the likelihood of OMB occurring and, as a result, minimize the financial, individual, and social costs associated with it. These interventions are assumed to influence the future recurrence of the misbehavior by affecting actors' intention to misbehave directly or indirectly. However, as is discussed, these interventions may also foster OMB.

The costs of OMB, real or projected, determine to a large extent the need for intervention as well as the type, timing, scope, and severity of the intervention. Whether the costs are real and the intervention comes as a reactive action or whether the intervention is aimed at the prevention of OMB is not important distinction. For example, fear of negligent-hiring lawsuits caused many United States companies to use selection tests aimed at detecting applicants' tendencies toward violence.

One major implication derived from this model suggests that the costs of OMB may have an adverse influence on the antecedents of OMB, thus enhancing the recurrence of a specific expression as well as inducing other forms of misbehavior. For example, chronic absenteeism or social loafing of one employee (expressions of production misbehavior) may increase the stress (individual-level antecedent) and pressure (task-level antecedent) of another, which in turn may result in violence toward a third party (expression of interpersonal misbehavior). When more than one employee is engaged in social loafing, it might become the group norm, leading even more employees to subperformance.

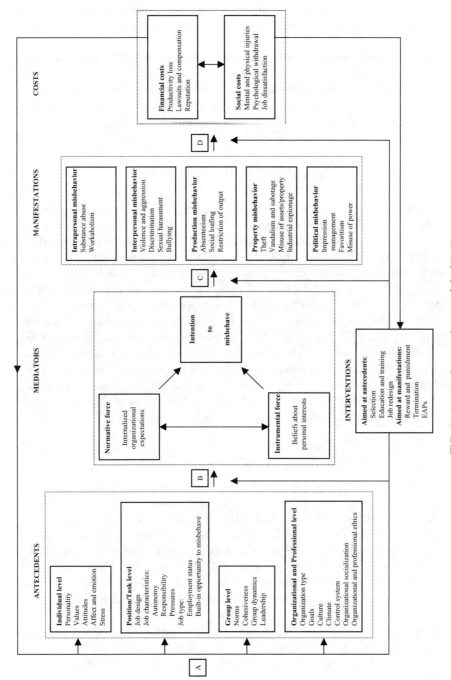

FIG. 11.1.   An integrative model of OMB.

Proposition: OMB bears significant financial and social costs, which in turn determine to a large extent the need for interventions and their type, timing, scope, and severity.

Proposition: OMB costs may have an adverse impact on the antecedents of OMB, thus enhancing the recurrence of the initial expression of OMB and inducing other forms of misbehavior. These secondary forms of misbehavior may be perpetrated by and targeted at the initial perpetrator(s) and target(s), as well as a third party.

OMB INTERVENTIONS

OMB interventions are defined as any planned actions taken by an organization to cope (i.e., prevent, control, or respond) with OMB with the intention of reducing its probability, frequency, scope, and costs. Fig. 11.1 suggests four points (marked A, B, C, and D) of intervention during the dynamic process of OMB, in which the organization may attempt to intervene and lower the possibility of OMB taking place. As depicted, these four action levers address the four main transitions in the process: Phase A, which is the costs ⇨ antecedents transition when dealing with second-order misbehavior, Phase B, which is the antecedents ⇨ intention transition, Phase C, which is the intention ⇨ expressions transition, and Phase D, which is expressions ⇨ the costs transition. More important, it is assumed that at all points the intervention influences the future recurrence of the misbehavior by affecting actors' and colleagues' intentions to misbehave either directly (Phases B and C) or indirectly (Phases A and D). These four points of intervention are elaborated in the following sections:

Phase A: Preemployment

The preliminary stage (Phase A) is the period in which the prospective employee has not yet entered the organization (preemployment stage); it represents the time frame in which one cycle of OMB has been completed and another one is about to begin (due to the adverse impact of the costs on the antecedents). At this stage, interventions can be designed to prevent misbehavior or alter the existing antecedents to prevent misbehavior. Use of selection techniques and careful job design and redesign methodologies are two examples of such interventions. The goal at this stage is keeping potential OMB-related antecedents out of the organization. However, note, that such tactics may sometimes be problematic, as with the case of a job that requires assertiveness (e.g., salespeople)—a personality trait usually desirable, yet not too dissimilar and not easily differentiated in the selection stage from aggressiveness, which might lead to violent behavior on the job.

Phase B: Socialization

As discussed earlier, the intention to misbehave is a function of two separate, although possibly related, forces: the normative force, reflecting internalized organizational expectations, and the instrumental force, reflecting beliefs about personal interests. Vardi and Wiener (1996) argued that variables such as organizational socialization, culture, cohesiveness, and goals affect the normative force, whereas personal circumstances, dissatisfaction, built-in opportunity to misbehave, and control systems contribute to the formation of the instrumental force. Variables such as the employees' primary socialization, personality, values, and cognitions attribute to both forces. The intention formation stage (Phase B) calls for two forms of intervention: one aimed at affecting the normative force, and one aimed at affecting the instrumental force. In both cases, the goal is to lower the possibility of a given antecedent(s) to trigger the intention to misbehave. Interventions at this stage need to enhance the identification of the sense of wrongdoing within the individual—the understanding that, for example, stealing is wrong or violence is not the solution—and reduce the instrumental motive to misbehave ("If I am caught stealing, I might get fired").

An intervention at Phase B may address a specific antecedent (e.g., personal attitudes and built-in opportunity) or, assuming that the antecedents have a common denominators(s), be designed to address one or more of the four possible antecedents levels: individual, task/position, group, and organization. For example, job redesign may reduce the built-in opportunity to misbehave (i.e., reduce the instrumental force), whereas a system-wide effort to disseminate, communicate, and implement a nonmisbehavior policy (i.e., cultural change) throughout the organization may reduce the normative force (Denenberg & Braverman, 1999). Some interventions may influence both normative and instrumental forces. For example, a formal mentorship program may help communicate values of proper conduct to newcomers (normative) as well as the possible sanctions facing misbehavior (instrumental).

Phase C: Behavior Control

The focus of intervention at this stage (note that the intention to misbehave already exists at this phase) shifts from prevention to deterrence—that is, from reducing the likelihood of the intention misbehave to arise to actively reducing the probability of this intention turning into an action. Naturally, reward, control, and sanction systems, which may deter employees from carrying out their intentions because of fear of the associated punishment, play a major role. Consider the use of tracking devices (control) combined with use of bonuses and employee stock options (rewards). Embittered employees may not choose to misbehave if they know that they are being closely monitored and that if caught they may lose a bonus or, in more serious cases, their job.

Phase D: Corrective Measures

Interventions in Phase D have three goals: minimizing the costs of the misbehavior, restoring the damage, and providing assistance (to both perpetrators and targets). For example, periodical drug tests may help identify substance abuse and thus lower the rate of accidents on the job. The substance abusers can participate in rehabilitation programs. Similarly, employee assistance programs (EAPs) for victims of violence or sexual harassment may contribute to their early return to work and reduce the possibility of second-order misbehavior perpetrated against their assessor(s) or a third party. They may reduce the possibility of victims sueing their employer. As in Phase A, interventions at this stage may address a specific expression (e.g., theft and sexual harassment) or, assuming a common denominator(s), one or more of the five categories of expressions (i.e., production, property, interpersonal, intrapersonal, and political misbehavior). Hence, sanctions may reduce future absenteeism, whereas team-building interventions can be designed to cope with high levels of observed interpersonal misbehavior (e.g., aggression, bullying, withholding information, and lack of cooperation) associated with a specific group or team within the organization.

> *Proposition: OMB management may reduce the frequency, scope, severity, and costs of OMB using varied action plans designed to minimize the relationship among the different variables associated with this process in four main phases of intervention along the OMB cycle.*

The complex, dynamic, and highly contingent nature of the OMB phenomenon suggests that a generic, one-size-fits-all solution to OMB is unlikely. Moreover, as Analoui and Kakabadse (1992) argued, the multidimensional factors involved in the inception, emergence, and expression of each act of OMB make it difficult, if not impossible, to predict the exact time or place of its occurrence. Hence, every organization needs to constantly monitor its situation, assess its own needs (i.e., types of misbehavior and associated costs), and design its own means (i.e., interventions) of coping with the problem. That is, we suggest that, for OMB management to be effective, the general phenomenon of OMB should be examined thoroughly and carefully analyzed (antecedents and/or expressions), and that a successful coping strategy be devised. It may be a combination of several interventions aimed at different types and categories of OMB to be applied simultaneously. Note that applying such a strategy means, in fact, a culture change—delivering a clear organization-wide message of OMB nontolerance.

The model depicted in Figure 11.1 may help management analyze the dynamics of the process at varied levels and design relevant interventions. As mentioned earlier, it is possible to analyze the dynamics of OMB in two major directions: antecedent ⇨ expressions and expression ⇨ antecedents. Thus, using this model as a managerial tool enables one to forecast possible expressions given a specific antecedent and vice versa. One may zoom in on a certain antecedent (e.g., stress) and check for the possible outcomes (e.g., absenteeism, violence, and substance abuse) that need to be handled. Similarly, one can focus on an expression (e.g., violence) and trace its causes (e.g., stress and sense of injustice).

Try to think of a situation in which the yearly job attitude survey and the performance appraisal system indicate that employees report high levels of job dissatisfaction and that they attribute this dissatisfaction to a sense of pay inequity. What are the forms of misbehavior that we may expect? Research indicates that such frustration can lead to individual or group complaints (which are a legitimate action grounded in labor relations) and to production misbehavior (e.g., restriction of output), property misbehavior (e.g., sabotage), interpersonal misbehavior (e.g., violence toward supervisor), and interpersonal misbehavior (e.g., substance abuse).

From another standpoint, assume that one unit of the company reports high rates of absenteeism and rule breaking. A thorough inquiry should be made to determine the causes of this phenomenon especially with regard to the different antecedent factors. Prevalent rule breaking may indicate the presence of inadequate and noncomprehensive normative and substantive rules and/or a lack of concern or skills on the part of the management to enforce protective regulation (Analoui & Kakabadse, 1992). Absenteeism and rule breaking may also be forms of protest against an authoritarian leadership style. Hence, solutions may range from sending the group manager to a management skills development program to transferring or terminating this manager and appointing a new one. However, if these behaviors reflect a built-in opportunity to be absent and taking advantage of a lax enviroment, a job redesign intervention may be needed.

Proposition: The complex, dynamic, and highly contingent nature of OMB prohibits a generic, one-size-fits-all approach, but a localized and specific solution.

Obviously this does not mean that there are no remedies for OMB, but rather that the general phenomenon of OMB needs to be carefully analyzed—broken down into its component parts (antecedents and/or expressions)—before devising and applying interventions, and that solutions need to be carefully tailored to match the unique needs of the situation and the organizational context.

A word of caution is in order: As can be easily understood from the discussion thus far, OMB interventions might have an adverse impact on misbehavior. That is, OMB interventions, if not designed and applied carefully and correctly, might foster OMB. For example, punishment needs to be perceived as justified and proportional relative to the severance of the act to be accepted as legitimate (Noe, Hollenbeck, Gerhart, & Wright, 1997; Scarlicky & Folger, 1997). If sanctions are perceived to be unjustified or nonproportional to the severity of the offense, the levels of dissatisfaction and frustration may increase, resulting in a more severe form of misbehavior, as in the following case reported by Analoui and Kakabadse (1992):

Wastage and destruction were used as forms of unconventional behavior and were observed to be employed in both overt and covert forms, in order to show the discontent experienced. For example, security cameras were installed in bar (L) and as a consequence the staff could not "help themselves" to an occasional drink or two; even those which were genuine mistakes or rejects brought back by customers. The staff then threw everything away instead of attempting to sell or save some of them as they were requested by the management. Phrases such as, "If I don't get, he (manager) doesn't either," were used. These phrases showed the intentions of the actors involved. (p. 22)

Consider too the case of Arturo Reyes Torres, a highway worker for Caltrans, a Californian transportation organization, who was discharged for theft in 1997 after 15 years of service. Overtaken with anger and feelings of perceived unfairness, he returned to his former workplace and killed his former supervisor, along with three other employees, whom he held responsible for his termination (Denenberg & Braverman, 1999). We cannot overemphasize that OMB interventions need to be carefully designed and implemented so that the interventions do not induce further, secondary, and perhaps more costly and severe types of misbehavior.

> *Proposition: OMB interventions may have an adverse impact on the antecedents of OMB, thus enhancing the recurrence of the initial expression as well as inducing other forms of misbehavior. These secondary forms of misbehavior may be perpetrated by and targeted at the initial perpetrator(s) and target(s), as well as a third party.*

SUMMARY

The suggested guidelines for OMB management and interventions for its control are the following. First, OMB management is a dynamic, ongoing process similar to the other conventional practices of administration and development and are, in fact, part of it. Second, there is no panacea for OMB. Control mechanisms for its reduction need to be based on the specific needs of the organization, the members, and the organizational context.

Third, there are four main phases of intervention through which the organization may attempt to control OMB. The intervention phases differ in relation to their focus, yet the general purpose of all OMB interventions should be minimizing (i.e., weakening) the relationships among antecedents, mediators, expressions, and consequences of the OMB cycle with the intention to prevent undesirable behaviors (just as OD interventions are designed to enhance desirable ones). Obviously some interventions or mechanisms may be used in more than one point throughout this process, and different interventions may be applied simultaneously. For example, in a transportation company whose drivers were involved in accidents (costs) due to substance abuse (expression), it may be wise to establish periodical drug-testing programs and send substance abusers to rehabilitation programs (Phase D interventions). Also, new employees may be tested for substance abuse prior to hiring as part of the selection process (Phase A interventions). A successful coping strategy calls for applying a combination of interventions at different stages simultaneously.

Fourth, OMB interventions should be designed so that they are perceived by employees as legitimate and justified to be effective. Perceived lack of fairness may lead to more severe forms of misbehavior in reaction to the sanctions imposed. This leads to the assertion that OMB interventions, like any other managerial practices, need to be constantly assessed for efficiency and effectiveness relative to their goals. Finally, while designing interventions, managers should consider the possibility that an intervention may have undesired effects (e.g., faulty design, improper application, or inappropriateness) and may even trigger misbehavior.

RESEARCH IMPLICATIONS

As noted, research into OMB is much less frequent in scope and depth than OB research. Thus, there is still a tendency to focus on the positive aspects of work at the expense of exposing the dark side of organizations. Most methodological and conceptual handicaps remain. We discussed these at length in the previous chapter and raised some useful suggestions for future endeavors. We still have a lot to learn, but we do have a good start. We believe the OMB framework presented in this book sheds light on the topic and contributes to our understanding. It also offers a broad canvas for future research, which may proceed in varied directions:

1. The systematic study of the direct relationships between specific types of antecedents and expressions—for example, the examination of the relationship between personality traits (e.g., the Big Five) and predisposition to violence.
2. The exploration of the interaction between two or more variables within a level (e.g., the individual level) and their contribution to the intention to misbehave—for example, personality × stress ⇨ intention to misbehave. Similarly, the interaction between antecedents across levels—for example, values (individual level) × built-in opportunity (task level) ⇨ intention to misbehave.
3. The exploration of the relationships between one or more antecedents and one or more specific types of misbehavior (with the intention to misbehave

as mediator)—for example, personality × stress ⇨ theft, attitudes × job characteristics ⇨ sabotage.

4. The examination of the interactions between expressions within or across categories—for example, theft × sabotage, violence × sexual harassment, and drug use × aggression.

This model also draws a framework for the development and assessment of specific models of interventions aimed at the following:

1. Specific antecedent or expression (e.g., selection tests designed to detect personality traits considered as predictors of violence).
2. Aggregate level of antecedents or expressions (e.g., team-building interventions at the group level and EAPs for rehabilitation to help victims of inter- or intrapersonal misbehavior).
3. The systemwide level (e.g., designing a formal senior function to coordinate all efforts of OMB management).

A major implication of this model for both researchers and practitioners is that it eliminates the distinction between prevention and response strategies; it offers a means for determining the appropriate strategy for OMB assessment and control and the different intervention(s) by their efficacy, rather than continuing the search for the single most effective way. We are now in a better position to examine the results of a given intervention (or interventions) in lowering the rate and the costs of a given type of OMB. We can better examine the effect that drug testing has on lowering the rate and costs of accidents in a given organization or the effects of integrity testing on lowering the rate and costs of employee theft. Future research regarding the probability of a given intervention to meet its goals is needed.

SUMMARY

In this chapter, we reviewed the phenomenon of OMB and suggested an integrative model of OMB management with implications for management as well as directions for future research. The framework posits that OMB and the management of such behaviors are part of a dynamic, intentional, ongoing process in which the intention to misbehave is assumed to mediate the relationship between the antecedents and expressions of OMB. The intention, in turn, is a function of two distinct, yet possibly related forces—an instrumental force reflecting beliefs about personal interests, and a normative force reflecting internalized organizational expectations. The varied antecedents in this model are grouped into categories reflecting four possible organizational levels of analysis: individual, task/position, group, and organization. Manifestations are classified into five distinct categories of misbehavior: intrapersonal, interpersonal, production, property, and political.

There are four main phases of intervention, or action levers, along the OMB cycle in which the organization may act to control the possibility of OMB to occur, thus reducing its associated costs. These four phases differ in their timing (regarding the OMB process), and thus in their focus, and call for an ongoing organizational effort to control OMB through the constant use of multiple interventions aimed at multiple forms of misbehaviors in varied steps of their formation and execution. If not applied sensitively and correctly, OMB interventions, might in fact foster OMB. Hence, OMB interventions require extremely cautious consideration, preparation, implementation, and evaluation. The model also implies that the distinction between prevention and response strategies is of less importance than the question of the probability that a given intervention (or type of interventions) will lower the rate and costs of a given type of OMB.

The framework proposes that the costs of OMB—real or projected—determine to a large extent the type, timing, scope, and severity of the intervention(s) to be used. Other considerations are by and large legal. Perhaps the most important lesson one may draw from this model is the assertion that, because of the highly contingent and dynamic nature of OMB, there cannot be a one best solution. Every organization needs to assess its own situation and design its own means of coping with these phenomena.

In summary, the proposed integrative model may help management analyze the dynamics of the process in varied levels and design appropriate intervention(s). It may also contribute to future research by drawing a general framework for the study of OMB in varied settings, such as the study of interactions among different variables in varied levels of analysis. Finally, this framework can be extended to encompass a wide range of organizational behaviors, and it can be developed into a general model of organizational behavior management and development.

References

Abdel Halim, A. A. (1978). Employee affective responses to organizational stress: Moderating effects of job characteristics. *Personnel Psychology, 31,* 561–578.

Abrahamson, E. (1996). Management fashion. *Academy of Management Review, 21,* 254–285.

Abrahamson, E. (1997). The emergence and prevalence of employee management rhetoric: The effects of long waves, labor union, and turnover, 1875 to 1992. *Academy of Management Journal, 40,* 491–533.

Academy of Management (August, 2002). *Newsletter.* Radcliff Manor, NY: Author.

Ackroyd, S., & Thompson, P. (1999). *Organizational misbehaviour.* London: Sage.

Adams, J. S. (1963). Toward an understanding of inequity. *Journal of Abnormal and Social Psychology, 67,* 422–436.

Adams, J. S. (1965). Inequity in social exchange. In L. Berkowitz (Ed.), *Advances in experimental social psychology* (Vol. 2, pp. 267–299). New York: Academic Press.

Adams, S. (1996). *The Dilbert principle.* New York: Harper Business.

Aguinis, H., Henle, C. A., & Ostroff C. (2001). Measurement in work and organizational psychology. In N. Anderson, D. S. Ones, H. K. Sinangil, & C. Viswesvaran (Eds.), *Handbook of industrial, work and organizational psychology* (Vol. 1, pp. 27–50). London: Sage.

Ailon-Souday, G. (2001). *Merging ourselves apart: A study of identities in an Israeli high-tech corporation undergoing a merger with an American competitor.* Unpublished doctoral dissertation, Tel Aviv University, Israel.

Ajzen, I. (1985). From intentions to actions: A theory of planned behavior. In J. Kurhl & J. Beckman (Eds.), *Consistency in social behavior: The Ontario Symposium* (Vol. 2, pp. 3–15). Hillsdale, NJ: Lawrence Erlbaum Associates.

Ajzen, I., & Fishbein, M. (1980). *Understanding attitudes and predicting social behavior.* Englewood-Cliff, NJ: Prentice-Hall.

Akeroyd-Lear, J. (2001). DrugPolicy.com. http://www.hr.com

Aldrich, H. E. (1979). *Organizations and environments.* Englewood Cliffs, NJ: Prentice-Hall.

Allcorn, S. (1994). *Anger in the workplace: Understanding the causes of aggression and violence.* Westport, CT: Quorum Books.

Allen, V. L., & Greenberger, D. B. (1980). Destruction and perceived control. In A. Baum & J. E. Singer (Eds.), *Applications of personal control* (Vol. 2 pp. 85–109). Hillsdale, NJ: Lawrence Erlbaum Associates.

Allinson, R. E. (1998). Ethical values as part of the definition of business enterprise and part of the internal structure of the business organization. *Journal of Business Ethics, 17,* 1015–1028.

Allison, G. T. (1971). *Essence of decision: Explaining the Cuban missile crisis.* Boston: Little, Brown.

Allport, F. H. (1924). *Social psychology.* Cambridge, MA: Riverside.

Allport, G. W. (1961). *Pattern and growth in personality.* New York: Holt, Rinehart & Winston.

Altheide, D. L., Adler, P. A., Adler, P., & Altheide, D. A. (1978). The social meanings of employee theft. In J. M. Johnson & J. D. Douglas (Eds.), *Crime at the top* (pp. 90–124). Philadelphia: Lippincott.

American Psychological Association. (1996). Task force on statistical inference: Initial report. http://www.apa.org/science/tfsi.html

Amernic, J. (2000). Applicant background checks. http://www.hr.com

Analoui, F., & Kakabadse, A. (1992). Unconventional practices at work: Insight and analysis through participant observation. *Journal of Managerial Psychology, 7,* 1–31.

Analoui, F., & Kakabadse, A. (1991). *Sabotage: How to recognize and manage employee defiance.* London: Mercury.

Andersson, L. M. (1996). Employee cynicism: An examination using a contract violation framework. *Human Relations, 49,* 1395–1418.

Andersson, L. M., & Bateman, T. S. (1997). Cynicism in the workplace: Some causes and effects. *Journal of Organizational Behavior, 18,* 449–469.

Andersson, L. M., & Pearson, C. M. (1999). Tit for tat? The spiraling effect of incivility in the workplace. *Academy of Management Review, 24,* 452–471.

Anthony, R. N., & Dearden, J. (1976). *Management control systems: Text and cases* (3rd ed.). Homewood, IL: Irwin.

Archer, E. R. (1994). Words of caution on the temporary workforce. *HR magazine, 39,* 168–170.

Archer, D. (1999). Exploring "bullying" culture in the para-military organization. *International Journal of Manpower, 2,* 94–105.

Argyris, C. (1957). *Personality and organization: The conflict between system and the individual.* New York: Harper.

Argyris, C. (1960). *Understanding organizational behavior.* Homewood, IL: Dorsey.

Argyris, C. (1964). *Integrating the individual and the organization.* New York: Wiley.

Arthur, M. B., Claman, P. H., & DeFillippi, R. J. (1995). Intelligent enterprise, intelligent careers. *Academy of Management Executive, 9,* 7–22.

Ashforth, B. E. (1985). Climate formation: Issues and extensions. *Academy of Management Review, 10,* 837–847.

Ashforth, B. E. (1994). Petty tyranny in organizations. *Human Relations, 47,* 755–778.

Ashforth, B. E., & Humphrey, R. H. (1995). Emotions in the workplace: A reappraisal. *Human Relation, 48,* 97–125.

Ashkanasy, N. M., & Jackson, C. R. A. (2001). Organizational culture and climate. In N. Anderson, D. S. Ones, H. K. Sinangil, & C. Viswesvaran (Eds.), *Handbook of industrial, work and organizational psychology* (Vol. 2, pp. 398–415). London: Sage.

Ashton, M. C. (1998). Personality and job performance: The importance of narrow traits. *Journal of Organizational Behavior, 19,* 289–303.

Astor, S. D. (1972). Twenty steps for preventing theft in business. *Management Review, 61,* 34–35.

Avolio, B. (1999). *Full leadership development: Building the vital forces in organizations.* Thousand Oaks, CA: Sage.

Bacharach, S. B. (1989). Organizational theories: Some criteria for evaluation. *Academy of Management Review, 14,* 496–515.

Bacharach, S. B., Bamberger, P., & Sonnenstuhl, W. J. (2002). Driven to drink: Managerial control, work related risk factors and employee drinking behavior. *Academy of Management Journal, 45,* 637–658.

Bacharach, S. B., & Lawler, E. J. (1980). *Power and politics in organizations.* San Francisco: Jossey-Bass.

Bachman, R. (1994). *Violence and theft in the workplace.* Washington, DC: Bureau of Justice Statistics, U.S. Department of Justice.

Bamberger, P. A., & Sonnenstuhl, W. J. (1998). Introduction: Research on organizations and deviance—some basic concerns. In S. Bacharach (Ed.), *Research in the sociology of organizations* (Vol. 15, pp. vii–xviii). Greenwich, CT: JAI.

Bandura, A. (1969). *Principles of behavior modification.* New York: Holt, Rinehart & Winston.

Bandura, A. (1973). *Aggression: A social learning analysis.* Englewood Cliffs, NJ: Prentice-Hall.

Baritz, L. (1960). *The servants of power: A history of the use of social science in American industry.* Middletown; CT: Wesleyan University Press.

Baron, R. A., & Neuman, J. H. (1996). Workplace violence and workplace aggression: Evidence on their relative frequency and potential causes. *Aggressive Behavior, 22,* 161–173.

Baron, S. A. (1993). *Violence in the workplace: A prevention and management guide for businesses.* Oxnard, CA: Pathfinder.

Barrick, M. R., & Mount, M. K. (1991). The big five personality dimensions and job performance: A meta-analysis. *Personnel Psychology, 44,* 1–27.

Barrick, M. R., & Mount, M. K. (1993). Autonomy as a moderator of the relationships between the big five personality dimensions and job performance. *Journal of Applied Psychology, 78,* 111–118.

Barrick, M. R., Mount, M. K., & Strauss, J. P. (1993). Conscientiousness and performance of sales representatives: Test of the mediating effects of goal setting. *Journal of Applied Psychology, 78,* 715–722.

Barrick, M. R., Mount, M. K., & Strauss, J. P. (1994). Antecedents of involuntary turnover due to reduction in force. *Personnel Psychology, 47,* 515–536.

Bartram, D. (1994). Computer-based assessment. In C. L. Cooper & I. T. Robertson (Eds.), *International review of industrial and organizational psychology* (Vol. 9, pp. 31–69). Chichester, England: Wiley.

Baruch, Y. (2000). *Bullying on the net: Adverse behavior on the e-mail and its impact.* Unpublished manuscript, University of East Anglia, Great Britain.

Bateman, T. S., & Organ, D. W. (1983). Job satisfaction and the good soldier syndrome: The relationship between affect and employee citizenship. *Academy of Management Journal, 26,* 587–595.

Baucus, M. S., & Near, J. P. (1991). Can illegal corporate behavior be predicted? An event history analysis. *Academy of Management Journal, 34,* 9–36.

Becker, T. E., & Martin, S. L. (1995). Trying to look bad at work: Methods and motives for managing poor impressions in organizations. *Academy of Management Journal, 38,* 174–199.

Bejsky, M. (1986). *Report of the inquest committee on the regulation of bank shares.* Jerusalem, Israel: Government of Israel.

Bendix, R. (1956). *Work and authority in industry: Ideologies of management in the course of industrialization.* New York: Harper & Row.

Bennett, R. J., & Robinson, S. L. (2000). Development of measure of workplace deviance. *Journal of Applied Psychology, 85,* 349–360.

Bensman, J., & Gerver, I. (1963). Crime and punishment in the factory: The function of deviancy in maintaining the social system. *American Sociological Review, 28,* 588–598.

Berelson, B. (1971). *Content analysis in communication research.* New York: Hafner.

Berger, P. L., & Luckmann, T. (1966). *The social construction of reality: A treatise on the sociology of knowledge.* Garden City, NY: Anchor Books.

Beugré, C. D. (1998). Understanding organizational insider-perpetrated workplace aggression: An integrative model. *Research in Sociology of Organizations, 15,* 163–196.

Bies, R. J., & Tripp, T. M. (1995). The use and abuse of power: Justice as social control. In R. Cropanzano & K. M. Kacmar (Eds.), *Organizational politics, justice, and support: Managing the social climate at the workplace* (pp. 131–145). Westport CT: Quorum.

Bies, R. J., & Tripp, T. M. (1996). Beyond distrust: "Getting even" and the need for revenge. In R. M. Kramer & T. R. Tyler (Eds.). *Trust in organizations: Frontiers of theory and research* (pp. 246–260). Thousand Oaks, CA: Sage.

Bies, R. J., & Tripp, T. M. (1998). Revenge in organizations: The good, the bad and the ugly. In R. W. Griffin, A. M. O'Leary-Kelly, & J. M. Collins (Eds.), *Dysfunctional behavior in organizations: Non-violent dysfunctional behavior* (Vol. 23, Part B, pp. 49–67). Stamford, CT: JAI.

Bies, R. J., Tripp, T. M., & Kramer, R. M. (1997). At the breaking point: Cognitive and social dynamics of revenge in organizations. In R. A. Giacalone & J. Greenberg (Eds.), *Antisocial behavior in organizations* (pp. 18–36). Thousand Oaks, CA: Sage.

Biran, A. (1999). *Job autonomy as chance or temptation: The relationship between autonomy, personal and organizational variables, and misbehavior at work.* Unpublished master's thesis, Tel Aviv University, Israel.

Blau, G. J. (1987). Using a person-environment fit model to predict job involvement and organizational commitment. *Journal of Vocational Behavior, 30,* 240–257.

Blau, P. M. (1964). *Exchange and power in social life.* New York: Wiley.

Blauner, R. (1964). *Alienation and freedom: The factory worker and his industry.* Chicago: The University of Chicago Press.

Bliss, E. C., & Aoki, I. S. (1993). *Are your employees stealing you blind?* San Diego, CA: Pfeiffer.

Bolino, M. C. (1999). Citizenship and impression management: Good soldiers or good actors? *Academy of Management Review, 24,* 82–98.

Bologna, P. S., & Shaw, P. (2000). *Avoiding cyberfraud in small businesses: What auditors and owners need to know.* New York: Wiley.

Bommer, M., Gratto, C., Gravander, J., & Tuttle, M. (1987). A behavioral model of ethical and unethical decision making. *Journal of Business Ethics, 6,* 265–280.

Bowie, N. E., & Dunka, R. F. (1990). *Business ethics.* Englewood Cliffs, NJ: Prentice-Hall.

Boyd, R. G. (1990). How employee thievery can plague an acquisition. *Mergers and Acquisitions, 24,* 58–61.

Boye, M. W., & Jones, J. W. (1997). Organizational culture and employee counterproductivity. In R. A. Giacalone & J. Greenberg (Eds.), *Antisocial behavior in organizations* (pp. 172–184). Thousand Oaks, CA: Sage.

Bozeman, D. P., & Kacmar, K. M. (1997). A cybernetic model of impression management processes in organizations. *Organizational Behavior and Human Decision Processes, 69,* 9–30.

Braithwaite, J. (1985). White collar crime. *Annual Review of Sociology, 11,* 1–25.

Brass, D. J., Butterfield, K. D., & Skaggs, B. C. (1998). Relationships and unethical behavior: A social network perspective. *Academy of Management Review, 23,* 14–31.

Braverman, H. (1974). *Labor and monopoly capital: The degradation of work in the twentieth century.* New York: Monthly Review Press.

Breaugh, J. A. (1985). The measurement of work autonomy. *Human Relations, 38,* 551–570.

Brief, A. P., & Motowidlo, S. J. (1986). Prosocial organizational behaviors. *Academy of Management Review, 11,* 710–725.

Briner, B., & Hockey, R. G. (1988). Operator stress and computer-based work. In C. L. Cooper & R. Payne (Eds.), *Causes, coping, and consequences of stress at work* (pp. 115–140). New York: Wiley.

Brown, M. A. (1976). Values—a necessary but neglected ingredient of motivation on the job. *Academy of Management Review, 1,* 15–23.

Brummer, J. (1985). Business ethics: Micro and macro. *Journal of Business Ethics, 4,* 81–91.

Bruner, J. S. (1964). The course of cognitive growth. *American Psychologist, 19,* 1–15.

Bryant, C. D. (Ed.). (1974). *Deviant behavior: Occupational and organizational bases.* Chicago: Rand McNally.

Bryson, J. B. (1977, August). *Situational determinants of the expression of jealousy.* Paper presented at the annual meeting of the American Psychology Association, San Francisco, CA.

Bureau of Labor Statistics. (1999). *Fatal occupational injuries by event and exposure, 1993–1998.* Washington, DC: U.S. Department of Labor.

Burke, R. J. (1999). Workaholism in organizations: The role of personal beliefs and fears. *Anxiety, Stress and Coping, 13,* 53–65.

Buss, A. H. (1961). *The psychology of aggression.* New York: Wiley.

Buss, D. (1993). Ways to curtail employee theft. *Nation's Business, 81,* 36–37.

Caldwell, D. F., & O'Reilly, C.A., III. (1982). Responses to failure: The effects of choice and responsibility on impression management. *Academy of Management Journal, 25,* 121–136.

Cappelli, P., & Chauvin, K. (1991). An interplant test of the efficiency wage hypothesis. *The Quarterly Journal of Economics, 106,* 769–787.

Cappelli, P., & Sherer, P. D. (1991). The missing role of context in OB: The need for a meso-level approach. In B. M. Staw & L. L. Cummings (Eds.), *Research in organizational behavior* (Vol. 13, pp. 55–110). Greenwich, CT: JAI.

Chappell, D., & Di Martino, V. (1998). *Violence at work.* Geneva: International Labor Organization.

Carr, A. Z. (1968). Is business bluffing ethical? *Harvard Business Review, 46,* 143–153.

Carroll, A. B. (1978). Linking business ethics to behavior in organizations. S.A.M. *Advanced Management Journal, 43,* 4–11.

Caudron, S. (1995). Fighting the enemy within. *Business Week, 244, 16,* 36–40.

Chatman, J. A. (1989). Improving interactional organizational research: A model of person-organization fit. *Academy of Management Review, 14,* 333–349.

Cherniss, C. (1980). *Staff burnout: Job stress in the human service.* Beverly Hills, CA: Sage.

Cherrington, D. J. (1980). *The work ethic: Working values and values that work.* New York: Amacom.

Cherrington, D. J., & Cherrington, J. O. (1985). The climate of honesty in retail stores. In W. Terris (Ed.), *Employee theft: Research, theory, and applications* (pp. 51–65). Park Ridge , IL: London House Press.

Cleveland, J. N., & Kerst, M. E. (1993). Sexual harassment and perceptions of power: An underarticulated relationship. *Journal of Vocational Behavior, 42,* 49–67.

Cleveland, J. N., Stockdale, M., & Murphy, K. R. (2000). *Women and men in organizations: Sex and gender issues at work.* Mahwah, NJ: Lawrence Erlbaum Associates.

Clinard, M. B., & Quinney, R. (1968). *Criminal behavior systems: A typology.* (2nd ed.) New York: Holt, Rinehart & Winston.

Cohen, G. (1999). *The relationship between different types of commitment in the workplace and organizational misbehavior.* Unpublished master's thesis, Tel Aviv University, Israel.

Cohen, M. D., March, J. G., & Olsen, J. P. (1972). A garbage can model of organizational choice. *Administrative Science Quarterly, 17,* 1–25.

Cohen, S. (1973). Property destruction: Motives and meanings. In C. Ward (Ed.), *Vandalism* (pp. 23–53). London: Architectural Press.

Coleman, J. W. (1985). *The criminal elite: The sociology of white-collar crime.* New York: St. Martin's Press.

Coleman, J. W. (1987). Toward an integrated theory of white-collar crime. *American Journal of Sociology, 93,* 406–439.

Collins, J. M., & Griffin, R. W. (1998). The psychology of counterproductive job performance. In R. W. Griffin, A. M. O'Leary-Kelly, & J. M. Collins (Eds.), *Dysfunctional behavior in organizations* (pp. 219–242). Stamford, CT: JAI.

Collins, J. M., & Schmidt, F. L. (1993). Personality, integrity, and white collar crime: A construct validity study. *Personnel Psychology, 46,* 295–311.

Collins, O., Dalton, M., & Roy, D. (1946). Restriction of output and social cleavage in industry. *Applied Anthropology, 5,* 1–14.

Cooper, C. L., & Rousseau, D. M. (Eds.). (1999). *The virtual organization. Trends in organizational behavior* (Vol. 6). New York: Wiley.

Cornwall, H. (1987). *Datatheft: Computer fraud, industrial espionage, and information crime.* London: Heinemann.

Costa, P. T., & McCrae, R. R. (1988). Personality in adulthood: A six-year longitudinal study of self-reports and spouse ratings on the NEO personality inventory. *Journal of Personality and Social Psychology, 54,* 853–863.

Crawford, N. (1999). Conundrums and confusion in organizations: The etymology of the word "bully." *International Journal of Manpower, 20,* 86–93.

Cressey, D. R. (1953). *Other people's money: The social psychology of embezzlement.* New York: The Free Press.

Crino, M. D., & Leap, T. L. (1988). *Sabotage: Protecting your company means dealing with the dark side of human nature. Success, 35*(1), 52–55.

Crowne, D. P., & Marlowe, D. (1960). A new scale of social desirability independent of psychopathology. *Journal of Consulting Psychology, 24,* 349–354.

Crozier, M. (1964). *The bureaucratic phenomenon.* London: Tavistock Publications.

Cullen, J. B., Victor, B., Stephens, C. (1989). An ethical weather report: Assessing the organization's ethical climate. *Organizational Dynamics, 18,* 50–63.

Cummings, L. L. (1982). Organizational behavior. *Annual Review of Psychology, 33,* 541–579.

Dabney, D. A., & Hollinger, R. C. (1999). Illicit prescription drug use among pharmacists. *Work and Occupation, 26,* 77–106.

Daboub, A. J., Rasheed, A. M. A., Priem, R. L., & Gray, D. A. (1995). Top management team, characteristics and corporate illegal activity. *Academy of Management Review, 20,* 138–170.

Daft, R. L. (1980). The evaluation of organization analysis in ASQ, 1959–1979. *Administrative Science Quarterly, 25,* 623–636.

Daft, R. L. (1995). *Organization theory and design.* St. Paul, MN: West.

Daft, R. L. (2000). *Management.* Fort Worth, TX: Dryden.

Daft, R. L., & Lewin, A. Y. (1993). Where are the theories for the "new" organizational form? An editorial essay. *Organizational Science, 4*(4), i–iv.

Daft, R. L., & Noe, R. A. (2001). *Organizational behavior.* New York: Harcourt.

Daft, R. L. & Marcic (2004). *Understanding Management* (4th ed.). Cincinnati, OH: South-Western.

Dalton, D. R., Johnson, J. L., & Daily, C. M. (1999). On the use of "Intent To . . ." variables in organizational research: An empirical and cautionary assessment. *Human Relations, 52,* 1337–1350.

Dalton, M. A. (1999). *Learning tactics inventory: Facilitator's guide.* San Francisco: Jossey-Bass.

Danet, B. (1981). Client-organization relationships. In P. C. Nystrome & W. H. Starbuck (Eds.), *Handbook of organizational design* (Vol. 2, pp. 382–417). New York: Oxford University Press.

De George, R. T. (1986). Theological ethics and business ethics/replies and reflections on theology and business ethics. *Journal of Business Ethics, 5,* 421–437.

Delaney, J. (1993). Handcutting employee theft. *Small Business Report, 18,* 29–38.

Delgado, A. R., & Bond, R. A. (1993). Attenuating the attribution of responsibility: The lay perception of jealousy as a motive for wife battery. *Journal of Applied Social Psychology, 23,* 1337–1356.

DeMore, S. W., Fisher, J. D., & Baron, R. M. (1988). The equity control model as a predictor of vandalism among college students. *Journal of Applied Social Psychology, 18,* 80–91.

Denenberg, R. V., & Braverman, M. (1999). *The violence-prone workplace: A new approach to dealing with hostile, threatening, and uncivil behavior.* Ithaca, NY: ILR Press.

Deutsch, M. (1985). *Distributive justice: A social-psychological perspective.* New Haven, CT: Yale University Press.

DeVries, D., & Vardi, Y. (2002). The bank-shares regulation affairs and illegalism in Israeli society: A theoretical perspective of unethical managerial behavior. *Israel Affairs, 8*, 226–252.

Diamond, M. A. (1997). Administrative assault: A contemporary psychoanalytic view of violence and aggression in the workplace. *American Review of Public Administration, 27*, 228–247.

Digman, J. M. (1990). Personality structure: Emergence of the five-factor model. *Annual Review of Psychology, 41*, 417–440.

Ditton, J. (1977). Perks, pilferage, and the fiddle: The historical structure of invisible wages. *Theory and Society, 4*, 39–71.

Drory, A. (1993). Perceived political climate and job attitudes. *Journal of Applied Psychology, 83*, 392–407.

Drory, A., & Romm, T. (1990). The definition of organizational politics: A review. *Human Relations, 43*, 1133–1154.

Dubinsky, A., & Loken, B. (1989). Analyzing ethical decision making in marketing. *Journal of Business Research, 19*, 83–107.

Dubois, P. (1976). *Sabotage in industry*. Middlesex, England: Pelican.

Duffy, M. K., Ganster, D. C., & Pagon, M. (2002). Social undermining in the workplace. *Academy of Management Journal, 45*, 331–351.

Dworkin T. M. & Near, J. P. (1997). A better statutory approach to whistleblowing. *Business Ethics Quarterly, 7*, 1–16

Ehrlich, H. J., & Larcom, B. E. K. (1994). *Ethnoviolence in the workplace*. Baltimore: Center for the applied study of Ethnoviolence.

Edwards, R. (1979). *Contested terrain: The transformation of the workplace in the twentieth century*. New York: Basic Books.

Egozi, E. (2002). *Towards a general framework of organizational misbehavior*. Unpublished master's thesis, Tel Aviv University, Israel.

Eisenhardt, K. (1985). Control: Organizational and economic approaches. *Management Science, 31*, 134–149.

Eisenhardt, K. (1989). Agency theory: An assessment and review. *Academy of Management Review, 14*, 57–74.

Elangovan, A. R., & Shapiro, D. L. (1998). Betrayal of trust in organizations. *Academy of Management Review, 23*, 547–566.

Ellis, S., & Arieli, S. (1999). Predicting intentions to report administrative and disciplinary infractions: Applying the reasoned action model. *Human Relations, 52*, 947–967.

Erez, M., & Early, P. C. (1993). *Culture, self, and identity*. New York: Oxford University Press.

Etzioni, A. (1961). *A comparative analysis of complex organizations*. Glencoe, IL: The Free Press.

Ewing, J. A. (1984). Detecting alcoholism: The CAGE questionnaire. *Journal of the American Medical Association, 252*, 1905–1907.

Fallan, J. D., Kudisch, J. D., & Fortunato, V. J. (2000, April). *Using conscientiousness to predict productive and counter productive work behavior*. Paper presented at the 15th annual conference of Society for Industrial and Organizational Psychology, New Orleans, LA.

Fallding, H. (1965). A proposal for the empirical study of values. *American Sociological Review, 30*, 223–233.

Fandt, P. M., & Ferris, G. R. (1990). The management of information and impressions: When employees behave opportunistically. *Organizational Behavior and Human Decision Processes, 45*, 140–158.

Farrell, D. (1983). Exit, voice, loyalty, and neglect as responses to job dissatisfaction: A multidimensional scaling study. *Academy of Management Journal, 26*, 596–607.

Farrell, D., & Petersen, J. C. (1982). Patterns of political behavior in organizations. *Academy of Management Review, 7*, 403–412.

Feldman, D. C. (1981). The multiple socialization of organization members. *Academy of Management Review, 6*, 309–318.

Ferrell, O. C., & Fraedrich, J. (1994). *Business ethics: Ethical decision making.* Boston: Houghton Mifflin.

Ferrell, O. C., & Gresham, L. G. (1985). A contingency framework for understanding ethical decision making in marketing. *Journal of Marketing, 49,* 87– 96.

Ferrell, O. C., Gresham, L. G., & Fraedrich, J. (1989). A synthesis of ethical decision modes in marketing. *Journal of Macro Marketing, 9,* 55–64.

Ferris, G. R., & Kacmar, K. M. (1988, March). *Organization politics and affective reactions.* Paper presented at the annual meeting of the Southwest Division of the Academy of Management, San Antonio, TX.

Ferris, G. R., & Aranya, N. (1983). A comparison of two organizational commitment scales. *Personnel Psychology, 36,* 87–98.

Ferris, G. R., Russ, G. S., & Fandt, P. M. (1989). Politics in organizations. In R. A. Giacalone & P. Rosenfeld (Eds.), *Impression management in the organization* (pp. 143–170). Hillsdale, NJ: Lawrence Erlbaum Associates.

Festinger, L. (1954). A theory of social comparison processes. *Human Relations, 7,* 117–140.

Festinger, L. (1957). *A theory of cognitive dissonance.* Stanford, CA: Stanford University Press.

Fiedler, F. E. (1967). *A theory of leadership effectiveness.* New York: McGraw-Hill.

Fimbel, N., & Burstein, J. S. (1990). Defining the ethical standards of the high-technology industry. *Journal of Business Ethics, 9,* 929–948.

Fishbein, M., & Ajzen, I. (1975). *Belief, attitude, intention and behavior: An introduction to theory research.* Readings, MA: Addison-Wesley.

Fisher, C. D., & Ashkanasy, N. M. (2000). The emerging role of emotions in work life: An introduction. *Journal of Organizational Behavior, 21,* 123–129.

Fisher, J. D., & Baron, R. M. (1982). An equity-based model of vandalism. *Population and Environment, 5,* 182–200.

Fitness, J. (2000). Anger in the workplace: An emotion script approach to anger episodes between workers and their supervisors. *Journal of Organizational Behavior, 21,* 147–162.

Fitzgerald, L. F. (1993). Sexual harassment: Violence against women in the workplace. *American Psychologist, 48,* 1070–1076.

Fitzgerald, L. F., Drasgow, F., Hullin, C. L., Gelfand, M. J., & Magley, V. J. (1997). Antecedents and consequences of sexual harassment in organizations: A test of an integrated model. *Journal of Applied Psychology, 82,* 578–589.

Fitzgerald, L. F., Shullman, S. L., Bailey, N., Richards, M., Swecker, J., Gold, Y., Ormerol, A. J., & Weitzman, L. (1988). The incidence and dimensions of sexual harassment in academia and the workplace. *Journal of Vocational Behavior, 32,* 152–175.

Fleishman, E. A. (1953). The measurement of leadership attitudes in industry. *Journal of Applied Psychology, 37,* 153–158.

Fleishman, E. A., & Harris, E. F. (1962). Patterns of leadership behavior related to employee grievance and turnover. *Personnel Psychology, 15,* 43–56.

Foa, E. B., & Foa, V. G. (1980). Resource theory: Interpersonal behavior as exchange. In M. K. Gergen, M. S. Greenberg, & R. H. Willis (Eds.), *Social exchange* (pp. 77–102). New York: Plenum.

Folger, R., & Skarlicki, D. P. (1998). A popcorn metaphor for employee aggression. In R. W. Griffin, A. M. Oleary-Kelly, & J. M. Collins (Eds.), *Dysfunctional behavior in organizations* (pp. 43–81). Stamford, CT: JAI.

Fox, S., & Spector, P. E. (1999). A model of work frustration–aggression. *Journal of Organizational Behavior, 20,* 915–931.

Fraedrich, J. P., & Ferrell, O. C. (1992). The impact of perceived risk and moral philosophy type on ethical decision making in business organizations. *Journal of Business Ethics, 24,* 281–295.

Freeman, R. E., & Gilbert, D. R. Jr. (1988). *Corporate strategy and the search for ethics.* Englewood Cliffs, NJ: Prentice-Hall.

Friedlander, R., & Greenberg, S. (1971). Effects of job attitudes, training and organizational climate on performance of hard-core unemployed. *Journal of Applied Psychology, 55,* 287–295.

Friedlander, R., & Margulis, N. (1969). Multiple impacts of organizational climate and individual value systems upon job satisfaction. *Personnel Psychology, 22,* 171–183.

Friedman, M. (1979). The social responsibility of business. In T. L. Beauchamp & N. E. Bowie (Eds.), *Ethical theory and business* (pp. 81–83). Englewood Cliffs, NJ: Prentice-Hall.

Frijda N. H. (1993). Moods, emotion episodes and emotions. In M. Lewis & J. M. Haviland (Eds.), *Handbook of emotions* (pp. 381–403). New York: Guilford.

Furnham, A,, & Zacherl, M. (1986). Personality and job satisfaction. *Personality and Individual Differences, 7,* 453–459.

Gabriel, Y. (1998). An introduction to the social psychology of insults in organizations. *Human Relations, 51,* 1329–1354.

Gaertner, K. N. (1980). The structure of organization careers. *Sociology of Education, 53,* 7–20.

Galbraith, J. R. (1977). *Organization design.* Reading, MA: Addison-Wesley.

Gale, E. K. (1993). *Social influences on absenteeism.* Unpublished doctoral dissertation, Purdue University, Lafayette, IN.

Galmor, E. (1996). *The effect of employment status (temporary/permanent) on the organizational misbehavior.* Unpublished master's thesis, Tel Aviv University, Israel.

Galperin, B. L., & Aquino, K. (1999, August). *Individual aggressiveness and minority status as moderators of the relationship between perceived injustice and workplace deviance.* Paper presented at the Academy of Management meeting, Chicago, IL.

Ganot, S. (1999). *Subjective pressure, job satisfaction and workplace misbehavior among R&D employees in a high-tech organization.* Unpublished master's thesis, Tel Aviv University, Israel.

Ganster, D. C. (1989). *Stress, personal control and health.* London: Wiley.

Gardner, H. (1983). *Frames of mind.* New York: Basic Books.

Gardner, W. L., III, & Martinko, M. J. (1998). An organizational perspective of the effects of dysfunctional impression management. In R. W. Griffin, A. M. O'Leary-Kelly, & J. M. Collins (Eds.), *Dysfunctional behavior in organizations: Non-violent dysfunctional behavior* (pp. 69–125). Stamford, CT: JAI.

Gayford, J. J. (1979). Battered wives. *British Journal of Hospital Medicine, 22,* 496–503.

George, J. M. (1989). Mood and absence. *Journal of Business Psychology, 74,* 317–324.

George, J. M., & Brief, A. P. (1996). Motivational agendas in the workplace: The effects of feelings on focus of attention and work motivation. *Research in Organizational Behavior, 18,* 75–109.

Giacalone, R. A., & Greenberg, J. (1997). *Antisocial behaviors in organizations.* Thousand Oaks, CA: Sage.

Giacalone, R. A., Riordan, C. A., & Rosenfeld, P. (1997). Employee sabotage: Toward a practitioner–scholar understanding. In R. A. Giacalone & J. Greenberg (Eds.), *Antisocial behavior in organizations* (pp. 109–129). Thousand Oaks, CA: Sage.

Giacalone, R. A., & Rosenfeld, P. (1987). Reasons for employee sabotage in the workplace. *Journal of Business Psychology, 1,* 367–378.

Giacalone, R. A., Rosenfeld, P. (1991) (Eds.). *Applied impression management: How image-making affects managerial decisions.* Thousand Oaks, CA: Sage Publications.

Gladstein, D. (1984). Groups in context: A model of task group effectiveness. *Administrative Science Quarterly, 29,* 499–517.

Glomb, T. M., Richman, W. L., Hulin, C. L., & Drasgow, F. (1997). Ambient sexual harassment: An integrated model of antecedents and consequences.*Organizational Behavior and Human Decision Processes, 71,* 309–328.

Goffman, E. (1959). *The presentation of self in everyday life.* Garden City, NY: Doubleday Anchor.

Goffman, E. (1971). *The presentation of self in everyday life.* New York: Penguin.

Goldberg, L. R. (1992). The development of marker variables for the big-five factor structure. *Psychological Assessment, 4,* 26–42.

Goldman, O. (1992). *Deviant behavior in work organizations: Constructs, dimensions, and factors influencing individual involvement in deviance.* Unpublished master's thesis, Tel Aviv University, Israel.

Goldshmid-Avon, L. (1997). *Individual and organizational antecedents of workaholism.* Unpublished master's thesis, Tel Aviv University, Israel.

Goleman, D. (1995). *Emotional intelligence.* New York: Bantam Books.

Goleman, D. (1998). *Working with emotional intelligence.* New York: Bantam Books.

Goleman, D., & Cherniss, C. (Eds.). (2001). *The emotionally intelligent workplace: How to select for, measure, and improve emotional intelligence in individuals.* San Francisco: Jossey-Bass.

Golembiewski, R. T., & Munzenrider, R. (1975). Social desirability as an intervening variable in interpreting OD effects. *Journal of Applied Behavioral Science, 11,* 317–332.

Gouldner, A. W. (1954). *Patterns of industrial bureaucracy.* New York: The Free Press.

Granovetter, M. S. (1985). Economic action and social structure: The problem of embeddedness. *American Journal of Sociology, 91,* 481–510.

Granovetter, M. S. (1992). Problems of explanation in economic sociology. In N. Nohria & R. G. Eccles (Eds.). *Networks and organizations: Structure, form and action* (pp. 25–56). Boston: Harvard Business School Press.

Gray-Toft, P., & Anderson, J. G. (1981). The nursing stress scale: Development of an instrument. *Journal of Behavioral Assessment, 3,* 11–23.

Graziano, W. G., & Eisenberg, N. (1997). Agreeableness: A dimension of personality. In R. Hogan, J. Johnson, & S. R. Brrigs (Eds.), *Handbook of personality psychology* (pp. 795–824). San Diego, CA: Academic Press.

Green, R. M. (1994). *The ethical manager: A new method for business ethics.* New York: Macmillan.

Greenberg, D. B., & Strasser, S. (1986). Development and application of a model of personal control in organizations. *Academy of Management Review, 11,* 164–177.

Greenberg J. (1998). The cognitive geometry of employee theft: Negotiating "the line" between stealing and taking. In R. W. Griffin, A. M. O'Leary-Kelly, & J. M. Collins (Eds.), *Dysfunctional behavior in organizations: Non-violent dysfunctional behavior* (Vol. 23, Part B, pp. 147–193). Stamford, CT: JAI.

Greenberg, J. (1990a). Employee theft as a response to underemployment inequity: The hidden cost of pay cuts. *Journal of Applied Psychology, 75,* 561–568.

Greenberg, J. (1990b). Organizational justice: Yesterday, today and tomorrow. *Journal of Management, 16,* 399–432.

Greenberg, J. (1993). Stealing in the name of justice: Informational and interpersonal moderators of theft reactions to underpayment inequity. *Organizational Behavior and Human Decision Processes, 54,* 81–103.

Greenberg, J. (1994) (Ed.). *Organizational behavior: The state of the science.* Hillsdale, NJ: Lawrence Erlbaum Associates.

Greenberg, J. (1995). Employee theft. In N. Nicholson (Ed.), *The Blackwell encyclopedic dictionary of organizational behavior* (pp. 154–155) Oxford, United Kingdom: Blackwell.

Greenberg, J. (1997). The steal motive: Management the social determinants of employee theft. In R. A. Giacalone & J. Greenberg (Eds.), *Antisocial behavior in organizations* (pp. 85–107). Thousand Oaks, CA: Sage.

Greenberg, J., & Alge, B. J. (1998). Aggressive reactions to workplace injustice. In R. W. Griffin, A. M. O'Leary-Kelly, & J. M. Collins (Eds.), *Dysfunctional behavior in organizations: Violent and deviant behavior* (Vol. 23, Part A, pp. 83–117). Stamford, CT: JAI.

Greenberg, J. (2002). Who stole the money? Individual and situational determinants of employee theft. *Organizational Behavior and Human Decision Processes, 89,* 985–1003.

Greenberg, J., & Barling, J. (1996). Employee theft. In C. L. Cooper & D. M. Rousseau (Eds.), *Trends in organizational behavior* (pp. 49–64). New York: Wiley.

Greenberg, L., & Barling, J. (1999). Predicting employee aggression against coworkers, subordinates and supervisors: The roles of person behaviors and perceived workplace factors. *Journal of Organizational Behavior, 20,* 897–913.

Greenberg, J., & Baron, R. B. (1997). *Behavior in organizations* (6th ed.). Englewood Cliffs, NJ: Prentice-Hall.

Greenberg, J., & Scott, K. S. (1996). Why do workers bite hands that feed them? Employee theft as a social exchange process. In B. M. Staw & L. L. Cummings (Eds.), *Research in organizational behavior* (Vol. 18, pp. 111–156). Greenwich, CT: JAI.

Greengard, S. (1993). Theft control starts with HR strategies. *Personnel Journal, 72,* 80–88.

Griffin, R. W., O'Leary-Kelly, A. M., & Collins, J. M. (Eds.). (1998a). *Dysfunctional behavior in organizations: Non-violent dysfunctional behavior* (Vol. 23, Part B). Stamford, CT: JAI.

Griffin, R. W., O'Leary-Kelly, A. M., & Collins, J. M. (1998b). Dysfunctional work behaviors in organizations. In C. L. Cooper & D. M. Rousseau (Eds.), *Trends in organizational behavior* (pp. 65–82). New York: Wiley.

Grover, S. L. (1993). Lying, deceit and subterfuge: A model of dishonesty in the workplace. *Organizational Science, 4,* 478–495.

Gruys, M. L. (1999). *The dimensionality of deviant employee performance in the workplace.* Unpublished doctoral dissertation, University of Minnesota, Minneapolis, MN.

Guinsel, J. (1997). *Cyberwars: Espionage on the Internet.* Cambridge, MA: Perseus Books.

Guion, R. M., & Gottier, R. F. (1965). Validity of personality measures in personnel selection. *Personnel Psychology, 18,* 135–164.

Gutek, B. A. (1985). *Sex in the workplace.* San Francisco: Jossey-Bass.

Guzzo, R. A., & Dickson, M. W. (1996). Teams in organizations: Recent research on performance and effectiveness. *Annual Review of Psychology, 47,* 307–338.

Hackett, R. D. (1989). Work attitudes and employee absenteeism: A synthesis of the literature. *Journal of Psychology, 62,* 235–248.

Hackman, J. R., & Oldham, G. R. (1976). Motivation through the design of work: Test of a theory. *Organization Behavior and Human Performance, 16,* 250–279.

Hackman, J. R., & Oldham, G. R. (1980). *Work redesign.* Reading, MA: Addison-Wesley.

Hall, D. T. (1976). *Careers in organizations.* Pacific Palisades: Goodyear.

Hall, D. T., & Schneider, B. (1972). Correlates of organizational identification as a function of career pattern and organizational type. *Administrative Science Quarterly, 17,* 340–350.

Hall, R. H. (1999). *Organizations: Structures, processes and outcomes.* Englewood Cliffs, NJ: Prentice-Hall.

Halverson, R. (1998). Employee theft drives shrink rate. *Discount Store News, 9,* 2–12.

Hanisch, K. A., & Hulin, C. L. (1991). General attitudes and organizational withdrawal: An evaluation of a causal model. *Journal of Vocational Behavior, 39,* 110–128.

Harper, D., & Emmert, F. (1963). Work behavior in a service industry. *Social Forces, 42,* 216–225.

Harrell, T., & Alpert, B. (1979). The need for autonomy among managers. *Academy of Management Review, 4,* 259–267.

Harris, M. M., & Greising, L. A. (1998). Alcohol and drug abuse as dysfunctional workplace behaviors. In R. W. Griffin, A. M. O'Leary-Kelly, & J. M. Collins (Eds.), *Dysfunctional behavior in organizations: Non-violent dysfunctional behavior* (Vol. 23, Part B, pp. 21–48). Stamford, CT: JAI.

Hegarty, W. H., & Sims, H. P. (1978). Some determinants of unethical decision behavior: An experiment. *Journal of Applied Psychology, 63,* 451–457.

Helldorfer, M. C. (1987). Church professionals and work addiction. *Studies in Formative Spirituality, 8*(2), 199–210.

Hellriegel, D., & Slocum, J. W. (1974). Organizational climate: Measures, research and contingencies. *Academy of Management Journal, 17,* 255–280.

Hellriegel, D., Slocum, J. W., & Woodman, R. W. (2001). Organizational behavior (9th ed.). Cincinnati, OH: South-Western College Publishing.

Hersey, P., & Blanchard, K. (1982). Management of organizational behavior (4th ed.). Englewood Cliffs, NJ: Prentice-Hall.

Herzberg, F. (1968). One more time: How do you motivate employees? *Harvard Business Review, 46,* 53–62.

Hirschi, T. (1969). *Causes and delinquency.* Berkeley: University of California Press.

Hirschman, A. O. (1970). *Exit, voice, and loyalty: Responses to decline in firms, organizations and states.* Cambridge, MA: Harvard University Press.

Hochschild, A. R. (1983). *The managed heart: Commercialization of human feeling.* Berkeley, CA: University of California Press.

Hofstede, G. (1993). Cultural constraints in management theories. *Academy of Management Executive, 7,* 81–94.

Hogan, J., & Hogan, R. (1989). How to measure employee reliability. *Journal of Applied Psychology, 74,* 273–279.

Hogan, R., & Ones, D. S. (1997). Conscientiousness and integrity at work. In R. Hogan, J. A. Johnson, & S. R. Brigs (Eds.), *Handbook of personality psychology* (pp. 849–870). San Diego, CA: Academic Press.

Holland, J. L. (1985). *Making vocational choices: A theory of vocational personalities and work environment* (2nd ed.). Englewood Cliffs, NJ: Prentice-Hall.

Hollinger, R. C. (1986). Acts against the workplace: Social bonding an employee deviance. *Deviant Behavior, 7,* 53–75.

Hollinger, R. C. (1991). Neutralizing in the workplace: An empirical analysis of property theft and production deviance. *Deviance Behavior: An Interdisciplinary Journal, 12,* 169–202.

Hollinger, R. C., & Clark, J. (1982). Employee deviance: A response to the perceived quality of the work experience. *Work and Occupations, 9,* 97–114.

Hollinger, R. C., & Clark, J. (1983). Deterrence in the workplace: Perceived certainty, perceived severity and employee theft. *Social Forces, 62*(2), 398–418.

Holsti, O. R. (1968). Content analysis. In G. Lindzeye & E. Aronson (Eds.). *The handbook of social psychology* (Vol. 2, pp. 596–692). Reading, MA: Addison-Wesley.

Holtsman-Chen, E. (1984). *The effects of entry jobs on the chances for promotion.* An Unpublished master's thesis, Tel Aviv University, Israel.

Homans, G. C. (1950). *The human group.* New York: Harcourt, Brace.

Horning, D. N. M. (1970). Blue collar theft: Conceptions of property, attitudes toward pilferage, and work group norms in a modern industrial plant. In E. O. Smigel & H. L. Ross (Eds.), *Crimes against bureaucracies* (pp. 46–64). New York: Van Nostrand Reinhold.

Hosmer, T. L. (1987). Ethical analysis and human resource management. *Human Resource Management, 26,* 313–330.

Hosmer, T. L. (1991). *The ethics of Management.* Boston: Irwin.

Hough, L. M. (1992). The "big-five" personality variables-construct confusion: Description versus prediction. *Human Performance, 5,* 139–155.

Hough, L. M., Eaton, M. K., Dunnette, M. D., Kamp, J. D., & McCloy, R. A. (1990). Criterion-related validities of personality constructs and the effect of response distortion on those validities. *Journal of Applied Psychology, 75,* 581–595.

Hough, L. M., & Schnieder, R. J. (1996). Personality traits, taxonomies, and applications in organizations. In K. R. Murphy (Ed.), *Individual differences and behavior in organizations* (pp. 31–88). San Francisco: Jossey-Bass.

House, R. J., & Singh, J. V. (1987). Organizational behavior: Some new directions for I/O psychology. *Annual Review of Psychology, 38,* 669–718.

House, R. J., Schuler, R. S., & Levanoni, E. (1983). Short notes, role conflict and ambiguity scales: Reality or artifacts. *Journal of Applied Psychology, 68,* 334–337.

House, R. J., & Podsakoff, P. M. (1994). Leadership effectiveness: Past perspectives and future directions for research. In J. Greenberg (Ed.), *Organizational behavior: The state of the science* (pp. 45–82). Hillsdale, NJ: Lawrence Erlbaum Associates.

House, R., Rousseau, D., & Themas-Hurt, M. (1995). The meso paradigm: A framework for the integration of micro and macro organizational behavior. *Research in Organizational Behavior, 17,* 71–114.

Humphreys, L. G. (1977). Predictability of employee theft: Importance of the base rate. *Journal of Applied Psychology, 62,* 514–516.

Hunt, S. T. (1996). Generic work behavior: An investigation into the dimensions of entry level, hourly job performance. *Personnel Psychology, 49,* 51–83.

Ilgen, D. R., & Klein, H. J. (1989). Organizational behavior. *Annual Review of Psychology, 40,* 327–351.

Ilgen, D. R., O'Driscoll, M. P., & Hildreth, K. (1992). Time devoted to job and off job activities, interole conflict and affective experiences. *Journal of Applied Psychology, 77,* 272–279.

Isaac, R. G. (1993). Organizational culture: Some new perspectives. In R. T. Golembiewski (Ed.), *Handbook of organizational behavior* (pp. 91–112). New York: Marcel Dekker.

Isen, A. M., & Baron, R. A. (1991). Positive affect as a factor on categorization. In L. L. Cummings & B. M. Staw (Eds.), *Research in organizational behavior* (Vol. 13, pp. 1–53). Greenwich, CT: JAI.

Ivancevich, J. M., & Matteson, M. T. (1990). *Organizational behavior and management.* Boston, MA: Irwin.

Izraeli, D. (1994). *Marketing: Theory and practice.* Tel Aviv: Cherikover.

Jaccard, J., & Davidson, A. R. (1975). A comparison of two models of social behavior: results of a survey sample. *Sociometry, 38* (4), 497–517.

James, G. G. (1984). In defense of whistle blowing. In W. H. Shaw & V. Barry (Eds.), *Moral issues in business* (6th ed., pp. 409–417). Belmont, CA: Wadsworth.

Janis, I. L. (1982). *Victims of groupthink:* A psychological study of foreign-policy decisions and fiascoes (rev. ed.). Boston: Houghton-Mifflin.

Janoff-Bulman, R. (1992). *Shattered assumptions: Towards a new psychology to trauma.* New York: The Free Press.

Jansen, E., & Von Glinow, M. A. (1985). Ethical ambivalence and organizational reward systems. *Academy of Management Review, 10,* 814–822.

Jensen, G. F., & Hodson, R. (1999). Synergies in the study of crime and the workplace. *Work and Occupations, 26,* 6–20.

Jermier, J. (1988). Sabotage at work: The rational view. *Sociology of Organizations, 6,* 101–134.

Jick, T. D. (1979). Mixing qualitative and quantitative methods: Triangulation in action. *Administrative Science Quarterly, 24,* 602–611.

John, O. P. (1989). Towards a taxonomy of personality descriptions. In D. M. Buss & N. Cantor (Eds.), *Personality psychology: Recent trends and emerging directions* (pp. 261–271). New York: Springer-Verlag.

Johns, G. (1997). Contemporary research on absence from work: Correlations, causes and consequences. *International Review of Industrial and Organizational Psychology, 12,* 115–174.

Johns, G. (2001). The psychology of lateness, absenteeism, and turnover. In N. Anderson, D. S. Ones, H. K. Sinangil & C. Viswesvaran (Eds.), *Handbook of industrial, work and organizational psychology* (Vol. 2, pp. 232–252). London: Sage.

Johnson, P., & Gill, J. (1993). *Management control and organizational behavior.* London: Paul Chapman.

Johnson, P. R., & Indvik, J. (1994). Workplace violence. *PUBLIC personnel Management, 23,* 515–523.

Jones, E. E., & Gerard, H. B. (1967). *Foundations of social psychology.* New York: Wiley.

Jones, G. R. (1984). Task visibility, free riding, and shirking: Explaining the effect of structure and technology on employee bahavior. *Academy of Management Review, 9,* 684–695.

Jones, J. W., & Terris, W. (1983). Predicting employees theft in home improvement centers. *Psychological Reports, 52,* 187–201.

Jones, T. M. (1991). Ethical decision making by individuals in organizations: An issue-contigent model. *Academy of Management Review, 16,* 366–395.

Judge, T. A., Matocchio, J. J., & Thoresen, C. J. (1997). Five-factor model of personality and employee absence. *Journal of Applied Psychology, 82,* 745–755.

Kacmar, K. M., & Carlson, D. S. (1998). A qualitative analysis of the dysfunctional aspects of political behavior in organizations. In R. W. Griffin, A. M. O'Leary-Kelly, & J. M. Collins (Eds.), *Dysfunctional behavior in organizations: Non-violent dysfunctional behavior* (Vol. 23, Part B, pp. 195–218). Stamford, CT: JAI.

Kacmar, K. M., & Carlson, D. S. (1994). Using impression management in women's job search processes. *American Behavioral Scientist, 37,* 682–696.

Kahn, R. L., Wolfe, D. M., Quinn, R. P., Snoek, J. D., & Rosenthal, R. A. (1964). *Organizational stress: Studies in role conflict and ambiguity.* New York: Wiley.

Kanji, G. K. (1999). *100 Statistical tests.* London: Sage.

Kanter, D. L., & Marvis, P. H. (1989). *The cynical Americans: Living and working in an age of discontent and disillusion.* San Francisco: Jossey-Bass.

Kantor, H. (1999). *Misbehavior among social workers in welfare agencies: Its relationship with professional commitment, burnout at work, and the violence of patients.* Unpublished master's thesis, Tel Aviv University, Israel.

Karasek, R. A., & Theorell, T. (1990). *Healthy work: Stress, productivity, and the reconstruction of working life.* New York: Basic Books.

Karau, S. J., & Williams, K. D. (1993). Social loafing: A meta-analytic review and theoretical integration. *Journal of Personality and Social Psychology, 65,* 681–706.

Katz, D., & Kahn, R. L. (1966). *The social psychology of organizations.* New York: J Wiley.

Katz, D., & Kahn, R. L. (1978). *The social psychology of organizations.* New York: Wiley.

Katzell, R. A., & Austin, J. T. (1992). From then to now: The development of industrial-organizational psychology in the United States. *Journal of Applied Psychology, 77,* 803–835.

Kemper, T. D. (1966). Representative roles and the legitimization of deviance. *Social Problems, 13,* 288–298.

Kets de Vries, M. F. R., & Miller, D. (1984). *The neurotic organization.* San Francisco: Jossey-Bass.

Kidwell, R. E., & Bennett, N. (1993). Employee propensity to withhold effort: A conceptual model to intersect three avenues of research. *Academy of Management Review, 18,* 429–456.

Killinger, B. (1991). *Workaholics: The respectable addicts.* New-York: Simon & Schuster.

Kilman, R. H. (1985). Managing your organization's culture. *Nonprofit World Report, 3,* 12–15.

Kipnis, D., Schmidt, S. M., & Wilkinson, I. (1980). Intraorganizational influence tactics: Exploration in getting one's way. *Journal of Applied Psychology, 65,* 440–452.

Klein, R. L., Leong, G. B., & Silva, J. A. (1996). Employee sabotage in the workplace: A biopsychosocial model. *Journal of Forensic Sciences, 41,* 52–55.

Knoke, D. (1990). *Organizing for collective action: The political economies of associations.* Hawthorne, NY: Aldine de Gruyter.

Kochan, N., & Whittington, B. (1991). *Bankrupt: The BBCI fraud.* London: Gollancz.

Kohlberg, L. (1969). Stage and sequence: The cognitive-developmental approach to socialization. In D. A. Goslin (Ed.), *Handbook of socialization theory and research* (pp. 347–480). Chicago: Rand McNally.

Kohlberg, L. (1984). *The psychology of moral development.* New York: Harper & Row.

Konovsky, M. A., & Cropanzano, R. (1991). Perceived pairness of employee drug testing as a predictor of employee attitudes and job performance. *Journal of Applied Psychology, 76, 5,* 698–707.

Konrad, A. M., & Gutek, B. A. (1986). Impact of work experiences on attitudes toward sexual harassment. *Administrative Science Quarterly, 31,* 422–438.

Korman, A. K. (1971). Organizational achievement, aggression and creativity: Some suggestions toward an integrated theory. *Organizational Behavior and Human Performance, 6,* 593–613.

Korman, A. K. (1976). Hypothesis of work behavior revisited and an extension. *Academy of Management Review, 1,* 50–63.

Kotter, J. P. (1973). The psychological contract: Managing the joining up process. *California Management Review, 15,* 91–99.

Kraut, A. I. (1975). Predicting turnover of employee from measured job attitudes. *Organizational Behavior and Human Performance, 13,* 233–243.

Kravitz, D. A., & Martin, B. (1986). Ringelmann rediscovered: The original article. *Journal of Personality and Social Psychology, 50,* 936–941.

Kreitner, R., & Kinicki, A. (1995). *Organizational behavior* (3rd ed.). Chicago: Irwin.

Krigel, K. (2001). *Relationship between personality traits (Big 5), organizational justice, and organizational misbehavior: A conceptual model.* Unpublished master's thesis, Tel Aviv University, Israel.

Kunda, G. (1992). *Engineering culture.* Philadelphia, PA: Temple University Press.

Kurland, N. B. (1995). Ethical intentions and the theories of reasoned action and planned behavior. *Journal of Applied Social Psychology, 25,* 297–313.

Kurland, O. M. (1993, June). Workplace violence. *Risk Management,* p. 76.

Kurmar, K., & Beyerlein, M. (1991). Construction and validation of an instrument for measuring ingratiatory behaviors in organizational settings. *Journal of Applied Psychology, 76,* 619–627.

Laabs, J. (2000). Employee sabotage: Don't be a target. *www.workforceonline.com/feature/00/03/17*

Landau, A. (1981). *Organizational-climate and work performance (Absenteeism and performance appraisal).* Unpublished master's thesis, Tel Aviv University, Israel.

Landy, F. J. (1985). *Psychology of work behavior* (3rd ed.) Homewood, IH: Dorsey Press.

Langer, E. J. (1983). *The psychology of control.* Beverly-Hills, CA: Sage.

Lasley, J. R. (1988). Toward a control theory of white collar offending. *Journal of Quantitative Criminology, 4*(4), 347–362.

Latané, B., Williams, K., & Harkins, S. (1979). Many hands make light the work: The causes and consequences of social loafing. *Journal of Personality and Social Psychology, 37,* 822–832.

Lazarus, R. S. (1991). *Emotion and adaptation.* New York: Oxford University Press.

Leatherwood, M. L., & Spector, L. C. (1991). Enforcements, inducements, expected utility and employee misconduct. *Journal of Management, 17,* 553–569.

Leavitt, H. J. (1972). *Managerial psychology* (3rd ed.). Chicago: University of Chicago Press.

Lee, C., Ashford, S. J., & Bobko, P. (1990). Interactive effects of "Type A" behavior and perceived control on worker performance, job satisfaction, and somatic complaints. *Academy of Management Journal, 33,* 870–881.

Lee, R. M. (1993). *Doing research on sensitive topics.* London: Sage.

Lehman, W. E. K., & Simpson, D. D. (1992). Employee substance use and on the job behavior. *Journal of Applied Psychology, 77,* 309–321.

Lerner, H. (1980). Internal prohibitions against female anger. *American Journal for the Advancement of Psychoanalysis, 40*(2), 137–148.

Levin, D. (1989). *Investigating the concept of violence among social-workers in welfare agencies.* Unpublished master's thesis, Tel Aviv University, Israel.

Lewin, K. (1951). *Field theory in social science: Selected theoretical papers .* New York: Harper Bros.

Lewis, K. M. (2000). When leaders display emotions: How followers respond to negative emotional expression of male and female leaders. *Journal of Organizational Behavior, 22,* 221–234.

Lewis, P. V. (1985). Defining "business ethics": Like nailing Jello to a wall. *Journal of Business Ethics, 4,* 377–383.

Lichtenstein, Y. (2000). *Employee jealousy and envy and their behavioral outcomes.* Unpublished master's thesis, Tel Aviv University, Israel.

Liden, R., & Green, S. (1980, August). *On the measurement of career orientation.* Paper presented at the Midwest Academy of Management Meeting, Cincinnati, OH.

Lind, E. A., & Tyler, T. (1988). *The social psychology of procedural justice.* New York: Plenum.

Linden, R. C., & Mitchell, T. R. (1988). Ingratiatory behaviors in organizational settings. *Academy of Management Review, 13,* 572–587.

Linstead, S. (1985). Breaking the purity rule: Industrial sabotage and the symbolic process. *Personnel Review, 15,* 12–19.

Lipman, M., & McGraw, W. R. (1988). Employee theft: A $40 billion industry. *Annals of the American Academy of Political and Social Science, 498,* 51–59.

Litwin, G. H., & Stringer, R. A. (1968). *Motivation and organizational climate.* Cambridge, MA: Harvard University Press.

Locke, E. A. (1968). Theory of task motivation and incentives. *Organizational Behavior and Human Performance, 3,* 157–189.

London House Press (1980). *Personnel selection inventory.* Park Ridge, IL: Author.

Lovelock, C. H. (1983). Classifying services to gain strategic advantages: Marketing insights. *Journal of Marketing, 47,* 9–20.

Luthans, F., & Kreitner, R. (1985). *Organizational behavior modification and beyond: An operant and social learning approach.* Glenview, IL: Scott, Foresman.

Machlowitz, M. (1980). *Workaholics, living with them, working with them.* Reading, MA: Addison-Wesley.

Maclagan, P. (1998). *Management and morality: A developmental perspective.* Thousand Oaks, CA: Sage.

Maidment, F., & Eldridge, W. (2000). *Business in government and society: Ethical, international decision-making.* Englewood Cliffs, NJ: Prentice-Hall.

Mangione, T. W., & Quinn, R. P. (1975). Job satisfaction, counterproductive behavior, and drug use at work. *Journal of Applied Psychology, 60,* 114–116.

Mangione, T. W., Howland, J., & Lee, M. (1998). *New perspectives for worksite alcohol strategies: Results from a corporate drinking study.* Boston: JSI Research and Training, Inc.

Manning, F. V. (1981). *Managerial dilemmas and executive growth.* Reston, VA: Reston.

Mantell, M. (1994). *Ticking bombs: Defusing violence in the workplace.* Burr Ridge, IL: Irwin.

March, J. G., & Simon, H. A. (1958). *Organizations.* New York: Wiley.

Marcus, A. I., & Segal, H. P. (1989). *Technology in America: A brief history.* San Diego, CA: Harcourt, Brace, Jovanovich.

Mars, G. (1973). Chance, punters and the fiddle: Institutionalized pilferage in a hotel dining room. In M. Warner (Ed.), *The sociology of the workplace* (pp. 200–210). New York: Halsted.

Mars, G. (1974). Dock pilferage: A cause stdy in occupational theft. In P. Rock & M. McIntosh (Eds.), *Deviance and social control* (pp. 209–228). London: Tavistock.

Mars, G. (1982). *Cheats at work: An anthropology of workplace crime.* London: George Allen & Unwin.

Mars, G. (1987). Longshore drinking, economic security and union politics in Newfoundland. In M. T. Douglas (Ed.), *Constructive drinking* (pp. 91–101). Cambridge, England: Cambridge University Press.

Martin, T. C. (1996). The comprehensive terrorism prevention act of 1995. *Seton Hall Legislative Journal, 20*(1), 201–248.

Martinko, M. J., & Zellars, K. L (1998). Toward a theory of workplace violence and aggression: A cognitive appraisal perspective. In R. W. Griffin, A. M. O'Leary-Kelly, & J. M. Collins (Eds.), *Dysfunctional behavior in organizations: Violent and deviant behavior* (Vol. 23, Part A, pp. 1–42). Stamford, CT: JAI.

Maslow, A. H. (1954). *Motivation and personality.* New York: Harper & Row.

Masuch, M. (1985). Vicious circles in organizations. *Administrative Science Quarterly, 30,* 14–33.

Mayo, E. (1933). *The human problems of an industrial civilization.* New York: Macmillan.

Mazzeo, J., & Harvey, A. L. (1988). *The equivalence of scores from automated and conventional educational and psychological tests: A review of the literature.* Princeton, NJ: Educational Testing Service.

McCrae, R. R., & Costa, P. T. (1997). Conceptions and correlates to openness to experience. In R. Hogan, J. A. Johnson, & S. R. Briggs (Eds.), *Handbook of personality psychology* (pp. 825–846). San Diego, CA: Academic Press.

McCrae, R. R., & John, O. P. (1992). An introduction to the five-factor model and its applications. *Journal of Personality, 60,* 175–215.

McFarlin, S. K., & Fals-Stewart, W. (2001, August). *Workplace absenteeism and alchohol use: A day-to-day examination.* Paper presented at the Academy of Management Meeting, Washington, DC.

McGarvey, M. (1992). The challenge of containing health-care costs. *Financial Executive, 8,* 34–40.

McGrath, J. E. (1976). Stress and behavior in organizations. In M. D. Dunnette (Ed.), *Handbook of industrial and organizational psychology* (pp. 1351–1395). Chicago: Rand McNally.

McGurn, R. (1988). Spotting the thieves who work among us. *Wall Street Journal,* p. 164.

McGregor, D. (1960). *The human side of enterprise.* New York: McGraw-Hill.

Mclean Parks, J. (1997). The fourth arm of justice: The art and science of revenge. In R. J. Lewicki, R. J. Bies, & B. H. Sheppard (Eds.), *Research on negotiation in organizations* (Vol. 6, pp. 113–144). Greenwich, CT: JAI.

Meglino, B. M. (1977). Stress and performance: Are they always incompatible? *Supervisory Management, 22,* 2–12.

Meglino, B. M., Ravlin, E. C., & Adkins, C. L. (1989). A work values approach to corporate culture: A field test of the value congruence process and its relationship to individual outcomes. *Journal of Applied Psychology, 74,* 424–432.

Mensch, B. S., & Kandel, D. B. (1988). Do job conditions influence the use of drugs? *Journal of Health and Social Behavior, 29*(2), 169–184.

Merriam, D. H. (1977). Employee theft. *Criminal Justice Abstracts, 9,* 375–410.

Merton, R. K. (1953). *Social theory and social structure.* Glencoe, IL: The Free Press.

Merton, R. T. (1938). Social structure and anomie. *American Sociological Review, 3,* 672–682.

Meyer, J. P., & Allen, N. J. (1997). *Commitment in the workplace: Theory, research, and application.* Thousand Oaks, CA: Sage.

Miceli, M. P., & Near, J. P. (1992). *Blowing the whistle: The organizational and legal implications for companies and employees.* New York: Lexington.

Miceli, M. P., & Near, J. P. (1997). Whistle blowing as antisocial behavior. In R. A. Giacalone & J. Greenberg (Eds.), *Antisocial behavior in organizations* (pp. 130–149). Thousand Oaks, CA: Sage.

Miles, R. E., & Snow, C. C. (1978). *Organizational strategy, structure and process.* New York: McGraw-Hill.

Mintzberg, H. (1983). *Power in and around organizations.* Englewood Cliffs, NJ: Prentice-Hall.

Mitchell, T. R. (1979). Organizational behavior. *Annual Review of Psychology, 30,* 243–281.

Mitroff, I. I., & Kilmann, R. H. (1984). *Corporate tragedies: Product tampering, sabotage, and other catastrophes.* New York: Praeger.

Moberg, D. J. (1997). On employee vice. *Business Ethics Quarterly, 7,* 41–60.

Molstad, C. (1988). Control strategies used by industrial brewery workers: Work avoidance, impression management and solidarity. *Human Organization, 47,* 354–360.

Moore, G. A. (1995). *Inside the Tornado: Markeing strategies from Silicon Valley's cutting edge.* New York: Harper Business.

Moorman, R. H., & Podaskoff, P. M. (1992). A meta analytic review and empirical test of the potential confounding effects of social desirability response sets in organizational behavior research. *Journal of Occupational and Organizational Psychology, 65,* 131–149.

Moran, E. T., & Volkwein, J. F. (1992). The cultural approach to the formation of organizational climate. *Human Relation, 45,* 19–47.

Morin, W. J. (1995). Silent sabotage: Mending the crisis in corporate values. *Management Review,* July, 10–14.

Mosier, S. K. (1983). *Workaholics: An analysis of their stress, success and priorities.* Unpublished master's thesis, University of Texas, Austin.

Mount, M. K., & Barrick, M. R. (1995). The big five personality dimensions: Implications for research and practice in human resources management. *Research in Personality and Human Resource Management, 13,* 153–200.

Mowday, R. T., & Sutton, R. I. (1993). Organizational behavior: Linking individuals and groups to organizational contexts. *Annual Review of Psychology, 44,* 195–229.

Muchinsky, P. M. (2000). Emotions in the workplace: The neglect of organizational behavior. *Journal of Organizational Behavior, 21,* 801–805.

Murphy, K. R. (1996). Individual differences and behavior in organizations: Much more than g. In K. R. Murphy (Ed.), *Individual differences and behavior in organizations* (pp. 3–30). San Francisco: Jossey-Bass.

Murry, W. D., Sivasubramaniam, N., & Jacques, P. (1999, August). *The leader's role in organizations: The moderating effects of leader behavior on perceived sexual harassment.* Paper presented at the Annual Meeting of the Academy of Management, Chicago.

Nadler, D. A., & Tushman, M. L. (1980). A model for diagnosing organizational behavior: Applying a congruence perspective. *Organizational Dynamics, 9,* 35–51.

National Council on Crime and Deliquency (1975). *Workplace crime: Proceedings and resources of the internal business theft conference.* Chicago: Author.

Naughton, T. J. (1987). A conceptual view of workaholism and implications for career counseling and research. *Career Development Quarterly, 35*(3), 180–187.

Near, J. P., Baucus, M. S., & Miceli, M. P. (1993). The relationship between values and practice: Organizational climates for wrongdoing. *Administration & Society, 25,* 204–226.

Near, J. P., Dworkin, T. M., & Miceli, M. P. (1993). Explaining the whistle-blowing process: Suggestions from power theory and justice theory. *Organization Science, 4,* 392–411.

Near, J. P., & Miceli, M. P. (1984). The relationship among beliefs, organizational position, and whistle-blowing status: A discriminant analysis. *Academy of Management Journal, 27,* 687–705.

Near, J. P., & Miceli, M. P. (1985). Organizational dissidence: The case of whistle-blowing. *Journal of Business Ethics, 4,* 1–16.

Near, J. P., & Miceli, M. P. (1986). Retaliation against whistle blowers: Predictors and effects. *Journal of Applied Psychology, 71,* 137–145.

Near, J. P., & Miceli, M. P. (1995). Effective whistle-blowing. *Academy of Management Review, 20,* 679–708.

Neuman, J. H., & Baron, R. A. (1997). Aggression in the workplace. In R. A. Giacalone & J. Greenberg (Eds.), *Antisocial behavior in organizations* (pp. 37–67). Thousand Oaks, CA: Sage.

Neven, T. (2001). Employee theft on the rise, but shoplifting losses fall (online). www.homecenternews.com

Noe, R., Hollenbeck, J. R., Gerhart, B., & Wright, P. (1997). *Human resource management: Gaining a competitive advantage.* Chicago: Irwin.

Nomani, A. Q. (1995, October). Women likelier to face violence in the workplace. *The Wall Street Journal,* p. A16.

Norman, W. T. (1963). Toward an adequate taxonomy of personality attributes: Replicated factor structure in peer nomination personality ratings. *Journal of Abnormal and Social Psychology, 66,* 483–574.

Oates, W. E. (1971). *Confessions of a workaholic: The facts about work addiction.* New York: World.

Ofer, R. (2003). *How do new employees learn to misbehave? The unexpected influence of organizational socialization.* Unpublished master's thesis, Tel Aviv University, Israel.

O'Leary-Kelly, A. M., Paetzold, R. L., & Griffin, R. W. (2000). Sexual harassment as aggressive behavior: An actor-based perspective. *Academy of Management Review, 25,* 372–388.

O'Leary-Kelly, A. M., Griffin, R. W., & Glew, D. J. (1996). Organization-motivated aggression: A research framework. *Academy of Management Review, 21,* 225–253.

O'Leary-Kelly, A. M., Duffy, M. K., & Griffin, R. W. (2000). Construct confusion in the study of antisocial behavior at work. *Research in Personnel and Human Resource Management, 18,* 275–303.

Ones, D. S., Viswesvaran, C., & Schmidt, F. L. (1993). Comprehensive meta-analysis of integrity test validities: Findings and implications for personnel selection and theories of job performance. *Journal of Applied Psychology, 78,* 679–703.

O'Reilly, C. A. III. (1991). Organizational behavior: Where we've been, where we're going. *Annual Review of Psychology, 42,* 427–458.

Organ, D. W. (1988). *Organizational citizenship behavior: The good soldier syndrome.* Lexington, MA: Lexington Books.

Ozer, D. J., & Reise, S. P. (1994). Personality assessment. *Annual Review of Psychology, 45,* 357–388.

Painter, K. (1991). Violence and vulnerability in the workplace: Psychological and legal implications. In M. J. Davidson & J. Earnshaw (Eds.), *Vulnerable workers: Psychsocial and legal issues* (pp. 159–178). New York: Wiley.

Pazy, A., & Zin, R. (1987). A contingency approach to consistency: A challenge to prevalent views. *Journal of Vocational Behavior, 30,* 84–101.

Pearson, C. M., Andersson, L. M., & Porath, C. L. (2000). Assessing and attacking workplace incivility. *Organizational Dynamics, 29,* 123–137.

Peiperl, M., & Jones, B. (2001). Workaholics and overworkers: Productivity or pathology? *Group & Organization Management, 26,* 369–393.

Peled, Y. (2000). *Sexual harassment: Attitudes and behavior among doctors and nurses in a general hospital.* Unpublished master's thesis, Tel Aviv University, Israel.

Perrow, C. (1984). *Normal accidents: Living with high risk technologies.* New York: Basic Books.

Perrow, C. (1986). *Complex organizations: A critical essay.* (3rd ed.). New York: McGraw-Hill.

Petrick, J. A., & Manning, G. E. (1990). Developing an ethical climate for excellence. *Journal for Quality and Participation,* March 84–90.

Petrick, J. A., Wagley, R. A., & Thomas, J. (1991). Structured ethical decision-making improving the prospects of managerial success in business. *SAM Advanced Management Journal, 56,* 28–34.

Pfeffer, J. (1981). *Power in organizations.* Marshfield, MA: Pitman.

Pillai, R., Schriesheim, C. A., & Williams, E. S. (1999). Fairness perceptions and trust as mediators for transformational and transactional leadership: A tow-sample study. *Journal of Management, 25,* 897–933.

Pines, A. (1981). *Job stress and burnout: Research, theory and intervention perspectives.* Beverly Hills, CA: Sage.

Pines, A., & Kanner, A. D. (1982). Nurses' burnout: Lack of positive conditions and presence of negative conditions as two sources of stress. In E. A. McConnell (Ed.), *Burnout in the nursing profession* (pp. 139–145). St. Louis, MO: Mosby.

Plutchik, R. (1993). Emotion and there vicissitudes:. Emotions and psychopathology. In M. Lewis & J. M. Haviland (Eds.), *Handbook of emotion* (pp. 53–66). New York: Guilford.

Pomazal, R. J., & Jaccard, J. J. (1976). An informational approach to altruistic behavior. *Journal of Personality and Social Psychology, 33,* 317–326.

Porter, G. (1996). Organizational impact of workaholism: Suggestions for researching the negative outcomes of excessive work. *Journal of Occupational Health Psychology, 1*(1), 70–84.

Porter, L. W., & Lawler, E. E. (1968). *Managerial attitudes and performance.* Homewood, IL: Irwin

Porter, L. W., Lawler, E. E., & Hackman, J. (1975). *Behavior in organizations.* New York: McGraw-Hill.

Porter, L. W., & Steers, R. M. (1973). Organizational work, and personal factors in employee turnover and absenteeism. *Psychological Bulletin, 80,* 151–176.

Porter, L. W., Steers, R. M., Mowday, R. T., & Boulian, P. V. (1974). Organizational commitment, job satisfaction and turnover among psychiatric technicians. *Journal of Applied Psychology, 59,* 603–609.

Price, A. V. (1982). *Type A behavior pattern: A model for research and practice.* New York: Academic Press.

Pritchard, R. D., & Karasick, B. W. (1973). The effects of organizational climate on managerial job performance and job satisfaction. *Organizational Behavior and Human Performance, 9,* 110–119.

Puffer, S. M. (1987). Prosocial behavior, noncompliant behavior, and work performance among commission salespeople. *Journal of Applied Psychology, 72,* 615–621.

Punch, M. (1996). *Dirty business: Exploring corporate misconduct: Analysis and cases.* London: Sage.

Quinney, E. R. (1963). Occupational structure and criminal behavior: Prescription violation by retail pharmacists. *Social Problems, 11,* 179–185.

Raelin, J. A. (1984). An examination of deviant/adaptive behaviors in the organizational careers of professionals. *Academy of Management Review, 9,* 413–427.

Raelin, J. A. (1986). An analysis of professional deviance within organizations. *Human Relations, 39,* 1103–1130.

Raelin, J. A. (1987). The professional as the executive's ethical aide de camp. *The Academy of Management Executive, 1,* 171–182.

Raelin, J. A. (1994). Three scales of professional deviance within organizations. *Journal of Organizational Behavior, 15,* 483–501.

Rafaeli, A., & Sutton, R. I. (1987). Expression of emotion as part of the work role. *Academy of Management Review, 12,* 23–37.

Rafaeli, A., & Sutton, R. I. (1989). The expression of emotion in organization life. In L. L. Cummings & B. M. Staw (Eds.), *Research in Organizational Behavior* (Vol. 11, pp. 1–42). Greenwich, CT: JAI.

Rahamim, Y. (1979). *Organization climate as a mediator between personal characteristics (ability and personality) and personal behavior (performance and satisfaction).* Unpublished master's thesis, Technion, Israel.

Randall, D. M., & Gibson, A. M. (1990). Methodology in business ethics research: A review and critical assessments. *Journal of Business Ethics, 9,* 457–471.

Ravid-Robbins, T. (1999). *The relationship between attitudes, perceptions and personal characteristics & organizational misbehavior among hospital nurses.* Unpublished master's thesis, Tel Aviv University, Israel.

Reddin, W. J. (1967). The 3–D management style theory: A typology based on task and relationships orientations. *Training and Development Journal, 21,* 8–17.

Reichers, A. E., & Schneider, B. (1990). Climate and culture: An evolution of constructs. In B. Schneider (Ed.), *Organizational climate and culture* (pp. 5–39). San Francisco, CA: Jossey-Bass.

Reichers, A. E., Wanous, J. P., & Austin, J. T. (1997). Understanding and managing cynicism about organizational change. *Academy of Management Executive, 11*(1), 48–59.

Reimann, B. C., & Wiener, Y. (1988). Corporate culture: Avoiding the elitist trap. *Business Horizons, 31,* 36–44.

Reiss, A., & Biderman, A. (1980). *Data sources on white collar lawbreaking.* Washington, DC: National Institute of Justice.

Reshef-Tamari, I. (1999). *Perceived organizational climate, job satisfaction and misbehavior among R&D employees in high-tech organization.* Unpublished master's thesis, Tel Aviv University, Israel.

Rest, J. R. (1986). *Moral development: Advances in research and theory.* New York: Praeger.

Riordan, C. M., & Vandenberg, R. J. (1994). A central question in cross-cultural research: Do employees of different cultures interpret work-related measures in an equivalent manner? *Journal of Management, 20,* 643–671.

Robinson, S. L. (1996). Trust and breach of the psychological contract. *Administrative Science Quarterly, 41,* 574–599.

Robinson, S. L., & Bennett, R. J. (1995). A typology of deviant workplace behaviors: A multidimensional scaling study. *Academy of Management Journal, 38,* 555–572.

Robinson, S. L., & Bennett, R. J. (1997). Workplace deviance: Its definition, its manifestations, and its causes. In R. J. Lewicki, R. J. Bies, & B. H. Sheppard (Eds.), *Research on negotiation in organizations* (Vol. 6, pp. 3–27). Greenwich, CT: JAI.

Robinson, S. L., & Greenberg, J. (1998). Employees behaving badly: Dimensions, determinants and dilemmas in the study of workplace deviance. In C. L. Cooper & D. M. Rousseau (Eds.), *Trends in organizational behavior* (Vol. 5, pp. 1–30). New York: Wiley.

Robinson, S. L., & O'Leary-Kelly, A. M. (1998). Monkey see, monkey do: The influence of work groups on the antisocial behavior of employees. *Academy of Management Journal, 41,* 658–672.

Robinson, S. L., & Rousseau, D. M. (1994). Violating the psychological contract: Not the exception but the norm. *Journal of Organizational Behavior, 15,* 245–259.

Roethlisberger, F. J., & Dickson, W. J. (1964). *Management and the worker.* Cambridge, MA: Harvard University Press.

Rokeach, M. (1973). *The nature of human values.* New York: The Free Press.

Rosen, L. (2001a). How firms handle workers' drug tests (online). http://www.hr.com

Rosen, L. (2001b). What employers can—and can't—find out about applicants (online). http://www.hr.com

Rosenbaum, R. W. (1976). Predictability of employee theft using weighted application blanks. *Journal of Applied Psychology, 61,* 94–98.

Rosenbaum, D. P., & Baumer, T. L. (1984). Measuring and controlling employee theft: A national assessment of the state of the art. *Journal of Security Administration, 5,* 67–80.

Ross, L., Greene, D., & House, P. (1977). The "false consensus effect." An egocentric bias in social perception and attribution processes. *Journal of Experimental Social Psychology, 13,* 279–301.

Rothschild, J., & Miethe, T. D. (1999). Whistle-blowing disclosures and management retaliation. *Work and Occupations, 26*(1), 107–128.

Rousseau, D. M. (1989). Psychological and implied contracts in organizations. *Employee Responsibilities and Rights Journal, 2,* 121–139.

Rousseau, D. M. (1990). New hires' perceptions of their own and their employer's obligations: A study of psychological contracts. *Journal of Organizational Behavior, 11,* 389–400.

Rousseau, D. M. (1995). *Psychological contracts in organizations: Understanding written and unwritten agreements.* Thousand Oaks, CA: Sage.

Rousseau, D. M. (1997). Organizational behavior in the new organizational era. *Annual Review of Psychology, 48,* 515–546.

Rousseau, D. M. (1998). Why workers still identify with their organizations? *Journal of Organizational Behavior, 19,* 217–233.

Rousseau, D. M., & Parks, J. M. (1993). The contracts of individuals and organizations. *Research in Organizational Behavior, 15,* 1–43.

Rousseau, D. M., & Tijoriwala, S. A. (1998). Assessing psychological contracts: Issues, alternatives and measures. *Journal of Organizational Behavior, 19,* 679–696.

Roy, D. F. (1952). Quota restriction and goldbricking in a machine shop. *American Journal of Sociology, 57,* 427–442.

Roy, D. F. (1959). Banana time: Job satisfaction and informal interaction. *Human Organization, 18,* 158–168.

Roznowski, M., & Hulin, C. (1992). The scientific merit of valid measures of general constructs with special reference to job satisfaction and job withdrawal. In C. J. Cranny, P. C. Smith, & F. S. Stone (Eds.), *Job satisfaction: How people feel about their jobs and how it effects their performance* (pp. 123–163). New York: Lexington Books.

Rubin-Kedar, Y. (2000). *Organizational misbehavior in a fast-food restaurant chain: Task and organization influences.* Unpublished master's thesis, Tel Aviv University, Israel.

Runice, J. F. (1988). Deviant behavior: Achieving autonomy in a machine-paced environment. In M. O. Jones, M. D. Moore, & R. C. Snyder (Eds.), *Inside organizations: Understanding the human dimension* (pp. 129–140). Newbury Park, CA: Sage.

Rusbult, C. E., Zembrotd, I. M., & Gunn, L. K. (1982). Exit, voice, loyalty and neglect: Responses to dissatisfaction in romantic involvements. *Journal of Personality and Social Psychology, 43,* 1230–1242.

Sackett, P. R., & DeVore, C. J. (2001). Counterproductive behaviors at work. In N. Anderson, D. S., Ones, H. K. Sinangil, & C. Viswesvaran (Eds.), *Handbook of industrial, work and organizational psychology* (Vol. 1, pp. 145–164). London: Sage.

Sagie, A. (1998). Employee absenteeism, organizational commitment, and job satisfaction: Another look. *Journal of Vocational Behavior, 52,* 156–171.

Salancik, G. R. (1977). Commitment and the control of organization behavior and belief. In B. M. Staw & G. R. Salancik (Eds.), *New directions in organizational behavior* (pp. 1–54). Chicago: St. Clair Press.

Salancik, G., & Pfeffer, J. (1978). A social information processing approach to job attitudes and task design. *Administrative Science Quarterly, 23,* 224–253.

Salovey, P., & Mayer, J. D. (1990). Emotional intelligence. *Imagination, Cognition and Personality, 9,* 185–211.

Salovey, P., & Rodin, J. (1986). The differentiation of social comparison jealousy and romantic jealousy. *Journal of Personality and Social Psychology, 50,* 1100–1112.

Sarchione, C. D., Cuttler, M. J., Muchinsky, P. M., & Nelson-Gray, R. O. (1998). Prediction of dysfunctional job behavior among law enforcement officer. *Journal of Applied Psychology, 83,* 904–912.

Savery, L. K. (1988). Comparison of managerial and non managerial employees' desire and perceived motivators and job satisfaction levels. *Leadership and Organization Development Journal, 9,* 17–22.

Scarlicki, D. P., & Folger, R. (1997). Retaliation in the workplace: The roles of distributive, procedural, and interactional justice. *Journal of Applied Psychology, 82,* 434–443.

Schein, E. H. (1969). *Process consultation:* Its role in organization development. Reading, MA: Addison-Wesley.

Schein, E. H. (1971). The individual, the organization and the career: A conceptual scheme. *Journal of Applied Behavioral Science, 7,* 401–426.

Schein, E. H. (1978). *Career dynamics: Matching individual and organizational needs.* Reading, MA: Addison-Wesley.

Schein, E. H. (1984). Coming to a new awareness of organizational culture. *Sloan Management Review, 25,* 3–16.

Schein, E. H. (1985). *Organizational culture and leadership: A dynamic view.* San Francisco: Jossey-Bass.

Schein, V. E. (1979). Examining an illusion: The role of deceptive behaviors in organizations. *Human Relations, 32,* 287–295.

Schmidt, F. L., & Hunter, J. E. (1992). Development of a casual model of processes determining job performance. *Current Direction in Psychology Science, 1,* 89–92.

Schmidt, W. C. (1997). World Wide Web survey research: Benefits, potential problems and solutions. *Behavior Research Methods, Instruments and Computers, 29*(2), 274–279.

Schminke, M. (1998). *Managerial ethics: Moral management of people and processes.* Mahwah, NJ: Lawrence Erlbaum Associates.

Schnake, M. E. (1983). An empirical assessment of the effects of affective response in the measurement of organizational climate. *Personnel Psychology, 36,* 791–807.

Schneider, B. (1975). Organizational climate: An essay. *Personnel Psychology, 28,* 447–479.

Schneider, B. (1980). The service organization: Climate is crucial. *Organizational Dynamics, 9,* 52–65.

Schneider, B. (1985). Organizational behavior. *Annual Review of Psychology, 36,* 573–611.

Schneider, B. (1987). The people make the place. *Personnel Psychology, 40,* 437–453.

Schneider, B., & Bowen, D. E. (1995). *Winning the service game.* Boston, MA: Harvard Business School Press.

Schneider, B., & Hall, D. T. (1972). Toward specifying the concept of work climate: A study of Roman Catholic diocesan priests. *Journal of Applied Psychology, 56,* 447–456.

Schneider, B., & Rentsch, J. (1988). Managing climates and cultures: A futures perspective. In J. Hage (Ed.), *Futures of organizations* (pp. 181–200). Lexington, MA: Lexington Books.

Schneider, K. T., Swan, S., & Fitzgerald, L. F (1997). Job-related and psychological effects of sexual harassment in the workplace: Empirical evidence from two organizations. *Journal of Applied Psychology, 82,* 401–415.

Schwartz, S. H., & Tessler, R. C. (1972). A test of a model for reducing measured attitude-behavior discrepancies. *Journal of Personality and Social Psychology, 24,* 225–236.

Scott, K. S., Moore, K. S., & Miceli, M. P. (1997). An exploration of the meaning and consequences of workaholism. *Human Relations, 50,* 287–314.

Scott, W. R. (1998). *Organizations: Rational, natural and open systems.* Upper Saddle River, NJ: Prentice-Hall.

Seibert, S. E., & Kraimer, M. L. (1999, August). *The five factor model of personality and its relationship with career success.* Paper presented at the Academy of Management meeting, Chicago, IL.

Selznick, P. (1957). *The organizational weapon.* New York: McGraw-Hill.

Sennewald, C. A. (1986, September). Theft maxims. *Security Management,* p. 85.

Setter, O. (2001). *Entitlements and obligations: Psychological contracts of organizational members.* Unpublished doctoral dissertation, Tel Aviv University, Israel.

Sewell, G. (1998). The discipline of teams: The control of team-based industrial work through electronic and peer surveillance. *Administrative Science Quarterly, 43,* 397–428.

Shain, M. (1982). Alcohol, drugs and safety: An updated perspective on problems and their management in the workplace. *Accident Analysis and Prevention, 14,* 239–246.

Shamir, B., House, R. J., & Arthur, M. B. (1993). The motivational effects of charismatic leadership: A self concept based theory. *Organization Science, 4,* 577–594.

Shapiro, S. P. (1990). Collaring the crime, not the criminal: Reconsidering the concept of white-collar crime. *American Sociological Review, 55,* 346–365.

Shaw, W. H., & Barry, V. (1995). *Moral issues in business* (6th ed.). Belmont, CA: International Thompson Publishing.

Shenhav, Y. (2002). *Manufacturing rationality: The engineering foundations of the managerial revolution.* New York: Oxford University Press.

Sheppard, B. H., Hartwick, J., & Warshaw, P. R. (1988). The theory of reasoned action: A meta-analysis of past research with recommendations for modifications and future research. *Journal of Consumer Research, 15,* 325–343.

Shirom, A. (1982). What is organizational stress? A facet analytic conceptualization. *Journal of Occupational Behavior, 3,* 21–37.

Shoham, S. G., Rahav, G., & Adad, M. (1987). *Criminology.* Tel Aviv: Shoken (Hebrew).

Sibbet, D. (1997). 75 years of management ideas and practice (1922–1997). *Harvard Business Review, 75,* 2–12.

Skarlicki, D. P., & Folger, R. (1997). Retaliation in the workplace: The roles of distributive, procedural, and interactional justice. *Journal of Applied Psychology, 82,* 434–443.

Skarlicki, D. P., Folger, R., & Tesluk, P. (1999). Personality as a moderator in the relationship between fairness and retaliation. *Academy of Management Journal, 42,* 100–108.

Slora, K. B. (1989). An empirical approach to determining employee deviance base rates. *Journal of Business and Psychology, 4,* 199–219.

Smelser, N. J. (1999). Looking back at 25 years of sociology and the *Annual Review of Sociology. Annual Review of Sociology, 25,* 1–18.

Smigel, E. O., & Ross, H. L. (1970). *Crimes against bureaucracies.* New York: Van Nostvand Reinhold.

Smith, P. C., Kendall, L. M., & Hulin, C. L. (1969). *The measurement of satisfaction in work and retirement.* Chicago: Rand McNally.

Somers, J. J., & Casal, J. C. (1994). Organizational commitment and whistle blowing: A test of the reformer and the organization man hypothesis. *Group & Organization Management, 19,* 270–284.

Sonnenstuhl, W. J. (1996). *Working sober: The transformation of an occupational drinking culture.* Ithaca, NY: Cornell University Press.

Sonnenstuhl, W. J., & Trice, H. M. (1991). The workplace as locale for risks and interventions in alcohol abuse. In P. M. Roman (Ed.), *Alcohol: The development of sociological perspectives on use and abuse* (pp. 295–318). New Brunswick, NJ: Rutgers Center of Alcohol Studies.

Snir, R., & Harpaz, I. (2000). Workaholism and the meaning of work. In M. Koslowski & S. Stashevsky (Eds.), *Proceedings of the 7th International Conference on Work Values and Behavior* (pp. 593–598). Jerusalem, Israel.

Spector, P. E. (1975). Relationships of organizational frustration with reported behavioral reactions of employees. *Journal of Applied Psychology, 60,* 635–637.

Spector, P. E. (1978). Organizational frustration: A model and review of the literature. *Personnel Psychology, 31,* 815–829.

Spector, P. E. (1986). Perceived control by employees: A meta analysis of studies concerning autonomy and participation at work. *Human Relations, 39,* 1005–1016.

Spector, P. E. (1997a). *Job satisfaction: Application, assessment, causes, and consequences.* Thousand Oaks, CA: Sage.

Spector, P. E. (1997b). The role of frustration in antisocial behavior at work. In R. A. Giacalone & J. Greenberg (Eds.), *Antisocial behavior in organizations* (pp. 1–17). Thousand Oaks, CA: Sage.

Spector, P. E. (2001). Research methods in industrial and organizational psychology: Data collection and data analysis with special consideration to international issues. In N. Anderson, D. S. Ones, H. K. Sinangil, & C. Viswesvaran (Eds.) *Handbook of industrial, work and organizational psychology* (Vol. 1, pp. 10–26). London: Sage.

Spence, J. T., & Robbins, A. S. (1992). Workaholism: Definition, measurement and preliminary results. *Journal of Personality Assessment, 58,* 160–178.

Sprouse, M. (1992). *Sabotage in the American workplace.* San Francisco: Pressure Drop Press.

Sprouse, M. (1994). *Sabotage in the American workplace: Anecdotes of dissatisfaction, mischief, and revenge.* San Francisco: Pressure Drop Press.

Staw, B. M. (1984). Organizational behavior: A review and reformulation of the field's outcome variables. *Annual Review of Psychology, 35,* 627–666.

Staw, B. M., Bell, N. E., & Clausen, J. A. (1986). The dispositional approach to job attitudes: A lifetime longitudinal test. *Administrative Science Quarterly, 31,* 56–77.

Staw, B. M., Sutton, R. I., & Pelled, L. H. (1994). Employee positive emotion and favorable outcomes at the workplace. *Organization Science, 5,* 51–71.

Steers, R. M. (1991). *Introduction to organizational behavior.* New York: Harper Collins.

Steers, R. M., & Mowday, R. T. (1977). The motivational properties of tasks. *Academy of Management Review, 2,* 645–658.

Steers, R. M., & Porter, L. W. (1979). *Motivation and work behavior.* New York: McGraw.

Steers, R. M., & Spencer, D. G. (1977). The role of achievement motivation in job design. *Journal of Applied Psychology, 62,* 472–479.

Stevens, S. S. (1968). Measurement, statistics, and the schemapiric view. *Science, 161,* 849–856.

Stein, B. A., & Kanter, R. M. (1993). Why good people do bad things: A retrospective of the Hubble Fiasco. *Academy of Management Executive, 7,* 58–62.

Strool, W. M. (1978). *Crime Prevention through physical security.* New York: Marcel Dekker.

Sukenik, N. (2001). *Goal-oriented mechanisms designed by organizations to promote safety are often used instead to promote profits.* Unpublished doctoral dissertation, Tel Aviv University, Israel.

Sutherland, E. H. (1940). White-collar criminality. *American Sociological Review, 5,* 1–12.

Sutherland, E. H. (1949). *White collar crime*. New Haven, CT: Yale University Press.

Szwajkowski, E. (1985). Organizational illegality: Theoretical integration and illustrative application. *Academy of Management Review, 10,* 558–567.

Sykes, G. M., & Matza, D. (1957). On neutralizing delinquent self-images. *American Sociological Review, 22,* 667–670.

Taylor, F. W. (1895). A piece rate system: A step toward partial solution to the labor problem. *ASME Transactions, 16,* 856–893.

Taylor, F. W. (1903). *Shop management*. New York: Harper.

Taylor, F. W. (1911). *The principles of scientific management*. New York: Norton.

Taylor, L., & Walton, P. (1971). Industrial sabotage: Motives and meanings. In S. Cohen (Ed.), *Images of deviance* (pp. 219–245). Baltimore, MD: Penguin.

Tedeschi, J. T., & Melburg, V. (1984). Impression management and influence in the organization. In S. B. Bacharach & E. J. Lawler (Eds.), *The social psychological processes: Research in the sociology of organizations* (Vol. 3, pp. 31–58). Greenwich, CT: JAI.

Tedeschi, J. T., & Reiss, M. (1981). Identities, the phenomenal self, and laboratory research. In J.T. Tedeschi (Ed.), *Impression management theory and social psychological research* (pp. 3–23). New York: Academic Press.

Tedeschi, J. T., Schlenker, B. R., & Bonoma, T. V. (1971). Cognitive dissonance: Private ratiocination or public spectacle? *American Psychology, 26,* 685–695.

Tett, R. P., Jackson, D. N., & Rothstein, M. (1991). Personality measures as predictors of job performance: A meta-analytic review. *Personnel Psychology, 44,* 703–742.

Thompson, J. D. (1967). *Organizations in action*. New York: McGraw-Hill.

Thompson, S. C. (1981). Will it hurt less if I can control it? A complex answer to a simple question. *Psychological Bulletin, 90,* 89–101.

Tichy, N. M. (1982, August). Managing change strategically: The technical, political, and cultural keys. *Organizational Dynamics,* pp. 59–80.

Toffler, B. L. (1986). *Tough choices: Managers talk ethics*. New York: Wiley.

Towler, J. (2001a). Finding employees with integrity (online). http://www.hr.com

Towler, J. (2001b). Don't hire a killer—how to avoid violence prone employees (online). http://www.hr.com

Trevino, L. K. (1986). Ethical decision making in organizations: A person-situation interactionist model. *Academy of Management Review, 11,* 601–617.

Trevino, L. K. (1992). The social effects of punishment in organizations: A justice perspective. *Academy of Management Review, 17,* 647–676.

Trevino, L. K., & Nelson, K. A. (1994). *Managing business ethics: Straight talk about how to do it right*. New York: Wiley.

Trevino, L. K., & Youngblood, S. A. (1990). Bad apples in bad barrels: A causal analysis of ethical decision-making behavior. *Journal of Applied Psychology, 75,* 378–385.

Trevino, L. K. Hartman, L. P. & Brown, M. (2000). Moral person and moral manager: How executives develop a reputation for ethical leadership. *California Management Review, 42,* 128–142.

Trice, H. M. (1993). *Occupational subcultures in the workplace*. Ithaca, NY: ILR Press.

Trice, H. M., & Beyer, J. M. (1993). *The cultures of work organizations*. Englewood Cliffs, NJ: Prentice-Hall.

Trice, H. M., & Sonnenstuhl, W. (1988). Drinking behavior and risk factors related to the workplace: Implications for research and prevention. *Journal of Applied Behavioral Science, 24,* 327–346.

Turgeman-Goldschmidt, O. (2001). *To become a deviant: Reality construction among computer delinquents*. Unpublished doctoral dissertation, Hebrew University, Jerusalem, Israel.

Turner, A. N., & Lawrence, P. R. (1965). *Industrial jobs and the worker: An investigation of response to task attributes*. Boston: Harvard University Press.

Turnispeed, D. L. (1988). An integrated, interactive model of organizational climate culture and effectiveness. *Leadership & Organizational Development Journal, 9*(5), 17–21.

Turnley, W. H., & Feldman, D. C. (1999). The impact of psychological contract violations on exit, voice, loyalty, and neglect. *Human Relations, 52,* 895–922.

Turnley, W. H., & Feldman, D. C. (2000). Re-examining the effects of psychological contract violations: Unmet expectations and job dissatisfaction as mediators. *Journal of Organizational Behavior, 21,* 25–42.

Tziner, A., & Vardi, Y. (1982). Effects of command style and group cohesiveness on the performance effectiveness of self- selected tank crews. *Journal of Applied Psychology, 67,* 769–775.

U.S. Department of Health and Human Services, Substance Abuse and Mental Health Services Administration. (2000). *1999 national household survey on drug abuse.* Rockville, MD: U.S. Government.

Usdiken, B., & Leblebici, H. (2001). Organization theory. In N. Anderson, D. S. Ones, H. K. Sinangil, & C. Viswesvaran (Eds.), *Handbook of industrial, work and organizational psychology* (Vol. 2, pp. 377–397). Thousand Oaks, CA: Sage.

Van Dyne, L., Graham, J. W., & Dienesch, R. M. (1994). Organizational citizenship behavior: Construct redefinition, measurement, and validation. *Academy of Management Journal, 37,* 765–802.

Van Maanen, J. (1979). The fact of fiction in organization ethnography. *Administrative Science Quarterly, 24,* 539–550.

Van Maanen, J., & Barley, S. R. (1984). Occupational culture and control in organizations. *Research in Organizational Behavior, 6,* 287–365.

Van Maanen, J., & Schein, E. H. (1979). Toward a theory of organizational socialization. *Research in Organizational Behavior, 1,* 209–264.

Vardi, Y. (1978). *Individual-level and organizational-level of career mobility patterns: An integrative model.* Unpublished doctoral dissertation, Cornell University. Ithaca, New York.

Vardi, Y. (2001) The effects of organizational and ethical climates on misconduct at work. *Journal of Business Ethics, 29,* 325–337.

Vardi, Y. & Weitz, E. (2001, August). *Lead them not into temptation: Job autonomy as an antecedent of organizational misbehavior.* Paper presented at the annual meeting of the Academy of Management Meeting, Washington, DC.

Vardi, Y., & Weitz, E. (2002a). Antecedents of organizational misbehavior among caregivers. In M. A. Rahim, R. T. Golembiewski, & K. D. Mackenzie (Eds.), *Current topics in management* (Vol. 7, pp. 99–116). New Brunswick, NJ: Transaction Publishers.

Vardi, Y., & Weitz, E. (2002b). Organizational misbehavior: Hypotheses, research, and implications. In M. L. Pava & P. Primeaux (Eds.), *Re-imaging business ethics: Meaningful solutions for a global economy* (Vol. 4, pp. 51–84). New York: JAI.

Vardi, Y., & Weitz, E. (2002c). Using reasoned action theory to predict organizational misbehavior. *Psychological Reports, 91,* 1027–1040.

Vardi, Y., & Wiener, Y. (1992, August). *Organizational misbehavior (OMB): Toward a motivational model.* A paper presented at the annual meeting of Academy of Management, Miami Beach.

Vardi, Y., & Wiener, Y. (1996). Misbehavior in organizations: A motivational framework. *Organization Science, 7,* 151–165.

Vaughan, D. (1998). Rational choice, situated action, and the social control of organizations. *Law & Society Review, 32*(1), 23–61.

Vaughan, D. (1999). The dark side of organizations: Mistake, misconduct, and disaster. *Annual Review of Sociology, 25,* 271–305.

Vecchio, R. P. (1995). It's not easy being green: Jealousy and envy in the workplace. In G. R. Ferris (Ed.), *Research in personnel and human resources management* (Vol. 13, pp. 201–244). Stamford CT: JAI.

Vecchio, R. P. (1997). Categorizing coping response for envy: A multidimensional analysis of workplace perceptions. *Psychological Reports, 81,* 137–138.

Vecchio, R. P. (2000). Negative emotion in the workplace: Employee jealousy and envy. *International Journal of Stress Management, 7*(3), 161–179.

Victor, B., & Cullen, J. B. (1987). A theory and measure of ethical climate in organizations. *Research in Corporate in Social Performance and Policy, 9,* 51–71.

Victor, B., & Cullen, J. B. (1988). The organizational bases of ethical work climates. *Administrative Science Quarterly, 33,* 101–125.

Vigoda, E. (1997). *Organizational politics: Characteristics, antecedents, and implications of interpersonal influence processes on employee performance in the Israeli public sector.* Unpublished doctoral dissertation, University of Haifa, Israel.

Villanova, P., & Bernardin, H. J. (1989). Impression management in the context of performance appraisal. In R. A. Giacalone & P. Rosenfeld (Eds.), *Impression management in the organization* (pp. 299–314). Hillsdale, NJ: Lawrence Erlbaum Associates.

Vinchur, A. J., Schippmann, J. S., Switzer, F. S., & Roth, P. L. (1998). A meta-analytic review of predictors of job performance for salespeople. *Journal of Applied Psychology, 83,* 586–597.

Vinten, G. (Ed.). (1994). *Whistleblowing: Subversion or corporate citizenship?* London: Paul Chapman.

Von Glinow, M. A. (1988). *The new professionals: Managing today's high tech employees.* Cambridge, MA: Ballinger.

Vroom, V. H. (1964). *Work and motivation.* New York: Wiley.

Wayne, S. J. Y., & Kacmar, K. M. (1991). The effects of impression management on the performance appraisal process. *Organizational Behavior and Human Decision Processes, 48,* 70–88.

Weber, J. (1996). Influences upon managerial moral decision making: Nature of the harm and magnitude of consequences. *Human Relations, 49,* 1–22.

Weick, K. E. (1979). *The social psychology of organizing.* Reading, MA: Addison-Wesley.

Weiner, B. (1974). *Achievement motivation and attribution theory.* Morristown, NJ: General Learning Press.

Weiss, H. M., & Adler, S. (1984). Personality and organizational behavior. *Research in Organizational Behavior, 6,* 1–50.

Weiss, H. M., & Cropanzano, R. (1996). Affective events theory: A theoretical discussion of the structure, causes and consequences of affective experiences at work. In B. M. Staw & L. L. Cummings (Eds.), *Research in organizational behavior* (Vol. 18, pp. 1–74). Stamford, CT: JAI.

Weitzman, M. (1985). *The relationship between climate dimensions and performance measures in military operational units.* Unpublished master's thesis, Tel Aviv University, Israel.

Welch, E. (1997). Business ethics in theory and practice: Diagnostic notes: A prescription for value. *Journal of Business Ethics, 16,* 309–313.

Welsh, S. (1999). Gender and sexual harassment. *Annual Review Sociology, 25,* 169–190.

West, M. A. (2001). The human team: Basic motivations and innovations. In N. Anderson, D. S. Ones, H. K. Sinangil, & C. Viswesvaran (Eds.), *Handbook of industrial, work and organizational psychology* (Vol. 2, pp. 270–289). London: Sage.

Westman, M. (1992). Moderating effect of decision latitude on stress-strain relationship: Does organizational level matter? *Journal of Organizational Behavior, 13,* 713–722.

Wheeler, H. N. (1976). Punishment theory and industrial discipline. *Industrial Relations, 15,* 235–243.

White, G. L., & Mullen, P. E. (1989). *Jealousy: Theory, research, and clinical strategies.* New York: Guilford.

Whitener, E. M. (1999, August). *The effects of cynicism on the development of interpersonal trust.* Paper presented at the annual meeting of the Academy of the Management, Chicago, IL.

Wiener, Y. (1982). Commitment in organizations: A normative view. *Academy of Management Review, 7,* 418–428.

Wiener, Y. (1988). Forms of value systems: A focus on organizational effectiveness and cultural change and maintenance. *Academy of Management Review, 13,* 534–545.

Wiener, Y., & Vardi, Y. (1980). Relationships between job, organization and career commitment and work outcomes—an investigative model. *Organizational Behavior and Human Performance, 26,* 81–96.

Wiener, Y., & Vardi, Y. (1990). Relationship between organizational culture and individual motivation: A conceptual integration. *Psychological Reports, 67,* 295–306.

Wiggins J. S., & Pincus, A. L. (1992). Personality: Structure and assessment. *Annual Review of Psychology, 43,* 473–504.

Williams, C. L., Giuffre, P. A., & Dellinger, K. (1999). Sexuality in the workplace: Organizational control, sexual harassment, and the pursuit of pleasure. *Annual Review Sociology, 25,* 73–93.

Wilpert, B. (1995). Organizational behavior. *Annual Review of Psychology, 46,* 59–90.

Wimbush, J. C., & Dalton, D. R. (1997). Base rate for employee theft: Convergence of multiple methods. *Journal of Applied Psychology, 82,* 756–763.

Withey, M. J., & Cooper, W. H. (1989). Predicting exit, voice, loyalty, and neglect. *Administrative Science Quarterly, 34,* 521–539.

Wolfgang, A. P. (1988). Career satisfaction of physicians, nurses and pharmacists. *Psychological Reports, 62,* 938–941.

Women's Bureau, U.S. Department of labor. (1994). *Sources of information on the incidence of domestic violence at work and its effects* (Briefing memo). Washington, DC: U.S. Government.

Wood, R. E., & Mitchell, T. R. (1981). Manager behavior in a social context: The impact of impression management on attributions and disciplinary actions. *Organizational Behavior and Human Performance, 28,* 356–378.

Wortman, C. B., & Breham, J. W. (1975). Responses to uncontrollable outcomes: An integration of reactance theory and the learned helplessness model. In L. Berkowitz (Ed.), *Advances in experimental social psychology* (pp. 278–336). New York: Academic Press.

Yanai, D. (1998). *Sexual harassment in the workplace: Women battery.* Unpublished master's thesis, Tel Aviv University, Israel.

York, K. M. (1989). Defining sexual harassment in workplaces: A policy-capturing approach. *Academy of Management Journal, 32,* 830–850.

Yosifon, H. (2001). *The relationship between job satisfaction and organizational misbehavior among employees.* Unpublished master's thesis, Tel Aviv University, Israel.

Zerbe, W. J., & Paulhus, D. L. (1987). Socially desirable responding in organizational behavior: A re-conception. *Academy of Management Review, 12,* 250–264.

Zeitlin, L. R. (1971). A little larceny can do a lot for employee morale. *Psychology Today, 14,* 22.

Zey-Ferrell, M., & Ferrell, O. C. (1982). Role set configuration and opportunity as predictors of unethical behavior in organizations. *Human Relations, 35,* 587–604.

Appendix 1

Overall OMB Questionnaire—Others (Vardi & Weitz)

The following items (translated from Hebrew) pertain to different behaviors at work. Please indicate how often people in this organization behave this way:

Item	Very Often	Often	Hardly Ever	Never
1. Make private phone calls from the factory phone during work hours or breaks	3	2	1	0
2. Are late to work or leave it earlier without permission	3	2	1	0
3. Accept bribes or presents from suppliers, customers, or other sources	3	2	1	0
4. Use the copying machine for private purposes	3	2	1	0
5. Take a longer lunch break than permitted	3	2	1	0

(Continued)

(Continued)

Item	Very Often	Often	Hardly Ever	Never
6. Drink alcohol before or during work or during breaks	3	2	1	0
7. Take unnecessary risks by ignoring safety regulations	3	2	1	0
8. Use the expense account not according to formal procedure	3	2	1	0
9. Attend to personal or political matters during work hours	3	2	1	0
10. Sabotage factory machines or equipment	3	2	1	0
11. Work slowly on purpose	3	2	1	0
12. Waste factory money or materials	3	2	1	0
13. Take factory equipment or materials home without permission	3	2	1	0
14. Miss work without a reasonable justification	3	2	1	0
15. Favor a certain employee	3	2	1	0
16. Report on their colleagues	3	2	1	0
17. Blame colleagues for their own mistakes	3	2	1	0
18. Sexually harass colleagues	3	2	1	0
19. Verbally abuse colleagues	3	2	1	0
20. Steal from their colleagues	3	2	1	0
21. Endanger their colleagues	3	2	1	0
22. Fire an employee without justification	3	2	1	0
23. Go against management decisions	3	2	1	0

Appendix 2

An Alphabetic List of OMB Manifestations, Definitions, and Models

Behaviors	Authors	Definition	Model/Typology/ Subcategories
Absenteeism	Farrell (1983)		
	Cascio (1991)	"Any failure to report for or remain at work as scheduled, regardless of the reason." (p. 59)	
Active aggression	Greenberg & Alge (1998)	"Violent acts, such as actual or threatened physical attacks." (p. 87)	
Alcohol/drug abuse	Griffin et al. (1998, 1998b)		
Assault	Neuman & Baron (1997)		
Attacking protege	Neuman & Baron (1997)		
Attempting to appear incompetent	Becker & Martin (1995)		
Belittling opinions	Neuman & Baron (1997)		

(Continued)

(Continued)

Behaviors	Authors	Definition	Model/Typology/ Subcategories
Breach of confidentiality	Griffin et al. (1998, 1998b)		
Causing others to delay action	Neuman & Baron (1997)		
Chiseling	Smigel & Ross (1970)	"Implying an effort to get "something for nothing," which is recognized as generally being "against the law" but to which the ordinary connotations and stigma of "criminal" do not attach. It emphasizes the idea of shrewdly turning a situation to one's own advantage." (p. 60)	
Consuming needed resources	Neuman & Baron (1997)		
Damning with faint praise	Neuman & Baron (1997)		
Defacing property	Neuman & Baron (1997)		
Delaying work to make target look bad	Neuman & Baron (1997)		
Deliberate output restriction	Ackroyd & Thompson (1999)		
Destruction of organization assets/property	Griffin et al. (1998, 1998b)		
Disruptive practices	Analoui & Kakabadse (1992)		
Dirty looks	Neuman & Baron (1997)		
Distorting data	Vardi & Wiener (1996)		
Doing little	Mangione & Quinn (1975)	Producing output of poor quality or low quantity.	
Dysfunctional impression management behaviors	Griffin et al. (1998, 1998b)		
Dysfunctional political behaviors	Griffin et al. (1998, 1998b)		
Electronic fraud	Greenberg & Scott (1996)		
Embezzlement	Black's Law Dictionary, St. Paul: West Publishing Co, 1933, p. 633 Cited in Cressey (1953)	"The fraudulent appropriation to his own use or benefit of property or money entrusted to him by another, on the part of a clerk, agent, trustee, public officer, or other person acting in a fiduciary capacity." (p. 740)	
	Cressey (1953)	"The criminal violation of financial trust." (p. 741)	
	Cressey (1953) Cited in Greenberg & Scott (1996)	"The destruction or misappropriation of another's money or property entrusted to one's care." (p. 118)	

(Continued)

(Continued)

Behaviors	Authors	Definition	Model/Typology/ Subcategories
Employee theft	Greenberg & Scott (1996)	"A nonviolent form of property deviance toward a company committed by an employee of that company for personal gain." (p. 111)	Petty theft (pilferage) Grand theft Societal attitudes toward employee theft: The cycle of acceptance. (p. 119)
	Merriam (1977, pp. 375–376) Cited in Greenberg & Scott (1996)	"The unlawful taking, control, or transfer of an employer's property with the purpose of benefiting the employee or another not entitled to the property." (p. 118)	
	Greenberg (1995) Greenberg & Scott (1996)	"Employee theft includes, but is not limited to, the removal of products, supplies, materials, funds, data, information, or intellectual property." (p. 118)	
Expressions of hostility	Greenberg & Alge (1998)	Verbal or symbolic gestures such as giving "Giving one dirty looks or talking negatively behind one's back." (p. 87)	
Failing to defend target	Neuman & Baron (1997)		
Failing to deny false rumors	Neuman & Baron (1997)		
Failing to protect the target's welfare	Neuman & Baron (1997)		
Failing to return phone calls	Neuman & Baron (1997)		
Failing to transmit information	Neuman & Baron (1997)		
Failing to warn of impending danger	Neuman & Baron (1997)		
Failure to work very hard	Ackroyd & Thompson (1999)		
Falsifying records	Vardi & Wiener (1996)		
Favoritism	Kacmar & Carlson (1998)	"Activities in which the political actor made a decision that favored a friend over another individual." (p. 205)	
Fiddling	Greenberg & Scott (1996)		
Flaunting status	Neuman & Baron (1997)		

(Continued)

(Continued)

Behaviors	Authors	Definition	Model/Typology/ Subcategories
Fraud	Bologna & Shaw (2000)	"An intentional deception of another whose property the perpetrator hopes to take by stealth or guile. In that sense, fraud is lying, cheating and stealing." (p. 11)	A taxonomy on fraud
Free riding	Jones (1984)	A negative incentive to control or minimize production costs. (p. 686)	
Gender discrimination	Kacmar & Carlson (1998)	"Less favorable outcomes being realized by an individual because of her gender." (p. 206)	
General unsafe work practices	Griffin et al. (1998, 1998b)		
Giving target the silent treatment	Neuman & Baron (1997)		
Goldbricking	Hollinger & Clark (1982)		
Grand theft	Smigel & Ross (1970) Cited in Greenberg & Scott (1996)	"Taking valuable items." (p. 118)	
Harassing peers	Vardi & Wiener (1996)		
Hiding needed resources	Neuman & Baron (1997)		
Homicide/workplace homicide	Neuman & Baron (1997)		
Inappropriate absenteeism/tardiness	Griffin et al. (1998, 1998b)		
Indiscipline	Analoui & Kakabadse (1992)		
Informal coworker interaction	Hollinger & Clark (1982)		
Ingratiation	Wortman & Linsen (1977)	"Behaviors employed by a person to make himself more attractive to another" (p. 134)	
	Tedeschi & Melburg (1984)	"A set of assertive tactics which have the purpose of gaining the approbation of an audience that controls significant rewards for the actor." (p. 37)	
	Liden & Mitchel (1988)	"An attempt by individuals to increase their attractiveness in the eyes of others" (p. 572)	A model of ingratiatory behavior (p. 575) Assessment of risk in the choice of an ingratiation strategy (p. 577)

(Continued)

(Continued)

Behaviors	Authors	Definition	Model/Typology/ Subcategories
	Kurmar & Beyerlein (1991)	"A set of assertive tactics that are used by organizational members to gain the approbation of superiors who control significant rewards for them . . . ingratiation involves strategic behaviors design to enhance one's interpersonal attractiveness." (p. 619)	
Insubordination	Robinson & O'Leary-Kelly (1998)		
Insults and sarcasm	Neuman & Baron (1997)		
Intentional work slowdowns	Neuman & Baron (1997)		
Interrupting others	Neuman & Baron (1997)		
Lateness	Farrell (1983)		
Leaving area when target enters	Neuman & Baron (1997)		
Lying	Robinson & O'Leary-Kelly (1998)		
Misuse/theft of organization assets/property	Griffin et al. (1998, 1998b)		
Misuse of facilities	Analoui & Kakabadse (1992)		
Moral hazard	Robinson & Bennett (1997)		
Nepotism	Kacmar & Carlson (1998)	"Favoritism with regard to one's relatives." (p. 206)	
Noncooperation	Analoui & Kakabadse (1992)		
Not working at all	Ackroyd & Thompson (1999)		
Obscene gestures	Neuman & Baron (1997)		
Obstructionism	Greenberg & Alge (1998)	Behaviors that impede one's ability to perform his or her job effectively, such as failing to return phone calls. (p. 87)	
Petty theft	Smigel & Ross (1970) cited in Greenberg & Scott (1996)	"Taking items in small quantities and/or items of limited values." (p. 118)	
Petty tyranny	Ashforth (1994)	"A petty tyrant is defined as one who lords his or her power over others." (p. 755)	Proposed antecedents and effects of petty tyranny. (p. 758)
Physical violence	Griffin et al. (1998, 1998b)		
Pilferage	Hollinger & Clark (1982)		
Playing dumb	Becker & Martin (1995)		
Practical joking	Ackroyd & Thompson (1999)		
Preventing target from expressing self	Neuman & Baron (1997)		

(Continued)

(Continued)

Behaviors	Authors	Definition	Model/Typology/ Subcategories
Quota restricting	Robinson & Bennett (1997)		
Refusing target's request	Neuman & Baron (1997)		
Refusing to provide needed resources	Neuman & Baron (1997)		
Removing needed resources	Neuman & Baron (1997)		
Restriction of output	Hollinger & Clark (1982)		
Revenge	Bies & Tripp (1996)		
Rule braking	Analoui & Kakabadse (1992)		
Sabotage	Hollinger & Clark (1982)		
Self-serving behavior	Kacmar & Carlson (1998)	"Activities undertaken by an individual to help ensure that an outcome will be favorable to him or her." (p. 207)	Impression management, self-promotion, "brown nosing" Sabotage Back stabbing Controlling access to information Aligning with powerful others Not holding opinions Lying Misrepresenting the truth Going behind someone's back
Selling secrets	Vardi & Wiener (1996)		
Sexual assault	Neuman & Baron (1997)		
Sexual harassment	Griffin et al. (1998, 1998b) Neuman & Baron (1997)		
Sexual misconduct	Ackroyd & Thompson (1999)		
Shirking	Jones (1984)	"A positive incentive to supply less effort." (p. 686)	
Showing up late for meetings	Neuman & Baron (1997)		
Smoking	Griffin et al. (1998, 1998b)		
Social loafing	Robinson & Bennet (1997)		
Specific unsafe work practices	Griffin et al. (1998, 1998b)		
Spreading rumors	Neuman & Baron (1997)		
Stealing	Vardi & Wiener (1996)		
Stealing intangibles	Greenberg & Scott (1996)		Taking long brakes
Stealing valuable intellectual property	Greenberg & Scott (1996)		Stealing trade secrets Stealing competitive information
Stonewalling	Jansen & Von Glinow (1985)	"Witholding and hiding relevant information." (p. 817)	
Strikes/"wildcat" strikes	Hollinger & Clark (1982)		

(Continued)

Behaviors	Authors	Definition	Model/Typology/ Subcategories
Suicide	Griffin et al. (1998, 1998b)		
Sustained sub-optimal performance	Griffin et al. (1998, 1998b)		
Talking behind target's back	Neuman & Baron (1997)		
Theft	Hollinger & Clark (1982)		
Threats	Neuman & Baron (1997)		
Transmitting damaging information	Neuman & Baron (1997)		
Unauthorized use of time-saving tools	Hollinger & Clark (1982)		
Underworking ("soldiering")	Taylor (1903)	"Deliberately working slowly so as to avoid doing a full day's work." (p. 13)	
Unethical decision making	Robinson & Bennett (1997)		
Unfair performance evaluation	Neuman & Baron (1997)		
Use of power—upward	Kacmar & Carlson (1998)	"Behaviors in which an actor "went over the head" of someone . . . took his or her problem to a higher authority in an effort to secure what he or she wanted." (p. 206)	
Use of power—downward	Kacmar & Carlson (1998)	"The use of power to politically influence an individual of lower standing." (p. 207)	
Verbal/Psychological violence	Griffin et al. (1998, 1998b)		
Violation of laws, codes, and regulations	Griffin et al. (1998, 1998b)		
Whistle blowing	Near & Miceli (1985)	"The disclosure of perceived wrongdoing by organization members to parties who may be able to halt it." (p. 2)	
White-collar crime	Sutherland (1940, 1949)	"A crime committed by a person of respectability and high social status in the course of his occupation. Consequently, it excludes many crimes of the upper class, such as most of their cases of murder, adultery, and intoxication, since these are not customarily a part of their occupational procedures. Also, it excludes the confidence games of wealthy members of	

(Continued)

(Continued)

Behaviors	Authors	Definition	Model/Typology/ Subcategories
		the under-world, since they are not persons of respectability and high social status." (1940, p. 9)	
	Gibbons & Garrity (1962)	Criminals acts in which employees steal or violate the law for the benefit of their employer (although the individual employee may benefit from these violations too).	*Organizational crimes* [are] committed with support from an organization, that is, at least in part, furthering its own ends.
	Coleman (1987)	"Violations of the law committed in the course of a legitimate occupation or financial pursuit by persons who hold respected positions in their communities." (p. 406)	*Occupational crimes* [are] committed for the benefit of individual criminals without organizational support.
	Collins (1998)	"White-collar offences profit first and foremost business or corporate organizations and not ant individual directly. The concept, therefore, is synonymous with 'corporate crime' ... 'organized occupational crime' ... or simply 'organizational crime.	White-collar offense is a 'crime that benefits the corporation [through enhancing] corporate profits'.... White collar crimes are labeled offences by virtue of the fact that they violate statutes falling beneath the jurisdiction of regulatory agencies
Withdrawal	Robinson & Bennett (1995)		
Withholding effort	Robinson & Bennett (1995)		
Yelling	Neuman & Baron (1997)		

Appendix 3

Constructs, Definitions, and Manifestations of OMB

Term Used	Author(s)	Definition	Manifestations
Antisocial behavior	Giacalone & Greenberg (1997)	"Any behavior that brings harm, or is intended to bring harm to the organization, its employees, or its stakeholders." (p. vii)	
Blue-collar crime	Horning (1970) Cited in Smigel & Ross (1970)	"Illegal acts which are committed by non salaried workers and which involve the operative's place of employment either as the victim (e.g., the theft of materials, the destruction of company property, the falsification of production records) or as a contributory factor by providing the locus for the commissions of an illegal act (e.g., fighting on company property, the theft of personal property, gambling on company premises, the selling of obscene literature on company premises)." (pp. 47–48)	Theft of materials Destruction of company property Falsification of production record Fighting on company property Theft of personal property Gambling on company premises, selling of obscene literature on company premises
Counterproductive workplace behavior	Sackett & DeVore (2001)	"Any intentional behavior on the part of an organization member viewed by the organization as contrary to its legitimate interests." (p. 145)	A hierarchical perspective of counterproductive behaviors at work: 1. A general counterproductivity factor. 2. A series of group factors (e.g., organizational deviance and interpersonal deviance). 3. Specific behavior domains (e.g., theft, absence and drug use).
Dysfunctional behavior in organizations	Griffin, O'Leary-Kelly, & Collins (1998a) Cited in Cooper & Rousseau (1999)	"Motivated behavior by an employee or group of employees that has negative consequences for an individual within the organization, and/or the organization itself." (1998c, p. 67)	Categories of dysfunctional behavior in organizations: • *Behaviors injurious to human welfare* —Behaviors that harm others: Verbal/psychological violence Physical violence

Sexual harassment

General unsafe work practices

—Behaviors that harm self:

  Alcohol/drug abuse

  Smoking

  Specific unsafe work practices

  Suicide

• *Behaviors injurious to the organization*

  —Behaviors that have specific costs:

  Inappropriate absenteeism/tardiness

  Misuse/theft of organization assets/property

  Destruction of organization assets/property

  Violation of laws, codes, and regulations

  —Behaviors that have general costs:

  Dysfunctional political behaviors

  Dysfunctional impression management behaviors

  Breach of confidentiality

  Sustained suboptimal performance

| Employee deviance | Hollinger & Clark (1982) | "Unauthorized acts by employees which are intended to be detrimental to the formal organization." (p. 97) |

• *Property deviance:*

"Those instances where employees acquire or damage the tangible property or assets of the organization without authorization."

Examples: theft, pilferage, embezzlement, sabotage.

• *Production deviance:*

"Behaviors which violate the formally proscribed norms delineating the quality and quantity of work to be accomplished."

Examples: unauthorized use of time-saving tools, restriction of output, "goldbricking," informal coworker interaction, "wildcat" strikes. (p. 98)

(Continued)

(Continued)

Term Used	Author(s)	Definition	Manifestations
Employee misconduct	Leatherwood & Spector (1991)	"Employee decisions to pursue self-interest at the expense of their principles or employer." (p. 553)	Misuse of company's resources, tools, or equipment Unauthorized markdowns Vandalism Kickbacks Theft of company's cash, merchandise, or time
Misconduct	Trevino (1992)	"Behavior that falls short of the [punishing] agent's moral or technical (work) standards." (p. 648)	Employee theft Drug or alcohol abuse Tardiness Excessive absenteeism or sick leave use Insubordination Below standards work performance
Nonperformance	Mangione & Quinn (1975)		• Doing little or nothing (e.g., poor quality or quantity of output) • Doing something, from an employer's perspective, counterproductive (e.g., damaging an employer's product on purpose)
Occupational crime	Colman (1985) Cited in Greenberg & Scott (1991)	"White collar crime committed by an individual or a group of individuals exclusively for personal gain." (p. 117)	Employee theft
Occupational crime	Turner & Stephenson (1993) Cited in Greenberg & Scott (1991)		• *Occupational crimes perpetrated by employees against their coworkers:* Examples: Taking credit for another person's sale Stealing cash from a coworker's wallet • *Occupational crimes perpetrated by employees against their organization:* Example: Employee theft

Occupational crime	Green (1997) Cited in Jensen & Hodson (1999)	Typology of occupational crime (p. 18):
		• *Organizational occupational crime*
		crimes in which the employing organization benefits
		• *State authority occupational crime*:
		criminal abuses of authority by officials
		• *Professional occupational crime*:
		crimes by professionals in their capacity as professionals
		• *Individual occupational crime*:
		crimes by individuals
		• *Overt*:
		  —*Strikes*
		  —Work slowdowns
		  —Grievances
		  —Lawsuits
		• *Covert*:
		  —Sabotage
		  —Secret withholding of output
		  —Stealing

Organizational aggression	Spector (1978)	"Any behavior intended to hurt the organization." (p. 821)
Organizational aggression	O'Leary-Kelly, Griffin, & Glew (1996)	General definition: "Any injurious or destructive actions that affect organizational employees, property, or relationships." (p. 228) Restricted definition: "Injurious actions and events that are prompted by some factor in the organization itself." (p. 228)

(Continued)

Term Used	Author(s)	Definition	Manifestations
		Organization-motivated aggression (OMA): "Attempted injurious or destructive behavior initiated by either an organizational insider or outsider that is instigated by some factor in the organizational context." (p. 229) Organization-motivated violence (OMV): "Significant negative effects on person or property that occur as a result of organizational-motivated aggression." (p. 229)	
OMB	Vardi & Wiener (1996)	"Any intentional action by members of organizations that violates core organizational and/or societal norms." (p. 151)	A typology of OMB (p. 151) • OMB Type S: misbehavior that intends to benefit the self. Examples: Distorting data Stealing Selling secrets Harassing peers • OMB Type O: misbehavior that intends to benefit the organization. Example: Falsifying records • OMB Type D: misbehavior that intends to inflict damage. Example: Sabotage
OMB	Ackroyd & Thompson (1999)	"Anything you do at work you are not supposed to do." (p. 2)	Failure to work very hard Not working at all Deliberate output restriction Practical joking

Organizational retaliation behavior	Skarlicki & Folger (1997)	"Adverse reactions to perceived unfairness by disgruntled employees toward their employer." (p. 434).	Pilferage Sabotage Sexual misconduct
Political behavior	Kacmar & Carlson (1998)	"Social influence attempts directed at those who can provide or limit rewards that will help promote or protect the self interests of the actor . . . can be deemed dysfunctional when the influence attempts result in negative consequences for other individuals or the organization." (p. 197)	• *Functional political behavior:* "actions that help organizations achieve goals." (p. 195) • *Dysfunctional political Behavior:* "behaviors that can be described as self-serving and organizationally non-sanctioned." (p. 196) Examples: Favoritism Nepotism Gender discrimination Use of power—Upward Use of power—Downward Self-serving

Political behavior in organizations	Farrell & Petersen (1982)	"Those activities that are not required as part of one's organizational role but that influence, or attempt to influence, the distribution of advantages and disadvantages within the organization." (p. 405)	A Typology of Political Behavior in Organizations (p. 407)
			LEGITIMATE LATERAL
			  VERTICAL Coalition forming
			  Direct voice Exchange favors
			  INTERNAL Reprisals
			  Complain to supervisor
			  Bypassing chain of command
			  Obstructionism
			  EXTERNAL Talk with counterpart from another organization
			  Lawsuits Outside professional activities

(Continued)

(Continued)

Term Used	Author(s)	Definition	Manifestations
			ILLEGITIMATE
			VERTICAL LATERAL
			Sabotage Threats
			INTERNAL Symbolic protest
			Mutinies
			Riots
			EXTERNAL Whistleblowing Organizational duplicity
			Defections
Unconventional practices at work	Analoui & Kakabadse (1992)		A Typology of Unconventional Practices at Work
			• Pilferage and theft
			• Rule braking (indiscipline)
			• Destructive practices (sabotage)
			• Noncooperation
			• Disruptive practices
			• Misuse of facilities
Workplace aggression	Greenberg & Alge (1998)	"Injurious actions and events that are prompted by some factor in the organization . . . excluding sources of aggression steaming from outside the organization, such as robbery." (p. 85)	• *Expressions of hostility:* Verbal or symbolic gestures, such as giving one dirty looks or talking negatively behind one's back
			• *Obstructionism:* Behaviors that impede one's ability to perform his or her job effectively, such as failing to return phone calls
			• *Active aggression:* Violent acts, such as actual or threatened physical attacks

Author Index

Subject Index